Crafting Digital Media

Audacity, Blender, Drupal, GIMP, Scribus, and Other Open Source Tools

Daniel James

Apress®

Crafting Digital Media: Audacity, Blender, Drupal, GIMP, Scribus, and Other Open Source Tools

ISBN-13 (pbk): 978-1-4302-1887-6

ISBN-13 (electronic): 978-1-4302-1888-3

Printed and bound in the United States of America 9 8 7 6 5 4 3 2 1

President and Publisher: Paul Manning
Lead Editor: Frank Pohlmann
Development Editors: Michelle Lowman and Matt Wade
Technical Reviewer: Trevor Parsons
Editorial Board: Clay Andres, Steve Anglin, Mark Beckner, Ewan Buckingham, Tony Campbell, Gary Cornell, Jonathan Gennick, Michelle Lowman, Matthew Moodie, Jeffrey Pepper, Frank Pohlmann, Ben Renow-Clarke, Dominic Shakeshaft, Matt Wade, Tom Welsh
Coordinationg Editor: Jim Markham
Copy Editor: Tiffany Taylor
Compositor: Nancy Wright
Indexer: John Collin
Artist: April Milne
Cover Designer: Anna Ishchenko

Distributed to the book trade worldwide by Springer-Verlag New York, Inc., 233 Spring Street, 6th Floor, New York, NY 10013. Phone 1-800-SPRINGER, fax 201-348-4505, e-mail orders-ny@springer-sbm.com, or visit http://www.springeronline.com.

For information on translations, please contact Apress directly at 2855 Telegraph Avenue, Suite 600, Berkeley, CA 94705. Phone 510-549-5930, fax 510-549-5939, e-mail info@apress.com, or visit http://www.apress.com.

Apress and friends of ED books may be purchased in bulk for academic, corporate, or promotional use. eBook versions and licenses are also available for most titles. For more information, reference our Special Bulk Sales–eBook Licensing web page at http://www.apress.com/info/bulksales.

The source code for this book is available to readers at www.freesoftwarecreative.com.

For Martha.

Contents at a Glance

Contents

Foreword

Fifty years ago, I decided to try to play a musical instrument. After a brief attempt at the trumpet, my parents and I settled on the clarinet, mostly (I think) because my parents realized that I couldn't play the clarinet and sing at the same time, and this was important to peace and harmony in the Hall household.

Fifty years ago, if a young person wanted to record and distribute their music, it was almost impossible. Although tape recorders existed, they were expensive. The average person couldn't afford even the simplest of tape recorders, much less very expensive mixing equipment. Editing of tape was often done with scissors, and to press a record was in the young artist's dreams.

Forty years ago (in 1969), I started working with computers. As a young college student, I couldn't afford the high prices of commercial computer software, so I joined an organization of computer users who wrote software and freely licensed it to anyone who wanted to use it. These people weren't necessarily paid to write programs. They included mathematicians, scientists, business people, and (yes) musicians. For the most part, they wrote the software because they needed it for their own purposes, and they hoped other people would enjoy it or (perhaps) help them make it better.

Fast-forward to this century. Modern-day computer equipment can turn a decent set of microphones and audio/video equipment into a sound or video studio at little incremental cost over the computer system itself. Fairly good software is available for relatively little money—or even at no cost, pulled down from the Internet.

However, while the software that is available is often free of cost, is it truly free? Can the musician who needs a slight change to the software affect the closed-source software they use? Can the computer science student interested in audio/video techniques see the source code to real audio/video software used by real musicians, and therefore learn how to improve that software?

Although the scope of the book is limited to showing you some of the software that is available and how to use it to complete audio and video projects, it really illustrates two freedoms: the freedom to produce your own type of music and the freedom of a system that allows (and encourages) you to change that software.

In addition, we hope that musicians and video people who like computers, and computer programmers who like music and video, will help to make these programs even better than they are today.

Most of all, we hope you enjoy this book as an introduction to the wonderful world of Free and Open Source Software.

Warmest regards,

Jon "Maddog" Hall
President Linux International

About the Author

**Daniel James** is the director of 64 Studio Ltd, a company developing custom GNU/Linux distributions for multimedia products. He was the founder and the original director of the linuxaudio.org consortium. Based in the UK, Daniel formerly worked on *LinuxUser & Developer* magazine, serving as Editor from the autumn of 2005 until early 2007. He has also contributed articles on music recording and related technology to *Linux Format* and *Sound on Sound* magazines.

Introduction

If you've picked up this book, then like me, you enjoy being creative—and you appreciate the sense of satisfaction that completing a project can bring. These days, computers have augmented or replaced the tools of the trade in many creative industries. Even if you aren't interested in computers for their own sake, you can still use one to realize your personal projects.

In this book, I'm going to take you on a guided tour of Free Software applications that can help you on your creative journey. You can install these programs on your own PC or Intel-based Mac, using the CD that comes with this book.

PART 1

■ ■ ■

Introduction

In Part 1, you'll learn how to install and configure Ubuntu GNU/Linux as the basis of your creative workstation. But first, you can read a little about the background to the Free Software phenomenon.

CHAPTER 1

■ ■ ■

Working with Free Software

The Two Meanings of Free

When you saw the words *Free Software* on the back cover of this book, you may have thought, "Great, I can save some money!" Or perhaps you thought that when it comes to software, quality costs—and programs that can be downloaded for free can't be any good. If the latter is the case, I don't blame you for being skeptical, because *Free!* is a much-abused word.

I'm using the phrase *Free Software* in two senses. It's literally true that all the software you look at in this book is available as a free download, gratis. However, it's also free in the sense of creative or personal freedom, and that's much more important to me. To explain why, this section offers you a short history of computer programs, from my highly partial point of view.

Did you ever see an old movie set at a time when a computer was the size of a wardrobe and had reels of tape spinning on the front? At the height of the Cold War in the 1960s and 70s, computers really looked like that (see Figure 1-1). In those days, software wasn't something you bought in a shrink-wrapped box at the mall. Most programs were written to order for a relatively small group of users or one institution. Software wasn't so much a product in its own right; it was more like the means to an end—making the very expensive computer hardware produce some useful output.

Figure 1-1. A Digital PDP-11/40 computer in the Vienna Technical Museum. Photo by Stefan Kögl, GNU Free Documentation License.

A lot of this software was written in research labs—for the military-industrial complex, for universities, or for the telephone company. At Bell Labs in the late 60s and early 70s, a bunch of programmers wrote an operating system called UNIX, which in time became the standard computer platform for bearded geeks across the world. The small, elite group of programmers who worked in these labs enjoyed sharing knowledge, impressing colleagues with their achievements, and playing with the machines. Some of these programmers called themselves *hackers*—which didn't mean they thought it was cool to breach security at the Pentagon or steal money from banks using a dial-up modem. Back then, to be a hacker meant that you enjoyed chipping away at complex computer problems, cutting and shaping program code in search of elegant solutions. Here's their secret: writing software is a creative process like any other.

The Internet hardly existed then, so hackers mailed each other reels of tape with programs on them. Getting your program distributed to all the UNIX labs on a tape of user-contributed software, known with hacker efficiency as *contrib*, meant you got kudos from your programming peers.

As computers became smaller, cheaper, and more widespread in the 70s and 80s, the environment in which software was written changed, too. A retail market in software products was beginning to emerge, which meant computer companies could make a lot of money if their program was a hit. Programming talent was enticed away from the labs and hired by commercial operations focused on selling software as a product. Not only were the labs losing programmers, but for confidentiality reasons, the hackers could no longer swap or even discuss software with their former peers. To make matters worse, their beloved UNIX was about to be fractured into several proprietary and incompatible versions.

One hacker in particular, who was working at MIT's Artificial Intelligence lab, got really upset about this problem. His name was Richard Stallman (Figure 1-2); and instead of resigning himself to the situation, he hatched an ambitious plan. He reasoned that if enough hackers cared about the problem, they could band together and eventually create a replacement for UNIX—a new operating system that would be free of the constraints imposed by the proprietary software vendors.

Figure 1-2. Richard Stallman in 2007. Photo by Bill Ebbesen.

Stallman called this project GNU, which stands for GNU's Not UNIX—it's a hacker's in-joke. Naturally, its symbol is a horned gnu (Figure 1-3), because all good teams have an animal mascot.

Figure 1-3. *The mascot of the GNU project, drawn by Etienne Suvasa.*

With the help of a couple of MIT professors, Stallman also set up a not-for-profit organization called the Free Software Foundation. The foundation holds the copyright of GNU software, and it campaigns on software issues.

GNU GPL: a Bill of Rights for Computer Users

The GNU project got under way in the early to mid 80s, with Stallman contributing large parts of the vital compiler program and a good deal of written material about the project's aims. As it turned out, one of the most important documents that Stallman wrote was the license under which the GNU software was released. The GNU General Public License (GPL) was designed specifically to make sure the project's software didn't fall into the trap of other freely available programs that had been written for UNIX.

Just imagine if you'd spent years writing a program that was your pride and joy, and you'd given it freely as your gift to the world, only to find out that it had been ripped off by a proprietary software vendor and turned into SuperDeLuxeProgram 2.0. When this happened, the original authors couldn't even get access to the source code of the new version for which people were now paying. The *source code* is the collection of files that human programmers write before the compiler software turns the code into a binary version, which the computer can then execute. Without having source code, you can't learn how the insides of a program work, and you can't fix it when it breaks down. Not having access to the code drives a hacker nuts; it's like a mechanic buying a new car and then finding out that the hood is welded shut. If the car broke down in the middle of the desert, you'd have no choice but to call the guy who sold you the vehicle and hope that he'd send out a tow truck.

With this in mind, Stallman declared in the GPL that all GNU software would grant its users four freedoms:

- The freedom to run the program for any purpose.

- The freedom to study how the program works and adapt it to your needs. (You can't do this without source code.)

- The freedom to redistribute copies so you can help your neighbor.

- The freedom to improve the program and release your improvements to the public, so that the whole community benefits. (You need source code for that, too.)

The GPL was different from more permissive Free Software licenses like the one used by the University of California for UNIX software written at its campus in Berkley. A clause in the GNU license means that people who distribute GPL software have to make the current, matching version of the source code available with the binary. It may seem like a minor distinction, but it makes all the difference to the software and the hackers that work on it. The GPL creates a positive feedback loop, or virtuous circle, which means that useful programs are maintained and updated over the years, even when the original author is no longer interested or available to do the work.

If a company rips off a piece of software released under the GNU GPL, by presenting it as the company's own work or hiding the source code from users, the company can be sued for copyright infringement by the original author. (Most GPL violations are settled out of court, because the terms of the license are very clear.) This legal enforcement is possible because GPL software is Free Software but isn't in the public domain. Some people call public-domain software *freeware*, which causes confusion with Free Software, but it's not the same thing at all. Many computer programs are offered gratis but without the four freedoms of the GPL, usually as part of a marketing ploy. Now you know why I keep typing *Free Software* with capital letters, so you don't make the same mistake.

■ **Note** Never, ever make the error of thinking that Free Software is cheap software. It's better to think of it as a gift from someone you've never met—a random act of kindness. Many Free Software authors have spent years working on their programs, so to have their work described as "cheap" is an insult. If you add up all the man-years and woman-years spent writing the millions of lines of source code in a typical GNU/Linux system, and multiply that number by the average salary of a programmer, you get a figure in the billions of dollars.

Is Free Software Un-American?

The proprietary software vendors weren't at all interested in this GNU GPL stuff. If people were allowed, or even encouraged, to make copies of software for their friends and neighbors, the "software as a product" business model wouldn't work. Because software costs very little to manufacture per unit once you've written it—close to zero, in the case of downloaded programs—the retail model can be extremely profitable. On the other hand, if you want to give it away, you can—it's not like making cars, where someone has to pay for all that steel, plastic, rubber, and glass.

When the idea of Free Software started to catch on with the public, it caused a panic among some proprietary software vendors. One senior executive at a well-known monopolist, based in Seattle, implied that Free Software was Not The American Way. This rather outlandish claim neglected the point that both UNIX and GNU were founded in the USA by Americans. MIT, UC Berkeley, and the other universities where Free Software flourished, along with the early Internet, were predominantly based in the USA.

I've described the GNU GPL as a Bill of Rights; not only does it grant specific freedoms to computer users, but it also attempts to limit the power of others to take those freedoms away. It's not hard to draw a parallel with the constitutional documents of the American Revolution, whose authors were keenly aware of the dangers of a monopoly on political power. The GPL attempts to limit the power of proprietary software monopolies by providing an alternative model, with four freedoms enshrined.

In contrast, proprietary software invites us to surrender our rights as a condition of using the program. Most likely you've installed software on Windows or a Mac and noticed a considerable amount of fine print that you're obliged to agree to in order to complete the installation. Nobody ever reads that text; life's too short. But when you click I Accept, you promise not to share that software with your neighbors and not to help your community, along with a great many other promises.

Another piece of misinformation was offered to the media by a different senior executive of that same software firm from Seattle. He claimed that the GNU GPL was a "cancer" that attached itself to other software, destroying it. (When otherwise sensible people start using language like that, you know they're panicking.) Although widely reported at the time, this assertion was incorrect—the GPL can only cover software that the author chooses to release under that license. In the case of modifications to an existing piece of software that a new developer has received under the GPL, it's entirely reasonable that the original author's license terms be respected. The same goes for *libraries*, which are reusable chunks of code that programs use to perform a specific task.

Throughout the 80s, work on Free Software programs continued, but the GNU Project wasn't yet at the point where users could download some software, install it on a PC, and have a complete Free Software system. Far away across the sea, that was about to change.

Linux: the Last Piece of the GNU Puzzle

A *kernel*, as its nutty name suggests, lies at the heart of the computer's operating system. The GNU project was working on a kernel called the Hurd, but at the beginning of the 90s, it wasn't in a usable shape. A student at the University of Helsinki, in Finland, with all the confidence of youth, decided that he would write a UNIX-like kernel. Linus Torvalds (Figure 1-4) wasn't American, and he wasn't attending a prestigious US university. Compared to the elite hackers at MIT, he was an outsider. But the Internet made it possible for Linus to share the development of his kernel with interested hackers around the world. Combined with the GNU software, Linus's kernel formed the basis of a usable UNIX-like system by 1992, and it was Free Software. Crucially, Linus decided to release his kernel under the GNU GPL license. With typical student humor, he wanted to call his project Freax (as in Free UNIX); but a friend who ran the server at the university hated the name, so the project was named Linux instead.

Figure 1-4. Linus Torvalds, the creator of Freax (also known as Linux), in 2002. Photo courtesy of Martin Streicher, Linux Magazine, under GNU FDL.

As Internet access became more widespread through the 90s, the GNU/Linux combination proved very popular with old UNIX hands and a new generation of geeks. It ran on ordinary PCs instead of big, expensive UNIX machines, and it was all Free Software—a powerful combination. GNU/Linux splurged out of the universities and into the business world as people became interested in the new World Wide Web. To keep a website going around the clock, you need a reliable server platform. UNIX was the obvious choice for a server back then, but GNU/Linux could be deployed on PCs much more cost-effectively. Pretty soon, fledging ISPs, search engines, and all kinds of crazy dot-com start-ups had hundreds or even thousands of GNU/Linux machines serving web pages and churning out e-mails. Free Software was entering the mainstream.

Hello Open Source

Over at the big UNIX vendors, management began to take more notice of Free Software. Engineers were finding ways to sneak GNU/Linux into the building when it did a better job than the company's own products. IBM, the granddaddy of proprietary computer systems, took a long look at the Free Software web-serving application Apache. It was much better than IBM's own web server product, which must have seemed somewhat counterintuitive: how could a bunch of bearded hippies on the Internet turn out better software than IBM, when the company had thousands of clean-cut, suit-and-tie-wearing engineers? Here's the second secret of Free Software—not everyone is motivated to do their best work by a pay check. If you consider writing software a creative activity, then this shouldn't come as a big surprise. The freedom to make the right choices for your project, and having the support and appreciation of your peers, count for a lot. (The third secret is that not all Free Software hackers fit the stereotype of bearded hippies; many of them look entirely normal, and a small proportion of them are women.) IBM began investing significant amounts in GNU/Linux development, allowing its engineers to spend time writing code for Free Software projects.

Within a couple of years, all the proprietary UNIX vendors had GNU/Linux-based products or were developing Free Software in some other way. Even Apple, whose computers had always been proprietary and nonstandard, switched from its own operating system to a variant of Berkley's UNIX, in the form of OS X. Significantly, Apple didn't adopt a core platform that was released under the GPL, so it wasn't obliged to share most of its enhancements to OS X with the Free Software community. (Apple does make some source code releases, but it's not practical for an ordinary computer user to create a complete, working operating system from them.)

Some people decided that the phrase *Free Software* was a problem for big-business adoption of GNU/Linux and related programs, and not just because of the potential for confusion with freeware. This is how the phrase *open source* came into being: as a way of emphasizing the technical benefits of source code availability while downplaying the four freedoms of the GPL. It remains a controversial rebranding, with old-school hackers like Stallman refusing to use the term *open source* (except to criticize it).

To make matters worse for the Free Software Foundation, as GNU/Linux began to get mainstream media attention in the late 90s, some people dropped the GNU part and called the operating system just Linux. This is technically inaccurate, because the Linux kernel can't work by itself—at the very least, it needs some low-level utilities to run alongside. Linux was a shorter and snappier name for the platform, but Stallman was infuriated. He no doubt felt that the GNU project and the aims of Free Software were belittled when media reports incorrectly attributed the creation of the "Linux operating system" to one guy in Finland. It had always been a team effort, and by this time the Free Software community included thousands of developers all over the world.

Distribution Explosion

Because the number of different companies, colleges, and individuals releasing Free Software grew so large by the early to mid 90s, it became impractical for users to locate and download all the available programs one at a time. The GNU GPL encourages sharing, so various people started to put together collections comprising GNU/Linux and programs that would run on it, a bit like the contrib tapes in the old days of the UNIX labs. Unlike with Windows or OS X, there was no one definitive version of the operating system, so these collections were known as *distributions* of GNU/Linux. At first, they were released on sets of floppy discs, but growing distribution sizes meant CD-ROMs soon became popular. The distribution projects released CD images on their web and FTP servers so that people could burn their own CD sets and share them locally.

One of the earliest GNU/Linux distributions was Slackware, created by Patrick Volkerding in 1993 and still maintained today. Red Hat was created as a commercially orientated distribution, produced by a company headed for the stock market. It remains widely adopted in the business sector, particularly in the US. In contrast, the Debian project is constituted as nonprofit, focuses on community, and elects its leader annually. In Europe, the SuSE and Mandrake distributions became popular, whereas some Japanese users favored Turbolinux, a version of Red Hat with Asian language support.

In time, hundreds of distribution projects sprang up all over the Internet. Most of them were based originally on Red Hat, Debian, or Slackware, but they diverged in form and function over the years. SuSE was acquired by proprietary software vendor Novell, and Mandrake became Mandriva after a trademark dispute with the Hearst Corporation (owners of the rights to comic strip "Mandrake the Magician"). In recent times, the Debian-based Ubuntu distribution has proved popular all over the world, but new distribution projects are still appearing. Some distributions are specialized and target one specific group of users—perhaps scientists doing high-energy physics research, or the speakers of a minority language in a remote country where market failure has meant that proprietary software in the local language isn't available.

The majority of code in a GNU/Linux distribution tends to be released under the GNU GPL, but other programs are released under Berkeley or MIT-style licenses. Some projects have written their own, unique Free Software licenses, but that practice tends to be discouraged nowadays because it can make combining code more complicated.

Another means of distributing Free Software programs took off in the 90s: project-hosting websites, where communities of developers share their latest code. One of the original hosting sites, and probably the largest to date, is SourceForge (`http://sourceforge.net`). Anyone can sign up for a SourceForge account, start a project, and begin recruiting developers. The site now claims 180,000 projects and more than 1.9 million registered users, although not all of these users are active developers. Some of the user accounts and projects are dormant; but even so, you can find a lot of software on SourceForge. The best projects on this and other, similar hosting sites are taken up and maintained within at least one of the GNU/Linux distributions.

The Year of the Linux Desktop

While GNU/Linux was becoming firmly entrenched on web and mail servers and gaining a foothold in high-performance computing, the new generation of hackers was getting fed up with having to use Microsoft Windows on desktop PCs. If you were working as a web-site designer in the mid 90s, as I was, you could do a lot of the text stuff on the command line of a GNU/Linux box. You had a basic desktop, a choice of editing programs, and a functional web browser on GNU/Linux, and you could teach yourself how to create web sites (with a little help from the browser's View Source menu item). Creating web graphics from scratch was another matter.

At UC Berkeley, two students named Spencer Kimball and Peter Mattis wrote a Free Software desktop graphics application, which they released under the name General Image Manipulation Program ("the GIMP"). By 1997, it had been adopted by the GNU project and renamed the GNU Image Manipulation Program. Early GIMP user Larry Ewing designed a mascot for the Linux kernel project: a cartoon penguin named Tux (Figure 1-5). (That's how GNU/Linux came to be associated with penguins.)

Figure 1-5. The outline of Tux the penguin, the Linux kernel mascot, as drawn by Larry Ewing and converted to EPS format by Neal Tucker.

The GIMP (shown in Figure 1-6) was the first creative tool to be written for GNU/Linux, but it was also the first cool desktop application for the platform generally. It was the right program at the right time for a lot of people working on GNU/Linux systems in web-design start-ups and dot-coms.

Figure 1-6. Version 1.2.1 of the GIMP, featuring multiple portraits of project mascot Wilber. Screenshot by Garrett LeSage.

Around the same time, movie studios in the Los Angeles area began to use large numbers of GNU/Linux systems to render computer animation. Most of these movie programs were written for in-house use—software as the means to an end—although a few were later released as proprietary applications. One exception was CinePaint, a program that developers working for the studios adapted from an early version of the GIMP. They were able to do this because of the four freedoms granted to them in the GNU GPL.

Desktop software for GNU/Linux improved rapidly, although predictions of a "year of the Linux desktop," when Free Software would displace Microsoft Windows from PCs, proved premature. Other kinds of creative applications began to be released for GNU/Linux: Inkscape for vector artwork, Blender for 3D modeling, Scribus for desktop publishing, Audacity for editing audio, and more. Internet communities of developers and users grew up around these Free Software programs, improving them with new features, fixing bugs, and providing support to new users. As people from outside the GNU/Linux world got involved with these community projects, alternative versions for Windows and the Mac began to be released. Today, enough good Free Software applications are available that some people get by without using any proprietary software at all—and are still able to realize their creative projects.

My Story

I'd been using GNU/Linux and Apache on web servers for a year or so when I was handed a box of Free Software CDs at work one day in the spring of 1997. Until that time, the idea of installing GNU/Linux on my PC at home hadn't occurred to me. I didn't even know that the GIMP existed—I was using a Mac at work, with the usual Adobe Photoshop and Illustrator combination.

I had a PC running Windows 95 at home, but I'd had some bad experiences with it. I'd bought a deluxe sound card for my PC with an on-board sampler so that I could try making music at home. As soon as I installed it and powered up the machine, it wouldn't boot. I wrestled with that sucker for two weeks of downtime before finding a workaround by trial and error. This involved removing the sound card, rebooting, reinstalling the driver, shutting down the PC, and refitting the sound card again. I got no help with the problem from the sound-card manufacturer, and Microsoft also doesn't generally offer one-to-one support to end users. That's a consequence of the "software as a product: model: it's easy to churn out millions of copies of a program but quite another to scale personal support to the same level. The experience left me feeling frustrated and alone—like being stranded next to a broken-down car in the desert.

Later, my sister sent me a CD of Red Hat 5.0 that had been given away on the cover of a computer magazine. By this time, GNU/Linux was easy enough to install that even a newbie like me could manage it. The desktop environment was simple—even crude, compared to Windows 95 or the Mac I was used to—but it worked. I was able to install the GIMP and Netscape Navigator, the forerunner of Mozilla Firefox.

By 1999, the GNU/Linux desktop had improved a great deal, and I was using it pretty much full-time. I enjoyed the support of the community that had formed around the software, and not just on the many mailing lists I had subscribed to. I noticed that the GNU/Linux community was frequently self-documenting, in that solutions to computer problems encountered were often posted to web pages and forums. This knowledge-sharing takes some effort on the part of individuals, but it has formed an invaluable reference resource—like a decentralized version of Wikipedia. Whenever I had a problem with my GNU/Linux system, a quick trip around the search engines usually turned up a solution. Of course, proprietary applications now have web forums too; but if you don't have source code or an understanding of how the internals of a program work, the degree to which you can help your neighbors is limited.

I was able to return to my interest in sound recording and set up a small studio based around a GNU/Linux system. Later, in 2005, I founded a new Free Software project called 64 Studio (see Figure 1-7). We were the first people to produce a fully native 64-bit GNU/Linux operating system for creative workstations, which I've been using every day since.

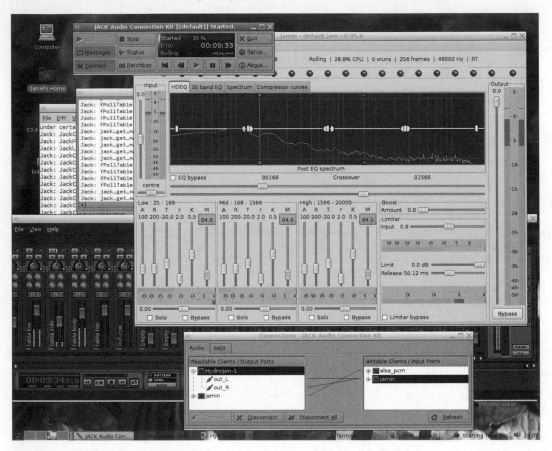

Figure 1-7. *The 64 Studio desktop, showing the JACK sound server and JACK client programs Hydrogen and Jamin*

What Free Software Is Good At, and Where There Are Gaps

Because Free Software applications are generally written to satisfy a personal need for a particular program, rather than a perceived market demand, many excellent tools do one job each and do it well. Bloated do-it-all programs are comparatively rare, and it's interesting to note that several of the largest Free Software desktop applications (in terms of lines of code) started life as proprietary products.

When a proprietary application is written as part of a wider business model—for example, to lock users into a particular format—there is often no exact equivalent in Free Software. In particular, with multimedia software and the associated hardware, this happens for a number of reasons:

- Business interests that seek to control user behavior (for example, forcing the use of a particular portable audio player with the company's own music store on the Web) don't publish details of their file formats. This makes it difficult for Free Software authors to support those formats, although sometimes they figure them out anyway. Unfortunately, reverse engineering a format is considered illegal in some countries, even though it's something that all kinds of software developers have to do on a regular basis.

- Some countries around the world, including the USA, allow patents to be filed on software and formats in addition to physical inventions. This leaves Free Software authors in danger of patent-infringement claims, even if they build support for these patented formats into their programs completely independently. (Imagine if you had ten million downloads of your Free Software video application, and then you got a lawyer's letter saying you owed five dollars per unit, plus damages.)

- In the case of a particular item of hardware, it may be that no one who purchased the device has written a GNU/Linux driver for it. This scenario is made more likely if the manufacturer of the device doesn't publish full specifications for it, or if it doesn't work very well. In contrast, the manufacturers of the worst hardware always provide proprietary drivers for Windows, because they have a vested interest in selling junk to the mass market. This driver problem often affects Mac users, too.

Despite these three factors, if you choose your hardware and software carefully, you can minimize compatibility problems. As far as proprietary lock-in and copy-restricted formats go, these are best avoided on any platform. You don't want to be locked out of an archived project in five or ten years because of a file format that you can no longer open.

Being a Good Free Software Citizen

From time to time, when I'm reading a mailing list for a Free Software application, I see a posting like this:

> From: dave@somerandom.net
> To: application-users@someprogram.org
> Subject: your program is lame
> Hi I downloaded your program but it crashed. It sux. Im going back to Windows cos Linus crashes all the time.
> whatever
> Dave

Perhaps I'm exaggerating for comic effect; most people aren't quite that rude. I think people get used to that stranded-by-the-car-in-the-desert feeling whenever something goes wrong with their computer. They take out their frustration on anyone who will listen, without realizing that the Free Software community includes a lot of helpful people. Having said that, it can be difficult to help people like Dave, particularly when they don't provide enough information about the problem. For example:

- Which exact version of the software is Dave using? (That's very important, because the bug may have been fixed already.)

- What was Dave doing with the application at the time of the crash or other problem? Details matter.

- Did any text appear on the screen, where the application provided details of what had gone wrong?

- Did Dave try any experiments to track down the cause of the problem?

Providing this kind of information would help Dave get a positive response. However, Dave should remember that most of the people who hang out on Free Software mailing lists, in forums, and in chat rooms are volunteers. They aren't obliged to help Dave with his problems in any way. As Dave learns more about the program, he may be able to help other new users with simple problems. If he docs, he will be more likely to get help from the experienced users and developers of that application. That's what community support is all about.

Beta Testing and Bug Reporting

Whenever you find a bug in a program, the first thing to do is check whether you're running the current release. Typically, the release version number is shown in the About dialog box for the program, which is often found on the Help menu. You can compare this number with the versions available from the application project's homepage.

An actively developed Free Software application has frequent releases, particularly for minor updates. Between major stable releases, development versions are likely to be available, which you can test. These are generally in one of three categories:

- *Alpha*: Early version, likely to be unstable. Only for the curious.

- *Beta*: Improved version, quite stable but may still have bugs.

- *Release candidate*: Mostly bug free, but still needs testing.

These terms are, of course, relative. As is the case for any kind of software, versions labeled *stable* can still have bugs, even crashing bugs—although they shouldn't take your computer down in flames. If you report a bug in a stable release—for example, on a mailing list—you will often be invited to test a beta or release-candidate version by a member of the development team. Performing these tests and providing good-quality feedback is part of the virtuous circle that improves Free Software applications. If, as part of this testing, you are asked to perform a task that you don't understand, don't be shy about saying so. It's much better to admit that you don't know how than for communication to go silent, because then the development team doesn't know if the problem you found has been fixed for you or not.

Some software projects offer a semi-automated system on the Web for reporting and tracking bugs. Examples of this type of system include Bugzilla, Trac, and Launchpad. These web-based systems often require you to fill in a form with your e-mail address so that follow-up questions can be sent to you. If you use this kind of form to report a bug, make sure you use an e-mail address with good spam filtering, because spammers have been known to harvest addresses from bug trackers.

Jargon-Busting Guide

If you subscribe to a Free Software development mailing list, you may encounter some technical terms that are unfamiliar. Here's a quick guide to some of the more common terms:

- *Distro*: Short for *GNU/Linux distribution*. A collection of software including both the operating system and applications. Hundreds of distros are available, but some are much more popular than others.

- *Tarball*: An archive file format used for distributing source code and some binary programs. It's an old UNIX term; the extension `.tar` is short for *tape archive*, and such files are usually distributed in compressed form.

- *gzip, bzip2*: Compression formats, equivalent to `.zip` files on Windows or `.sit` files on the Mac. When a tarball is compressed with gzip, it has the extension `.tar.gz`, whereas compression with bzip2 results in the extension `.tar.bz2`.

- *deb, rpm*: Package formats for Debian- and Red Hat-based GNU/Linux distributions, respectively. These are generally the easiest way to install software on GNU/Linux, because they're ready-prepared for a specific version of a distribution.

- *cvs, svn, git, bzr*: Source code tools that developers use to keep track of changes in their projects. Downloading a bleeding-edge version of an application often requires the use of one of these tools.

- *Checkout*: A download of source code for the bleeding-edge version of a program. When a developer has made a change to their local copy of the source code, they perform a *checkin* or *commit* so that other developers can get the update.

- *Recompile*: To create a fresh version of the binary program, usually after making a modification to the source code. The Linux kernel can be recompiled to improve performance on a specific machine or to enable a less commonly used feature.

- *gdb*: The GNU debugger. A program that helps developers identify what's going wrong with a program that crashes.

- *Backtrace*: Output from a program that crashes, showing what the program was doing immediately before it went down.

Mouse Conventions Used in This Book

In the chapters ahead, you will install and use a lot of different Free Software programs, but there's something I need to make clear first. When I write *left-click*, I mean you should click the main mouse button—the one you press with your index finger. Most operations are performed with a left-click, so if I just write *click*, that's the button I mean. If, like many creative people, you're left-handed, you may have your mouse set up so that this button is on the right side of the device.

When I write *right-click*, I mean to click the button that most people press with their middle or ring finger. If you have a Mac, you may only have one button on your mouse, in which case a left-click means to tap the button and a right-click means to hold it down longer.

Freesoftwarecreative.com

While you're reading this book, you may want to visit the accompanying website at `http://www.freesoftwarecreative.com`. This site is the best place to leave your comments and feedback on the text, discuss the topics covered in the chapters with other readers, and download example materials used in the application tutorials. I hope to see you there!

Further reading

Rebel Code by Glyn Moody (Allen Lane, 2001, ISBN-13: 978-0738206707) is a highly recommended history of the Free Software movement's early days. It's since been published by Perseus Books and Basic Books in the USA. It's also been published as a Penguin paperback in the UK (ISBN-13: 978-0140298048). *Just for Fun: The Story of an Accidental Revolutionary* (HarperCollins, 2002, ISBN-13: 978-0066620732) is Linus Torvald's autobiography.

CHAPTER 2

■ ■ ■

Getting Started

Distro or No?

Before you can begin using creative Free Software applications, the first thing you need to decide is whether to install a GNU/Linux operating system on your computer. This step isn't essential, because many of the applications I'll cover are also available for Windows or the Mac. If you're nervous about potentially deleting the wrong thing from your computer and screwing it up, it may be best to try these creative applications on your existing operating system first.

On the other hand, if you're familiar enough with your computer's software that you could reinstall it from scratch if necessary, then you may want to try running a full GNU/Linux system. In this chapter, you look at installing and using Ubuntu, which is one of the most popular GNU/Linux distributions. Ubuntu is available in both desktop and server editions, as well as several specialist versions. You examine the desktop edition, because it provides a good foundation for a creative GNU/Linux system and has the easiest install routines of the bunch. You can also run Ubuntu directly from the CD or install it side by side with Windows, as you'll see.

■ **Caution** The most likely time that you'll accidentally delete some file or program from your PC is during the installation of new software. You should make a full, tested, back-up of any files or programs that you wish to keep, before installing any of the software mentioned in this book.

Ubuntu Compatibility

Most people who install Ubuntu use one of the official CD-ROM images available for download from www.ubuntu.com. These .iso images are generally under 700MB and can be burned to a standard blank CD-R disk using any good CD-burning software. Some distros are larger and require a DVD-R disk.

The Ubuntu desktop install image is available in both 32-bit and 64-bit builds. The 32-bit version (sometimes labeled i386, indicating the first compatible Intel chip) works well on pretty much any PC or laptop made in the last five years and on most of the Intel-based Macs. This is the version of Ubuntu supplied with this book.

It's possible to run Ubuntu on very old PCs, but doing so can be a false economy. Generally, any PC that was originally supplied with Windows XP is fine. If you have less than 256MB RAM, or a CPU running at less than 800MHz clock speed in your PC, it could be time for an upgrade. GNU/Linux is considerably more efficient than Windows Vista, so if you're on a tight budget, many inexpensive, useful PCs that were discarded during Vista upgrades are available on the second-hand market. Also, Ubuntu takes up a comparatively small amount of disk space for itself, so even an old 10GB or 20GB hard drive can be used to install the GNU/Linux operating system. If your Windows PC has a full C: drive, adding a second hard disk may be the easiest way to begin enjoying Ubuntu.

The older Macs with PowerPC CPUs are no longer officially supported by Ubuntu, although an alternative PowerPC installer is produced by members of the Ubuntu community. Installing Ubuntu on a Mac is less common, and much less straightforward, than installing on a PC. This is because even though Macs now have similar CPUs to Windows PCs, they're still a little nonstandard. A Mac install can be achieved if you have enough patience—step-by-step instructions are provided in the Ubuntu documentation for several specific models of Apple hardware.

The 64-bit build of Ubuntu is based on the same source code as the 32-bit version but is optimized for the CPUs found in newer PCs and recent Intel Macs. It's sometimes named *amd64* after the first 64-bit CPUs from AMD to use the x86 architecture found in PCs, but it also works on the Intel 64 chips, such as the Core 2 Duo. Although there are sometimes compatibility problems with 32-bit proprietary and legacy applications, the 64-bit build is generally recommended if you have one of these newer machines. However, the 64-bit version won't work on a 32-bit machine; if you aren't sure what kind of CPU you have, it's best to check before you begin the installation attempt.

The steps that follow detail the standard install method for PCs and apply to both 32-bit and 64-bit machines. This method is based on booting from CD and works whether the PC already has Windows installed or has a blank hard disk.

Booting from the Optical Drive

Newer PCs offer direct access to a boot menu (via a function key such as F8, F10, or F12) as soon as they're switched on. You can use this menu to select the Ubuntu CD, and the boot of the Linux kernel begins. Many older Windows PCs don't have this boot menu and are set to boot from the C: drive first. If your PC is set up this way, it won't boot from the Ubuntu install CD when switched on.

To fix this, immediately after the machine is switched on, press whichever key on the keyboard allows you to access the computer's BIOS settings. This may be the Delete key, the Escape key, or the F10 key—usually, a small line of text on the computer's screen says "Press Esc for Setup" or something similar. If not, you may have to check the manual that came with your PC or laptop. If you don't have a printed manual, try searching on the Web for a PDF version. Failing that, you may find a manual for the specific motherboard used in your machine, if you can identify the motherboard model number. When you access the BIOS setting screens, you see an option called Boot Order or Boot Priority. The options available are something like the following:

- C only
- C,A,CD
- A,C,CD
- CD,A,C
- CD,C,A

The list may include references such as Hard Drive, Optical Drive, and Floppy Drive. If your PC or laptop is a relatively recent model, you may also have the option to boot from a USB or network device.

Usually, you have to select one of these options using the cursor keys on your keyboard or the Page Up and Page Down keys. Make sure CD or similar is at the beginning of the priority list you select. This applies even if you have a DVD drive—as far as the BIOS is concerned, booting from a CD or a DVD is pretty much the same thing. If you've changed this setting, you must press another key to save the new value to the BIOS memory chip on your motherboard. This may be one of the F keys, indicated by "Save to CMOS and Exit" or some such phrase.

The Ubuntu Live CD

Now you're ready to put the Ubuntu disk in your CD or DVD drive, and reboot the PC. After you see the usual power-on screen, the optical drive should start to spin the CD. Sometimes, the BIOS displays the message "Booting from CD-ROM." A couple of seconds pass, and an Ubuntu welcome screen appears. You have the option to select a language at this stage; if you do nothing, the default of English is selected automatically after 30 seconds. Or you can choose a different language and then select "Try Ubuntu without any change to your computer." In the next step, an orange progress bar moves across the screen as Ubuntu boots. This takes a minute or two, depending on the speed of your PC.

If your sound card is detected automatically, which should be the case for most common audio hardware, and your PC's loudspeakers are switched on, you now hear the Ubuntu start-up sound. (I think it's meant to sound like a choir plus a couple of xylophone players, but you can be the judge of that.) Shortly afterward, the Ubuntu live desktop appears (see Figure 2-1). The software isn't installed on the hard disk of your computer yet, so if you've jumped a step ahead, it's not too late to go back to the beginning of this chapter and reread the warning about backups!

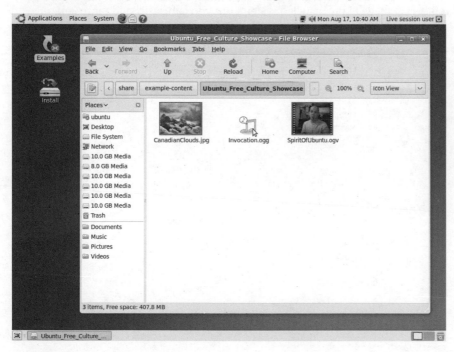

Figure 2-1. The initial desktop of the live Ubuntu session

The live desktop is a fully functional operating system, even though it's running from a CD. It's a bit slower than an installed Ubuntu system, and no user accounts are set up yet, but the live system lets you confirm that your hardware is supported by GNU/Linux drivers.

■ **Note** If you don't hear the Ubuntu start-up sound or see the desktop, it means your hardware hasn't been automatically detected and configured properly. It should still be possible for you to run Ubuntu on this PC, but you may have to do a little more work to get it running right. The best approach in this situation is to research which piece of hardware is causing the trouble, by searching the Web. Most likely, another person has run into the same problem with Ubuntu on this particular model of computer. If you enter **ubuntu** plus the model number of your PC or laptop into any good search engine, you're likely to find the answer to your problem. If an error message appears on the screen, enter that into the search engine, too.

Ubuntu Desktop installation

If you've made that backup and you're ready to proceed with the Ubuntu installation, double-click the Install icon at upper left on the desktop. A Welcome window appears, which gives you a second chance to select your native language—again, the default is English (see Figure 2-2). Whichever language you choose here will be the default language of the installed system, but you can easily add more languages later.

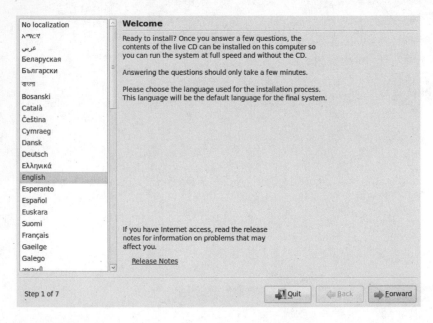

Figure 2-2. Language selection is the first step toward permanent Ubuntu installation.

Click the Forward button, and the second step appears: the selection of your nearest city and time zone (see Figure 2-3). New York is the default, but a very thorough list of alternatives is offered, from Abidjan on the Ivory Coast to Zaporozhye in the Ukraine. OK, it also has Zurich, but you probably guessed that already. It's actually more fun to click the dots on the interactive world map and select your nearest city that way.

Figure 2-3. *The time-zone selector includes most major cities in the world.*

Next is the "Keyboard layout" window (see Figure 2-4). Based on your language selection, the installer makes an educated guess about the kind of keyboard you have. If you aren't sure this setting is correct, there is a box at lower left into which you can type a few words to test it. The QWERTY keys are generally correct; but if you have the wrong keyboard variant set, then some of the symbol keys like ~, #, and | may not be in the right places. Watch out for currency symbols like £, ¥, and €, too.

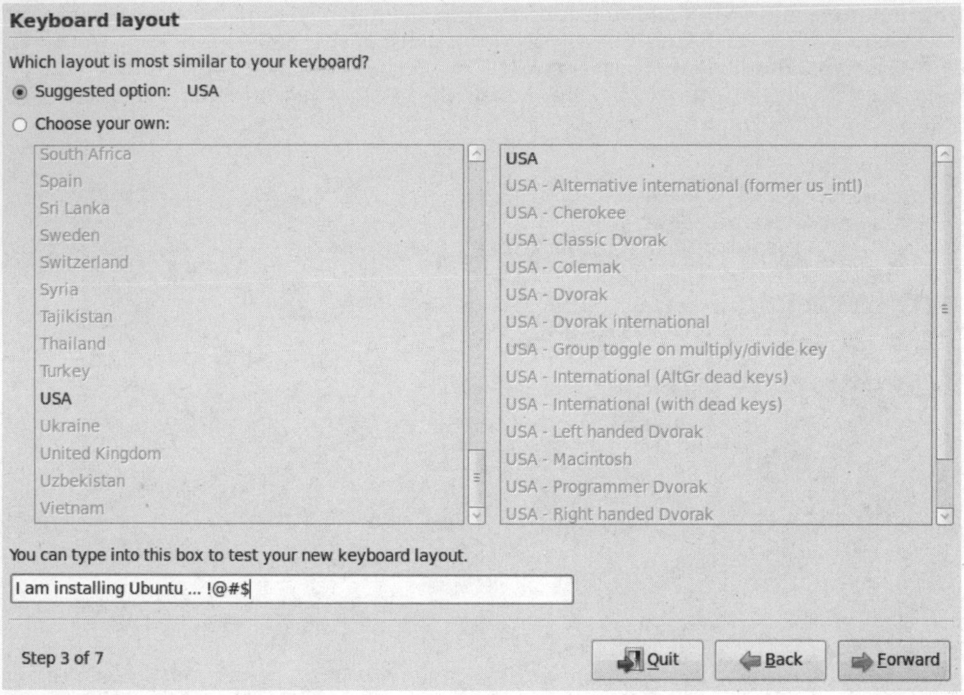

Keyboard layout

Which layout is most similar to your keyboard?

⦿ Suggested option: USA

◯ Choose your own:

South Africa	USA
Spain	USA - Alternative international (former us_intl)
Sri Lanka	USA - Cherokee
Sweden	USA - Classic Dvorak
Switzerland	USA - Colemak
Syria	USA - Dvorak
Tajikistan	USA - Dvorak international
Thailand	USA - Group toggle on multiply/divide key
Turkey	USA - International (AltGr dead keys)
USA	USA - International (with dead keys)
Ukraine	USA - Left handed Dvorak
United Kingdom	USA - Macintosh
Uzbekistan	USA - Programmer Dvorak
Vietnam	USA - Right handed Dvorak

You can type into this box to test your new keyboard layout.

I am installing Ubuntu ... !@#$|

Step 3 of 7   ↵| Quit   ⬅ Back   ➡ Forward

Figure 2-4. The Ubuntu installer tries to guess your keyboard layout.

Partitioning

Clicking the Forward button again, you come to the most critical part of the installation: partitioning the hard disk. To avoid the potential for conflict between operating systems, most permanent GNU/Linux installations use their own partition on the hard disk, separate from or instead of a Windows partition (still known under Windows as the C: drive, even though floppy drives A: and B: are obsolete now).

Partitioning is good practice even if you only use Windows, because it helps keep the operating system and applications separate from your files and other data. However, the C: drive legacy means that most Windows PCs today are delivered with one huge partition, even if it's hundreds of gigabytes in size. (If you've ever had to do an emergency C: drive reformat and reinstall on Windows, you probably already know how dangerous that can be for your personal files, especially if you didn't make a backup first.)

The Ubuntu installer attempts to guide you toward a partitioning scheme for your computer, making use of any empty space on the disk first (see Figure 2-5). If a partition (such as the Windows C: drive) fills the whole disk, the installer suggests shrinking that partition to make space. The partitions are color coded, with the current situation shown on the upper of two bars and the installer's proposed partitions on the lower bar. The lower bar has a small white handle on it, dividing the proposed partitions. You can drag this handle sideways to set how much disk space is allocated to each operating system.

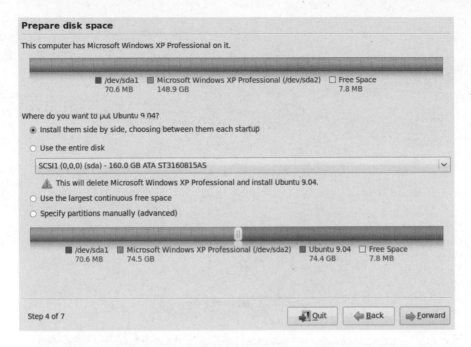

Figure 2-5. *If it goes wrong, partitioning can mess up your computer—so take it slowly, and make sure you understand what's going on.*

In the event that your C: drive uses the entire disk and is completely full of files, resizing the partition won't work, because there is no free space into which to shuffle the files. If that's the case, you have the option to do some housekeeping on the Windows partition and return to the install later, or perhaps get a larger or additional hard disk.

The alternative for guided partitioning is to use the entire hard disk. Be careful with this option—unless you're very sure you want to wipe Windows completely. If you have more than one disk installed, a choice of install targets is offered, with the disk size, type, and model number listed to help you identify which disk it is. For example, 60.0GB ATA ST960821A is the hard disk in my laptop, whereas 160.0GB ATA ST3160815AS is the disk in my desktop machine.

The Windows disk letters for the C: drive and D: drive have no meaning here. Windows gives the name C: to the first partition on the first hard disk it finds. On the other hand, GNU/Linux gives each disk a name starting with `/dev/`, followed by letters that represent the type of disk (`sd` for SCSI disk emulation, in this case), and then a letter to indicate a specific piece of hardware. In most PCs with a single hard disk, this is referred to as `/dev/sda`. Each partition on this disk has a number, so you may have partitions named `/dev/sda1`, `/dev/sda2`, and so on.

Your other option, which most experienced users choose, is to set up the partitions manually (see Figure 2-6). If you go down this route, there must be at least one partition for the system, known as the *root partition*. The root partition is labeled with the mount point of a forward slash: `/`. You must also have a *swap partition*, which is for virtual memory and is similar to the page file in Windows—except that because it has its own dedicated partition, it can't grow beyond that partition's size. You can specify other partitions as required. For a permanent installation, I always recommend the creation of a `/home` partition, where your personal files live. It makes sense to keep these separate from the operating system.

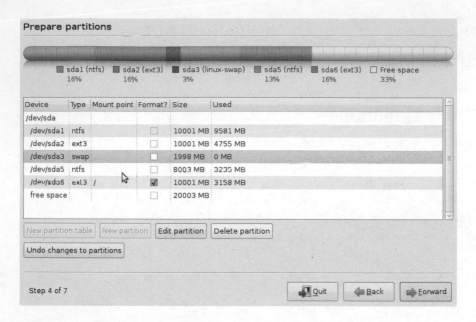

Figure 2-6. Here's a more complicated example, featuring logical partitions. Manual partitioning offers the greatest control over resizing and formatting options.

Select the option to format the partitions to use for Ubuntu, as long as you're sure there is no software or data in those partitions that you wish to keep. Each operating system has its own format for organizing files, which the installer must set up on the appropriate partition. The partition type for the root / and any other Ubuntu partitions (except swap) should be **ext3** (see Figure 2-7). This is the standard GNU/Linux filesystem, and it's resilient against faults caused by events such as sudden power failure in the PC.

Edit a partition

New partition size in megabytes (1000000 bytes):	10001
Use as:	Ext3 journaling file system
Format the partition:	☑
Mount point:	/

Cancel   OK

*Figure 2-7. The **ext3** filesystem is the default in Ubuntu, so choose this for the root and home partitions unless you know you definitely need one of the alternatives.*

Any Windows partitions are probably formatted with ntfs and should be left as they are if you want Windows to be able to read them. GNU/Linux is pretty good at reading the filesystems of other operating systems, but Windows isn't so obliging in the other direction.

For more information about the subject of partitioning, check out the Ubuntu community documentation at http://help.ubuntu.com/community/HowtoPartition.

Completing the Installation

Click Forward again, and the Ubuntu installer asks you some questions about your user account (see Figure 2-8): your real name, the name you want to use for logging in, the password you would like, and the hostname (the name of the computer on the network). Unless you have a network administrator in your building who has something specific in mind, you can make up a hostname or accept the installer's automatic suggestion. There is also a check box that enables you to be logged in automatically when the computer is switched on, but this isn't a good option if your computer is used in a public place—then other people could easily read your email or look through your personal files.

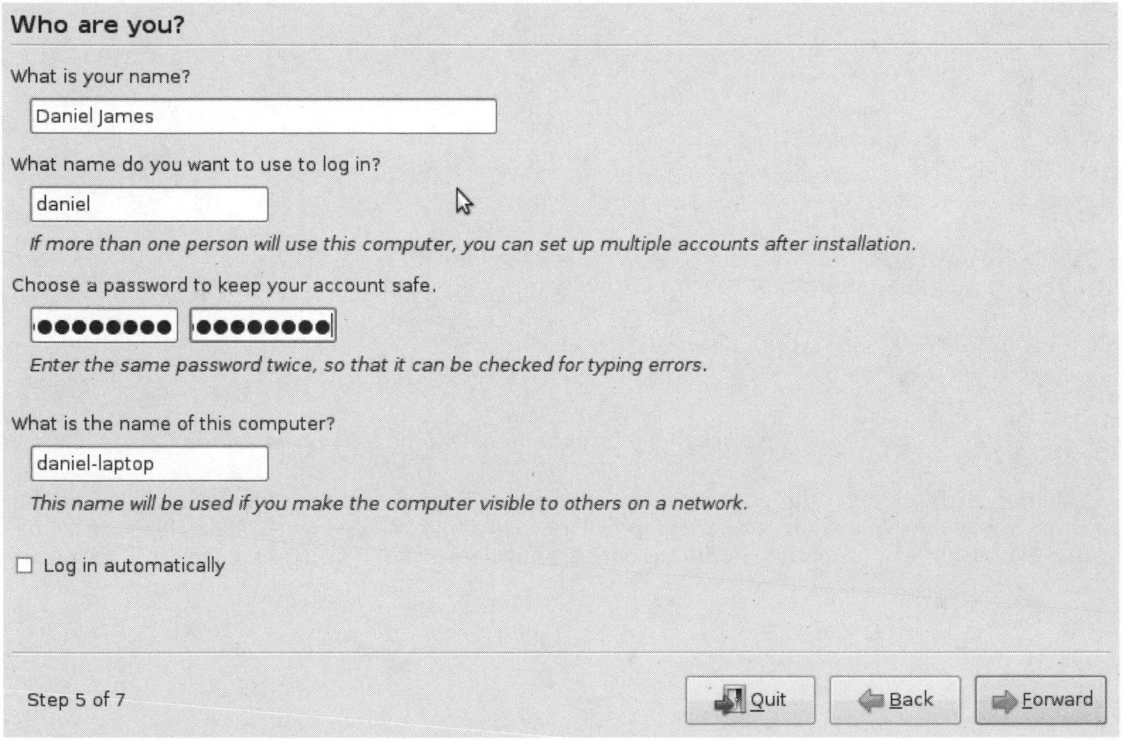

Who are you?

What is your name?

    Daniel James

What name do you want to use to log in?

    daniel

If more than one person will use this computer, you can set up multiple accounts after installation.

Choose a password to keep your account safe.

    ●●●●●●●●   ●●●●●●●●

Enter the same password twice, so that it can be checked for typing errors.

What is the name of this computer?

    daniel-laptop

This name will be used if you make the computer visible to others on a network.

☐ Log in automatically

Step 5 of 7   Quit   Back   Forward

Figure 2-8. The installer needs a few personal details for your user account.

Next comes the "Migrate documents and settings" window (see Figure 2-9). This part of the installer can copy across a few specific types of file from Windows or another GNU/Linux system on the same machine. You probably shouldn't rely on this feature to copy across all of your data, but it's useful for

25

migrating things like browser settings. If your Windows system has very large amounts of data—for example, in My Documents, My Pictures, or My Music—there's no point in copying all of it, because doing so doubles your disk usage and may exceed the space you've allotted for your Ubuntu partition. You can access these files on the Windows partition after you've installed Ubuntu.

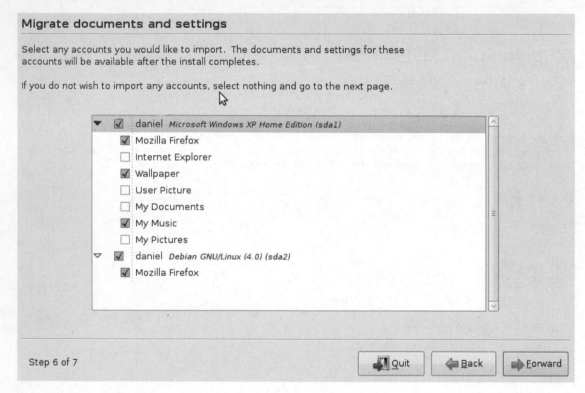

Figure 2-9. Ubuntu can copy across some files from existing systems on the same machine.

Finally, the installer presents a list of the options chosen in the previous six windows, giving you the opportunity to review your choices before you click the Install button (see Figure 2-10). There is also the warning that deleting or formatting partitions destroys any data present, so this is the point of no return.

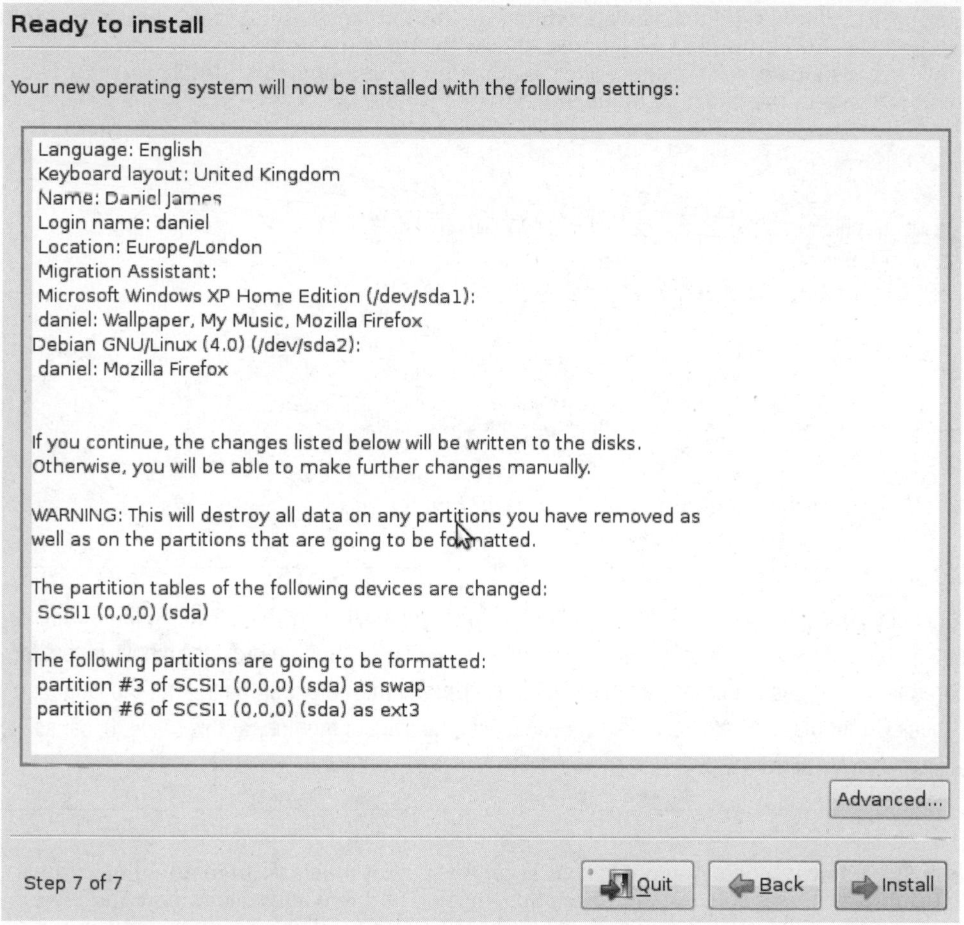

Ready to install

Your new operating system will now be installed with the following settings:

Language: English
Keyboard layout: United Kingdom
Name: Daniel James
Login name: daniel
Location: Europe/London
Migration Assistant:
Microsoft Windows XP Home Edition (/dev/sda1):
 daniel: Wallpaper, My Music, Mozilla Firefox
Debian GNU/Linux (4.0) (/dev/sda2):
 daniel: Mozilla Firefox

If you continue, the changes listed below will be written to the disks.
Otherwise, you will be able to make further changes manually.

WARNING: This will destroy all data on any partitions you have removed as
well as on the partitions that are going to be formatted.

The partition tables of the following devices are changed:
SCSI1 (0,0,0) (sda)

The following partitions are going to be formatted:
 partition #3 of SCSI1 (0,0,0) (sda) as swap
 partition #6 of SCSI1 (0,0,0) (sda) as ext3

Advanced...

Step 7 of 7

Quit   ← Back   ➡ Install

Figure 2-10. Last chance to change your mind before the installation begins.

After you click Install, a progress bar shows the installation under way (see Figure 2-11). Depending on the speed of your computer, this stage can take 20 minutes or half an hour, so you've got time to order a pizza.

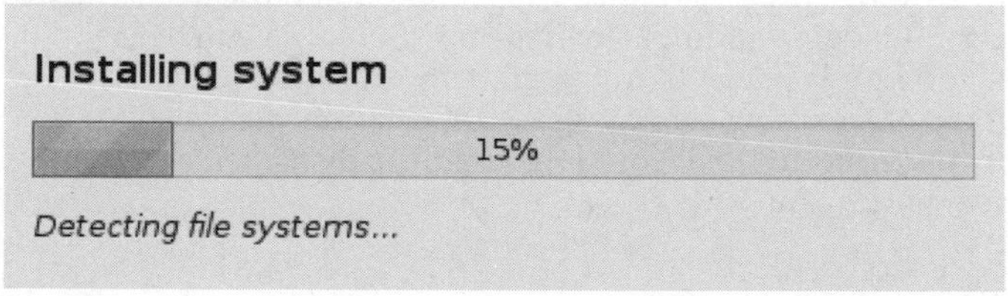

Installing system

15%

Detecting file systems...

Figure 2-11. Let the Ubuntu installer do its work while you think about dinner.

Returning to your PC or laptop, if the installation has gone smoothly, you see a dialog box informing you that you need to restart the computer (see Figure 2-12). As the machine powers down, you're prompted to remove the installation CD—otherwise, the machine could boot from the CD again (unless you change the BIOS settings or use the boot menu).

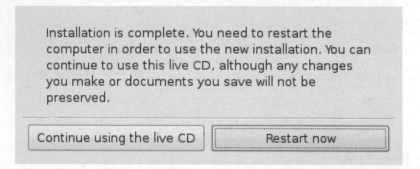

Figure 2-12. Installation is finished, but the live desktop is still functional.

■ **Tip** If the installation begins well but doesn't complete successfully, the most likely reason is that the CD media is faulty. This can be a problem with both factory-made and homemade CDs, so Ubuntu provides a built-in test for this possibility. Boot from the CD again; but instead of selecting Try Ubuntu from the first menu after the language selection, select "Check CD for defects". You can also choose to test the system memory at this stage, because faulty RAM can cause installation errors.

Although it's possible to carry on using the live desktop, there's not much point in doing so—you now have the full Ubuntu system installed. After rebooting, instead of the machine loading Windows or Ubuntu automatically from the hard disk, you should see the GRUB menu. This acronym stands for Grand Unified Boot Loader, and it describes a little piece of software that lets you boot multiple operating systems on the same machine. The menu lists entries for Ubuntu and any other systems installed previously, such as Windows XP. You can use the cursor keys on your keyboard to select a specific entry in the list, or do nothing to boot the new default system, which is likely to be Ubuntu in this case. If that's not appropriate, later you can change the operating system that GRUB selects as the default. There's more information about GRUB at http://help.ubuntu.com/community/GrubHowto.

When Ubuntu is booted, you see the same orange progress bar as when you booted the live CD. The screen then goes blank for a second as the Ubuntu login window is loaded, at which time you hear Ubuntu's login sound. (To me, this sounds like a bongo player trying to grab my attention with a theatrical flourish.) Type in the username and password you set during the installation, and you're logged in to the Ubuntu desktop again—only this time, for real. Your login name is displayed at upper right on the desktop, between the clock and the red logout button.

Installation from the Internet with Wubi

If you're not sure the full Ubuntu installation is for you, but you're after something more usable than the live desktop, there is a middle way. Wubi is a program that runs inside Windows and installs the Ubuntu operating system as if it was a Windows application. If you decide later that you want to proceed with the full Ubuntu installation, you can remove the Wubi install just like you would any Windows program.

To get Wubi up and running, you need a Windows 98, 2000, XP, or Vista PC with an Internet connection and at least 256MB RAM. You also need a minimum of 5GB disk space free to make room for Ubuntu. If you don't have an Ubuntu CD available, you can point your web browser at www.wubi-installer.org and download the wubi.exe program, which is very small (about 1MB); see Figure 2-13.

Figure 2-13. If you don't have an Ubuntu CD handy, the first step is to download the small Wubi program.

I recommend defragmenting the Windows drive on which you intend to install Ubuntu, because NTFS drives can get to be a real mess, just with everyday Windows use. You can do this in Windows XP by right-clicking the drive icon in My Computer and selecting Properties. Then, select the Tools tab, and click the Defragment Now button.

When that's done, run the Wubi program, ignoring the warning that Windows offers about Wubi potentially harming your computer (see Figure 2-14). This warning isn't based on any detailed analysis of the file other than it being an executable (a binary program).

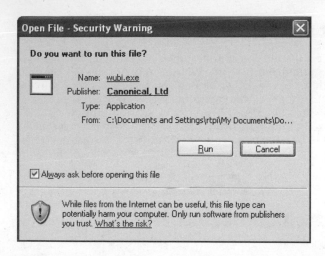

Figure 2-14. Windows displays a security warning about Wubi.

Next, a window appears that asks for the target hard drive for the installation, such as the C:, D:, or E: drive in Windows-speak (see Figure 2-15). You have to set up a username and password here, and you can also choose a language other than the default of English.

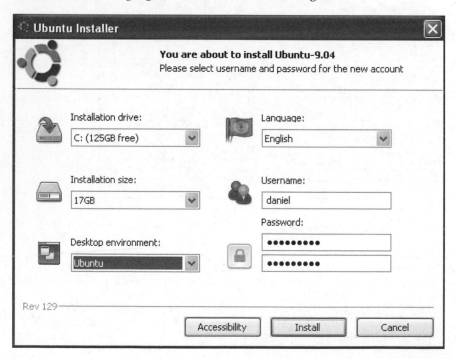

Figure 2-15. Choose the target hard drive and initial Ubuntu user account.

Some accessibility options are available, such as running the install with high-contrast fonts or magnification, for the benefit of partially sighted people. There are also keyboard aids for people with impaired mobility (see Figure 2-16).

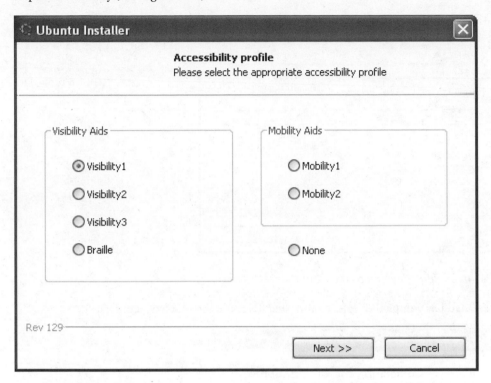

Figure 2-16. *Some accessibility options are available to help people with disabilities.*

Click Next, and the download of Ubuntu begins (see Figure 2-17). Because the install image is just under 700MB, this step can take half an hour or more on a domestic broadband connection to the Internet. On a dial-up connection, it may take several hours.

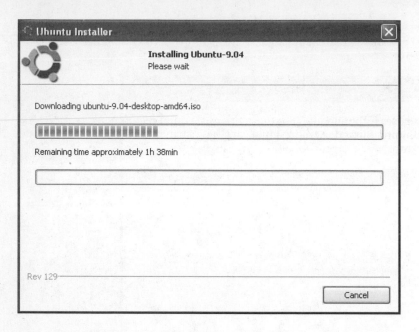

Figure 2-17. *The Wubi installer downloads the Ubuntu install image.*

When the download has completed, you're prompted to reboot the PC (see Figure 2-18).

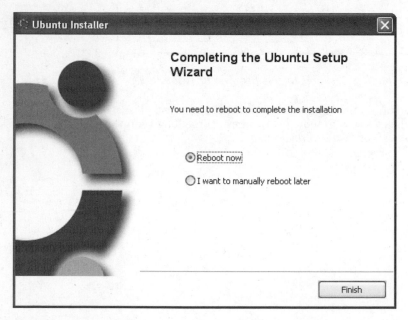

Figure 2-18. *Now it's time to reboot into Ubuntu.*

After the reboot, instead of the machine booting straight into Windows, a bootloader menu offers a choice of Windows or Ubuntu. This is the Windows bootloader, so it's not quite the same as GRUB. Select Ubuntu, and the Ubuntu logo and orange progress bar are displayed as Ubuntu boots. After this, you can log in to Ubuntu using the username and password that you entered in the Wubi dialog.

An Ubuntu installation based on Wubi has to use a different filesystem from the tried-and-tested GNU/Linux standard of ext3—a filesystem that isn't as robust as ext3 against sudden power failures. It also depends on Windows to some extent, because it lives in the same partition as the Windows installation (see Figure 2-19) and uses its bootloader. For these reasons, I don't recommend using Wubi for a long-term installation of Ubuntu. But it does represent a very low-risk method for Windows users to experience the GNU/Linux desktop.

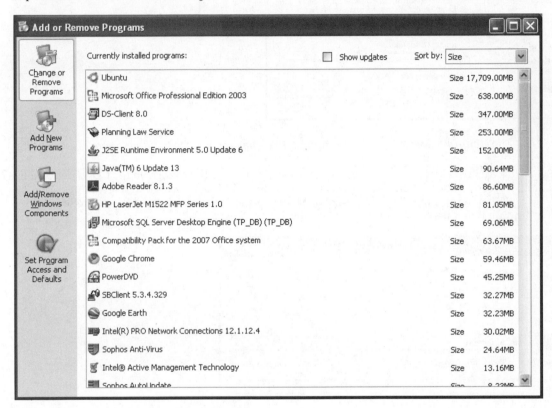

Figure 2-19. The Wubi installation of Ubuntu can easily be managed using XP's Add or Remove Programs dialog, as if it were a Windows application.

Running Wubi from CD

If you have the Ubuntu CD that comes with this book, or any recent Ubuntu Desktop CD, then there's a much quicker way to install Wubi than the download method you just read about. When you insert the Desktop CD into a Windows PC, a dialog pops up with three options: reboot to the live CD and perform a conventional install, install Wubi from the CD, or learn more about Ubuntu (see Figure 2-20).

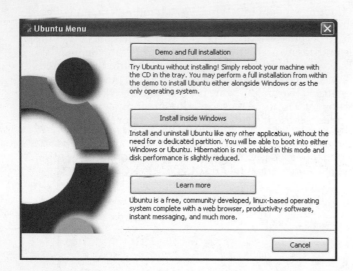

Figure 2-20. The Ubuntu Desktop CD includes a small welcome program for Windows users.

If you click the Install inside Windows button, Wubi uses the Ubuntu image on the CD to perform its installation, instead of downloading an image (see Figure 2-21). This step takes only a few minutes, instead of half an hour or more like the download. As long as the CD contains an up-to-date release of Ubuntu, running Wubi direct from the disk saves time.

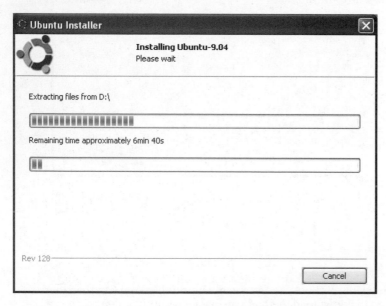

Figure 2-21. Copying Ubuntu from the CD instead of downloading it saves you time when installing Wubi. In this example, the CD drive on the Windows machine is labeled D:\.

A Tour of GNOME

Many different desktop environments and interfaces are available for GNU/Linux, but the one provided by default in Ubuntu is called GNU Object Model Environment (GNOME). It's based on the graphical toolkit originally developed for the GIMP project, and it has lots of user-friendly features. GNOME is comparable to the desktop interface of Windows Vista or Apple's OS X but is a clone of neither. Fortunately, it doesn't take long to come to grips with.

Starting in the upper-left corner, you see the Ubuntu logo: a red and orange circle with three blobs around it. (I think it's meant to represent a group hug, with the blobs being the heads of the participants and the circle being their arms.) Click the logo or the word Applications next to it, and a small start menu pops out (see Figure 2-22). This menu is divided into six fairly self-explanatory categories: Accessories, Games, Graphics, Internet, Office, and Sound & Video. A separate Add/Remove item appears at the bottom; as you'd expect, it refers to a basic software package manager that helps you install some programs recommended by Ubuntu. This chapter returns to the subject of software installation later.

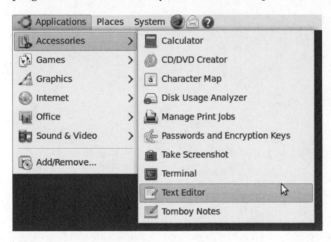

Figure 2-22. Ubuntu's main Applications menu offers access to a good number of programs out of the box.

You get a much more comprehensive set of applications in the basic Ubuntu installation than you do with a typical Windows or OS X machine, which is all the more remarkable considering that Ubuntu fits on a single CD. Not only do you get the OpenOffice.org suite as standard, but you get the GIMP too— and these aren't feature-limited or demo versions, but the full Free Software programs.

To the right of the Applications menu are two more menus: Places and System. The Places menu allows you to find directories (also known as *folders* on a graphical desktop) quickly, by providing shortcuts to the most likely locations on the GNU/Linux filesystem (see Figure 2-23). First is your personal folder in the /home partition, which is /home/daniel/ in my case. As additional users are added to the system, they get their own directories called, for example, /home/katie/ or /home/steve/. This keeps everyone's personal files properly separated. GNOME's Places menu provides a Home icon that points to the directory belonging to the user logged in at the time. There is also a Desktop icon, where files downloaded from a web browser, such as Firefox, often end up. Within your home directory, Ubuntu sets up folders to organize typical file types: Documents, Music, Pictures, and Videos.

Figure 2-23. The Places menu offers shortcuts to commonly used directories, devices, and networks.

The next section on the Places menu refers to hardware. There is an icon for the computer itself, which provides an overview of disks and the network. Any optical drives, external hard disks, and USB memory sticks available to the system are linked from here, too.

The third section on this menu has links to the network overview and a program used for connecting to remote servers, and the final section features a local file-search tool and a link listing recently accessed documents.

■ **Note** Removable storage devices are also represented as desktop icons, which you can double-click to open in GNOME's File Browser. To make sure the file-writing process has completed before you disconnect a USB device, right-click this icon and select Unmount Volume before unplugging it. This is equivalent to the Safely Remove Hardware routine in Windows XP.

Last of the three main menus is System, which, as its name suggests, provides access to preference settings and administration tools (see Figure 2-24). You probably don't need to tweak anything here right away—but as you become more proficient with your Ubuntu system, you can begin customizing it to suit you better. On the System menu, you also find shortcuts to the built-in help documentation.

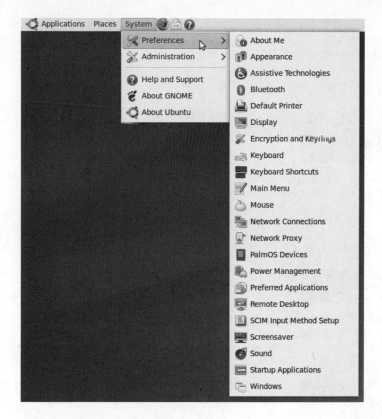

Figure 2-24. The System menu offers access to preferences, administration, and help functions.

To the immediate right of the three main menus are shortcut icons for the Firefox web browser, the Evolution mail client, and the help system.

In the upper-right corner of the desktop are alert icons from the system, which may include the following:

- An *orange burst icon* that notifies you about any updated software packages available. Mouse over it to find out how many are available to download. All Ubuntu package updates are managed with the same tool, so hundreds of updates may be available; but each package tends to be small. This icon turns into a gray arrow pointing downward as the package files are fetched from the Internet.

- A *PC card icon* that, when clicked, informs you about additional hardware drivers that are available. These typically aren't Free Software drivers, so they're labeled as restricted. Sometimes, using a restricted driver can offer better 3D graphics or wireless Internet performance, but you have to rely on the hardware vendor to fix any bugs in that driver.

- A *network monitor icon* showing two computer screens, which describes any network interfaces present when moused over. This applet handles both wired (Ethernet) and wireless (Wi-Fi) connections; left-click it to select from available wireless networks, or right-click to set network options.

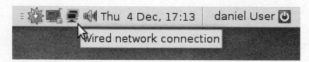

- A *sound-card volume icon* that lets you adjust or mute the audio output. Right-click this icon to open the soundcard mixer.

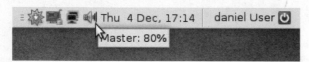

- To the right of the clock, a *red logout button*. This also enables you to shut down the machine. If you have a laptop, or a PC with power-management features, you also see Suspend and Hibernate options. In addition, you can lock the screen or begin a guest login session from this menu.

In the lower-left corner of the GNOME desktop is a handy button with an icon that looks like a picture frame (see Figure 2-25). This allows you to see whatever files and folders you have on the desktop without closing the programs you're running at the time. This is particularly useful if you're the kind of person who likes to keep their work-in-progress files on the desktop. You can always use the Places menu to file away this work later.

Figure 2-25. *Use the lower-left corner button to show files on the desktop.*

In the lower-right corner are two squares that represent virtual desktops (see Figure 2-26). This concept may be unfamiliar if you're used to Windows or OS X, but it's a standard GNU/Linux desktop feature. If you have two or more displays (monitors) on your PC, then you're used to the idea that windows can be dragged from one to the other. Related programs can be bunched together on a particular display, so you can switch your attention from one to the other without a lot of minimizing and maximizing. Ubuntu gives you a minimum of two virtual desktops (called *workspaces*) as standard, even if you have only one hardware display. This virtual desktop feature works very well, because you can only look at one display at a time.

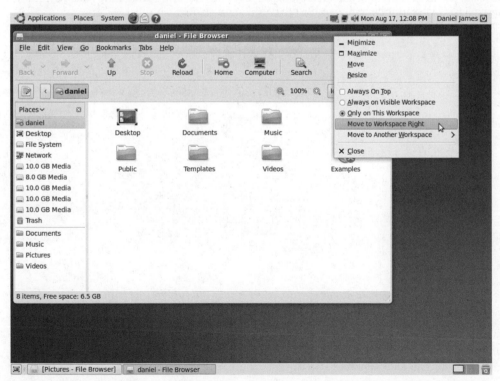

Figure 2-26. *GNOME's workspaces give you two desktops for the price of one.*

Left-click either of the squares in the lower-right corner of the desktop to switch between workspaces. If you want to move a particular window from one workspace to the other, right-click its title bar, and select Move to Workspace Right, or Move to Workspace Left. You can also select Always on Visible Workspace, in which case the window moves with your attention.

Finally, in the lower-right corner is an orange wastebasket icon. Left-click this icon to see what's inside, or right-click it and select Empty the Deleted Items Folder.

Network Configuration

It's not absolutely critical to connect a GNU/Linux machine to the Internet—it works perfectly well as a stand-alone system. But you can get the most out of Ubuntu by connecting it to the network. This step may enable you to download extra software, find creative materials on the Web, or share the fruits of your projects with others.

If you have a wired broadband router that connects to your PC via Ethernet cables, you may find that Ubuntu has established a link to the Internet automatically. Most Ethernet-based routers use a system called Dynamic Host Configuration Protocol (DHCP), which can assign an Internet Protocol (IP) address, gateway, and name server to your PC as soon as GNOME's network applet asks for them.

To set up an Ethernet connection with a static IP address, first right-click the network icon near the clock in the upper-right corner of the desktop. Select Edit Connections; then, on the Wired tab, click the PC's Ethernet interface, which is probably labeled eth0 (see Figure 2-27). (Some machines have multiple Ethernet cards, so GNU/Linux numbers them eth0, eth1, eth2, and so on.)

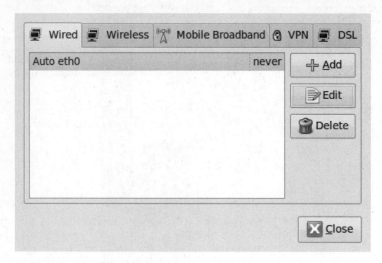

Figure 2-27. *GNOME's Network Manager enables control over most kinds of Internet connections.*

Click the Edit button, and then click the IPv4 tab (see Figure 2-28). Select Manual from the Method drop-down menu; then, enter the IP address, gateway, and domain name server (DNS) details that your network administrator or ISP has provided.

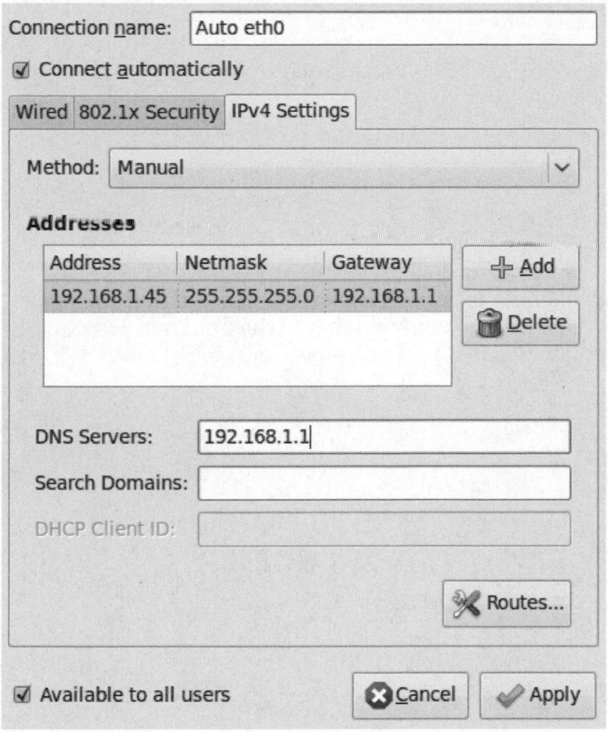

```
Connection name:  [ Auto eth0                            ]
☑ Connect automatically

[ Wired | 802.1x Security | IPv4 Settings ]

  Method:  [ Manual                              ⌄ ]

  Addresses

  ┌──────────────┬────────────────┬──────────────┐    ┌──────────┐
  │ Address      │ Netmask        │ Gateway      │    │ ✛ Add    │
  ├──────────────┼────────────────┼──────────────┤    └──────────┘
  │ 192.168.1.45 │ 255.255.255.0  │ 192.168.1.1  │    ┌──────────┐
  │              │                │              │    │ 🗑 Delete │
  │              │                │              │    └──────────┘
  └──────────────┴────────────────┴──────────────┘

  DNS Servers:     [ 192.168.1.1|                      ]
  Search Domains:  [                                   ]
  DHCP Client ID:  [                                   ]

                                    [ ✗ Routes... ]

☑ Available to all users       [ ✗ Cancel ]  [ ✓ Apply ]
```

Figure 2-28. DHCP is enabled by default, but you can also set an IP address manually.

Wireless Internet is slightly more complicated, first because some Wi-Fi chips rely on a proprietary driver that isn't installed as standard with Ubuntu, and second because several different methods are used to authenticate Wi-Fi connections. To get started, make sure your Wi-Fi chip is switched on—many laptops and netbooks have a button that disables the chip and its radio device (to improve security or save battery power). Next, click the Wireless tab in the Network Connections window; if your Wi-Fi device isn't listed, this probably means the driver isn't loaded. In this scenario, I recommend that you connect your Ubuntu machine to the Internet using a wired connection while you find out which driver is needed for your hardware.

If you have no luck with Free Software drivers, a ready-packaged driver may be available from Ubuntu's Restricted Drivers section. If the PC card icon is no longer visible in the upper-right corner of the GNOME desktop, you can find the corresponding dialog by going to the System menu and selecting Administration and then Hardware Drivers. For a wireless device listed in this window, click the Activate button to download the proprietary driver (see Figure 2-29).

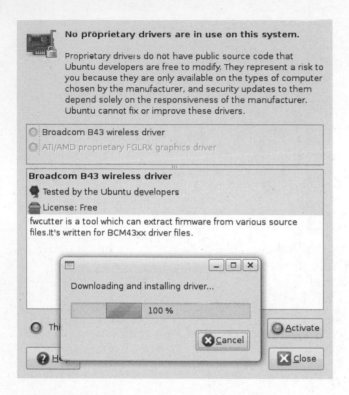

Figure 2-29. Ubuntu provides a tool for downloading proprietary drivers, including those required for many Wi-Fi chipsets.

When you have a driver loaded for your Wi-Fi hardware, you can proceed to set up the connection. Right-click the networking icon in the upper-right corner of the GNOME desktop, and select Edit Connections. On the Wireless tab, click the Add button, or the Edit button if a connection is set up already. At the very least, you have to set the SSID (network name) of the wireless network and the mode. To connect to a known access point, you probably want to set Infrastructure rather than Ad-hoc mode. If the access point uses encryption, you need to click the Wireless Security tab and set the type of encryption in use. For a domestic broadband connection, it's likely to be either Wired Equivalent Privacy (WEP) or Wi-Fi Protected Access 2 (WPA2) Personal. You must also set the password or key, of course—using the "Show password" check box helps avoid typing mistakes. On the IPv4 tab, Method should almost always be set to DHCP—because of the transient nature of Wi-Fi connections, it's much less common to use static IP addresses for these.

When the Wi-Fi connection has been made, the GNOME network icon turns into a bar graph of signal strength (see Figure 2-30). Left-click this graph to display the signal strength relative to any other access points detected in the area. You can also connect to an access point that doesn't broadcast its SSID, as long as you know what that SSID is! Passwords for multiple access points can be stored using the Create New Wireless Network option.

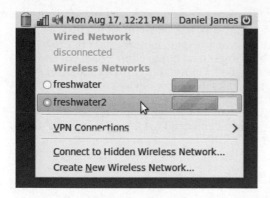

Figure 2-30. The Network Manager applet in GNOME displays Wi-Fi signal strength.

When storing or retrieving Wi-Fi passwords, you may be prompted by GNOME to allow access to the keyring and to enter your user password. This is an extra security measure, designed to make sure Wi-Fi network passwords that you type in can't be read by other users on your system or through shared directories on your local network, if you have one.

The setup for broadband delivered via the cell-phone network (also known as 3G, Universal Mobile Telecommunications System [UMTS], or High Speed Packet Access [HSPA]) is different than that used for Wi-Fi. Perhaps because of the relative complexity of these mobile broadband connections, or a lack of standardization, Ubuntu provides a wizard to help you set them up. In the Network Connections window, click the Mobile Broadband tab, and then click the Add button. You then have to select your country, your cellular phone company, and the type of subscription you have (see Figure 2-31). When that's done, you can edit the new connection to enter the dial-in number, username, and password given to you by the phone company when you set up the account.

Figure 2-31. Ubuntu provides a wizard to help you set up mobile broadband (3G) connections.

If you have wired broadband via a phone line but don't have a router, the fifth tab in the Network Connections window is for you. Perhaps your phone company has supplied you with an Ethernet modem for asymmetric digital subscriber line (ADSL), in which case the attached computer has to handle the authentication process. As with setting up a mobile broadband connection, you must enter the username and password that your phone company has supplied. Ubuntu also provides support for the cheap and nasty USB modems supplied by some ADSL providers, but these devices often aren't worth the trouble it takes to set them up. Usually, upgrading to a proper router is a better option, especially if you have more than one computer in your house or building. A web search on *ubuntu* plus the make and model of the adapter in question should tell you what you need to know.

Additional Software Installation

As hinted earlier, software management tends to be centralized on GNU/Linux systems. Using Windows or OS X, you may have to visit a number of different websites and gather a variety of CD-ROMs and DVD-ROMs in order to install the applications you need. Apart from the time this effort can take for each new install, it can be very annoying on Windows when half a dozen different applications pop up a message, prompting you to update each one individually.

If you open the Add/Remove Applications program at the foot of GNOME's Applications menu, you're prompted for your password before you can install any new software (see Figure 2-32). Other people who have access to your computer can't sit down and install random programs that they found in the shadier corners of the Internet. This is one of the key features that keeps GNU/Linux systems more secure and reliable than typical Windows machines. However, it's still possible for programs to be installed and run from your /home directory if your session stays logged in while the machine is unattended. That's why Ubuntu has screen-locking and guest session options on its logout menu, in the upper-right corner of the desktop.

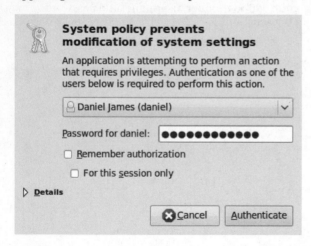

Figure 2-32. All software installed system-wide on Ubuntu requires your password, entered here into a dialog box. Don't check the "Remember authorization" box if anyone else has access to your computer; if you do, the password check is bypassed.

Because of the redistributable nature of Free Software, most of the GNU/Linux distributions offer large online package repositories containing all the popular programs in a tested and ready-to-run format. Typically, these packages are divided into sections according to their perceived importance, and Ubuntu is no exception. In the Add/Remove Applications tool, you can select "All Open Source applications" or "Canonical-maintained applications" from a drop-down list. (Canonical is the commercial organization that produces the Ubuntu distribution.)

In Ubuntu, the section of applications maintained by Canonical is known as *main*, and the section of packages maintained by the wider Free Software community is known as *universe*. Many of the best creative applications for GNU/Linux are in the Ubuntu universe repository. There is also a section called *restricted* that contains the Canonical supported but non–Free Software packages available for Ubuntu, and a section known as *multiverse* for non–Free Software packages without Canonical support.

One package you're likely to need from the multiverse section is flashplugin-installer, which downloads Adobe's proprietary Flash plug-in for Firefox and other browsers. Many contemporary websites won't work without it. Although Free Software alternatives to the plug-in are under development by the Gnash and Swfdec projects, for now at least, Adobe's plug-in remains the most functional choice for multimedia websites like YouTube and MySpace. See www.gnu.org/software/gnash/ for more details about Gnash.

To locate the package you're interested in, either browse the categories at left in the Add/Remove Applications window or type a search term into the box at upper right. The search tool can find packages by their description, so you don't need to know the exact name of the software in question to locate it. Then, check the box next to the package name, and click the Apply Changes button at lower right (see Figure 2-33).

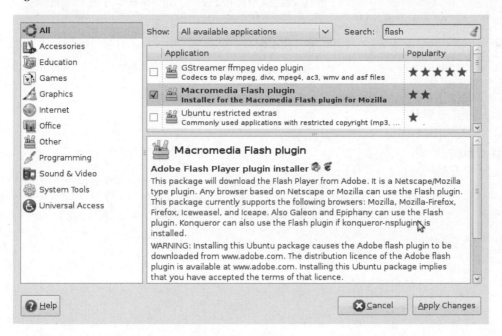

Figure 2-33. The downloader for Adobe's Flash plug-in is one of the more useful packages in the multiverse section.

Occasionally, this program prompts you to update the list of packages available, which you can do with a single click (as long as the machine is connected to the Internet); see Figure 2-34.

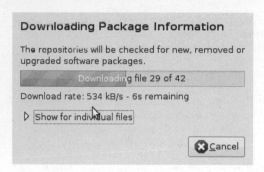

Figure 2-34. Ubuntu needs to refresh its list of packages to check for critical updates.

Refreshing this list of packages often causes Ubuntu's Update Manager to begin working in the upper-right corner of the GNOME desktop. As you saw earlier, an orange burst icon appears, and it's important not to ignore this. In addition to critical bug fixes, Update Manager downloads security fixes that help keep your PC and data safe when you use the Internet. GNU/Linux has a pretty solid security record so far, with almost zero virus or spyware activity—but as the Free Software platform becomes ever more widespread, that may not always be the case. It's best not to put off downloading the package updates for too long, unless you're right in the middle of an important project.

If you've just installed Ubuntu for the first time, there are likely to be a large number of packages that have been updated since the release of that version (see Figure 2-35). After this major update, it should settle down to just a few packages per day.

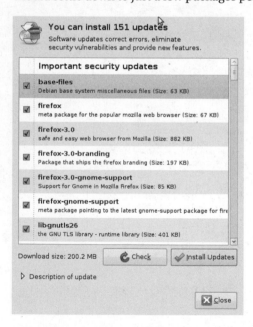

Figure 2-35. The first update of a new Ubuntu system can contain hundreds of packages improved since the original distribution release.

When an update has completed, sometimes a new Linux kernel has been installed. This is one of the few times when a GNU/Linux machine must be powered down and restarted, because nearly all other updates can be made on the fly (see Figure 2-36). If this is the case, then Update Manager prompts you to reboot the PC.

Figure 2-36. Update Manager lets you know if the machine has to be rebooted, but this is comparatively rare with GNU/Linux.

Setting Up a Printer

When your Ubuntu machine is running smoothly, connected to the Internet, and downloading new applications, most creative users want to perform one more task before going any further. Fortunately, printer setup on GNU/Linux is smooth these days. Support for most popular printer models is built in, and most USB printers can be auto-detected. With your printer plugged in to the computer and switched on, you may find that it has been set up for you already (see Figure 2-37).

Figure 2-37. With printers like this Epson Stylus inkjet, getting the device working is as simple as plugging it in. You don't even have to click through a wizard!

It only remains for you to click the Configure button and set options such as the print quality mode, paper size, and paper type (see Figure 2-38).

Figure 2-38. The printer configuration utility offers control over all options made available by the driver.

If your printer is connected properly and powered on, but not detected automatically, you can go to the System menu, select Administration, and then select Printing. Click the New button, and you can then specify a network printer location or a particular driver that should be used. This printer administration tool is also useful for managing your printer (or printers) when in use later.

Further Reading

This chapter has been a short introduction to the GNU/Linux desktop, with just enough information to get a typical PC up and running with Ubuntu. If you'd like to know more about configuring and running the operating system, I recommend *Beginning Ubuntu Linux, 4th edition*, by Keir Thomas and Andy Channelle with Jaime Sicam (Apress, 2009, ISBN-13: 978-1-4302-1999-6). (I was a technical reviewer on the third edition of that best-selling title.) If you'd like some help with the OpenOffice.org suite included with Ubuntu, I suggest *Beginning OpenOffice 3*, by Andy Channelle, my colleague at *Linux Format* magazine (Apress, 2008, ISBN 978-1-4302-1590-5).

PART 2

■ ■ ■

Tools

This section of the book explains how to use the leading Free Software creative tools, with enough detail that you can begin using these applications for real projects of your own.

CHAPTER 3

■ ■ ■

Photography

Getting Photos into the Computer

If you're working with a digital still camera, it almost certainly has a USB socket. Using the USB cable supplied with the camera is often the quickest and simplest way to get your photos on to your computer. Although programs like F-Spot (GNU/Linux), included with Ubuntu by default, can help you manage your photo collection, it isn't strictly necessary to use them. This is because GNU/Linux can access the memory card inside a USB-equipped camera as if it were any other storage device.

When you plug the camera into the computer and switch it on, Ubuntu detects the make and model of the camera via the USB cable. At the same time, an icon for the camera appears on the GNOME desktop in the upper-left corner. You can use this icon to view the photo files stored on the camera's memory card or to unmount it by right-clicking—just as if the camera was a USB memory stick. Proper unmounting makes sure all writes to the camera's memory card have completed before you pull out the plug, which reduces the risk of file corruption.

After camera detection and mounting, a dialog pops up, giving you the choice of opening the photo files in F-Spot or Nautilus (GNU/Linux, Mac), the regular file manager included with the GNOME desktop (see Figure 3-1). Nautilus has a snail shell icon and is labeled Open Folder here.

When you've decided which method you prefer, check the "Always perform this action" box to save your preference. You can also choose to unmount the camera's memory card from this dialog box, if this wasn't the camera you wanted to access, after all.

Figure 3-1. Ubuntu recognizes the make and model of camera and offers a choice of applications for photo file management.

If you choose to open the camera memory card in Nautilus, you access the filesystem on the card directly. There are probably a couple of directories with names like `store_00010001`, which are created by the camera—don't delete these unless you want to reformat the card. Typically, the photos are stored in one of these folders, perhaps in a subdirectory; the other folders contain the settings file for the camera. A little trial and error locates the images you're after. In the case of the Kodak DX6490 camera I use, the images are stored under the `store_00010001/DCIM/100K6490` directory. Note that in Figure 3-2, the camera has its own icon in Nautilus's Places sidebar.

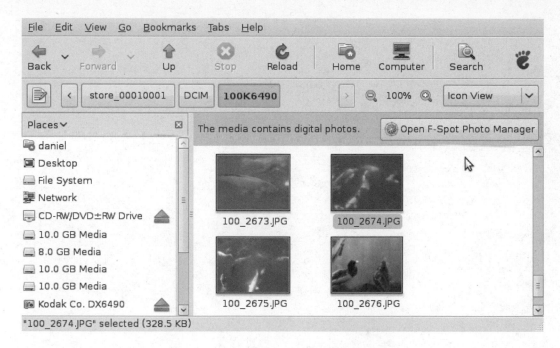

Figure 3-2. You can use Nautilus to drag and drop photo files from the camera's memory card.

The images on the camera are thumbnailed; a left click opens each one in the default application, whereas a right click presents a list of alternative programs. Photos can be dragged and dropped, or copied and pasted, like any other file. There is also a button that opens F-Spot directly from this Nautilus window.

■ **Tip** Don't leave your camera connected to the computer and switched on for too long. If the camera goes into a power-saving mode, the memory card inside may not be unmounted correctly by Ubuntu, resulting in an error message. If this happens, switch off the camera completely, and then switch it on again. You may also need to remove the USB plug from the computer and reinsert it before switching on the camera.

Using F-Spot to Import Photos

F-Spot works slightly differently than Nautilus. Instead of accessing the camera's memory card directly, the program invites you to begin by copying selected photos to your personal /home directory on the hard disk. F-Spot first unmounts the camera, if it's mounted (the desktop icon for it disappears), and then downloads previews of the photos (see Figure 3-3).

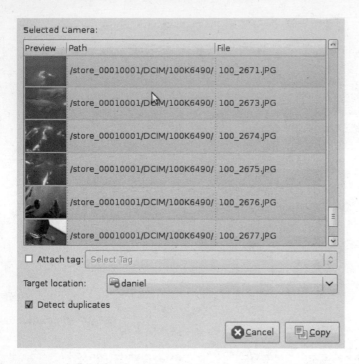

Figure 3-3. *F-Spot asks you to select the photos that you wish to copy to your* /home *directory.*

By default, all the photos in the preview window are selected and are highlighted in orange. If you don't need to download all of them, Shift+click to select adjacent photos, or Ctrl+click to select noncontiguous groups of photos.

At this point, you can tag your photos to help you organize them later. The default tags available are Favorites, Hidden, People, Places, and Events, but you can also create your own custom tags. Tags aren't added to the photo files permanently unless you select the "Write metadata to file" check box under Edit ➤ Preferences on the main F-Spot menu bar. If you choose this option, other compatible software should be able to read the tags, too.

The target location for your images may be /home/dave/Photos or /home/sue/Pictures, depending on your username and how your computer is set up.

Click the Copy button, and F-Spot transfers the photo files from the camera; it lets you know when it has completed the task. You can now switch off the camera and unplug the USB cable, because its memory card was unmounted earlier.

Next, F-Spot's main window opens, displaying thumbnails of your photos beneath a timeline (see Figure 3-4). The timeline has a bar graph that represents the number of photos taken each month, based on the information stored by the camera. You can drag the rectangular slider along the timeline with your mouse to reveal how many photos were taken each month.

Figure 3-4. F-Spot features a photo timeline and a bar graph of monthly totals.

If you've never gotten around to setting the date on your camera, or if it has blinked 1/1/2000 ever since you changed the batteries, now would be an excellent time to put that date right!

To begin with, F-Spot is in Browse mode, which is something like a light box. By clicking the Edit Image button above the timeline, you can view individual photos in close-up (see Figure 3-5). Alternatively, double-click the photo you want to view or edit.

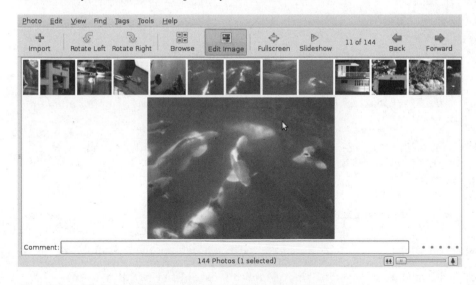

Figure 3-5. Click the Edit Image button for close-ups of your photos.

Depending on the size of your computer's screen, you'll probably have to maximize the F-Spot window to see the Back and Forward buttons on the right side. There are also buttons for rotating images or running a slideshow.

F-Spot's image-editing capabilities are basic compared to what the GIMP can achieve; but F-Spot does have tools for common tasks, hidden at left (see Figure 3-6)—you may need to click and drag out the left side of the window to see these tools. They include buttons for cropping, red-eye reduction, and adjusting the color of your photos. Note that when you make an edit using the tools in F-Spot, there is no Undo button. Instead, you can revert to the unmodified image by selecting original from the Version drop-down menu in the left-side toolbar.

Figure 3-6. The editing tools in F-Spot are well hidden but may prove useful for basic photo-manipulation tasks.

F-Spot is primarily a photo import, management, and cataloging tool, rather than an editor. In its favor, it presents an easy-to-use and consistent interface for your photo collection, whatever make and model of digital camera you happen to use.

GThumb: An Alternative to F-Spot

Many older digital cameras that use a serial cable are supported by a program called gThumb (GNU/Linux, Mac). This application also works very well for USB cameras. gThumb isn't installed on Ubuntu by default, but it's available via the Add/Remove Applications tool on GNOME's main Applications menu. One of the most useful features of gThumb is that it can automatically create image galleries for static web sites (simple sites that don't require a database). To do this, select Create Web Album from gThumb's Tools menu. Like F-Spot, gThumb also has photo cataloging and basic editing features.

Card Readers and Bluetooth

You may have a camera memory-card reader fitted to your computer; but when you're running Ubuntu, you need to check whether a GNU/Linux driver is available for the reader device. The external card readers with a USB connection tend to work, but the internal readers fitted to laptops and some desktop machines can be problematic. Sometimes, an internal card reader works with certain types of memory card but not others.

The same rule about GNU/Linux drivers applies when you're transferring images from cameras or camera phones using Bluetooth wireless networking, for which Ubuntu has a wizard. If a Bluetooth device is detected on the computer, an icon is displayed near the clock at upper-right. To use the wizard, click the Bluetooth icon (a white, stylized *B* in a blue oval), and select "Setup new device" (see Figure 3-7).

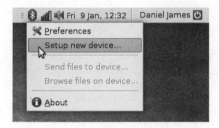

Figure 3-7. Ubuntu detects Bluetooth adaptors automatically, if your hardware has them.

Scanning Prints, Slides, and Negatives

If you need to work with archived photos that aren't available in a digital format, or you prefer film as the primary medium, you'll be pleased to know that Ubuntu includes scanner support out of the box. Of course, scanners are also useful for digitizing hand-drawn artwork and paintings. Most image scanners made recently have USB interfaces, but many older scanners with SCSI or parallel (printer port) interfaces are also supported under GNU/Linux.

First, you need to connect your scanner and power it on. If it's a SCSI scanner, make sure the SCSI chain is properly terminated and that there are no device ID number conflicts. Confusingly, some scanners made in the 1990s used the same 25-pin D-shaped socket, whether they were SCSI or parallel port models, so make sure you have the cable hooked up to the right place. (The SCSI logo is a square rotated 45 degrees, with the right corner changed to a horizontal bar; a parallel port is usually marked with a printer icon.)

Next, on GNOME's Applications menu, select Graphics, and then choose XSane Image Scanner. The XSane (GNU/Linux, Windows) program searches for scanners connected to your computer and then presents a list of the devices it has detected (if any). In my case, I use an Epson 2400 Photo scanner connected by USB. XSane detects my scanner as an Epson GT-9300 (see Figure 3-8), but I can click OK and it works, because both models of scanner can use the same driver. The program then loads three floating windows: the main XSane window, a preview window, and a histogram window.

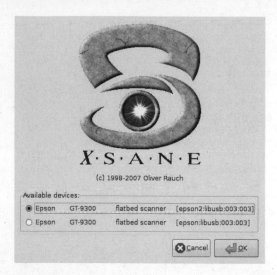

Figure 3-8. XSane automatically detects the scanning devices attached to the computer.

XSane's default scanning settings aren't likely to be very useful for creative photographic or illustration work. For instance, scans are set to be exported in the PNM image format on startup, which isn't commonly used for photos. In the Type drop-down box (see Figure 3-9), select JPEG, or perhaps TIFF if you're looking for higher quality and file storage space isn't an issue. You can also select the PNG format, used mostly for web graphics. Compression settings for these formats are in the Filetype tab of the Setup menu, which is located on the Preferences menu of the main XSane window's menu bar.

Figure 3-9. It's important to set appropriate scan settings in XSane before you begin.

Below the Type drop-down box is the setting for scan source (which defaults to the scanner's flatbed), used for photographic prints. If your scanner has a transparency unit for slides and negatives (lit from above, rather than below) or a document feeder, then it should be listed.

Next is the setting for scan mode, which defaults to Binary (black and white only). Again, this isn't well suited for our purposes; even black and white artwork looks better when scanned in grayscale mode, because of the subtle shades of gray on the edges between black and white areas. If you select Gray or Color in this drop-down menu, an additional box appears for color range. The default setting is for a full color range print, but you can also select Slide or Negative. Presets are available for Agfa, Fuji, Kodak, Konica, and Rossman negatives, varying by the photographic process used. You can also create your own presets in this dialog.

The final drop-down box in this dialog is for scan resolution. Scan resolutions are usually measured in pixels per inch (ppi), even when you're scanning metric-sized images and documents. Many people confuse scan ppi with dots per inch (dpi), a different measurement used in printing. Most modern scanners are capable of relatively high resolutions, so the resolution you choose should depend on how you intend to use the image and your available file storage space. The following section throws some light on these topics.

A Word or Two About Resolution

As a general rule of thumb, most magazine-quality printing requires a resolution of 300 ppi or higher—otherwise, artifacts of the digital process may be visible on the page. These artifacts may include individual pixels being visible; sometimes, file-compression techniques cause noticeable patterns or blurring among the pixels. Consider that digital photography is just an optical illusion that attempts to make you believe a real, continuous image is in front of you. The more pixels are in the scan, the closer the digital representation is to the real thing.

This resolution number has little to do with the size of the original image being scanned; instead, it describes how large the image can be printed without artifacts being visible. So, in the example of a magazine that specifies a 300 ppi minimum, a cover image printed ten inches high needs to have 3,000 or more pixels in the vertical dimension. If the original image is only five inches high, it must be scanned with at least 600 ppi, in order to include the necessary detail.

From this comparison, you can tell that when you're scanning 35mm slides and negatives, you usually need to scan at very high resolutions. A one-inch-high image on a slide, in the magazine cover example, would need to be scanned at 3,000 ppi. If the same image was to be printed at a smaller size on an inside page of the magazine, then a lower scan resolution might be acceptable. For instance, if the image was going to be printed three inches high, then it could be scanned at only 900 ppi, saving file space on the storage server.

Graphics destined for the web are a different matter, because a computer screen has a fixed maximum resolution. The computer screen I use has 1,280 pixels horizontally by 1,024 pixels vertically, and is about 13½ inches wide by 10½ inches high. By convention, computer screens are supposed to have a resolution of 72 ppi; so, you'll find a setting of this value in most scanning programs, including XSane. Most modern flat-screen displays have a resolution of around 100 ppi, as you can figure out from the dimensions I just gave for my screen. Some web tablet and netbook computers now have higher resolutions, squeezing more than 1,000 pixels horizontally into a display that may be only six inches across. Even at 170 ppi or greater, typical computer screens still have some way to go before they can match the resolution of good quality printing. This extra detail and sharpness on the printed page, which is particularly noticeable when reading text, may be one reason why people still read books!

An image printed at 100 ppi probably won't look as good on paper as it does on a screen of the same resolution, and yet the screen can't display any more pixels without zooming out to shrink the image. This is why it's common on the Web to show photographs as thumbnails perhaps 500 pixels wide, with a link to a higher-resolution version for printing that's maybe 3,000 pixels wide. Because turning a low-resolution image into a high-resolution one (by interpolating pixels) can't replace detail missing from the original scan, it makes sense to scan at print resolution and then scale down from this master image whenever a web version is required.

Making the Scan

Now it's time to put the image into the scanner. Back in XSane, make sure the preview window is visible (Window ➤ Show Preview). Click the "Acquire preview" button in the lower-left corner, and a progress bar indicates that a low-resolution preview scan is taking place. If you get an error message when trying to preview-scan, especially after leaving the computer idle for a while, it's possible that the scanner has gone into a power-saving mode—in that case, try again. This sometimes happens with modern, energy-efficient USB scanners.

Drag the dotted outline in the preview window around the part of the image you'd like to scan (see Figure 3-10). Then, click the Scan button in the main XSane window, and the full resolution scan begins. The scan is displayed in its own window at 100% of its pixel size, which may be larger than your computer screen can view at one time. At this point, you can perform some basic editing functions directly within XSane; but most likely you'll want to click the green disk icon to save the image file. XSane does a pretty good job of adjusting gamma, brightness, and contrast for the scan automatically. If you're not happy with the results, you can adjust the sliders for these settings manually in the main XSane window.

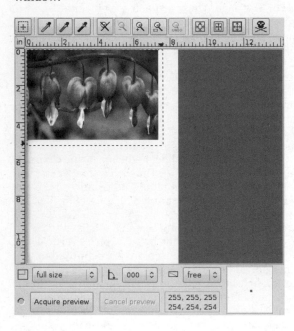

Figure 3-10. *Preview in XSane first, to make sure you've got the right area for the scan.*

Scanning within the GIMP

XSane has a plug-in that enables scanners to be used directly inside the GIMP (GNU/Linux, Windows, Mac). Because you'll get creative with your scanned and imported images, using the plug-in is often quicker and more convenient than using XSane in stand-alone mode. In Ubuntu, start the GIMP by choosing Applications ➤ Graphics ➤ GIMP Image Editor on the GNOME menu. After the main GIMP window fills your screen, select File ➤ Create ➤ XSane ➤ Device dialog; the XSane device-selection window appears again.

This time, though, because you're using the plug-in, scanned images open ready for editing and manipulation inside the GIMP, skipping the file-saving step (see Figure 3-11). Bear this fact in mind if you wish to keep unmodified versions of the scans; save each image before you begin work on it, in this case.

Figure 3-11. Scanning inside the GIMP enables a faster workflow.

___

■ **Tip** To compare scan resolution with digital camera resolution, multiply the vertical dimension of the scan, in pixels, by the horizontal dimension. 3,000 pixels vertically by 2,500 pixels horizontally equals 7,500,000 pixels, or 7.5 megapixels in camera marketing speak.

___

Which File Format to Use?

The GIMP can save image files in a wide variety of formats, including JPEG, TIFF, and PNG. For images that you'll work on later, it's best to use the GIMP's native XCF file format. This format isn't widely recognized by other graphics programs, so it's not a great choice for final output or sharing with people who use different software. Having said that, it's a high-quality format with support for saving layers, channels, and paths. In these respects, it's similar to the native PSD format used by Adobe Photoshop. The GIMP can also save and open PSD files, so if you're working side-by-side with Photoshop users, PSD may be a better choice for you (see Figure 3-12). Of course, these high-quality, multilayered formats take up more storage space, but they're considerably more flexible when it comes to making changes to the image later.

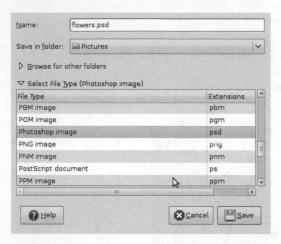

Figure 3-12. The GIMP can save images in Adobe Photoshop's PSD format, but they will probably be larger than native XCF files.

To give you an idea of the storage requirements, I scanned a roughly 7 inch by 5 inch print of a flower photograph at 300 ppi and saved it to XCF, PSD, and JPEG formats. File ➤ Save As offers you the same choice. The JPEG quality setting was 100%, to make sure the image had no compression artifacts, thereby allowing a fair comparison of quality. Subjectively, all three images appeared identical on my computer's display.
Here are the results:

- Image size: 2,192 x 1,459 pixels

- XCF image size: 9.2MB

- PSD image size: 17.9MB

- JPEG image size: 1.8MB

As you can see, even at 100% quality, the JPEG is only one-fifth the size of the XCF file and almost one-tenth of the PSD size. This is for an image straight from the scanner, with a single layer and no paths. (You look at layers and paths later.)

It's easy to appreciate why JPEG is the standard format for high-quality images on the Web, where download times and bandwidth used are crucial. However, on your creative workstation, you may have hundreds of gigabytes of storage, or even terabytes of disk space. You can afford the luxury of working in native image formats until the project is completed and needs to reach the outside world. Then, you can export your images to whichever format is required by your co-creators, colleagues, or local print shop.

The GIMP's Selection Tools

Notice that the GIMP has a floating Toolbox window, not unlike the one found in Photoshop. This Toolbox is divided into upper and lower halves; the top half contains tool icons, whereas the bottom half displays options for the currently selected tool (see Figure 3-13). Starting with the top row of tools, five different selection methods are available. Selections are crucial for detailed image manipulation, because you need to be able to move and apply effects to individual elements of the image. That's why the GIMP offers five different methods for the same task.

Figure 3-13. The lower half of the GIMP's Toolbox displays options for the current tool.

First is the Rectangle Select tool, at upper left, which is straightforward. With this tool selected, click anywhere in the image window; while holding down the button, drag the mouse pointer diagonally. This action results in a rectangle of tiny black and white dashes being drawn around your selection, sometimes called *marching ants* because of the motion of the dashes. Any operation you choose from the GIMP's Colors or Filters menu is now applied only to the area inside the rectangle, not the entire image.

If you select the wrong part of the image, you have three options for adjustment. First, you can mouse over a corner of the rectangular selection, and a small square appears just inside that corner; click and drag inside this square, and you can change the position of that corner of the selection (see Figure 3-14). Second, mouse over the middle of any of the sides, and then click and drag to adjust the rectangle in only that dimension. Or third, click the center of the selection, and, while holding down the mouse button, drag the entire selection to another part of the image without changing the selection's shape. If you're not happy with the selection, you can either click None on the GIMP's Select menu or click outside the existing selection to begin anew.

Figure 3-14. Click inside the corner of the rectangular selection to drag it inwards or outwards.

Next along in the top row of tools is the Ellipse Select tool; apart from its shape, it works the same way as the rectangle select tool. To make an elliptical selection that is a regular circle, select the Fixed check box and select "Aspect ratio" in the lower half of the GIMP's Toolbox.

After that comes the Free Select tool, represented by a lasso icon. With a mouse or laptop trackpad, free selections are most useful for roughly defining an area. If you have a touch-sensitive graphics tablet with a stylus, and a steady hand, you may also find the free select tool capable of more detailed work.

The next tool is the Fuzzy Select tool, which has a magic wand icon. This selects regions on the basis of similar color. Because a real photograph may have thousands of different colors or very few tones, this tool must have adjustable sensitivity in order to be useful. You make this adjustment using the Threshold control in the lower half of the GIMP's Toolbox. The default maximum color difference setting is 15, but you may have to increase this value to get the result you want. Hold down the Shift key to grow the selection with successive clicks. If you go too far and grow the selection to cover part of the image that you don't want, click Edit ➤ Undo Fuzzy Select, or press the keyboard shortcut for Undo (Ctrl+Z). It's well worth practicing with the Fuzzy Select tool, because you can use it to select complex shapes with great accuracy (see Figure 3-15).

Figure 3-15. The Fuzzy Select tool is very useful for selecting complex shapes.

The Select by Color tool works similarly to Fuzzy Select, except that it operates across the entire image instead of just the adjacent area. In the flower photo example, you can select all the areas that are the same shade of pink with just one click.

On the second row of tools are three more ways to create selections. First is the Scissor Select tool, which uses edge detection to help you trace the outline of shapes. With this tool active, click all around the object you want to select. The GIMP does its best to trace the outline of that object. How well it performs this task depends in part on how accurate your mouse clicks are, of course. When you return to the point at which you started the selection and complete the loop, click inside the selection to finalize it; the marching ants now appear (see Figure 3-16).

Figure 3-16. Scissor Select uses edge detection to trace shapes.

Next up is the Foreground Select Tool, which requires you to draw a lasso by clicking and dragging the cursor around the area you're interested in. As you release the mouse button, the lasso cursor changes to a paintbrush cursor. The rest of the image is now masked in a transparent blue to show that it's outside this area. (You can use the Toolbox options to mask in red or green, if you prefer.) After that, click a foreground part of the image, and the rest of the foreground is selected automatically (see Figure 3-17).

Figure 3-17. The Foreground Select tool can isolate parts of an image, with some help from your eye.

You can grow the foreground selection using the paintbrush cursor and successive clicks, or clicks and drags; unlike the Fuzzy Select tool, you don't have to hold down the Shift key to do this. If this tool automatically selects an area that isn't part of the foreground, hold down the Ctrl key, and the tool's icon changes from a paintbrush to an eraser; you can now remove the incorrect area from the selection. Press the Enter key when you're happy with the selection you've made, and the masked image changes to the marching ants again.

The Path Tool

The final selection tool in the box is a little different than the others. The Path tool has an icon like a fountain pen nib drawing a curved line. It works in a similar way to the path tools found in other graphics programs, with nodes (points) joining curves that can be edited and moved. When your path is where it needs to be, you can turn it into a selection or put a stroke (brushstroke) on the path, creating a border around the selected part of the image.

By default, the Path tool is in Design mode. This is a mode you can use to draw your first attempt at a path around the part of the image you want to select. Click in the image window with this tool selected, and a colored dot indicates the first node. Click again, a few pixels away, and the first segment of the path is drawn. The Path tool gets more interesting when you click, keep the button held down, and then drag the mouse: two handles appear, one on each side of the node; the further you drag, the curvier the line between the nodes becomes. Using these handles and a little practice, you can create complex curves in a way that is much quicker and more accurate than drawing freehand with a mouse.

Switching to Edit mode, using the Path options in the Toolbox, means you can go back to a node you created previously and move its handles to alter the curve (see Figure 3-18). By holding down the Shift key, you can also delete a node in this mode. If you need to move the entire path, switch to Move mode, and click and drag anywhere in the image.

Figure 3-18. You can use the Path tool to make editable selections.

When you're happy with the shape of your path, use Select ➤ From Path to turn the nodes and segments into a marching-ants selection.

The real power of the Path tool becomes apparent when you open its dockable dialog box. You've already seen how the Tool Options dialog is docked in the lower half of the Toolbox by default, but many other tool-related dialogs are available in the GIMP. You can leave these dialogs as free-floating windows or drag and drop them into the lower part of the Toolbox. Multiple docked dialogs appear as tabs, so you can flip through them with a mouse click.

Select Windows ➤ Dockable Dialogs ➤ Paths, and the Paths dialog pops up. Any paths drawn on the image are listed here, labeled Unnamed, Unnamed#1, Unnamed#2, and so on (see Figure 3-19). These paths are only visible on top of the image being edited while the Paths tool is active, unless you click the left column in the dialog to make an eye icon appear. The paths with eye icons are then visible when you use any other tool, although the individual nodes aren't shown.

Figure 3-19. The Paths dockable dialog lets you rename paths or make them visible when other tools are in use.

If you right-click a path's name, you can select Edit Path Attributes and rename the path something more memorable than Unnamed. Alternatively, double-click to change the name of the path. Now, you can recall and edit paths created earlier, and turn them into selections whenever you wish. The paths can also be reordered, duplicated, or stroked with an outline, using the small icons along the bottom edge of the dialog. Up and down arrows let you stack the individual paths in any order you wish.

■ **Tip** At upper-right in each dockable dialog is a small gray arrowhead icon, pointing to the left. Click this icon to add more tool tabs to the dock or to close one. Helpfully, the GIMP remembers the changes you make to tool tabs the next time you start the program.

Choosing Colors

After the Path tool, next along in the Toolbox is the Color Picker, which has a pipette icon. By default, the Color Picker sets the active foreground color used by brushes and other painting tools. When you hold down the Shift key, you can use this tool to pop up numerical color values for a particular shade, which is very useful when you're trying to match colors for a web graphic or print project (see Figure 3-20).

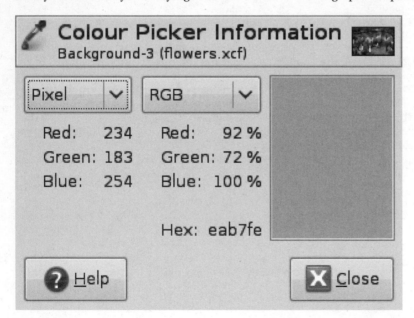

Figure 3-20. Hold down the Shift key when using the Color Picker to pop up a dialog with color values.

Otherwise, you can click the selected shade in the Foreground & Background chooser, which is at the bottom of the upper panel in the Toolbox. Doing so opens a dialog with a choice of color settings: hue, saturation, value (HSV), red, green and blue (RGB), and HTML hex value, ranging from 000000 (black) to ffffff (white); see Figure 3-21.

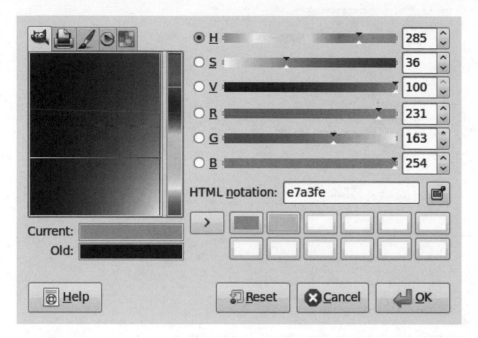

Figure 3-21. *The Change Foreground Color dialog, with the manual color picker box on the left*

On the left side of this dialog is a manual color picker in a rectangular box, with saturation on the vertical axis and value on the horizontal. You select the hue on a vertical bar to the right. The color values in this dialog change in real time, so you can select a color by eye alone or by clicking to adjust the numbers. There's also a pipette button, just to the right of the HTML notation box, which you can use to select a color from anywhere on your screen—not just a GIMP window.

Below this are 12 palette boxes, known as the *color history*. You can add any color you choose to the color history by clicking the arrow to the left of the palette buttons. Then, click one of these buttons to return to the saved color.

Above the rectangular color box are five tabs; Wilber, the GIMP's mascot, appears on the first. The printer icon lets you set CMYK (cyan, magenta, yellow, black) values, used in color printing, but no calibration profile is set up by default. For accurate results, you need to work with the same profile your print shop is using. If you know you're going to be working with CMYK values, choose Edit ➤ Preferences, click Color Management (see Figure 3-22), and choose "Select color profile from disk" from the CMYK profile drop-down menu to open a file dialog. The GIMP supports standard ICC color profiles, which have an `.icc` or `.icm` file extension. If you've been given a color profile by your print shop, locate the file on your hard disk or memory stick, select the file, and click Open. If you don't have a color profile, there are some standard profiles you can use in the `icc-profiles` package, available in Ubuntu's multiverse package repository. These profiles are installed in the **/usr/share/color/icc/** directory when you install the package.

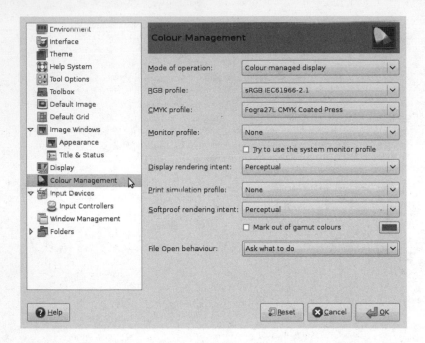

Figure 3-22. For accurate color matching, load an ICC profile into the GIMP.

■ **Note** You don't need to worry about CMYK values for regular photographic printing. Digital cameras and scanners are RGB devices by nature, and your print shop can do any conversion required for their particular printing machines. CMYK values are most useful for designers who have to match colors exactly on printed documents.

The next tab in the Change Foreground Color dialog is the Watercolor tab. This tab has a paintbrush icon and is more like mixing colors with real paint; the more you dab with your mouse button or touchpad stylus, the darker the currently chosen color becomes. This color chooser has a slider for adjustable pressure on the right of the box, making it a subtle tool. The last two tabs in this dialog feature a color wheel and a palette chooser, which are similar to the GIMP's default color chooser—click to set the new active color.

Zooming and Measuring

After the Color Picker pipette icon, next in the GIMP's Toolbox are the Zoom tool, which has a magnifying glass icon, and the Measure tool, which looks like the kind of compass used on a drawing board. The Zoom tool is straightforward; click to zoom in on an image, and Ctrl+click to zoom out. To save yourself switching tools constantly, you can use the keyboard shortcuts of plus (+) and minus (–).

The only problem with these default shortcuts is that on many keyboards, you have to hold down the Shift key to get a plus sign and zoom in, which makes it slight less convenient than using the minus sign for zooming out. (On the main GIMP menu, you can use Edit ➤ Keyboard Shortcuts to change these settings to any that you prefer.)

The Measure tool is particularly useful when you're working on graphics for the Web, because it can give you an idea of how an element in an image will appear in your web page layout without going to the trouble of cropping or resizing the image. Click point A, hold down the mouse button, and drag the cursor to point B—that's all there is to it. The number of pixels measured and the angle of the line you draw are displayed at the bottom of the image window. Optionally, you can select the "Use info window" check box in the Measure tool options to display a pop-up dialog with the information—but note that this dialog can sometimes get in the way of the measurement operation (see Figure 3-23).

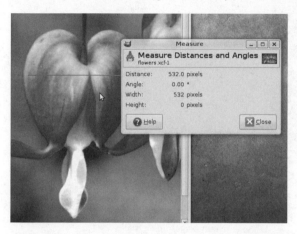

Figure 3-23. *The Measure tool's information window can sometimes get in the way of the image you're trying to measure—but it's switched off by default.*

The Move and Alignment Tools

You can use the GIMP's Move tool to drag layers, selections, and paths around the image window by holding down the left mouse button. The icon for the Move tool looks like a cross with arrow heads pointing vertically and horizontally. In the options panel of the GIMP's Toolbox, the default is to move the layer or guide you click; but you can choose to move the selection or path instead. By holding down the Shift key, you can move the active layer, or the active path when you're in path-moving mode.

Even if you haven't created any layers yet, you'll notice that if you drag the original image, it's treated as a layer on top of a transparent background. The GIMP represents transparency as a checkerboard of dark and light grey squares rather than showing you the window underneath. You can't move the transparent background, so when you mouse over the checkerboard with the Move tool, a small "no entry" sign appears next to the tool icon.

The Alignment tool sits next to the Move tool in the Toolbox, but it's more automatic than moving layers and other objects by hand. You can use it when you wish to place a layer in the exact center of the image, for instance (see Figure 3-24). Use the tool's pointing finger cursor to click the object you wish to move, and then click one of the six Align buttons in the lower half of the Toolbox to perform the operation. By default, the Alignment tool positions the object to be moved relative to the first item you click in the image. You can choose the entire image; the selection; or the active layer, channel, or path instead, using the drop-down list in the tool's options box.

Figure 3-24. You can use the Alignment tool to place a copied selection in the exact center of the image, even if not all of the image is visible.

Further down in the tool's options box are six buttons labeled Distribute, which you use to align multiple items with an offset, specified in pixels. Whether this offset is vertical or horizontal depends on the direction button you click.

Cropping and Rotation

These commonly used photographic tools are easy to get to grips with. The Crop tool's icon is a scalpel, in reference to darkroom days of the past. Click, hold down the mouse button, and drag around the area of the image you want to keep. When you release the mouse button, the area around the cropping selection darkens to show that it's about to be deleted from the image. In the four corners of the cropping selection are rectangular handles that enable you to move each corner of the area to be cropped. Clicking and dragging the edges of the cropping selection between the rectangles moves just that side of the area. If you click and drag in the center of the selection, you move all of it, keeping the shape intact (see Figure 3-25).

Figure 3-25. You can modify the Crop tool's selection by moving the corner rectangles or by dragging the selection edges.

When you're happy with how the crop looks, click once in the central area of the crop selection or press the Enter key on your keyboard to perform the cropping action. If the crop is too drastic, select Edit ➤ Undo Crop Image, or press the general keyboard shortcut for undoing the last action (Ctrl+Z).

If you're cropping photographs to be printed on a fixed size of paper—for example, a 6 inch by 4 inch landscape print at your local photo shop—the GIMP has a tool option in the lower half of the Toolbox that can help you. Select the Fixed check box, and leave the drop-down box at the default setting "Aspect ratio". This ensures that your image can be scaled to print at the correct size without losing detail from two of the edges or leaving white strips on either side of the print. If your original image doesn't have the correct aspect ratio for the print size you desire, you can type a width-to-height ratio, such as 6:4, into the box just underneath, instead of the default value Current. That way, you don't have to think too much about print resolution and exact pixel sizes when you're cropping, because if the aspect ratio is correct, the photo shop's computer should take care of scaling the image to fit the paper. Portrait and landscape buttons appear to the right of this box; they can help you switch quickly from 4:6 to 6:4 or whichever aspect ratio you require.

Most cathode-ray computer screens had a 4:3 ratio, just like their TV tube cousins. Perhaps because of this, many digital cameras capture images at exactly 4:3, but there are exceptions—including the Nikon D series of digital SLRs, which use a pixel ratio close to 6:4, or 4:6 for a portrait shot. Many of the newer flat-screen displays have a 16:9 aspect or other widescreen ratio, intended for movie or HDTV playback without black bars at the top and bottom.

Like the Move tool, the Rotate tool can be used on a layer, selection, or path. It has an icon with two blue boxes and two curving white arrows in the corners. By default, the pivot for the rotation is the center of the image, represented by a light blue crosshair in a circle. If you don't want to rotate the object around the exact center of the image, mouse over the crosshairs; a small Move tool cursor appears. You can then click and drag the pivot point anywhere in the image you prefer. Next, drag the slider in the Rotate pop-up window, or enter a numerical angle for the rotation (using a negative number for counterclockwise); see Figure 3-26. If you prefer, click the object itself, and drag it with the mouse around the rotation point. This manual method isn't very precise, but it does offer quick results.

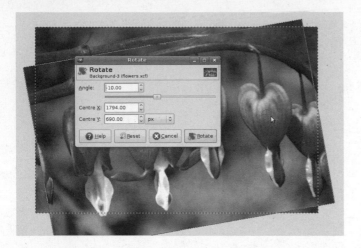

Figure 3-26. Move the crosshairs of the Rotate tool cursor to set the pivot point. Precise angles of rotation can be set using this tool's dialog box.

In addition to creating montages and special effects, one very useful application of the Rotate tool can be applied when the camera was inadvertently tilted to one side during the original shoot. The human eye is good at noticing when the horizon in a landscape shot isn't level, even if it's only by a fraction of a degree. The precise control offered by the Rotate dialog box lets you fix this common photographer's mistake quickly and easily. To help you get this operation right, you can click and drag out a horizontal or vertical guide from the GIMP's rulers at the top and left sides of the image window, respectively. A vertical guide can help you align the wall of a building, but watch out for distortions in perspective caused by the camera lens.

The Scale Tool

The Scale tool's icon is two adjacent blue boxes connected by a diagonal arrow. Scaling in the GIMP works similarly to rotation: a pop-up dialog box lets you enter precise figures, but you can also perform the required action by clicking and dragging on the image. In order to preserve the aspect ratio of the original image, you need to make sure the chain icon in the dialog box, to the right of the Width and Height numbers, is showing as linked, rather than broken. To toggle this setting, either click the chain icon or select the "Keep aspect" check box in the tool options part of the GIMP's Toolbox (see Figure 3-27). If you only need to lock the aspect ratio occasionally, you can hold down the Ctrl key while clicking and dragging the scale cursor. Getting this right is particularly important when you're scaling photographs of human subjects, because even a small change in aspect ratio can make the result look unnatural. No one ever complains about being made to look thinner, but they certainly will be unhappy if you add a few pounds to their figure!

By default, the Scale tool's dialog shows the target width and height of the scaling operation in pixels, but a drop-down box lets you select inches instead or express the scale as a percentage. Whichever measurement you choose, the final pixel size and resolution in ppi following the scale are displayed under the Width and Height boxes as a guide.

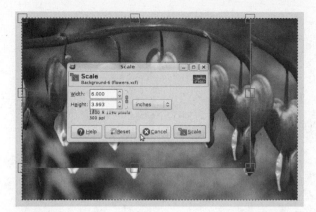

Figure 3-27. The chain icon in the Scale tool's dialog box enables aspect ratio to be preserved. After scaling down, this image will end up almost exactly 6 inches by 4 inches at 300 ppi.

Shear, Perspective, and Flip

Next is the Shear tool, which slants the layer, selection, or path to one side. Its icon is a slanting blue box being pushed by a right-pointing arrow. Use a negative value for "Shear magnitude X" in this tool's dialog box to shear the top of the image to the right (see Figure 3-28). Just like Rotate, you can also use the Shear tool by clicking and dragging.

Figure 3-28. The Shear tool slants the image towards one side—but watch out for parts of the image ending up outside the original boundary.

Note that as with the Rotate tool, any parts of the selection that end up outside the boundary of the original image are lost. To avoid this happening, use Image ➤ Canvas Size on the main GIMP menu to grow the canvas you're working on before performing the shear or other transformation.

The Perspective tool is similar to Shear, except that it shrinks the top part of the image to create a trapezoid shape. It has a blue trapezoid icon with two white arrows. One other difference is that you adjust the Perspective effect by eye, by clicking and dragging rectangles in the corners; this tool doesn't offer the option of entering numbers into a dialog box. In common with the Rotate tool, the Perspective tool features blue crosshairs in a circle, which enable you to specify the center of the effect by clicking and dragging (see Figure 3-29).

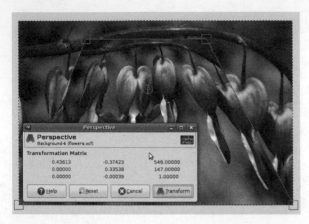

Figure 3-29. *You can fake perspective effects using the tool of the same name. The center of the effect is adjustable using the blue crosshairs.*

Flip is an extremely straightforward tool—all you have to decide is whether you want the layer, selection, or path flipped horizontally or vertically. You make this choice in the Toolbox options panel; horizontal is the default. You can temporarily switch to vertical flipping by holding down the Ctrl key as you click in the image.

■ **Note** Horizontal flips are commonly used in magazine layouts to make the image fit better on the page—but be careful with this technique. Tell-tale signs that an image has been flipped include background text that reads backward, bicycles with chains on the opposite side, and left-handed guitars being played by right-handed people!

Text and Fonts

For the sharpest possible results, typography should usually be done with vector graphics, which you look at in the next chapter. However, in some circumstances, using a bitmap (pixel-based) program like the GIMP to put text on an image is appropriate. Creating graphic buttons for the Web is a common example, because bitmaps should look the same in any web browser.

Click the icon for the Text tool, which is a big, black, bold letter A. In the options panel of the GIMP's Toolbox, you see the default font, size, and color. In the version of the GIMP that comes with Ubuntu GNU/Linux, this font is Sans, 18 pixels high, in black. When you click with the Text tool in a high-resolution photograph, notice that text 18 pixels high looks very small.

Your computer may have different fonts installed, particularly if you're running the GIMP on Windows or a Mac. You can easily download additional font packages for Ubuntu using System ➤

Administration ➤ Synaptic Package Manager on the main GNOME menu. Try searching for *font* or *ttf* among the package names; the latter is an acronym for TrueType Font.

Note that the height measurement is in pixels rather than the typographer's traditional measurement of *points*. (Computer printers have standardized on 72 points to the inch; but in the era of typesetting by hand, the exact size of a point varied from country to country.) If you prefer to work in points, or fractions of an inch, a drop-down menu to the right of the Size box lets you specify your choice.

When you click the image with the Text tool, a pop-up window appears in which you can type. You can also open a prepared file and import the text from that (see Figure 3-30). By default, the Text Editor window is set up for Western left-to-right languages, but the RTL button enables you to switch to right-to-left typing. As you type in the editor, the text appears on the image in your chosen font, size, and color. The text area has rectangular handles in the corners that you can use to reposition the type in either direction. Exactly where the text sits in this area depends on the justification and spacing options you choose in the GIMP's Toolbox. When you're done, click the Close button in the editor to hide the pop-up window; it reappear the next time you click the image with the Text tool active.

Figure 3-30. *The Text tool has a Text Editor window that can import text from a file. Drag the text area to the correct position, and then justify and space the text with the tool options.*

Text and the Layers Dialog

When you're working with text, it's vital to keep an eye on the image's layers. If you put text on the same layer as your original image, it's much harder to manipulate the text independently. In particular, if you have more than one item of text in your image, you can only edit the lettering on the current active layer. Fortunately, the GIMP puts each new item of text on its own layer, which helps keep all the elements of your image separate.

In the main GIMP menu, select Windows ➤ Dockable Dialogs ➤ Layers. (This is a frequently used window in the GIMP, so it also has a keyboard shortcut to open it: Ctrl+L.) In the Layers dialog, you see that the original image is thumbnailed and has the label Background. Double-click the label if you want to change this name to something more specific. To make a particular layer active, so that tools work on that layer and not the others, you have to click the layer name in this dialog so that it becomes highlighted. In the case of Ubuntu, the highlight color is a pale orange.

Figure 3-31. The Layers dialog displays thumbnails for image layers and indicative text for typographical layers.

On the far left of the image thumbnail is a small eye icon, which toggles the visibility of this particular layer. Between the eye and the thumbnail is a space for the chain icon, which indicates when the positions of two adjacent layers are locked together.

Text layers are indicated with a capital letter *T* instead of a thumbnail. The label of a text layer indicates the actual text that's been entered. Like any other layer, you can make text layers more transparent by using the Opacity slider in the Layers dialog, which defaults to a setting of 100. Just above this is the Mode drop-down box, which defaults to Normal—in other words, it treats each layer as if it were a static glass slide on top of the next layer. But because this is digital photography, you can apply effects or have multiple layers interact with each other. Try setting Opacity to 50 and Mode to Dissolve, or Opacity to 90 and Mode to Saturation.

Figure 3-32. *Font effect using Burn on a rotated text layer and Dissolve on the original image, above a new layer of white background. Notice how the burn effect changes the text as it passes over black to silver parts of the image underneath.*

Small icon buttons at the bottom edge of the Layers dialog provide shortcuts to common layer tasks. From left to right, these buttons create a new layer, raise a layer one place in the stack, lower a layer one place, duplicate a layer, anchor a floating layer, and delete the currently active layer. The active layer is the layer you happen to be working on at the time. For an image with many layers, this dialog is handy to keep open, because you can see at a glance the name and thumbnail or text of the active layer. When a tool doesn't work the way you expect it to, it's often because you're not working on the layer you think you are.

To access the full range of layer options, right-click any particular layer in the Layers dialog. One of the frequently used options is Merge Down, which combines the active layer with the layer beneath it in the stack. Don't forget that this means you can no longer edit items on the two layers independently. The right-click option Merge Visible Layers combines all layers that have the eye icon visible, whereas Flatten Image reduces the image to a single layer, including any invisible layers. Personally, I rarely flatten images, because if I need to export a single-layered image, the GIMP's File ➤ Save As action does the flattening job for me during the export, leaving the multilayered file intact. If you don't save a multilayered version of your file, you can't manipulate the layers later; so, it's a very good idea to save a master copy of your image in .xcf or .psd format.

Bucket Fill and Blends

Just about every pixel-painting program has a fill tool, but the GIMP's version has plenty of special effects to keep you amused. Imagine you want to give the red and yellow bicycle a makeover with some hot pink paint. Select the desired shade in the GIMP's color-selection dialog, and then click the icon for the Bucket Fill tool—a dripping pot of blue paint. In the tool's Toolbox options, set the mode to "Color erase". Duplicate the original image on a new layer, and begin clicking the red and yellow bike. The effect is a little too harsh; drop the opacity of the new layer to 50 so the original image underneath shows through (see Figure 3-33). I hope the owner of the bike likes the new colors!

Figure 3-33. *A pink bucket fill on a red bike*

The Blend tool, which has a square icon with a gray gradient fill, is a little different than Bucket Fill. You have to click the image to set the start and end points of the gradient—it isn't necessary to have the gradient cover the whole image. The default gradient is a linear blend from the GIMP's current foreground color to the current background color, but there are many other predefined gradients to choose from. Click the Gradient preview button in the Toolbox to open a dialog in which you can choose any setting you prefer, from metallic gradients to national flags. Just to the right of this is a blue double-headed arrow icon, which enables you to flip the direction of the gradient quickly.

In Normal mode, the Blend tool works like a painting tool—but as is true for the Bucket Fill tool, a selection of photographic effects are available on the Mode drop-down menu, including Dodge and Burn (see Figure 3-34). You can also set the opacity of the gradient effect in the Toolbox options. This setting isn't retroactive to previously applied gradients; if the gradient effect is too prominent, you can press Ctrl+Z, adjust the Opacity setting, and try again. As usual when applying effects, putting each gradient on its own layer makes it much easier to change your mind later.

Figure 3-34. Dodge and Burn blends in the corners of the image help the foreground stand out. Then, a transparent radial blend centers on the silver bicycle badge, progressively tinting the surrounding areas of the image with red.

To see the full selection of gradients available, select Windows ➤ Dockable Dialogs ➤ Gradients from the main GIMP menu. At the lower edge of this window, second from the left, is a small document icon with a white plus sign in a tiny orange circle, which you use to create custom gradients. You need to give your new gradient a name and then drag the small triangles in this window to set the gradient points.

It's not obvious from the Gradient Editor window, but you must right-click in the gradient's preview area to set the left and right colors and other more complex options (see Figure 3-35).

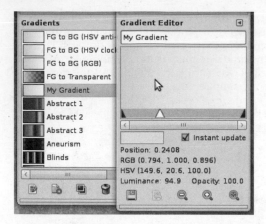

Figure 3-35. *Right-click in the Gradient Editor's preview window to set the left and right colors.*

You can use the small magnifying glass icons at the bottom of the Gradient Editor window to zoom in or out and to inspect the colors you set. When you're happy with the look of your gradient, don't forget to click the disk icon to save it.

Pencil and Paintbrush

These tools are much easier to handle if you have a USB pen tablet, but they're still quite useful if you only have a mouse. The Pencil tool is really a brush that paints pixels with a hard edge. I personally don't use it a great deal, but it may be useful for adding solid lines to the right kind of image. The default settings for the Paintbrush tool appear similar to the Pencil; but a close look at the results demonstrates that the Paintbrush tool fills the boundary of the painted area with intermediate color pixels, to achieve a softer effect on curved edges (see Figure 3-36).

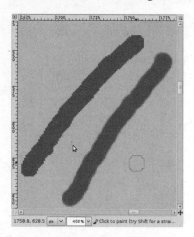

Figure 3-36. *Zoomed in to 400% of normal size, the difference in edge between the Pencil tool (left) and the Paintbrush tool (right) is obvious.*

You can achieve a far greater difference in effect depending on the brush you select to use with either tool. The current brush can be selected from the Toolbox options panel, but you can also open a dialog for brushes by choosing Windows ➤ Dockable Dialogs ➤ Brushes. The keyboard shortcut to open this window is Shift+Ctrl+B. For either the Pencil or Paintbrush tool, the default brush is a fairly hard-edged circle of 11 pixels; but you can select many different sizes and shapes, including soft-edged and patterned brushes. Because these brushes are specified by the number of pixels wide they are, the size they appear on-screen depends on how much you have zoomed in or out. Beneath the Brush button in the Toolbox options is the Scale slider, which enables you to grow or shrink the current brush without switching to a different size.

Below this, click the small triangle to the left of the Brush Dynamics label to access advanced configuration options (see Figure 3-37). Check boxes let you apply effects including brush fade-out, which is more like painting for real, and using color from a gradient.

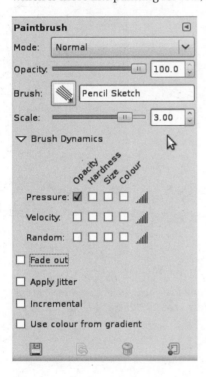

Figure 3-37. You can access advanced configuration options for the Paintbrush tool in the Toolbox options panel.

The Eraser Tool

This tool has a slightly misleading name, because it's a brush like any other. The only difference is that it removes pixels instead of adding them. Because it's really a brush, the Eraser tool has the usual options for size and pattern, as well as modes and opacity.

Note that the Eraser makes a transparent hole in a particular layer only if the layer has an alpha channel—if the layer doesn't have one of these, using the Eraser looks the same as painting with white pixels (see Figure 3-38). Should this prove to be a problem, in the Layers dialog, right-click the layer in question, and select Add Alpha Channel from the pop-up menu.

Figure 3-38. Using the Eraser on a layer without an alpha channel (the pink bike) means you see white pixels. The text layer with the word Bicycles *has an alpha channel, so when you use the eraser on the letter* s, *the layer underneath shows through. Note that the boundary of the text layer is shown by a black and yellow dashed line.*

Airbrush and Ink

The Airbrush tool is much like the Paintbrush, except that a single click results in a very light paint effect. You need to hold the mouse button down for a couple of seconds for the digital paint to build up, much as you would have to with a real airbrush—or, on a lower budget, a can of spray paint. You can adjust rate and pressure in the Toolbox options panel; these allow for subtle paint effects, even if you don't have a pen tablet device.

The Ink tool is intended for calligraphic effects, and although it has Mode and Opacity options like the other brushes, it also has some unique controls. There are adjustments for size and angle, sensitivity controls, and Type buttons that set the shape of the virtual nib (see Figure 3-39). Like the Pencil tool, the Ink tool probably delivers better results when used with a pen tablet than with a mouse.

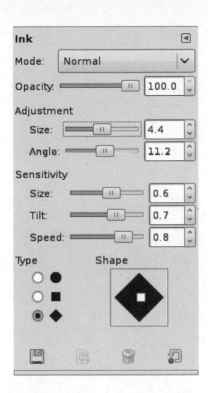

Figure 3-39. *The Ink tool has different options than the brush-based painting tools, including a setting for nib shape.*

Cloning and Healing

The color dialogs in the GIMP allow you to specify individual solid colors, which you can vary in opacity when using the painting tools. However, real photographs have many complex patterns of color, as you'll discover if you attempt to paint solid colors while performing edits—the results don't look natural. For detailed retouching work, you need to use the patterns already in the image and manipulate them using the GIMP's Clone, Healing, and Perspective Clone tools.

Often, when you're editing a photograph, you're trying to repair damage and get back that natural, continuous look you would have with a darkroom print from a fresh, clean negative. In reality, you must often deal with dust and scratches on the scan or on the camera lens. When you get tricky with digital manipulation, you sometimes have to use repair techniques to hide the tell-tale signs of your edits, too.

The first tool you should consider for repairs is the Clone tool, which has a rubber-stamp icon. This tool samples an area of pixels and then duplicates them in another part of the image, which is very useful for copying complex color textures to cover damaged areas. To specify the area to be cloned, first select an appropriate brush size from the Clone tool options in the lower half of the GIMP's Toolbox (see figure 3-40). You're looking for a brush size that's small enough to make an invisible repair but large enough that you won't be clicking the image all night, trying to cover the damage. You can also specify a fuzzy-edged brush to make the effect softer.

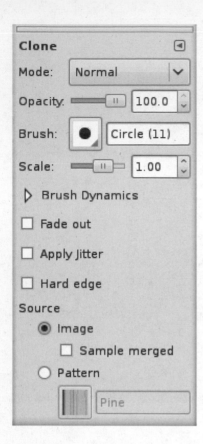

Figure 3-40. *Just like the painting tools, the Clone tool's options allow you to set the mode, opacity, brush size, scale, and dynamics of the effect.*

Next, find part of the image close by that has the color pattern you're looking to clone, hold down the Ctrl key, and click. You can now release the Ctrl key and click to clone the pattern on top of the damaged area. Note that if you hold down the mouse button and drag the Clone tool, the area being sampled moves with the mouse. If this isn't what you want, make individual clicks on the area to be repaired, instead.

As you move to different parts of the image, you must hold down the Ctrl key again to select a fresh area of pixels for cloning; otherwise, the results aren't likely to match. Sometimes, you want to clone the area to the immediate left of the repair; other times, the area on the right needs to be sampled. In a photograph, color patterns can change dramatically just a few pixels away, so this technique relies heavily on the artist's eye. With practice, you'll learn which parts of the image to repair and which to leave alone—it isn't always necessary to remove every last speck of dust.

The Healing tool is very similar to the Clone tool, except for the fact that it's explicitly designed to fix irregularities in the image. (The icon for this tool is a crossed pair of bandages.) Sometimes, these irregularities aren't artifacts of the photographic process, but exist in real life. For example, on the head badge of the bicycle in this photo, there are some cracks in the metal (see Figure 3-41). This kind of problem is commonly found when reprinting antique photos, just because of wear and tear on the original photographic print.

Figure 3-41. The Healing tool being used to fix real-life damage that ended up in the photo. On the left is the original image; on the right is the result of the first pass with the tool. It will take many clicks and Ctrl+clicks to do an invisible repair, but this is just one detail in a much larger image—so the repair may be good enough.

■ **Note** Manual repair with a mouse can be a painstaking process, and the level of detail required depends on the quality of the new print and the use it's put to. I remember a colleague of mine stitching together a composite image from three studio portraits of a young violin player who wasn't entirely happy with any of the shots. It took many hours of labor but resulted in the perfect publicity image that the subject desired.

Perspective Clone is one of the more obscure tools in the GIMP. It's a sort of hybrid between the Perspective tool and the Clone tool, so I suppose it's aptly named. The icon for this tool is the rubber stamp on top of a blue trapezoid. To use it, you must first modify the perspective of the image by dragging square handles—just like the regular Perspective tool. Then, you have to go to the Toolbox options panel and click the Perspective Clone radio button. Only after this can you Ctrl+click to set the clone source and begin painting with the cloning brush. The difference between this and the regular Clone tool is that the images you paint with the Perspective Clone tool are distorted according to the perspective you set.

Blur, Sharpen, and Smudge

Blur and Sharpen are part of the same tool, which has an icon like a droplet of blue water. By default, it's in Blur mode, but you can toggle Sharpen with the Ctrl key or click the Sharpen radio button in the

Toolbox options panel (see Figure 3-42). The rest of the options for this tool are similar to those for the painting tools, except for the Rate slider that controls the intensity of the effect.

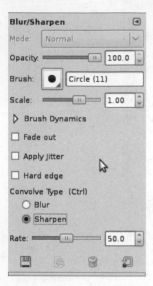

Figure 3-42. The Blur and Sharpen tools share one options panel. Toggle between them with the Ctrl key.

Blurring is often used in contemporary movie production to help crisp, clean computer-generated images blend in with real-life footage shot on film. The Sharpen effect can be used to a certain extent to improve bad photographs, but if you over-use it, the grain of the pixels becomes too obvious.

The Smudge tool has an icon like a right hand with the index finger extended—which represents what the tool does pretty well. It's like dragging a wet finger over a pastel drawing, so this is more for artistic effects than repair jobs. Like Blur/Sharpen, the Smudge tool has a Rate slider in the Toolbox options panel.

Dodge and Burn

The Dodge and Burn tools also share an icon, which looks like a black dodging stick from the darkroom days (a round disk on the end of a handle). For the benefit of young people who've never seen a photographic enlarger, this dodging stick was a crude device that allowed photographers to reduce the amount of light that fell on a specific part of the print by holding it between the enlarger lens and the photographic paper. Burning was the opposite technique, in which parts of the print were deliberately over-exposed to make them darker. The GIMP's Dodge/Burn tool is in Dodge mode by default; but like Blur/Sharpen, you can toggle Burn with the Ctrl key or click the radio button for it in the Toolbox options panel.

Dodge/Burn has a few extra settings, including Range for shadows, midtones, or highlights, and a slider for Exposure.

Other Useful Programs

This chapter has looked at some of the most popular Free Software programs for capturing, cataloging, and editing your photos—but many more are available. Here are four that I recommend you look at:

- *PhotoPrint* (GNU/Linux, Windows): A tool that does quick layout of multiple prints on single sheets of paper. Ideal for output to typical inkjet printers that are fed with US Letter or A4 paper. `www.blackfiveservices.co.uk`.

- *Rawstudio* (GNU/Linux, Mac): A specialist tool for owners of digital SLR cameras that can store images in the high-quality RAW format, including Nikon and Canon models. `www.rawstudio.org`.

- *Hugin* (GNU/Linux, Windows, Mac): A tool that creates panoramic images from multiple overlapping shots, without requiring a special camera or lens. `http://hugin.sourceforge.net`.

- *Stopmotion* (GNU/Linux): An animation tool that you can use to make movies from a sequence of still images. `http://stopmotion.bjoernen.com`.

All of these programs can be installed easily on Ubuntu GNU/Linux using the Add/Remove Applications tool.

Further Reading

If you'd like to delve deeper into the GIMP, *Beginning GIMP: From Novice to Professional, 2nd edition* by Akkana Peck (Apress, 2009, ISBN-13: 978-1-4302-1070-2) provides a thorough grounding in the program. I can also recommend *GIMP 2 for Photographers* by Klaus Goelker (Rocky Nook, 2006, ISBN-13: 978-1-933952-03-1)—even though this book is getting a little old for a software manual, it was beautifully produced. You can also check out *The Artist's Guide to GIMP Effects* by Michael J. Hammel (No Starch Press, 2007, ISBN-13: 978-1-59327-153-4).

■ ■ ■

## CHAPTER 4

Illustration and Font Design

Bitmaps vs. Vectors

When you're drawing or painting in the GIMP, you're working with bitmap files, which for color images are more correctly termed *pixmaps* (an abbreviation of *pixel maps*). As you have seen when editing photos, these pixmap files are just numerous rows and columns of identical size pixels in different colors and shades, like the tiles in a mosaic. This is a perfectly good way to represent typical photographic images, as long as you have enough pixels (resolution) for the job you're doing. A pixmap is sometimes referred to as a *raster image*, in reference to the way cathode ray tubes in older computer displays and TV sets drew images on the screen.

The pixmap method isn't so appropriate when you're trying to represent hard, curved edges accurately or scale the image up, down, and back up again at will. This is because the pixmap works by optical illusion, as mentioned in the previous chapter, and is only an approximation of the original, continuous image. The size of a pixmap file is directly proportional to the number of pixels and depth of color it contains; if you throw away pixels or reduce color depth to make the image file smaller, you can't retrieve the lost detail from the file later. Individual pixmap files can grow to dozens of megabytes, particularly if compression techniques aren't being used.

There is another way to represent an image using a computer, and it's a completely different approach from pixmaps or rasters. Instead of breaking down the image into a mosaic of tiny pixels, you can attempt to describe it by its mathematical properties or *vectors*. For example: a line from point A to point B has a certain thickness and color. When you have this mathematical information, you can make the line 10 times longer or 100 times thicker by simple multiplication. It doesn't matter what size the line was in the first place. You can zoom in as much as you like to a vector graphic, and its quality and detail remain the same, with not a pixel in sight (see Figure 4-1). Typical vector graphics are much smaller in file size than the same images saved as high resolution pixmaps. This is what makes vector formats like PDF so useful for sending formatted text documents over the Internet: they allow you to have reasonable file sizes while keeping the fonts crisp at all levels of zoom.

Free
Free

Figure 4-1. You can scale vector graphics to any size without losing quality, making them an excellent format for original artwork and typography. Above, a pixmap of a 48-point font scaled to 400%—below, the same font drawn as a vector, scaled to the same size.

Vectors are excellent for representing relatively simple shapes and abstract images, like line art or fonts, but they aren't as useful for photo-realistic images. This is because a real image contains many complex lines, colors, textures, and gradients, which an artist would have to work very hard to reproduce. That's not to say it can't be done—a skilled vector artist with enough time and computing power available can draw artwork that looks very real (see Figure 4-2).

Figure 4-2. In skilled hands, vector graphics tools can produce beautiful results from scratch. Image drawn by Mariana Sing for www.inkscapegallery.net*—Creative Commons attribution license.*

If you've ever tried screen printing a photograph onto fabric or paper, you've noticed how original detail can become lost among the bold, chunky colors—vector graphics converted from pixmaps can often look a little like that. You can use this effect to your advantage when designing a poster or other artwork, particularly if you're going for a retro, screen-printed look.

By choosing the most appropriate format for your graphics projects—vector, pixmap, or a combination of both—you can be sure to get the best quality results possible and avoid the pitfalls of either method.

Vector Graphic Formats

It used to be that most vector graphics file formats were handled best by the proprietary program that created them, whether that was Adobe Illustrator (for `.ai` files), CorelDRAW (`.cdr`), or, back in the day, Aldus FreeHand (`.fh3`). Many design studios also used the Encapsulated PostScript (`.eps`) format for vector graphics, although this was sometimes problematic when working cross-platform, because the PC and Mac versions of EPS are slightly different. The need for a truly open standard that would work the same way across all platforms resulted in the creation of the Scalable Vector Graphics format (`.svg`) by the World Wide Web Consortium (W3C).

This SVG format is fully editable with any up-to-date illustration program; but unlike its proprietary alternatives, it can also be viewed directly in web browsers and on many mobile devices. The SVG standard allows for the inclusion of pixmaps and text in a single file, making it an excellent choice for all kinds of illustration projects. It's particularly well supported by Free Software graphics applications and web browsers, and the GNOME desktop used by Ubuntu and other GNU/Linux distributions supports SVG natively too.

Inkscape: An SVG Drawing Tool

The leading Free Software application for working with two-dimensional vector graphics is Inkscape (GNU/Linux, Windows, Mac); see Figure 4-3. This program isn't usually included in a default installation of GNU/Linux, but if you're running Ubuntu, you can easily get Inkscape using the Add/Remove Applications tool. (You can find this tool at the foot of the main Applications menu, on the top left of Ubuntu's GNOME desktop.) Ready-made Inkscape packages are available for just about all other popular GNU/Linux distros aimed at desktop use; if you're running one of these distros, use your package manger of choice to download and install Inkscape automatically. On Windows or a Mac, visit the official Inkscape web site at `www.inkscape.org` to obtain a package of the application for your specific operating system.

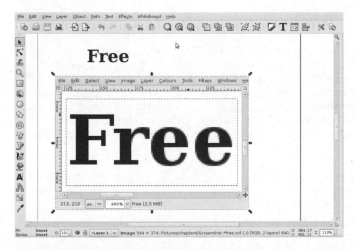

Figure 4-3. Inkscape is a Free Software vector artwork program available for all major platforms. Here, a pixmap of a screenshot from the GIMP has been placed within an SVG document. Scaling up the screenshot demonstrates the limitation of pixel-based formats.

Inkscape uses SVG as its native file format, but it can also export files in EPS, PDF, GIMP (`.xcf`), Adobe Illustrator (`.ai`), and AutoCAD (`.dxf`) formats, among others. On the import side, it can open PDFs and files from CorelDRAW and Adobe Illustrator version 9 or later, as well as import various pixmap formats. Pixmaps are placed in a new SVG document when opened directly, and can also be placed into an existing document.

To start working with a blank document in Inkscape, choose File ➤ New, and select a document size. Like the GIMP, Inkscape has a variety of preformatted document sizes available, including DIN A4 and US Letter paper sizes, CD and DVD cover dimensions, digital video frames, and desktop icons measured in pixels. By default, Inkscape opens with a blank document of DIN A4 paper size (210mm wide, 297mm high); if this isn't what you need, select File ➤ Document Properties, and choose a different setting.

Remember that because you're working with vector graphics, you can change the document size at any time and scale your drawing to fit. This is very handy when you're working on a drawing like a logo, which may need to be printed at a wide range of sizes.

■ **Tip** When you run Inkscape for the first time, you may find that the program's main window doesn't fit in your computer's screen very well, particularly if your display is 1024 x 768 pixels or less. This is because all of Inkscape's toolbars are visible by default, and it can be difficult to click menu items if the main window keeps shrinking and growing to fit the available space. To remedy this issue, press the keyboard shortcut for the View menu, which is Alt+V. Then, use your cursor keys to select the Show/Hide submenu. Press the right cursor key to jump across to this submenu, and then press the spacebar on your keyboard to uncheck either the Palette or the Statusbar.

Inkscape's Transformation Tools

Most of the Inkscape tools and commands are available through keyboard shortcuts. However, you don't have to learn these shortcuts to begin using the program, because all the commands are available from menus, too. When you select a particular tool, its parameters appear in the Tool Controls Bar beneath the Command Bar, which is just under the main menus.

The Toolbox runs down the left side of the main Inkscape window. First is the Select and Transform Objects tool, represented by a black arrowhead icon (see Figure 4-4). The corresponding mouse cursor is a white arrowhead of the same shape and size. Mouse over the center of an object on the Inkscape document, and the cursor turns into a clenched fist. This means you can click, hold the mouse button down, and reposition the object.

Figure 4-4. You can use Inkscape's selection tool to move, rotate, and flip objects in the document.

A single click turns the object's corner handles from resizing controls into rotation controls. You can constrain both rotation and resizing by holding down the Ctrl key while using the mouse on the corner handles. There are also buttons for fixed angles of rotation and flips on the Tool Controls Bar when this particular tool is active.

Below this is the Edit Paths by Nodes tool (see Figure 4-5), which has a black triangle icon and cursor and a lot in common with the Path tool in the GIMP. As you saw in the last chapter, a *node* is the point at which a line or curve can be made to change direction. Objects created in Inkscape aren't editable as paths by default; instead, they must first be converted to path outlines using the Path ➤ Object to Path menu item. After this, the nodes of the path appear as small gray squares. If you click one of these square nodes, you can drag it to another position, taking the path with it.

Figure 4-5. The Edit Paths by Nodes tool can produce many complex shapes, but only if the object has already been converted to a path.

The Tool Controls Bar includes buttons for adding and deleting nodes, and joining or splitting paths. Alternatively, you can change the shape of the path by changing a node from one type to another—a node can be a corner, smooth, or symmetric. For these three types of nodes, handles are displayed as long as the "Show the Bezier handles of selected nodes" button on the Tool Controls Bar is active, which it is by default. By experimenting with pulling in and out and adjusting the angle of these handles, you can produce pretty much any shape you imagine.

■ **Note** The word *Bezier* is used to describe curves with handles in graphics programs, in tribute to Pierre Étienne Bézier, the late French engineer, mathematician, and pioneer of computer drawing. He worked at car manufacturer Renault on an early computer system called UNISURF in the 1960s and early 70s. This system was used to help designers draw car bodies and other mechanical parts. The algorithm used for these curves was developed earlier, in the late 1950s, by Paul de Casteljau, a mathematician at rival French car maker Citroën.

You can turn adjacent nodes into a segment by holding down the Shift key and clicking the nodes. You can then make straight lines into a series of Bezier curves by clicking the "Make selected segments curves" button on the Tool Controls Bar. For those times when you need to go in the other direction, from curves to straight lines, you can use the "Make selected segments lines" button, just to the left.

The Tweak Objects by Sculpting or Painting tool, which is the next one down in the Toolbox, produces interesting effects. Its icon is a wave, and its cursor depends on the particular effect you've selected—Push, Shrink, Grow, Attract, Repel, Roughen, Paint, or Jitter. An orange circle around the cursor displays the width of the effect. This tool enables you to distort paths and color fills as if they were physical objects that you were able to push, pull, and paint on. In Figure 4-6, I've used the Push button on the Tool Controls Bar to give the text a ripple effect, as if it were painted on a bumpy surface.

Figure 4-6. *The Tweak Objects by Sculpting or Painting tool lets you manipulate paths as if in response to physical forces.*

Next is the Zoom In or Out tool, which, as you'd expect, is straightforward. It has the usual magnifying-glass icon and cursor. Click to zoom in to the document, or Shift+click to zoom out. Useful shortcut buttons are available on the main Commands bar: "Zoom to fit selection in window," "Zoom to fit drawing in window," and "Zoom to fit page in window." These buttons are duplicated on the Tool Controls Bar when the Zoom tool is active.

Shape Tools

Inkscape has a good selection of preformatted shape tools to satisfy the five-year old potato printer in you. These shape tools provide a useful way to start playing around with the possibilities of this application, and it's possible to achieve many different effects. You can manipulate the shapes via their nodes: small square ones for resizing, and round ones for reshaping. Drawn shapes are objects by default, rather than paths, but as usual you can convert them to paths with the Path ➤ Object to Path menu item.

First is the Create Rectangles and Squares tool (see Figure 4-7), which has the icon of a light blue square in the Toolbox, and a cursor with a cross and a black rectangle. Click and hold down the mouse button while you drag to create the shape you want. It's filled with the current active color, which you can change by clicking a color swatch on the Palette bar at the bottom of the main Inkscape window. (If you can't see the swatches, enable the Palette bar by checking the box at View ➤ Show/Hide ➤ Palette.)

Figure 4-7. The Create Rectangles and Squares tool is the first of Inkscape's shape tools. All five have similar resizing and reshaping handles.

If none of the colors in the Palette are quite what you have in mind, drag the slider directly under the swatches to access more colors. You can also click the chevron to the immediate right of the Palette to select alternative preset color schemes, including a Topographic palette for drawing maps. To select a custom color, click the paintbrush icon on the Commands Bar at the top of the main Inkscape window. A dialog box opens with a variety of color-selection methods; it looks similar to the GIMP's color dialog (see Figure 4-8).

Figure 4-8. Inkscape's color-selection dialog is very similar to the GIMP's. In this screenshot, a gray stroke has been applied to the rectangular object beneath the text.

By default, the path fill color is set in this dialog; but if you click the "Stroke paint" tab, you can set the color drawn on the path itself, or the boundary in the case of an object. Fills and strokes don't have to be solid colors; they can also be gradients or patterns (see Figure 4-9). The "Stroke style" tab in this dialog enables you to set the width, joins, and end shapes of the stroke on the currently active path or object boundary.

Figure 4-9. The same gradient fill and gray stroke applied to both the text object and the rectangle object.

The next tool down in the Toolbox is a little odd, because it's meant for creating three-dimensional objects; as I mentioned earlier in this chapter, Inkscape is really a 2D graphics program. Nevertheless, if you select the Create 3D Boxes tool, the icon for which is a light blue cube, you can create box shapes by clicking, holding down the mouse button, and dragging (see Figure 4-10). For a box object that's already been created, you can use this tool to alter the dimensions of the faux-3D box by clicking and dragging the corner nodes. While you're doing this, a small X is visible in the middle of the box; you can click it and drag to change the object's perspective.

Figure 4-10. The Create 3D Boxes tool feels a little out of place in a 2D program like Inkscape, but it does speed up the creation of faux-3D objects.

A tool for creating 3D objects is much more useful when you can place other objects onto the boxes you make. To do this, you need to use the Layers dialog, which again is similar to the dialog of the same name in the GIMP. In Inkscape, you can view this dialog on the right side of the window by choosing Layer ➤ Layers on the main menu, or by using the default keyboard shortcut Shift+Ctrl+L.

■ **Note** From these similarities with the GIMP, it's obvious that the authors of Free Software graphics programs are following each other's work, in order to provide an integrated experience for users—in other words, you and me. Developers of these programs meet up and present their latest ideas at an annual conference called the Libre Graphics Meeting, which is held in a different country each year.

To try this for yourself, use the plus-sign button in the Layers dialog to create a new layer, type in a name, select "Position: Below current," and click the Add button. Move your 3D box to this new layer by selecting it with the arrowhead tool, click the Layer main menu, and choose Move Selection to Layer Below. Any object on the current layer now appears to be floating above the 3D box. As with the GIMP's Layers dialog, you can adjust the opacity and blend of each layer here, too. Finally, you may need to adjust the shape of the object on the top layer to fit the perspective of the 3D object visible beneath it (see Figure 4-11).

Figure 4-11. *You can easily create a fake 3D effect by using layers to place a text object on top of a box object.*

An interesting feature of the 3D box tool is that you can convert the box object to a path, in the usual way (Path ➤ Object to Path), and then start bending or dismantling the box by adjusting the nodes and converting segments to curves (see Figure 4-12). You can also change the colors of the faces of the box this way and stroke the paths by using the Palette or colors dialog. However, if you perform this operation on a particular box, you can no longer adjust its perspective or shape with the 3D box tool.

Figure 4-12. *3D boxes can be exploded by converting them to paths—you can then manipulate the edges of the three back sides of the box as lines or Bezier curves.*

The Create Circles, Ellipses, and Arcs tool, which has a light pink circle icon, is superficially similar to the Create Rectangles and Squares tool. One difference is that you can use the small circle controls on the edge of the object to create closed (segment) and open (arc) shapes—or Pac-Man and potato-chip shapes, to be more descriptive (see Figure 4-13)! You can switch between the types using buttons on the Tool Controls Bar, which are visible when the Circles tool is active.

Figure 4-13. *You can use the Create Circles, Ellipses, and Arcs tool to make Pac-Man or potato chip shapes, as well as regular circles.*

The Create Stars and Polygons tool is cool and somewhat addictive. You can make all sorts of shapes with this tool, from mandalas to randomized ink-blot shapes to conventional stars. To achieve the more unusual shapes, adjust the "Spoke ratio," Rounded, and Randomised values in the Tool Controls Bar (see Figure 4-14).

Figure 4-14. *Adjust the values for the Create Stars and Polygons tool to create abstract shapes, or stick with the defaults for pentagons and five-pointed stars.*

Next up is the Create Spirals tool. It works similarly to the other shape tools, except that as you'd expect, its parameters on the Tool Controls Bar are different. Set the Turns, Divergence, and "Inner radius" controls to achieve the kind of spiral you're looking for. You can also use a fill and stroke color, gradient, or pattern with a spiral (see Figure 4-15).

Figure 4-15. Spirals can be filled or stroked, like other shape objects.

Line-Drawing Tools

The Draw Freehand Lines tool, which has the icon of an orange pencil drawing a wavy line, works best if you have a graphics tablet—just like the equivalent tool in the GIMP. To use it with a mouse, hold down the left button, and start your scribbling motion. However, because in Inkscape this is a path-based tool, it doesn't depend on a brush setting; instead, the properties of the line drawn depend on the stroke paint and style currently set. You can also set a fill for a freehand line, which even for noncontiguous curves fills the space enclosed by the shape.

Unlike when you're using the predefined shape tools, freehand lines are paths automatically, rather than objects that need to be converted to paths for detailed editing. If you draw one of these lines with the Draw Freehand Lines tool and switch to the Edit Paths by Nodes tool, you see that it already has Bezier handles (see Figure 4-16).

Figure 4-16. The Draw Freehand Lines tool creates Bezier curves, with width, color, and style set by the active Stroke properties. Switch to the Edit Paths tool, and the lines are ready to be modified.

Next in the Toolbox is the Draw Bezier Curves and Straight Lines tool, which is thankfully more precise than the Draw Freehand Lines tool when you're using a mouse alone. Its icon is a blue drafting pen drawing a Bezier curve, but its cursor looks more like an ink-pen nib. To construct linked straight lines, click with this tool, move the mouse, and click again. When the series of lines is complete, right-click to release the tool. If you need a curved line, hold the left mouse button down and drag out the Bezier handle to get the shape you desire. Then, move the mouse to the next intended node position, and repeat the process. You can combine clicks with hold-and-drags to achieve a line with a combination of straight and curved sections (see Figure 4-17).

Figure 4-17. You can use the Draw Bezier Curves and Straight Lines tool for precise line shaping with the mouse alone.

Finally, right-click to release the tool and stroke the line with the current active color and width. If this isn't the color and width that you wanted after all, you can change it in the Fill and Stroke dialog box (keyboard shortcut Shift+Ctrl+F), as long as the line remains selected.

The Draw Calligraphic or Brush Strokes tool works a little differently than the previous two line-drawing tools. It has an icon like an ink pen with a gold nib drawing a bold, curved line, and its cursor looks like a curled pen stroke. The blunt shapes you can achieve with this tool look like ink-pen strokes; and the Tool Controls Bar offers a number of variables that you can adjust to control the effect, including Thinning, Angle, and Fixation. More significantly, it doesn't draw a stroked line like the other two tools—it draws the outline of the ink as an enclosed, stroked path, and fills it with the current active fill color. If you draw a line with this tool and then switch to the Edit Paths by Nodes tool, you see that the calligraphic paths generated are relatively complex.

For calligraphic writing, it's useful to provide some guide lines, which you can pull out of the rulers on the top and left side of the document (keyboard shortcut Ctrl+R) just as you can in the GIMP. As with the Draw Freehand Lines tool, a graphics tablet is recommended if you're serious about your calligraphy; but for the dabbler, the mouse does fine. When you're done writing, you can adjust the fill and stroke and edit the Bezier curves to correct any slips.

The Fill Tool

The next tool in the Toolbox is Fill Bounded Areas, which is similar to the Bucket Fill tool in the GIMP. Its icon is a blue can of paint in the process of being spilled; and its cursor is similar, except in black and white. This tool is a quick and convenient way to fill large areas without needing to select them and adjust the fill each time in the Fill and Stroke dialog (see Figure 4-18). Instead, the area you click is painted with the current active fill, as long as it's enclosed by a path or object boundary. For this reason, it doesn't work on unbounded backgrounds—to achieve a background effect, you must draw a rectangle around your drawing, fill it, and send this rectangle to the bottom layer of the document. The exact shade of fill color visible depends, as usual, on the Opacity setting of the layer it's on.

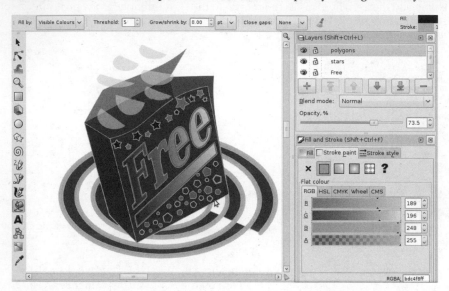

Figure 4-18. *The Fill Bounded Areas tool is useful for quickly coloring large areas with the same shade.*

The Tool Controls Bar includes a number of options for the Fill Bounded Areas tool, including the color to fill by, the threshold for the fill, and controls to grow or shrink the fill or close gaps.

The Text Tool

The Create and Edit Text Objects tool has options in the Tool Controls Bar for font family, size in pixels, alignment, and bold or italic attributes. It also has buttons that enable you to toggle between horizontal and vertical text. In addition, you can open the Text and Font dialog (keyboard shortcut Shift+Ctrl+T).

On the Text menu of the main Inkscape window, menu items let you put text on a path or remove it from a path. These options are very useful when you want text to follow a curve instead of the default straight line (see Figure 4-19). In order to put text on to a path, you must select both the text object and the path first; to do so, hold down the Shift key and click both items. If you select the path that shapes the text and click the X button in the Stroke Paint tab of the Fill and Stroke dialog, the path becomes invisible—leaving only the shaped text in position.

Figure 4-19. *The Create and Edit Text Objects tool has its own menu on Inkscape's main menu bar, which enables you to place text on a curved path (Text ➤ Put on Path).*

The text object remains editable as normal text, with an I-beam cursor and the Text and Font dialog, unless you convert it to a path outline using Path ➤ Object to Path on the main Inkscape menu. As when you use the Draw Calligraphic and Brush Strokes tool, this conversion can result in very complex paths; but it offers fine-grained control over the shape of the lettering (see Figure 4-20).

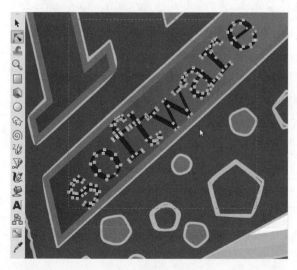

Figure 4-20. *Converting text to a path means it's no longer editable as text, but fine control over the text's shape becomes possible.*

While still in text mode, you can alter the kerning of individual pairs of letters or move them up and down relative to the baseline, which can produce some interesting effects. *Kerning* is a typographical term that refers to the horizontal spacing of letter shapes. Each font design has a preset kerning value; but you can adjust this manually by placing the text-editing cursor between two letters, holding down the Alt key, and using the left and right arrow keys to adjust the spacing. To reset the text to the font's default kerning, choose Text ➤ Remove Manual Kerns.

The *baseline* is an invisible horizontal guideline that normal lettering sits on, except for superscript (above baseline) or subscript (below baseline) characters. (The square sign ² and the cubed sign ³ are examples of common superscript characters, and the cedilla ¸ is a widely used subscript character in some European languages.) To manually adjust the height of letters relative to the baseline, select them with the text-editing cursor, hold down the Alt key, and press the up or down arrow key.

You can also make text flow inside a shape using a combination of the shape tools and Text ➤ Flow into Frame on the main Inkscape menu. As when you're putting text on a path, you have to select both the text object and the shape object by holding down the Shift key and clicking both before performing this operation.

■ **Note** SVG files use the fonts that are installed on the current system, so the look of your final design may change on different systems that don't have the same fonts installed. Converting all the text to paths before export works around this problem and also allows you to make further transformations. You can save a different copy of the file with the fonts preserved as objects, for use on your own system.

Diagram Connectors

A specialist tool that Inkscape offers is found next in the Toolbox: Create Diagram Connectors. It has an icon that looks like a collection of small boxes, but its cursor is a crooked arrow. Imagine that you're using Inkscape to create a flowchart. This tool helps you draw lines between objects that are automatically updated when those objects are moved.

To use this tool, mouse over the first object to be linked. A small square with a black outline is visible in the center of the object, which turns red when the cursor is directly over it. Click the small red square, and then move the mouse to the center of the second object to be linked. When the small square at the center of the second object turns red, click that to make the connection (see Figure 4-21). Despite the position you just clicked, the connecting line doesn't go from center to center; instead, it goes from the boundary of the first object to the boundary of the second.

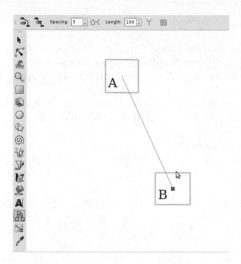

Figure 4-21. *The Create Diagram Connectors tool requires you to mouse over an object and click when the small square in the center turns red.*

The Create Diagram Connectors tool doesn't add arrowheads to the lines automatically. To create these, you have to look at the Stroke Style tab of the Fill and Stroke dialog, and select a start marker and an end marker (see Figure 4-22). You can also use a mid marker, if your line is a long one. Up in the Tool Controls Bar, buttons let you set how the connectors route around selected objects in the document, as well as the ideal connector length, spacing, and arrangement.

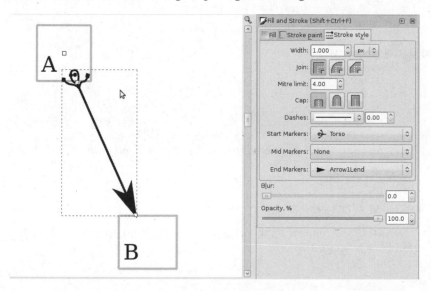

Figure 4-22. *Use the Start Markers and End Markers drop-down menus in the Fill and Stroke dialog to add arrowheads and tails to your connecting lines.*

Creating Gradients

Next is the Create and Edit Gradients tool, which has an icon that looks like two connected boxes on a greenish gradient background. Its cursor looks like these connected boxes in black and white, only vertically aligned. This tool is a little different from the drawing tools, because it doesn't do anything on a blank document. You have to select an object or path—a box shape, for instance—and then put a gradient inside it. It doesn't have to be a continuous path to have a gradient fill, but it must enclose at least some space—you can't put a gradient next to a straight-line path, any more than you can use a normal fill with it.

Using this tool is straightforward. Click inside the selected object or path where you want the gradient fill to start, hold the mouse button down, drag to the point where you want the gradient to end, and then release the mouse button (see Figure 4-23).

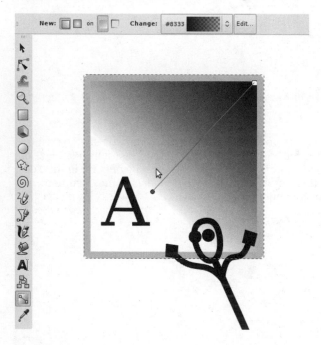

Figure 4-23. *You can use the Create and Edit Gradients tool to specify the start and end point of gradient fills.*

Selecting Colors from an Image

The final tool in the Inkscape toolbox is Pick Colors from the Image, which has a pipette icon and cursor just like the similar tool in the GIMP (see Figure 4-24).

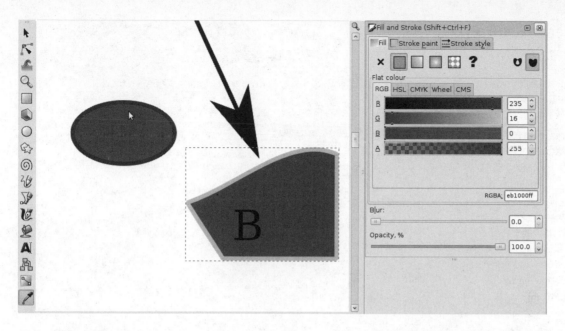

Figure 4-24. *The Pick Colors from the Image tool fills the currently selected object or path with whatever color is under the pipette cursor when it's clicked.*

There's a crucial difference from the GIMP's color-picker tool, however. Inkscape's color picker doesn't set the active fill color in the Fill and Stroke dialog unless at least one object or path is selected. When you make the color choice with the pipette cursor, that selected object or path gets filled with the color you just chose. If multiple objects or paths are selected, they're all filled with the chosen color—so you should use this tool with caution. If you fill the wrong object or path with color, there's always the Edit ➤ Undo option (keyboard shortcut Ctrl+Z).

Managing Colors

When you're working with color designs, it's useful to know that like the GIMP, Inkscape supports standard ICC color profiles. If you have any of these profiles installed on your system, using the method described in the last chapter, they appear in Inkscape's Preferences dialog when you choose File ➤ Inkscape Preferences ➤ Color Management ➤ Display Profile (see Figure 4-25).

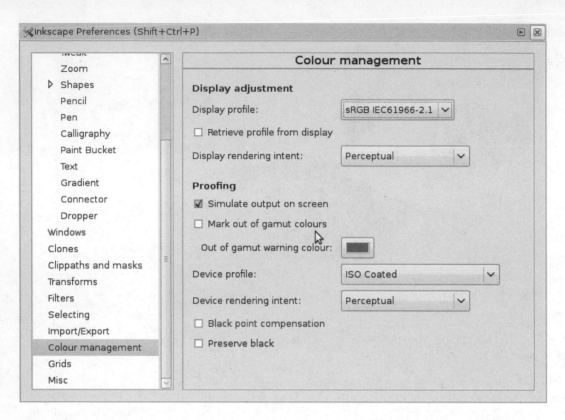

Figure 4-25. *Inkscape supports color-management features, both for display and for proofing.*

Pixmap-to-Vector Conversion

If you import pixmaps into an Inkscape document, they don't become vector graphics automatically. However, you can trace the outline of a placed pixmap. First, import the pixmap using the button on the Commands Bar, which looks like a piece of paper with an arrow pointing into it. Resize the pixmap if necessary, using the arrowhead tool on the corner arrows, holding down the Ctrl key as you do so to preserve the aspect ratio of the original pixmap. Make sure the pixmap in question is selected, and then choose Path ➤ Trace Bitmap on the main Inkscape menu. You probably need to try a few different options in the resulting dialog to get the result you want in the Preview window, so keep clicking the Update button as you change the variables (see Figure 4-26).

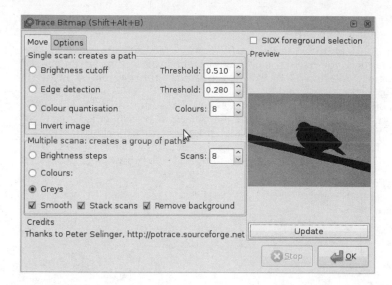

Figure 4-26. The Trace Bitmap dialog box. Some experimentation is required for the best results.

Click the OK button, and wait for the computer to do the tracing; this step involves a lot of processing. If your computer is on the old side, you may need to make yourself a cup of coffee while the tracing is completed. Then, close the dialog box, switch to the Edit Paths by Nodes tool, and check out the results (see Figure 4-27).

Figure 4-27. Bird on a wire: photographed in silhouette, and then traced into vectors automatically by Potrace, running in Inkscape. The path nodes are shown as squares.

Exporting Pixmaps

When you're happy with your design, save it in Inkscape's native SVG format. To use your artwork in programs that don't support vector graphics, you need to export it as a static pixmap. One advantage of this process is that the pixmap of your artwork should look exactly the same in any program or on any platform, regardless of SVG support or the fonts installed.

To do this, choose File ➤ Export Bitmap on the main Inkscape menu. The resulting dialog allows you to select the whole page for export, just your drawing, a particular selection, or a specified area of the page (see Figure 4-28). You can also specify the bitmap size and resolution and the export filename. Inkscape exports pixmaps in Portable Network Graphics format (`.png`) by default, which is a cross-platform, standard format understood by all modern graphics programs and web browsers.

Figure 4-28. Inkscape offers a range of choices for bitmap export.

If Inkscape can't export the pixmap format you need, you can import a PNG file into the GIMP and then save it in one of the wide array of pixel-based formats that the GIMP supports. You can also perform effects and transformations on the pixmap using the GIMP's tools and filters, some of which are difficult or impossible to achieve with a vector program like Inkscape.

■ **Tip** If you need to apply the same operation to many pixmap images, or repeat a specific operation at different times, it's well worth knowing about ImageMagick (GNU/Linux, Windows, Mac), a suite of command-line tools. This package comes as standard with many GNU/Linux distros, including Ubuntu. It's used behind the scenes on the servers of many photographic web sites, whenever images are converted automatically. For Windows and Mac versions, visit the ImageMagick web site at `www.imagemagick.org`.

Forging Fonts

One of the most arcane aspects of illustration is font design. Usually, people tend to regard fonts as something static that you buy or download from the Internet—and if you don't like the fonts you have available, it means searching through hundreds of alternatives to find one that you prefer. In reality, fonts on a computer are just a bunch of vector graphics, with nodes and Bezier curves like the shapes you've been looking at making in Inkscape.

Many of the well-known computer fonts are proprietary to the font foundries that produced them, but there are a growing number of Free Software fonts that you can download, modify, rename, and re-release. When you've had some practice working with font design, you can even try making your own unique font from scratch—although it helps to have read up on the theory of font design, handed down through the ages by generations of typographers.

Typefaces, Fonts, and Glyphs

A *typeface* is a collection of fonts with a similar or compatible visual style. In turn, a *font* is a collection of rendered glyphs organized into characters, and a *glyph* is made up of the contours and shapes that represent a character. The same character can be represented by several different glyphs. Computer fonts must contain information about how to map an input string of bytes into an output display of visual glyphs. This mapping is called an *encoding*. A font may also contain information on how to compose ligatures and accents.

The study of fonts and typefaces can become complex, but fortunately it isn't necessary to get too involved in the details in order to get started. That said, in order to produce results that look professional, clean, and easy on the eye, it's worth learning a little more about how fonts are displayed. I just deal with the basics here.

Font File Formats

Fonts are stored using various different file types:

- *PCF* is a type of binary bitmap font with a platform-independent representation. Bitmap fonts are occasionally used for screen display, but they don't resize well.

- *PostScript* fonts are vector fonts designed primarily for printing; this file type was originally developed by Adobe. PFA files are Type 1 PostScript fonts in text format, and a PFB is a Type 1 PostScript font in binary format. These outline vectors require an accompanying AFM or PFM file, which contains the font metrics.

- *TTF* files are TrueType fonts—single file vector fonts for screen display, originally developed by Apple, and supported on GNU/Linux by the FreeType library. TrueType fonts usually print well and are the most universal format nowadays, although a few applications still don't support them.

There are many other, less widely used, font formats, which you can safely ignore for now.

The size of a font is traditionally measured in *points* (abbreviated pt), a very small and old-fashioned unit. Before international standardization, the size of a printer's point varied from country to country. As mentioned in the last chapter, on a computer, the convention is that there are 72 pixels in one inch; and by convention, the same value is used for the number of points in an inch. Ordinary body text in a book is usually between 9 and 12 points, but newspaper headline fonts can be 72 points (one inch) high or even larger.

Sketching a Font

If you want to try designing a font from scratch, and you prefer a pen and paper to the mouse for quick drafting, you may want to try drawing an alphabet with a black felt-tip pen. This method is a practical starting point for font design, particularly if you have access to an image scanner. Make sure you leave enough space between the lines and keep the letters well separated, because the letters need to be cut out individually. When you like the look of the alphabet you've drawn, put the sheet of paper in the scanner and import the image into the GIMP using the File ➤ Acquire ➤ XSane ➤ Device dialog, as you saw in the last chapter. You need to perform a grayscale scan at a resolution high enough to capture the detail of your hand drawing (see Figure 4-29).

Figure 4-29. *The original hand-drawn sketch for Kenny, a font design by Tim Hall, scanned into the GIMP.*

If you don't have access to a scanner, there are many other ways to create your letters, including using the mouse and Bezier curves. Don't despair!

Forging Ahead

FontForge (GNU/Linux, Windows, Mac) is a design tool and editor for Type 1 PostScript and TrueType fonts, among other formats. It isn't a standard GNU/Linux distro package, but it's available via Ubuntu's Add/Remove Applications tool. You should also install the optional autotrace package using Synaptic (System ➤ Administration ➤ Synaptic Package Manager), because you'll use that shortly.

FontForge is Free Software and primarily made for UNIX-like platforms. Ready-made packages are also available for Windows and the Mac from the FontForge web site at http://fontforge.sourceforge.net.

When you run FontForge from Ubuntu's Applications ➤ Graphics menu, you're presented with an Open Font dialog. Click New, and you see an empty font-editing window (see Figure 4-30). Double-clicking a glyph space brings up an outline glyph window. This is where you can edit the Bezier splines that make up the individual contours.

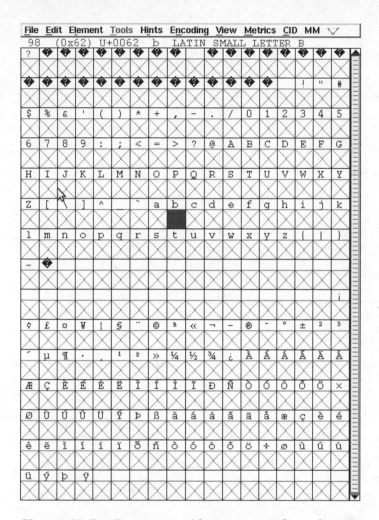

Figure 4-30. FontForge opens with a new, empty font—there are no glyphs in it yet.

Give your new font a name by choosing Element ➤ Font Info. You can also set a copyright notice here and a lot of other information that affects the font (see Figure 4-31). The defaults are suitable for PostScript fonts, so you can accept them for now. TrueType fonts may benefit from different settings; but fortunately, FontForge usually manages to do the right thing automatically. You may also wish to choose Encoding ➤ Reencode to change the characters that are available in your font. FontForge generally creates new fonts with an ISO 8859-1 encoding, which contains most of the characters needed for Western European languages such as English.

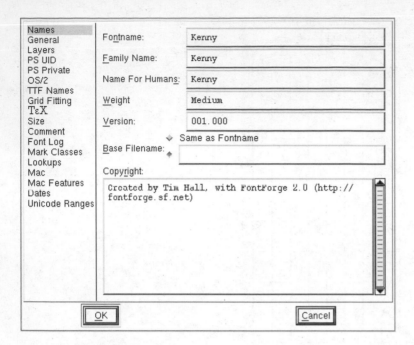

Figure 4-31. *The FontForge Font Info window allows you to specify basic settings, including the font's name and copyright information.*

Copying and pasting the scan of all your letter shapes from the GIMP into FontForge doesn't work well. Instead, use the GIMP to split the scan of the alphabet into separate PNG files, one for each letter, and then import them individually into FontForge by choosing File ➤ Import. Choose Format Image in the Import dialog box.

The FontForge native file format for creating fonts has a `.sfd` extension. This format is suitable for sharing and storing font designs, rather than installing for use as a font in other programs on your computer. Before you go any further, now is a good time to save your work in that format (File ➤ Save).

Editing the Font Images

After you import the pixmaps from the scan, you may need to resize them to fit correctly inside the FontForge 1000 x 1000 pixel box provided for each glyph. Double-click one of the glyphs, and, in the small floating Layers dialog, click the button in the E column next to Back; doing so enables you to edit the background pixmap. You can then drag the background image around so that it sits on the baseline and fits inside the box in an appropriate manner (see Figure 4-32).

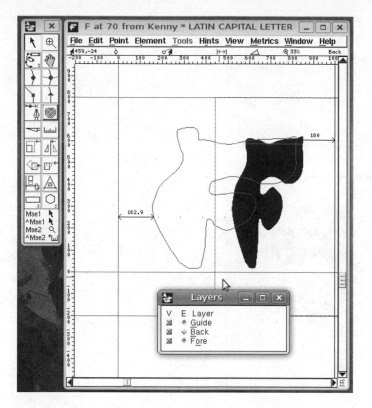

Figure 4-32. *Use the buttons in the Layers dialog to toggle visibility and editing of the guides, background and foreground.*

■ **Tip** If you're working from scratch, I recommend that you create a base glyph with all the lines your letters need. A circled cross is often a good starting point; you can edit it to create all the letters you require, starting with *A*, *R*, *O*, *H*, and *T*. Many letter shapes are related to one another, so you can create new glyphs by flipping shapes on the horizontal or vertical axis. This technique can be used to fill in glyphs that are missing from the original design, and produces consistency in the final look of the font.

If you have the autotrace program installed, you can generate an outline from the pixmap image by choosing Element ➤ AutoTrace (see Figure 4-33). Otherwise, you have to add the node points yourself. Make the Foreground layer editable, and select the Curve Point tool from the Tools dialog (its icon is a red circle on a curved line). Click around the shape on the corners and straight lines, preferably in a clockwise fashion, making sure you close the path by adding a new point on top of the old start point. It's then possible to fine-tune the contours using a combination of Point menu items and dragging the Bezier control points around with the mouse. Remember to select the Pointer tool, with the black arrow icon, for this task. The representation of the glyph changes in the font-view window as you edit, so you can easily check your progress.

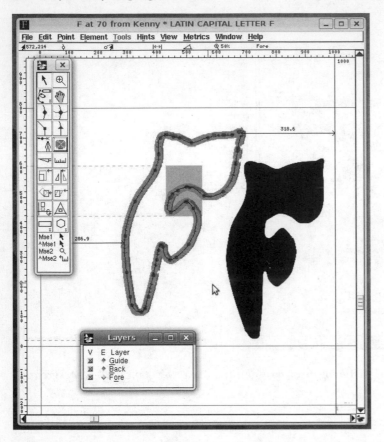

Figure 4-33. *Autotrace (highlighted in green) used on an imported pixmap for the letter F (filled with black). The path has been slanted ten degrees after the import, for a more oblique look.*

Note that the glyph for *O* has two contours: the inner and outer circles. If all you see is a big black dot, it's most likely because the inner contour is going in the wrong direction in relation to the outer contour. To solve this problem, flip the direction of the inner contour. In FontForge, all outer boundaries must be drawn clockwise, and all inner boundaries must be drawn counterclockwise. This condition applies to any glyphs involving enclosed spaces. You can choose Element ➤ Correct Direction to automatically correct this kind of error.

Importing Glyphs from Inkscape

If you've considered creating letter shapes in Inkscape, you'll be pleased to discover that FontForge can import Inkscape's SVG files directly (see Figure 4-34). Again, you need to save each glyph in its own file in order to import it into FontForge, but in this case you choose Format SVG from the Import dialog box. The Inkscape document for your glyph should be 1000 pixels high and 1000 pixels wide.

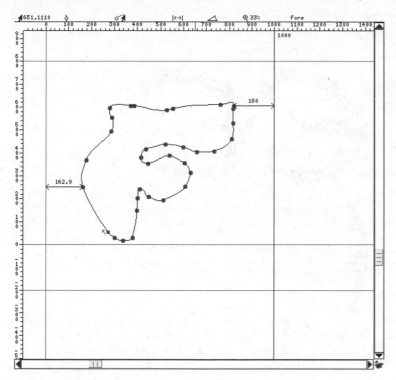

Figure 4-34. *A hand-drawn capital F from Inkscape saved in SVG format and imported directly into FontForge. The red dots are already present on the glyph—there's no need to autotrace or hand-draw the path.*

Spacing and Kerning

When you've created the glyph shapes, the next task is to specify the spacing between the glyphs. *Kerning* is the process of setting the spacing between specific pairs of letters. Open the Metrics window by choosing Window ➤ New Metrics Window (see Figure 4-35). Here, you can adjust the spacing of each letter relative to the others either by typing values into the text fields or by dragging the shapes and lines into the desired positions. You can set the widths of the glyphs and the kernings automatically from the Metrics menu, but doing so can produce alarming effects. This process can take quite a bit of fiddling around, and it's best to get the correct widths for the individual glyphs before you attempt to set any kernings.

Figure 4-35. *The font Metrics window, showing the spacing and kerning of the Kenny font.*

FontForge also has facilities to create hints to help the font renderer find horizontals and verticals, and produce consistent serifs and stem widths at small point sizes. It's possible to create ligatures, accents, and alternative glyphs as well. The program can also deal with right-to-left and vertical alignments and most conceivable encodings. It can handle Chinese, Japanese, and Korean fonts, and Arabic type styles.

To make your font usable, you need to save it in a standard font format (File ➤ Generate Fonts). Although it seems like you have a bewildering array of choices, you should choose PostScript Type1 or TrueType in most circumstances. The default settings will serve you for now.

Installing Your New Font

On GNU/Linux, fonts meant for personal use are stored in the hidden `.fonts` directory in your home directory. To find this directory on Ubuntu, open the file manager by choosing Places ➤ Home Folder from the main GNOME menu at upper left on the desktop. When your home directory appears, choose View ➤ Show Hidden Files (keyboard shortcut Ctrl+H) to see if the `.fonts` directory is there. If not, right-click any empty space in the file manager main window, select Create Folder from the pop-up menu, and give the new folder the name `.fonts`—making sure you include that leading period.

Double-click the `.fonts` folder icon to open it, and drag in the `.pfb` and `.afm` files (in the case of a Type 1 font) that you exported from FontForge.

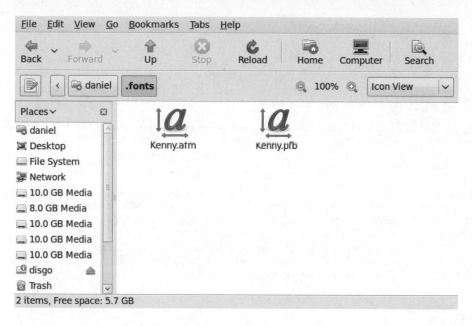

Figure 4-36. Create the hidden `.fonts` directory, if it doesn't exist already.

The next time you start a program like Inkscape, you should immediately see the name of your new font in the drop-down list. Your work is done, and your new font is ready to use.

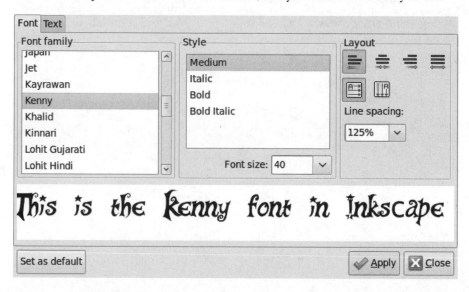

Figure 4-37. The Kenny font is now available for use in Inkscape and other programs. Note that the lowercase letter c still needs work, because it isn't displayed correctly.

Other Useful Programs

You can try many more vector illustration and design tools, including these:

- *Karbon 14* (GNU/Linux, Mac): A Free Software alternative to Inkscape that is part of the KOffice suite; `www.koffice.org/karbon/`.

- *Xara Xtreme* (GNU/Linux, Windows): Another vector graphics tool with some advanced features. The Linux version of Xara is Free Software, but the Windows version isn't, although a 30-day trial for Windows is available to download; `www.xaraxtreme.org`.

- *QCAD Community Edition* (GNU/Linux): a Free Software program for drawing 2D designs that engineering shops and house builders can make for you. It's designed to allow very precise measurements when drawing, and it supports natively the `.dxf` file format used by AutoCAD and other proprietary programs. QCAD Professional (GNU/Linux, Windows, Mac) has some additional features but isn't Free Software. A trial version of the Professional edition is available for all platforms from the QCAD web site at `www.ribbonsoft.com`.

Further Reading

Inkscape is well documented. Start by choosing Help ➤ Tutorials ➤ Inkscape Basic, and work your way through. The tutorials are in SVG format, so you can try things as you read them. The learning curve for Inkscape is gentle; you can work through the tutorials in a day, by which time you can come up with some designs and gain enough confidence to develop your ideas through further experimentation. Just as with Inkscape, the documentation that comes with FontForge is extensive and comprehensive.

■ ■ ■

## CHAPTER 5

Animation

Free Software for Movie Production

Hollywood studios make extensive use of the GNU/Linux platform for both animation and visual effects work. However, many of the applications that the studio artists rely on are created for exclusive in-house use and are treated as trade secrets. No wonder, because this application software forms part of a studio's competitive advantage over its box-office rivals. This kind of program is a classic example of software written to order, which you read about in Chapter 1. Some other animation applications used in the movie industry can be purchased from specialist proprietary software vendors, but the price tag often puts them out of reach of the average computer user.

Fortunately, several good and improving Free Software animation programs are now available for movie production. Like GNU/Linux, most of these applications are highly configurable, which is a big plus for creative people who crave the ability to modify and improve their software tools. These desktop-orientated animation applications are fairly new in the Free Software arena, and they don't all enjoy the large developer and user communities of some of the other tools covered in this book. Suddenly, you're a lot closer to the bleeding edge of software development than you may have hoped.

With the GIMP Animation Package (GAP) plug-in (GNU/Linux, Windows) it's possible to create flip-book style animation from a series of pixmaps (see Figure 5-1). Using the GIMP with this plug-in is more suited to creating animated web graphics than a full-length movie, although GAP does support video file export. When this plug-in is installed, it adds an extra menu—Video—to the GIMP's main toolbar.

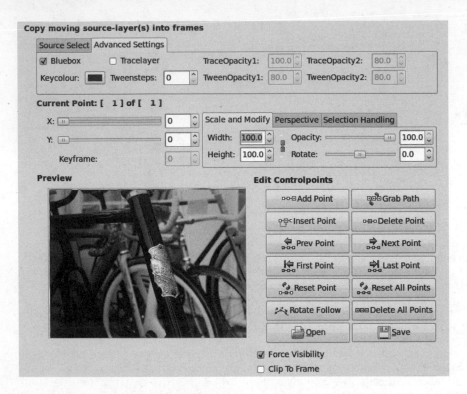

Figure 5-1. *The GIMP has an animation plug-in known as GAP. Checking compatibility with your installed GIMP version is recommended.*

The Ubuntu package for this plug-in is called gimp-gap; you can find it in the universe package repository. It isn't visible in Ubuntu's Add/Remove Programs application, but you can install this package using the more advanced software-management program by choosing System ➤ Administration ➤ Synaptic Package Manager on the main GNOME menu. Source code for GAP is available from `ftp://ftp.gimp.org/pub/gimp/plug-ins/`, and also ready-made binaries are available for Windows on various web sites.

■ **Note** At the time of writing, the GAP plug-in hasn't been updated to work with the current release of the GIMP, version 2.6—which makes GAP liable to crash frequently. If you want to use GAP, you may need to downgrade your GIMP installation.

A rare example of cross-industry collaboration on a Free Software movie-making application is CinePaint (GNU/Linux, Mac), briefly mentioned in Chapter 1. Adapted from an early version of the GIMP, CinePaint is intended for frame-by-frame retouching of film, including dust and wire-rig removal. This tool has been used on many well-known feature films, including *The Last Samurai* (2003), where it was used to add flying arrows (see Figure 5-2). It has also been used by still photographers who need greater color depth and fidelity than is available with other graphics applications. Currently, it isn't the easiest program to install, and few ready-made binary packages are available that are up to date. You can find out more about the program at www.cinepaint.org.

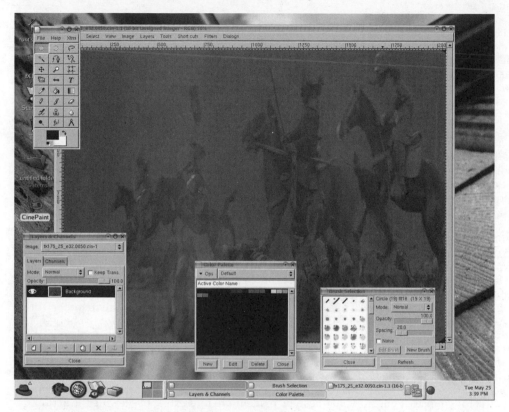

Figure 5-2. In this composite shot from The Last Samurai, CinePaint was used to touch up and enhance a live battle scene, with digital stunt doubles on digital horses added using other tools. The film frame is squished horizontally in this shot because the film was shot anamorphically. Image copyright 2003 Warner Bros.

The Importance of Storyboarding

Good quality, hand-drawn animation takes a lot of work for a lot of people, and that makes it expensive to produce. To create the optical illusion of smooth motion, a high frame rate is required—just as with a film or video camera—which means a lot of drawing for the artists to do. The exact number of frames per second depends on the film camera or video format being used; traditionally, these rates were from 24 frames up to 30 frames per second, but some newer high-definition video formats use even higher rates. Multiply the number of frames per second by the length of the animation in seconds, and you begin to get an idea of the work involved in making a feature-length animated movie.

Because of the high costs involved in animation, in time if not in money, preparation is essential. Before you begin drawing, you must make sure the concept behind the piece you're going to make is completely clear. If you have nothing to say, then all the software and techniques in the world can't help you. Just as when making a big-budget special effects movie, having a plot helps a lot! You don't even need a computer for this step.

Storyboarding is useful for capturing and refining ideas. It's a chance to plan the movie, develop the narrative, and visualize the action before it becomes too complicated. The storyboarding process helps you get an overview of the whole piece, to test whether your idea will work, to discover whether anything is missing, and to see what problems turn up. It can also serve as a common point of reference for the production team and help to speed up the process of preparing the content later.

The actual storyboard is a series of pictures that shows how each shot in a scene will be filmed. Storyboarding is like making a comic book of your movie idea. You can use it to plan how the titles will look, the order and duration of the visual images (either still or moving), and the audio and text that will accompany them. The storyboard should map out everything that will be seen, heard, or experienced by the final audience.

For a lengthy animation, it can be useful to divide the story into its logical parts, such as a lead-in paragraph, which explains the importance of this story; profiles of the main characters in the story; the event or situation; descriptions of how things work in the story; a map or overview of the area of action, if necessary; and the history behind the event. Next, you can divide the contents of the story into video, still photos, audio, graphics, and text. Decide which format is best to tell each part of the story, and decide which parts allow for user interaction (if you're going to have any).

To make the storyboard, find a piece of paper and draw some numbered frames in horizontal rows. Leave enough room for text underneath each frame, and keep the area you have to draw small. Some people like to use post-it notes so they can move frames around. If this idea appeals to you, you may want to find a large sheet of cardboard to stick the notes on. Sketch in pencil so you can make changes easily; you can ink in the images later. You don't need to be good at drawing; matchstick figures are fine, but the more attention to detail you pay at this stage, the more work you save later on. Remember, this is just a guide—a rough sketch. The storyboard is like a script to fall back on. You may want to change things as the project develops; some movie makers say that a good storyboard is never completed.

It's useful to get an idea of how long each action should take, along with the timing of any audio components. If you have a voice-over, every six words will take roughly three seconds to speak. And three seconds is about the ideal length for any still image to appear on the screen.

You can learn a lot about storyboarding by studying comic books and looking at the different kinds of shots a film director chooses. Your storyboard can be made more interesting by viewing the action from different positions and using wide, medium, and close-up shots to add drama. There are various ways of showing movement on the storyboard, either within the frame or by indicating camera panning using arrows. You can have text notes between the frames and floating frames within a larger landscape, in various combinations. Use whatever visual shorthand works for you, and let your imagination flow! When you're done scribbling, it's time to switch on the computer and realize your pen-and-ink vision in digital format.

KToon: a Tool for Cartoonists

Designed by animators and focused on the needs of the cartoon industry, KToon (GNU/Linux) is a Free Software 2D animation toolkit. It's available with Ubuntu's Add/Remove Programs application or as a download from the project's home page at ktoon.toonka.com.

Versions for the Mac and Windows are planned but not yet available. You're warned that KToon is still considered beta software and as such may crash or be missing functionality. More so than ever, when you're running beta or other bleeding-edge software, you should save your work early and often.

. When you start KToon for the first time, a dialog invites you to set up the environment for the program (see Figure 5-3). You can accept the defaults by clicking Next and then Finish.

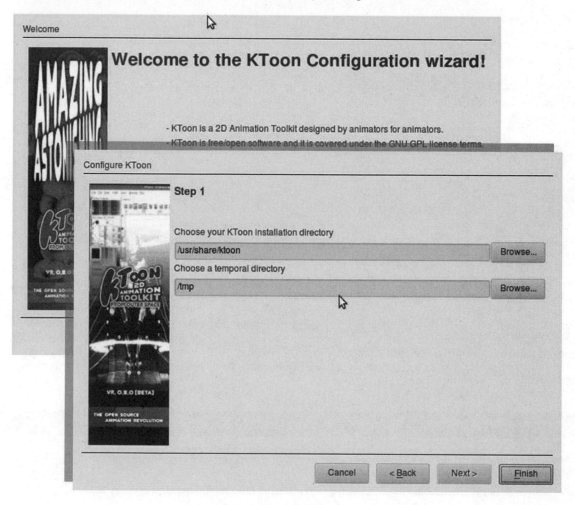

Figure 5-3. KToon features a wizard that sets up installation and temporary directories on a GNU/Linux system.

When the main KToon window opens, you see a large blank window with two tabs: Illustration and Animation. A "Tip of day" window floats in the center, which you can get rid of for now with the Close button. It's not immediately obvious what you're supposed to do next. This is because the drawing canvas and illustration tools aren't apparent until you create a project by choosing File ➤ New ➤ New Project. When you do, you're prompted for project and author names, the dimension of your animation in pixels, and the number of frames per second you require (see Figure 5-4). The default settings of a project 520 pixels wide and 340 pixels high with 24 frames per second are fine to start with. Later, you may prefer higher values for these settings; but bear in mind that this will mean more of you computer's processing and storage capabilities will be required to complete the project.

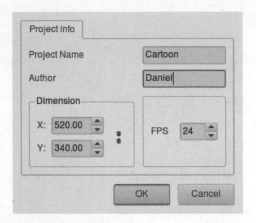

Figure 5-4. The KToon "Create a new project" dialog requires you to set names, dimensions, and frame rate before you can begin.

After you click the OK button in the "Create a new project" dialog, a window with a blank canvas with horizontal and vertical guidelines appears, along with toolbars, rulers, and four menus: Tools, Edit, View, and Filters. KToon now begins to look like a program you can actually use to create an animation.

On the left side of the canvas window, you see three small icons with drop-down menus to the immediate right. These are the Brushes, Selection, and Fill menus; they're similar to those you've seen in the GIMP and Inkscape in previous chapters. From the Brushes drop-down menu, which is the top icon, select the Pencil tool. You can also access this tool by choosing Tools ➤ Brushes ➤ Pencil on the canvas menus, as long as the Illustration tab is active.

Fixing KToon on Ubuntu Jaunty

There is a critical bug in the KToon package included with Ubuntu, up to at least the April 2009 release, 9.04, code-named Jaunty Jackalope. If none of the tools are visible when you click the icons or menus, it's because the system can't find them. To fix this, close KToon, open a terminal (Applications ➤ Accessories ➤ Terminal on the main GNOME menu), and enter the following command:

```
sudo ln -s /usr/lib/ktoon/plug-ins /usr/share/ktoon
```

You're prompted for your login password. Type it in (it isn't shown in the terminal, for security reasons), and press the Enter key. This command (ln -s) makes a soft link between the directory containing the tools (/usr/lib/ktoon/plug-ins) and the directory where KToon expects to find them (/usr/share/ktoon). The sudo part gives you administrator rights over the system (su stands for Switch User). The only feedback you get from the terminal to show that this command was successful is being returned to the command prompt without an error message. When you restart KToon, the tools should be visible.

KToon's Drawing Tools

Like the equivalent tool in the GIMP, the freehand Pencil tool in KToon is most useful if you have a graphics tablet (see Figure 5-5). With a mouse, the results tend to be a little shaky. The Rectangle, Ellipse, Line, and Shape Brush tools are likely to be more accurate (see Figure 5-6). There is also a Polyline tool, but it appears incomplete as of KToon version 0.8. With any of these tools, click and hold the mouse button down while you drag the mouse to draw the line or shape. The Text tool is just as straightforward, offering a selection of the fonts installed on the system.

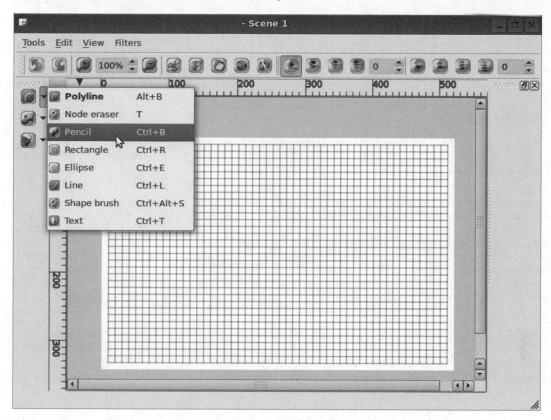

Figure 5-5. The drawing tools in KToon allow the construction of basic shapes.

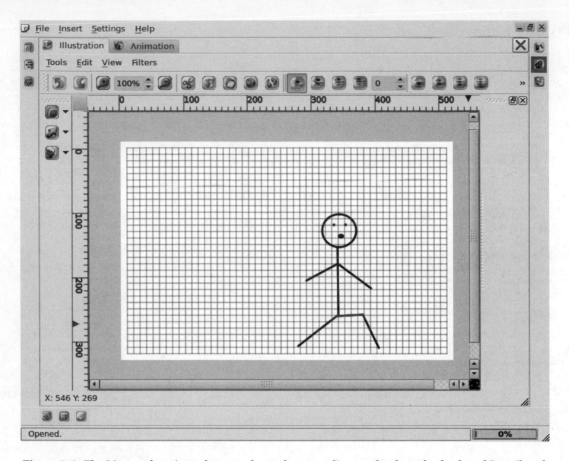

Figure 5-6. *The Line and various shape tools produce steadier results than the freehand Pencil tool.*

One of the current limitations of KToon is that it's difficult to see what you're drawing. The line or shape isn't visible while the mouse button is held down—only when you release it, which means you have to feel your way around the canvas.

If you make a mistake that Edit ➤ Undo can't fix, you can use the Selection tool to click and drag the mouse pointer around an object. The selection is highlighted with small blue squares in its corners. You can then press Ctrl+X, the usual keyboard shortcut for Cut, or the Delete key.

When you have a first drawing that you're happy with, click the middle icon of the three arranged vertically on the far right side of the main KToon window. Doing so opens the Exposure Sheet dialog, which provides an overview of the individual frames in the project (see Figure 5-7). Right-click your first image, which is labeled Drawing 1 by default, and select "Clone this Frame." A pop-up window asks how many cloned frames you require; 23 clones, to create a total of one second in your movie, may be a good number to start with. All 24 frames are labeled Drawing 1 in the Exposure Sheet dialog, but you can rename each frame by double-clicking its name. Any changes you make to the original drawing are automatically applied to all of its clones.

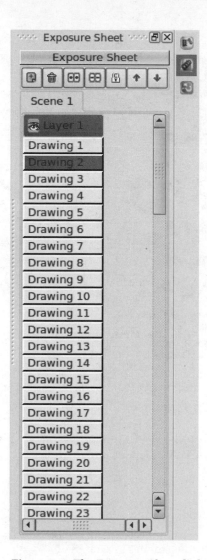

Figure 5-7. The Exposure Sheet dialog lists all the frames that make up the animation project.

Of course, if all the frames are identical clones, there isn't much going on in the animation. In the Exposure Sheet dialog, right-click the name of one of the frames you've already created, and select "Copy this Frame." If you click in one of the empty frame spaces below, a new frame is created automatically. Right-click its name, and select "Paste into this Frame." Unlike when cloning, you can modify this new frame without affecting the clone frames you made earlier.

After you've added a few different frames to the Exposure Sheet, click the Animation tab at the top of the main KToon window. The Render Camera Preview opens, which has Rewind, Play, Stop, and Fast Forward buttons. Click the Play button for a first look at your animation (see Figure 5-8).

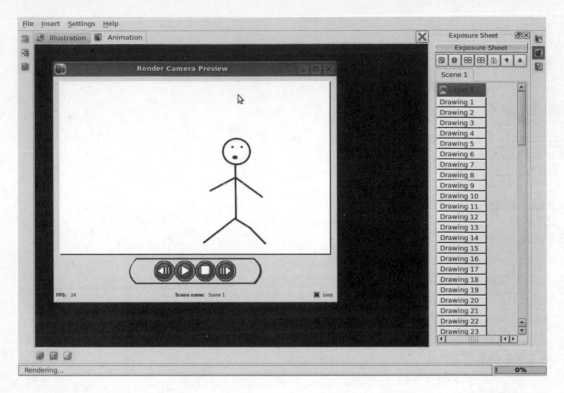

Figure 5-8. *The Render Camera Preview window helps test how your animation is progressing.*

If it's very short, you may want to select the Loop check box in the lower-right corner to see the animation over and over again. Click the Stop button if your animation is still looping, and then click the Illustration tab to switch back to Editing mode.

Exporting from KToon

KToon has its own native file format with a `.ktn` suffix for saving projects, but this is unlikely to be understood by any other program. You have the option to export individual frames as a series of numbered PNG or JPEG images; this approach is compatible with a wide range of graphics programs, but given the number of frames required in any animation of significant length, it isn't the most convenient format for playback. In order to put your animation in front of an audience, you need to save it in a standard format that is compatible with media player software. Just as with SVG, which you read about in the last chapter on vector graphics, a format designed for this purpose has been standardized by the World Wide Web Consortium (W3C). It's called *Synchronized Multimedia Integration Language (SMIL)*. In the implementation used by KToon, the `.smil` format comprises a directory full of PNG images and an XML file that describes the order in which the images should be played back. SMIL is supported in several up-to-date media players and should soon be supported directly in web browsers.

To make the export, first click the icon button for the Export dialog in the lower-left corner of the KToon main window. If the KToon package you're using has been compiled with video support, you see options to export directly to a video file. If you're using the Ubuntu package, though, you only see options for Image Arrays (a bunch of stills) and SMIL 2.0 in the list (see Figure 5-9). Select the export of all scenes, specify a file name, and click the Export button.

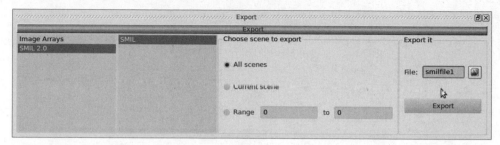

Figure 5-9. *Ktoon's Export dialog (in Ubuntu) offers a choice of a sequence of PNG or JPEG stills, or a SMIL file and data directory.*

■ **Note** If you decide to export in SMIL format, be careful about where KToon puts the still images referenced by the `.smil` file. By default, it saves the stills in a directory called `data`, with each still having the prefix of the project name and a suffix of the frame number: for example, `ktoon-project0004.png`. Therefore, when you copy or move a KToon project, it's essential that the correct data directory is copied together with the corresponding `.smil` file. If you had several KToon projects, all with their stills in directories called `data`, there would be plenty of room for confusion.

Hand-Drawing vs. Tweening

Even with today's digital inking and painting software, the animation process often relies on individual artists hand-drawing or correcting each frame, as you've seen with KToon. If you're trying to produce animation by yourself or in a small team, you may find the process prohibitively time-consuming or too boring. It can be done, but some animators have spent years on one short film—particularly when they were just starting out and had no one to help them. Commercial animation studios have often worked around this problem by having the lead artist draw the key frames of the action and then outsourcing the drawing of the in-between frames to less well-paid animators, often in countries where pay rates and labor laws are much less demanding.

If the key frames are drawn as a series of vectors, then it becomes possible to use the computer's number-crunching power to fill the gaps in time and space automatically using a process known as *tweening*, as in in-betweening. Essentially, this is an extension of the same vector techniques you looked at in Chapter 4. Letting the computer do the time-consuming, boring work potentially makes good-quality animation much more practical for individual artists and small teams.

Synfig: a Tweening Animation Tool

Synfig (GNU/Linux, Windows, Mac) is a vector-based 2D graphics application, designed to enable the production of feature-film quality animation with fewer people and resources (see Figure 5-10). It has both a server-side version and a graphical interface version that looks superficially similar to the GIMP. You can install the latter from the Add/Remove Programs tool in Ubuntu by selecting the package synfigstudio. If you install just the synfig package, you don't get the graphical interface. Ubuntu also has a package called synfig-examples that puts demo files in the `/usr/share/doc/synfig-examples/` directory on the system. If you use Ubuntu, the examples package should be installed automatically when you install the synfigstudio package; if not, you can find it with the Synaptic package manager.

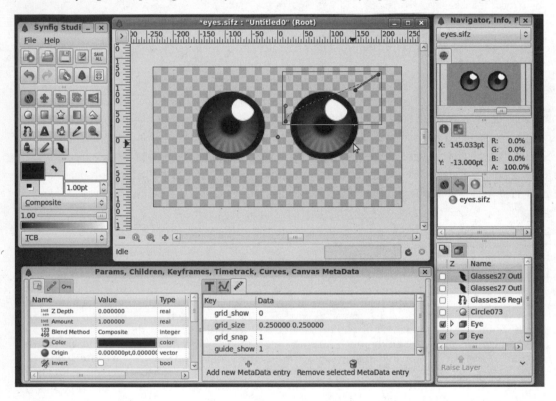

Figure 5-10. Synfig Studio is a Free Software application designed specifically to help smaller teams produce top-quality animation.

You can obtain versions of Synfig Studio for Windows and the Mac from the project's home page at `www.synfig.org`. There, you can also find many helpful tutorials, including video tutorials.

Broken Ubuntu Packages in Jaunty

Synfig has matured rapidly and is now relatively stable, but the original package of Synfig Studio released with Ubuntu Jaunty (9.04) was completely busted and reliably crashes on startup. As a workaround, you can download the following `.deb` packages from Debian GNU/Linux, Ubuntu's parent distribution (see Figure 5-11):

- `http://packages.debian.org/sid/libsynfig0` and `http://packages.debian.org/sid/libsynfigapp0`: The system library packages that Synfig Studio requires

- `http://packages.debian.org/sid/synfigstudio`: The application package

- `http://packages.debian.org/sid/synfig-examples`: The optional, but recommended, examples package

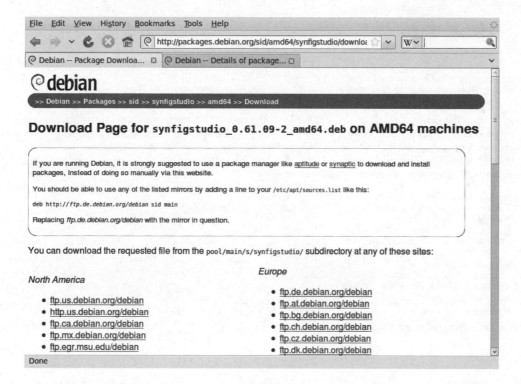

Figure 5-11. *Fixed Synfig Studio packages that run on Ubuntu Jaunty are available from the Debian project and can be installed manually.*

You need to download the correct binaries for your computer's architecture. This is most likely i386 for all Intel and AMD PCs, or amd64 for newer 64-bit CPUs made by AMD and Intel, such as the Athlon 64 or Intel Core 2 Duo. Whichever you choose, it must match the architecture of the version of Ubuntu you installed. Open these links to `packages.debian.org` in your web browser, and scroll to the bottom of the page, where there is a table of processor architectures. Follow the link for your architecture to a page of specific links for the package, mirrored in dozens of locations around the world.

Choose a mirror server close to you, and the package begins downloading. On Ubuntu, the Firefox browser recognizes the package .deb extension and prompts you to open the packages in gdebi, a simple helper application that installs the packages for you (see Figure 5-12).

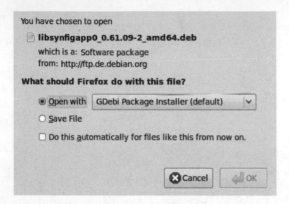

Figure 5-12. Firefox prompts you to open .deb packages with gdebi by default.

When gdebi is up and running, click the Install Package button in the upper-right corner to proceed. Repeat the process for the other Synfig packages you download. For those packages with additional dependencies that can be satisfied by the official Ubuntu repositories, gdebi takes care of the downloading and installation automatically (see Figure 5-13). This saves you a lot of boring searches and manual installations of standard packages.

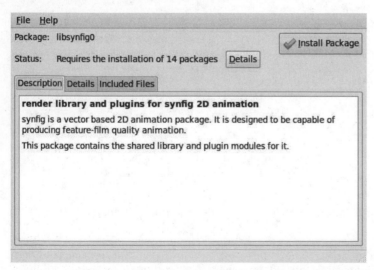

Figure 5-13. Gdebi downloads any additional packages required if they're available in the official Ubuntu repository.

Run on Ubuntu Jaunty, gdebi tells you that older versions of the Synfig packages are available from the official repository and that the official packages are recommended. In this case, you know that the official packages are broken, so the warning isn't very useful. Why would you be trying to update the package manually unless there was a problem with it, given the ease and convenience of using Synaptic? Gdebi also warns that installing packages manually from repositories other than Ubuntu's can be a security risk, and asks you for your password. However, because you're downloading packages from Debian or its mirrors, which is the same place Ubuntu gets them from, you have to consider that warning in context (see Figure 5-14).

Figure 5-14. *In this case, you can ignore warnings about package versions in official repositories.*

The exact version numbers of the packages, or the architecture suffix of `amd64.deb`, may be different on your machine. The important thing is that the library and application version numbers are the same; otherwise, the system complains. When gdebi has completed the installation of all relevant Synfig packages, you can start Synfig Studio using its entry on GNOME's Applications ➤ Graphics menu (see Figure 5-15).

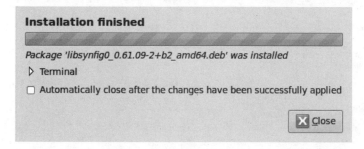

Figure 5-15. *When gdebi has done its work, your bug workaround is complete and Synfig Studio is ready for use.*

Getting Started with Tweening

It's best to start your experimentation with Synfig Studio by creating a simple background and an object to be the actor—this can be as basic as a bouncing ball, for the purposes of learning the ropes. You achieve animation with this program by creating key frames along a timeline, which are similar to the cartoon frames in your storyboard. The application fills in all the intervening positions automatically, using the process of tweening that you read about earlier in this chapter.

When you start Synfig Studio for the first time, several windows are visible, including a toolbox window and a blank canvas window with the title Synfig Animation 1. Because this application's interface is made up of many floating windows, you may prefer to close some of them before you start drawing, particularly if you have a small display on your computer. You can probably do without the Navigator and Params docked panels for now; if you want to, close them the usual way, by clicking the X icon in the upper-right corner.

In the upper-left corner of the blank canvas window, where the horizontal and vertical rulers meet, there is a small square button with a right-facing chevron. Clicking this button opens a pop-up menu that has many more options than the File and Help menus offered by the main Synfig Studio toolbox. The first item on the pop-up menu that you should look at is Edit ➤ Properties. This option opens a dialog in which you set the name and a short description of the animation project, under the heading Canvas Info (see Figure 5-16). Lower down, on the Image tab, you can set the animation size and resolution; the default resolution is again 72 pixels per inch. If you click the Time tab in this dialog, you can set the number of frames per second for your animation. Just as in KToon, the default is 24 frames per second—the traditional frame rate of movie film. You can also set the start and end times for your project, with a single-letter suffix either specifying the number of frames (where 0f is the beginning) or a number of seconds (such as 5s). Five seconds of animation is plenty for you to get started with, because it represents 120 frames at a rate of 24 frames per second.

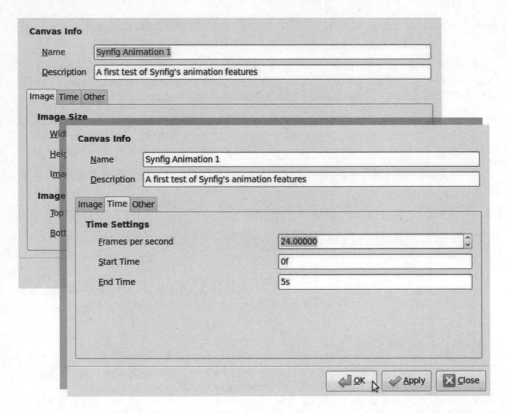

Figure 5-16. *Set the name of your project, its size, resolution, frame rate, and length in the Properties dialog.*

The Synfig Studio Toolbox has two groups of icon buttons. The upper group contains file operations; the Undo and Redo buttons; and the button for Help, which is a browser link to the documentation pages on the `www.synfig.org` web site. The lower group of buttons activate the transformation and drawing tools. In the second row of this lower group are the shape-drawing tools; the first on the left is the Circle tool, which you can use in your bouncing ball example. When you select the tool, which has an icon of a circle with a gray gradient fill and a little shadow underneath, the Tool Options window pops up.

With the Circle tool active, click anywhere in the empty canvas, which has a gray checkerboard pattern like the GIMP's canvas (see Figure 5-17). This tool has a white cross cursor to show the center of where the circle will go. Hold down the mouse button, and drag out the circle to a suitable size. The radius of the circle in pixels is displayed as you do this, as a guide. When you release the mouse button, the circle is filled with the current active foreground color (black, by default).

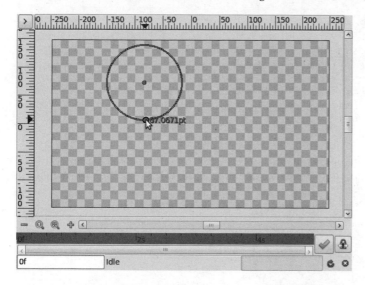

Figure 5-17. The Circle tool is one of several preformatted shape tools.

If you switch now to the tool directly above Circle in the Toolbox, which has an icon of a black arrowhead on a blue circle, the circle you just drew is surrounded by a square box and has a green dot in the center and a blue dot on the edge. This is the not-very-helpfully named Normal tool. Clicking and dragging the green dot moves the circle, and the same operation on the blue dot changes the size of the circle.

Creating the Animation

In order to create movement, you have to first put Synfig into Animate Editing mode by clicking the green check-mark icon in the lower-right corner of the canvas window. The green check then turns into a red light icon (see Figure 5-18); when you mouse over this red light, an In Animate Editing Mode tooltip appears. Also, the canvas is outlined with a thin red line.

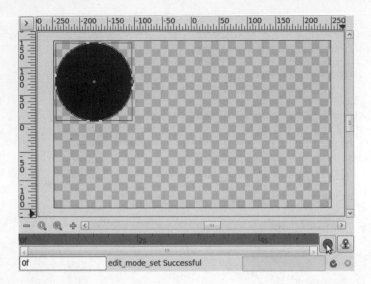

Figure 5-18. *The green check mark in the lower-right corner turns into a red light when Animate Editing mode is activated.*

Click in the gray timeline at the bottom of the main window; the timeline cursor moves, and the current time point is displayed in seconds and frames in a small box in the lower-left corner (see Figure 5-19).

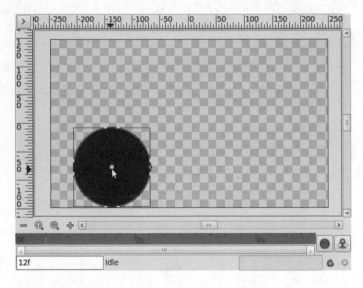

Figure 5-19. *The circle has been moved to the bottom edge of the canvas at 12 frames—half a second—into the animation.*

Now, use the Normal tool to move the circle object to the place you want it to be at that point in time. If you then click in between those timeline points, your object moves to a space between the start position and the place where you just moved the circle (see Figure 5-20).

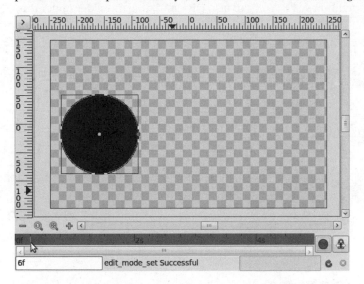

Figure 5-20. Without needing any manual intervention, Synfig Studio tweens the animation. At six frames into the action, the bouncing ball is drawn at a point midway between the top and bottom of the canvas.

When you're happy with the way your timeline is shaping up, click the chevron button in the upper-left corner of the canvas window, and select File ➤ Preview. This action opens a dialog in which you can select the zoom factor and frame rate of animation playback. The reason for this is that shrinking the preview or dropping the frame rate means the animation can be rendered more quickly (see Figure 5-21). This may be an advantage when the drawing gets complex and the number of frames starts to mount up. You can also specify one part of the animation to preview, using frame or second values in the Begin Time and End Time fields of this dialog.

General Settings

Zoom	0.50
Frames per second	12.0

Time Settings

☐ Begin Time	0f
☐ End Time	5s

[✖ Cancel] [Preview]

Figure 5-21. Set preview options to decrease render time. You can render at full quality later.

Click the Preview button in the lower-right corner, and the Preview window appears (see Figure 5-22). Because your animation isn't complicated and lasts only 120 frames, you shouldn't have to wait more than a few seconds for it to be rendered. Next, click the orange right-pointing arrow button at lower left in the Preview window; your animation starts. You can also click and drag the slider under the preview area to inspect a specific part of the action.

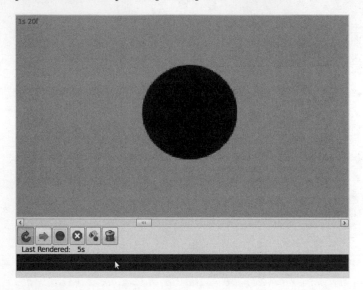

Figure 5-22. In the Preview window, the bouncing ball can be seen in real-time motion.

Layers and Colors

Like the GIMP and Inkscape, Synfig Studio works with layers; but in this program, each object gets its own layer. This can result in a lot of layers being created! Each layer has a set of parameters that define how it behaves, including distorting or modifying the layer below it. To create a background to sit behind your bouncing ball, you need to first choose the color and then create a new layer. In the Synfig Studio toolbox menus, select File ➤ Panels ➤ Layers. A small window pops up, which you may need to resize to see properly—particularly the Cut, Copy, and Paste buttons on the right. (You can do this by mousing over the lower-right corner of the window and then clicking and dragging out the corner using the diagonal arrow cursor.)

To fill the background of the animation, click the background square of the Color Picker in the Synfig Studio Toolbox (it's a white rectangle by default, just to the right of and below the black foreground Color Picker). This Colors dialog is simpler than the equivalent windows in the GIMP or Inkscape—you only get to choose colors by their RGB or YUV values (see Figure 5-23). You can also set the alpha channel (which corresponds to the degree of transparency). Now, use the double-headed arrow icon next to the Color Picker rectangles to flip the background color you selected to the foreground. This action keeps the previous foreground color ready to be flipped back again, so you have two colors saved at all times.

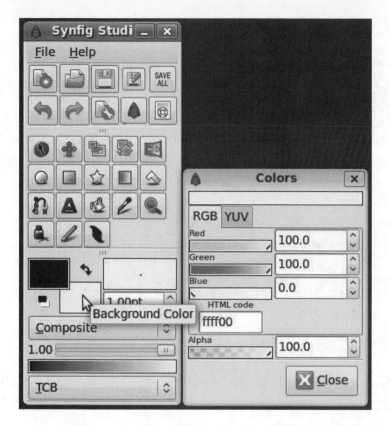

Figure 5-23. *The Colors window allows you to set RGB, YUV, and alpha values.*

The only layer listed in the Layers window is called something like Circle001. Right-click this layer name, and select New Layer from the pop-up menu that appears. Try New Layer ➤ Geometry ➤ Solid Color to start with; this option creates a layer that fills the whole canvas with the current foreground color. Lots of ready-made effects are available on the New Layer menu, from distortions and blurs to fractals.

Two layers are now listed in the Layers window (see Figure 5-24). You can toggle the visibility of each layer using the check box at far left. Either layer should become highlighted in pale orange if you click to select it, after which you can use the buttons along the bottom of the window to manipulate the layer in question. If your background ends up in front of your bouncing ball, use the Raise Layer or Lower Layer button in the Layers window to get things in order.

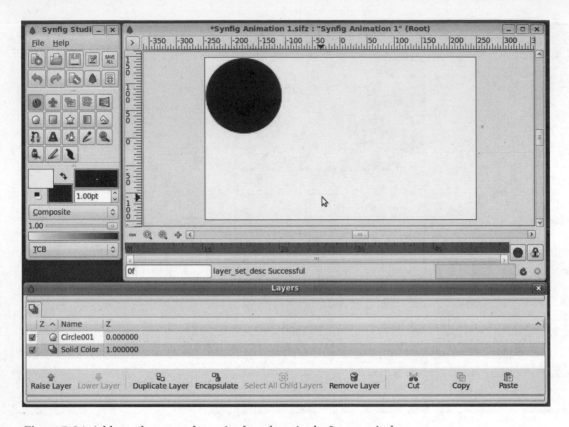

Figure 5-24. *Add new layers and manipulate them in the Layers window.*

You can use the Duplicate Layer button in the Layers window to save redrawing every similar layer. Use the Fill Tool from the Toolbox (with a paint-bucket icon) to fill the circle on the duplicated layer with the background color. Then, switch to the Normal tool, and drag the circle's size using the colored dot to make it slightly smaller. If you run the preview again, you see the outline of a circle moving across the screen.

You can draw and edit Bezier curves in Synfig Studio (see Figure 5-25); these are called BLines, and the tool has an icon like an ink pen nib drawing a curve.

Figure 5-25. *With the help of the Star Tool and BLine tool, your bouncing ball is now a bouncing smiley face.*

The BLine tool isn't yet as sophisticated as the Bezier tools found in Inkscape. Even so, with time and effort, it's possible to build up much more complex animated sequences and add sound files and visual effects to convey your message more dramatically.

Rendering and Exporting

When you're happy with the preview of your animation, you can render and export it in various formats by choosing File ➤ Render on the chevron menu (in the upper-left corner of the canvas window); see Figure 5-26. A series of PNG stills is compatible with other graphics programs, although it isn't much use for watching the animation directly. Alternatively, you can export to `.gif` for a webpage or `.dv` if you're working with material from a video camera, as discussed in a later chapter. DV format is certainly good quality, but the files are comparatively large.

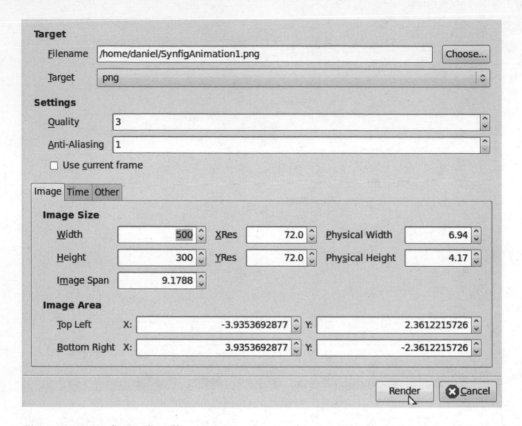

Figure 5-26. Synfig Studio offers a variety of export formats. The format you choose depends on the intended use for the animation.

Other Useful Programs

Although most Free Software animation tools are still new and raw, as you have seen in this chapter, several other interesting applications are being developed:

- *Stopmotion* (GNU/Linux): An animation tool you can use to make movies from a sequence of still images. http://stopmotion.bjoernen.com.

- *Pencil* (GNU/Linux, Windows, Mac): A program designed to help artists draw traditional 2D animation. www.pencil-animation.org.

- *Animata* (Windows, Mac): Real-time animation software, designed to create interactive background projections for concerts and theater performances. http://animata.kibu.hu.

## CHAPTER 6

3D Modeling

The Three Ages of Blender

Blender (GNU/Linux, Windows, Mac) is a Free Software 3D graphics program with animation, video compositing, and game creation features. This program is also available on two UNIX platforms: SGI Irix, which was popular for high-end graphics work before the GNU/Linux desktop came along, and Sun Solaris. On Ubuntu, you can install Blender using the Add/Remove Applications tool. Other GNU/Linux distributions are likely to include ready-made Blender packages, and you can download versions for Windows or the Mac direct from www.blender.org.

Originally developed as the in-house 3D tool of NeoGeo, a Dutch computer graphics studio, Blender was released as a proprietary product in the late 90s by the company Not a Number. In 2002, following the closure of Not a Number, the nonprofit Blender Foundation was created to raise funds from the program's user community, acquire the Blender source code, and release it under the GNU GPL. This program has therefore represented, at different times, all three of the main types of software you read about in Chapter 1—software as the means to an end, software as a retail product, and Free Software.

Showing its roots as an in-house tool for 3D graphics professionals, rather than a program aimed at beginners, Blender can hardly be considered user-friendly—that is, if user-friendliness is based on a shallow learning curve and a familiar look and feel. Instead, Blender was designed for fast workflow, with the assumption that users have one hand on the keyboard and one hand on the mouse at all times. The graphical interface is unique to Blender: it has no floating windows and is often initially incomprehensible, even to experienced graphic artists.

However, perseverance with Blender is well rewarded; it's a very powerful tool that can be used to create top-quality 3D animated movies and games. For once, this isn't merely an idle boast from the marketing department, as the Blender Foundation has proven by producing two animated shorts and a game using its own software (see Figure 6-1 and Figure 6-2).

Figure 6-1. Elephants Dream *was the first movie created by the Blender Foundation and one of the first high-definition animated movies made in Europe.*

A third short movie with a Japanese anime look and theme, under the codename Project Durian, is currently in production. The Foundation calls these movies and games *open projects*, as in the term *open source*. This openness isn't limited to downloading the final, finished versions and sharing them with your friends, although that right is granted. More significantly, all Blender project files and other source materials for the animations *Elephants Dream* (2005) and *Big Buck Bunny* (2007) and the game *Yo Frankie!* (2008) are available for download or on DVD. You can find out how these projects were made or make your own, alternative versions of them. That just doesn't happen with conventional movie studios and game-development houses, because too many trade secrets are involved in the production pipeline.

Figure 6-2. Big Buck Bunny *was the second open movie produced by the Blender Foundation. One of the characters from this animated short later starred in his own game,* Yo Frankie!

Starting Blender

If you look at Ubuntu's Applications ➤ Graphics menu after installing Blender, you notice that there are two different ways of starting the program: fullscreen and windowed. Fullscreen mode does give you slightly more space to work in, but you can't see GNOME's panel along the bottom edge of your display. Because of Blender's unique interface (see Figure 6-3), which is based on the OpenGL standard for 3D graphics, the integration of either mode with Ubuntu's GNOME desktop is less than perfect. You may also notice display quirks caused by bugs in the 3D video support on your system, which Blender makes heavy use of—like an application background window that doesn't go away when you close Blender, in the case of my laptop.

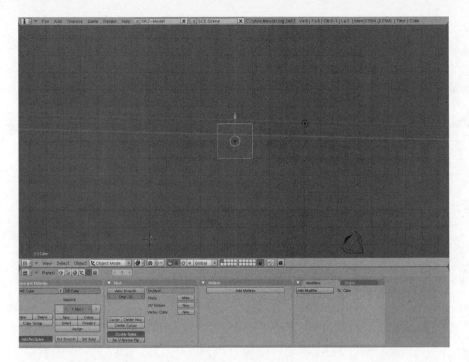

Figure 6-3. The Blender interface offers few clues to the uninitiated but contains many powerful tools.

Sometimes, you can improve the situation by choosing System ➤ Preferences ➤ Appearance on the main GNOME menu, selecting the Visual Effects tab in the preferences window that appears, and selecting None. Doing so disables the Compiz window manager that provides visual effects on the Ubuntu desktop, such as transparent windows. Very few, if any, of the visual effects that Compiz provides are genuinely useful on a creative workstation, so you can safely leave them disabled.

The Blender interface has a menu bar across the top of the main window and a darker gray workspace that takes up most of the display. Another menu bar appears just beneath this workspace, and below that a row of control panels is arranged along the lower edge of the display.

In the center of the workspace is a white circle with a green vertical arrow and a red horizontal arrow, which is Blender's 3D Transform Manipulator tool. To begin with, it sits on top of a gray square with a hot pink outline. This square is the default object created in any new Blender project, which you can use as the basis of your 3D model if you wish. The square is also useful, at this early stage, as a test object for learning to use Blender's unique selection and manipulation tools. In the lower-left corner of the workspace, a small graphic labels the red arrow as the X axis and the green arrow as the Y axis. In addition, there's a crosshair 3D cursor—four black lines at right angles, crossing the perimeter of a red and white circle—that operates independently of the 3D Transform Manipulator tool. There is also a regular mouse pointer that you use for placing cursors, selecting objects, and choosing menu items.

At lower right is the outline of a kind of diamond-shaped box. This box is the camera, which represents the viewpoint from which your 3D model is seen (see Figure 6-4). Just to the right of the square object are two concentric circles, dashed and solid, with a black dot in the middle. This marker represents the position of the lighting source in the 3D scene. As when you're taking photos or shooting a movie with a camera in the real world, you must consider the direction that Blender's artificial light comes from. The lighting marker sits on the end of a gray stick to show that its height is adjustable.

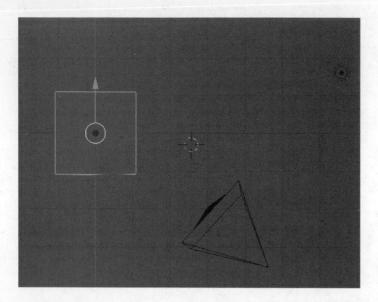

Figure 6-4. *The working area of the Blender interface features a camera, by default on at lower-right, which indicates the angle from which your 3D object is viewed. Above the camera and to the side of it, two circles and a black dot represent the lighting source.*

Changing Views

Blender's default view looks decidedly 2D. The default square object is a cube, but it doesn't yet appear to be one on the screen. This is because although you're working in a 3D space, the default view in Blender is from directly above the canvas. (Unlike the GIMP or Inkscape, Blender doesn't use a paint and brush metaphor, so it calls the canvas a *plane* instead.) On the left side of the menu bar directly beneath the Blender workspace is a View menu. Click this menu with your mouse, and select Camera. The keyboard shortcut for this action is the zero key on the numerical keypad, over on the right side of most desktop keyboards. On a laptop, you may have to hold down a function key to access the numerical keypad.

The workspace now switches to the kind of view you may have expected in a 3D graphics program (see Figure 6-5). A plane made up of gray squares stretches into the distance, like a tiled floor. Instead of a gray square in the center of the workspace, you now have a cube with a top and sides in different shades of gray. One side of the cube is shown as the darkest gray, but that doesn't necessarily mean it's in the shadow of the light source—you look at lighting effects later in this chapter. The red and green arrows are supplemented by a third, blue arrow, pointing upward. At lower left in the main window, you can see the blue arrow labeled as the Z axis (the third dimension).

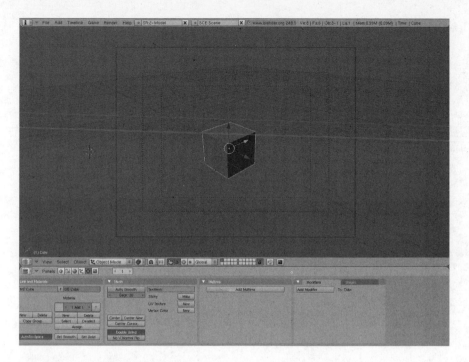

Figure 6-5. *Switch the view to Camera mode, and the object in the Blender workspace begins to look 3D.*

Changing the Selection

Looking at the default cube object in Camera view, you see a pink outline around the edges furthest away from you. This shows that the object is already selected. To the right of the View menu on Blender's lower toolbar, click the Select menu and choose Select/Deselect All; the pink outline around the cube disappears.

Blender offers a number of different methods for selecting objects in the 3D scene—try Select ➤ Select All by Type ➤ Mesh. Because you have only one mesh object at the moment, which is the default cube, only one object is selected with this command. By contrast, if you use the Select ➤ Select/Deselect All toggle again, and switch back to Top view on the View menu, both the camera and light source are selected (outlined in pink) as well as the cube (see Figure 6-6). This global selection means that any transformation tools used on the cube affect the position of the camera and light source, too.

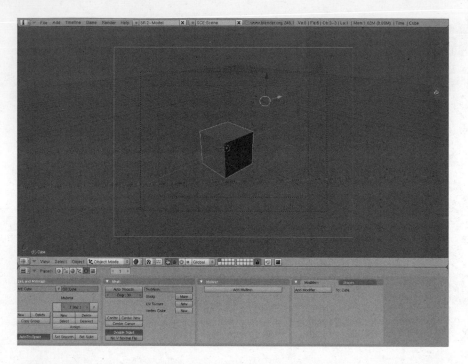

Figure 6-6. *The pink outer rectangle indicates that the camera and the object are selected. Note that the colored arrows have moved, too.*

In the Camera view, the selection of the camera is indicated by a pink outline around the largest rectangle in the window (because you can't see the camera itself in this view). Selecting multiple objects moves the colored arrows of the 3D Transform Manipulator tool away from the center of the cube.

However, the crosshair cursor stays in the center of the cube, demonstrating that it's moved independently from the 3D Transform Manipulator. The crosshair 3D cursor indicates where new objects that you create will be placed. To relocate it, click anywhere on the plane.

Right-clicking an individual object in Blender is supposed to select it, although this doesn't work on my laptop—probably due to buggy 3D driver support in Ubuntu for the ATI graphics chip inside. (Right-click selection does work on my desktop machine, which has a Matrox graphics card. If you're serious about working on a 3D project with Blender, you may need to invest in better hardware—or, at the very least, a graphics card with decent 3D performance.) Instead, I use Blender's Lasso Select tool by holding down the Ctrl key, clicking and holding down the left mouse button, and drawing a shape around the object I want to select. The shape of the lasso is drawn on the screen as a thin gray line, which can be hard to see against the gray default plane (see Figure 6-7).

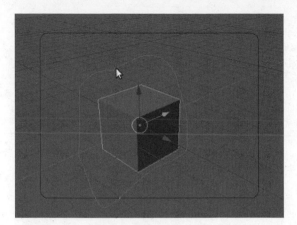

Figure 6-7. The Lasso Select tool is more reliable, on some laptops at least, than right-click object selections.

Moving, Rotating, and Scaling objects

With only the cube selected, click the red, green, or blue arrowhead of the 3D Transform Manipulator to drag the object in that direction and back again (see Figure 6-8). It's as if the object slides on a rail, and Blender provides thin red and green guidelines on the plane to help you remember which axis is which. Notice how the cube looks larger as it gets closer to the camera on the plane and smaller as it gets further away; that's 3D perspective. If this isn't working for you, then again it may be due to incomplete 3D driver support for your graphics hardware.

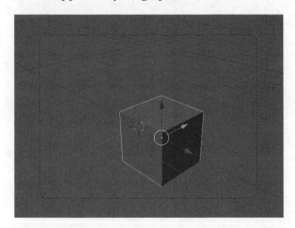

Figure 6-8. Click the arrowheads to move the object along one axis at a time. In this example, the cube is being dragged along the X axis, shown as a thin red line on the plane.

In the middle of the toolbar at the bottom of the main Blender window are four icons: a hand, a red triangle, a light green donut, and a small blue square. The hand icon toggles on or off the 3D Transform

Manipulator tool, and the other three buttons select its mode. By default, the red triangle button is active, which corresponds to Translate mode—the tool with the red, green, and blue arrowheads you've just been reading about. Click the green donut icon instead, and the colored arrows change into rings around the cube object, but in the same colors (see Figure 6-9). This is the rotation tool; you can flip the cube in the direction of any axis by clicking one of the rings, holding down the button, and making a circular motion with your mouse.

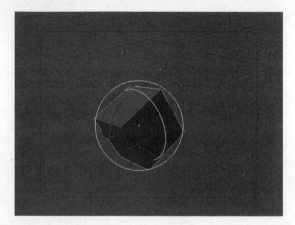

Figure 6-9. The Rotate mode of the 3D Transform Manipulator tool can flip your object in any direction.

Last of the three 3D Transform Manipulator modes is Scale, which has the small blue square icon. Click this icon, and you see that the tool in Scale mode looks similar to Translate, except that instead of arrowheads, you have a circular blob on the end of each colored line (see Figure 6-10). It works similarly to Translate; but instead of the whole object moving on the plane, only one face of the object moves. This way, Scale mode turns your default cube into brick-like shapes with rectangular sides.

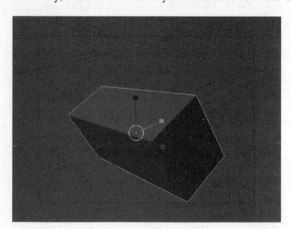

Figure 6-10. The 3D Transform Manipulator's Scale mode distorts the selected object along each of the three axes.

Free Object Manipulation

For free movement, click the object, hold down the button, and drag the cursor a little way to release the object from its current position (see Figure 6-11). (This takes a little practice to get right without making Blender's pop-up menu appear. A thin line is drawn on the object as you perform this action, but it's only temporary and doesn't appear on the 3D model.) Alternatively, press the keyboard shortcut G to grab the object. You can then position it up and down, or left and right in front of the camera—but notice that its size doesn't change with perspective. To use this method to move an object further away from or nearer to the camera, switch to Top view first.

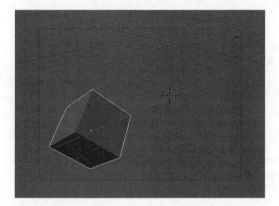

Figure 6-11. Free movement is possible without the 3D Transform Manipulator tool, albeit in two dimensions only.

You can also use this tool for free rotation by making a circular motion with the mouse as you hold down the left button and drag. The keyboard shortcut for rotation is R, as you may have guessed. A dotted line rotation handle appears; drag it toward the object to make large rotations quickly, or extend the handle away from the object to make more subtle adjustments (see Figure 6-12). The center of the rotation is shown by a pink blob on the end of the dotted handle.

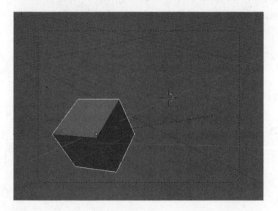

Figure 6-12. Free rotation is accomplished by dragging out the rotation handle to the length you require.

There is also a Free Scaling tool (keyboard shortcut S). It has a handle similar to that of the Free Rotation tool.

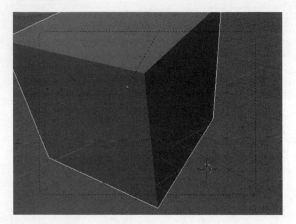

Figure 6-13. *The Free Scaling tool, like the Free Rotation tool, has a drag handle.*

Unlike the 3D Transform Manipulator, the Free Scaling tool changes the size of all faces of the object at once. You can use the Free Movement tool and its keyboard shortcuts alongside the 3D Transform Manipulator tool; but they also work when the hand icon in the lower toolbar is toggled off, disabling the 3D Transform Manipulator.

Panning and Zooming

To move your viewpoint around Blender's 3D workspace, hold down the middle mouse button and move the mouse to the left and right or up and down. Doing so pans or rotates your viewpoint around the center of the model (see Figure 6-14). You can even move your viewpoint under the tiled floor plane, if you wish. In a similar fashion, you can zoom in and out of the workspace by rolling the mouse scroll wheel forward and backward. Holding down the Shift key while you move the scroll wheel moves the viewpoint up and down in the vertical plane. On some mice, the scroll wheel is also the middle button, so you may have to switch quickly between holding the wheel down and rolling it with your middle finger.

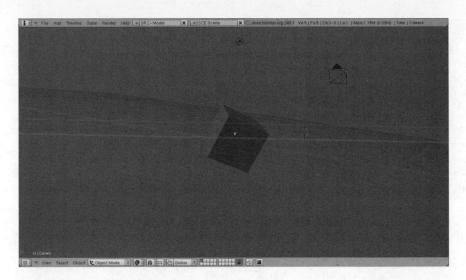

Figure 6-14. Use the middle mouse button and scroll wheel to pan and zoom around Blender's 3D workspace.

It's easy to become disorientated in a 3D space, particularly if you're new to modeling with Blender. If you do get lost, zoom out until you can see the whole plane, click to place the crosshair 3D cursor where you want to go, and use the keyboard shortcut C to center the viewpoint.

If you don't have a middle mouse button, don't worry! Mac mice have traditionally been single-buttoned, most laptops have only one or two mouse buttons, and mice on traditional UNIX workstations and GNU/Linux machines usually have three buttons. Sometimes you can emulate the middle button on a two-button mouse by holding down both buttons at once, and certain laptop track pads have a scroll wheel area to one side. If you intend to use Blender on a regular basis, then a new mouse with a middle button or scroll wheel is an inexpensive upgrade.

Creating Mesh Objects

You can access Blender's pop-up menu by clicking and holding down either the left or right mouse button in the workspace, as you would in other graphics applications. (A short left or right click isn't sufficient; you need to hold the button down for a second or two.) However, because Blender has been designed with a two-handed interface, you can also access the pop-up menu by pressing the spacebar on your keyboard (see Figure 6-15).

When the pop-up menu is visible, you can navigate it with either the mouse or the cursor arrow keys on your keyboard. For example, click somewhere on the plane to set the crosshair cursor, and then try selecting Add ➤ Mesh ➤ Cylinder from the pop-up menu. Because these aren't real, solid building blocks you're playing with, Blender doesn't care if you place new objects on top of or inside other objects.

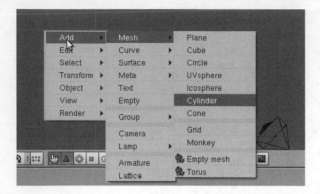

Figure 6-15. You can access Blender's pop-up menu via the spacebar or by the mouse click that other graphics applications use for this function.

A small dialog box pops up, asking about the dimensions you require for the object being created (see Figure 6-16). In addition to radius and depth, this dialog has a setting for the number of vertices; these are the corner points of the object. Vertices are similar in some respects to the corner node points in a 2D vector application, like Inkscape or Synfig, which you read about earlier in this book. The number of vertices you set determines how smooth the curves of an object are; the default for a cylinder is 32 vertices, but you can change this and the other values using the small gray triangles on either side of the bars in this dialog. Click OK in this dialog box or press the Enter key to create the cylinder.

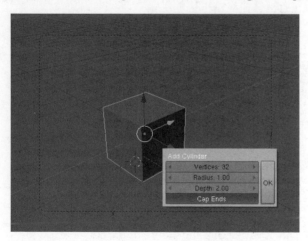

Figure 6-16. Use the Add Cylinder dialog to set the size of the 3D object and the number of vertices it will have.

The new cylinder object you just created should be visible somewhere near the cube. If it isn't in the right place, use the 3D Transform Manipulator or free movement tools to put the cylinder where it should be. As a newly created object, the cylinder is automatically selected, so it has the pink outline already (see Figure 6-17).

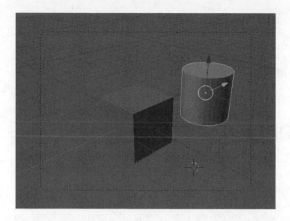

Figure 6-17. *Next to the cube, the pink selection outline of the cylinder you just created is visible.*

Saving Your Work

Before things get more complicated, this is a good time to save your project. From the File menu in the upper-left corner of the Blender interface, select Save. Because the project file is currently untitled, the Save As dialog opens. In Blender on Ubuntu, even this simple window looks complicated (see Figure 6-18). This is because by default, all the hidden system files (those with a name that begins with a period or dot) in your home directory are on display.

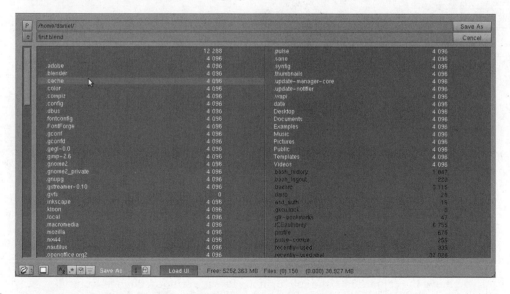

Figure 6-18. *Blender's Save As dialog looks more complicated than it is.*

The second field from the top of the Save As window contains the project file name, which has the suffix .blend for Blender's native file format. Click in this field, and a red cursor appears, after which you can delete untitled.blend and type in a file name of your choice. (If you're a famous conceptual artist, you can get away with calling all your projects untitled. It does make the files harder to find on your hard drive, though!) Unusually, the keyboard shortcut Blender offers for save is Ctrl+W, but the customary Ctrl+S works just as well.

Adding Color and Texture to an Object

So far, your cylinder is drab gray and doesn't look like a model of anything real. Adding colors and textures to your objects can help a lot. In the Panels section of the Blender window, at the bottom of the display, are a number of tools for manipulating the properties of objects in your 3D scene. You can rearrange these panels by dragging and dropping them left and right, or minimize them by clicking the small white triangle to the left of the panel's name. Because Blender has been designed to run on high-resolution displays, the ability to minimize panels that you aren't currently using is very handy on a smaller screen. Panels can be dropped into each other, to create space-saving tabs, and tabs can be dragged out into separate panels.

At upper left in the Panels area of the Blender interface is a row of small icon buttons. The third button from the left has the icon of a small gray sphere and provides access to shading options. With the cylinder object selected, click this button or use its keyboard shortcut (F5). Doing so brings up a Links and Pipeline panel, which has a Link to Object drop-down menu that shows the option Add New (see Figure 6-19). Click Add New, and select Material (the selection may happen automatically as you click).

Figure 6-19. *Clicking the gray sphere icon button causes the Links and Pipeline panel to appear. Click Add New to create a material for your cylinder object.*

When the new material has been linked to the cylinder object, the lower part of Blender's interface changes again to show a panel titled Preview. This panel has two tabs—Material and Ramps—and several other tabbed panels. In the Material tab are horizontal sliders for Red, Green, Blue, and Alpha values, which may be familiar from the chapter on the GIMP (see Figure 6-20). (To recap, the RGB sliders allow you to mix colors, and the Alpha slider sets the transparency value.) There is also a small button that lets you switch the Material tab into HSV (hue, saturation, value) mode, if you prefer to specify colors that way. As you move the color sliders, the sphere in the Preview window changes color automatically. Any object in the Blender workspace that you've selected, such as the cylinder object you made, changes to the same color simultaneously.

Figure 6-20. *The Material tab (or separate panel, as shown here) contains sliders for setting object color according to either RGB or HSV values. Note that the Texture panel, labeled with a T, has been minimized and dragged to the left for now.*

To add a texture to an object, move your mouse to the Texture panel (or tab), which is at far right by default, and click the Add New button. Above the panels, a second group of buttons become visible, to the right of the buttons that were there originally. In this second group, the third button from the left has an icon that looks a little like leopard-print fabric. This is the Texture button (keyboard shortcut F6). When you click this button or press its shortcut, the panels change to show a different Preview window, which is black to start with—your colored sphere disappears. That's because this preview is just for the texture that's being selected, rather than the original material.

On the Texture panel or tab is a Texture Type drop-down menu, from which you can select a variety of ready-made texture patterns including Wood, Marble, and Clouds. As you perform this selection, another panel opens to display the properties of the texture you choose (see Figure 6-21).

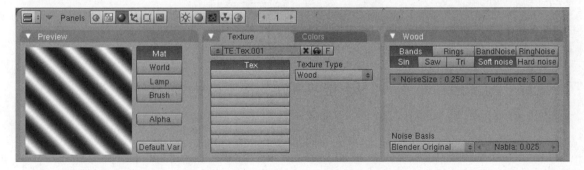

Figure 6-21. *Blender includes a number of ready-made patterns and textures that can be used on your 3D model. Here, the Wood texture has been set in the Texture Type drop-down menu.*

Switch back to Material mode by clicking the small red sphere icon to the immediate left of the leopard print Texture button (keyboard shortcut F5). The Preview window updates to show your original material decorated with the texture you selected (see Figure 6-22).

Figure 6-22. *Switch back to Material mode to see how the texture looks when applied to your object.*

If you don't like the second color that Blender sets for the texture, you can change it by clicking the Map To tab that appears when the program is in Material mode. The Map To tab contains horizontal sliders for RGB colors and also lets you set the texture-blending mode—somewhat like the layer modes in the GIMP. The default texture-blending setting is Mix, but other settings available include Lighten, Darken, Difference, and Multiply (see Figure 6-23).

Figure 6-23. *Adjust the RGB sliders and blending mode on the Map To tab to set the color of the texture.*

Don't worry if the cylinder object you selected in the Blender workspace doesn't yet display the same color or texture as in the Preview window. The objects in the workspace aren't yet fully *rendered*, or finalized. (You look at final rendering later in this chapter.) For a sneaky look at how your 3D model will turn out, select View ➤ Render Preview from Blender's lower toolbar. This command opens a small, resizable window that renders just the part of the model you're working on, saving time compared to a full render (see Figure 6-24). The more complicated your model is, the longer a full render takes—but the simple models featured in this chapter won't take more than a couple of seconds to produce.

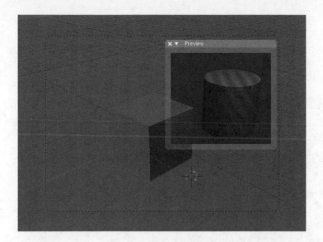

Figure 6-24. *The Render Preview feature gives you a quick look at a detail of the model you're working on.*

Using Edit Mode

Although the cubes and cylinders you've been reading about are useful as starting points for your 3D model, objects in Blender aren't restricted to simple geometric shapes. To make manual tweaks to the vertices of an object, you need to switch from Blender's default Object mode to Edit mode. To do so, use the pop-up menu on Blender's lower toolbar, to the immediate right of the View, Select, and Object menus. Alternatively, press the Tab key to toggle between Object and Edit mode. Deselect the object you created by pressing the A key, and then switch to Edit mode. Your object changes into a series of lines indicating its vertices, with pink dots showing the control points (see Figure 6-25).

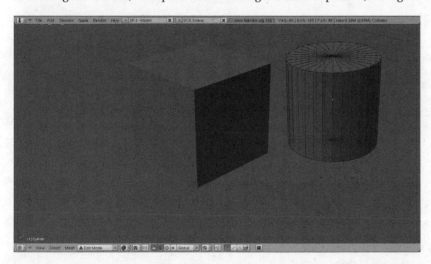

Figure 6-25. *Before individual objects can be modified, you need to switch Blender into Edit mode by pressing the Tab key.*

By selecting individual control points with a right-click of the mouse and modifying their position with the 3D Transform Manipulator or free movement tools, you can deform a regular object into any shape you like (see Figure 6-26). It's also possible to select multiple control points by holding down the Shift key and right-clicking them, or using the Lasso Select tool (hold down the Ctrl key, and draw a circle around the points). The selected control points then move together as one.

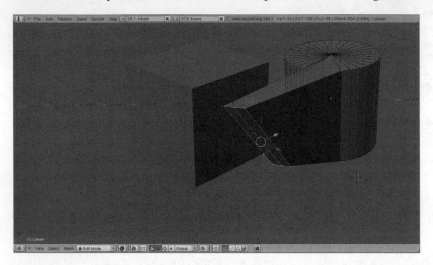

Figure 6-26. You can move multiple control points together if they're selected before the manipulation.

Copying and Grouping Objects

Rather than create and manipulate many similar objects individually, you can use the Object menu on Blender's lower toolbar to perform copying and grouping operations. For example, if you make a 3D model of a drum, you can then create a five-piece drum kit from your original model without needing to make each object from scratch. You can get away with this time-saving shortcut because all drums in a kit are basically similar, apart from their size and orientation. The same principle applies to many other models with repeated elements, such as a bowl of cherries or a crowd of people. First, delete Blender's default gray cube by right-clicking it and pressing the Delete key on your keyboard. A small dialog box asks you to confirm that you want to erase the selected object.

A typical drum has a shell made of wood covered with a plastic wrap, a chromed steel hoop holding down a white plastic skin at both ends, and bolts holding the whole thing together. The shell can be made from a cylinder object; but make sure the Cap Ends option isn't selected in the Add Cylinder pop-up dialog, because you want your wooden drum shell to be hollow, like the real thing. As for size, the default cylinder radius of 1.00 and depth of 2.00 will do fine. You can make the plastic skin by choosing Add ➤ Mesh ➤ Circle from Blender's spacebar pop-up menu. The default circle radius of 1.0 matches the size of the cylinder you created; make sure the Fill button is selected, or the circle will be just an outline. You also need to adjust the values in the Materials panel to give the drum skin a different color from the cylindrical, wooden shell. You may find that you need to switch from Camera to Top view and back again, or use pan and zoom, to place the skin correctly on the top of the shell; it's easy to get confused about the Z axis and end up with a circle that floats above the cylinder (see Figure 6-27).

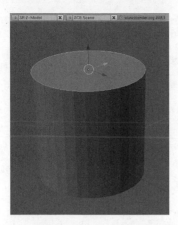

Figure 6-27. Create a circle object, and move it so that it sits on top of the cylinder.

With the drum skin selected, choose Object ➤ Duplicate from Blender's lower toolbar. The duplicated skin is already selected; drag it downward on the Z axis (the opposite direction from the blue arrowhead) until it sits below the drum. Then, hold down the middle mouse button, and drag the mouse around to flip your view to the underside of the drum. You can then position the lower drum skin so that it sits neatly on the shell.

After that, create the metal drum hoops by making another open-ended cylinder, but slightly larger in diameter and much thinner. A diameter of 1.02 and depth of 0.1 are about right. In real life, the drum hoop must be seated on the outside of the shell and raised slightly above the skin; to make your model as realistic as possible, you have to do the same. When you're happy with the look of the hoop, duplicate it, and move it along the Z axis until it's roughly in position. Then, flip the view, and finalize the position of the hoop copy over the lower drum skin (see Figure 6-28).

Figure 6-28. With duplicated skins and hoops, your drum model is starting to take shape.

Next, you need to model the bolts that hold the metal hoop onto the wooden shell, tensioning the drum skin. If you aren't sure what these look like, refer to a close-up picture of a drum kit on the

Internet. Depending on the size and quality of the drum, anywhere from 4 to 12 bolts hold down the hoop on each side. Bass or kick drums have the most bolts, because they're the largest drums in the kit. For the sake of simplicity, this example uses six bolts, properly known as *tension rods*, on each drum. In real life, these bolts pass through holes in the metal hoops; the other end goes into a lug that's fixed to the outside of the drum shell. The first bolt can be modeled using a small cylinder with cap ends, using the same metal material you set for the hoops (see Figure 6-29).

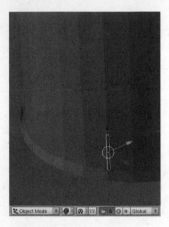

Figure 6-29. A drum tension rod can be modeled using a cylinder with cap ends.

To create the lug for the tension rod to fit into, make a cube by choosing Add ➤ Mesh ➤ Cube. It's large by default, so resize the cube by pressing S (for scale) and dragging the dashed handle toward the center of the object. Right-click the new cube if it isn't already selected, and then switch to Edit mode with the Tab key. You can now manipulate the vertices of the cube until it becomes the shape you want (see Figure 6-30). Real drum lugs are roughly equal size in the X and Y dimensions but taller in the Z dimension. They vary in shape but are usually thinner at one end than the other. Again, refer to a picture on the Internet if you aren't sure what shape to go for.

Figure 6-30. You can make the drum lug from Blender's standard cube object, using Edit mode.

Until you gain experience with Edit mode, you may prefer to manipulate the shape of the lug (see Figure 6-31) in a different part of the Blender workspace than your drum model, so you don't select and move, scale, or rotate the wrong vertices by mistake.

Figure 6-31. *Model the drum lug by selecting and moving or scaling control points to create an irregular shape.*

Next, move the lug into position on the end of the tension rod—you probably have to scale or rotate it until it looks right. Keep checking the front and side views (using the View menu, on the lower toolbar) to make sure the position is correct in all three dimensions. Then, select the lug and the tension rod by holding down the Shift key and right-clicking both objects.

On the Object menu from the lower toolbar, choose Object ➤ Join Objects, and click OK to confirm in the dialog box that pops up. The pink selection outline of the two objects changes to the perimeter of the new compound object (see Figure 6-32). If you use the 3D Transform Manipulator or free movement tools on these joined objects, they move together as one—even if you select only one of the original objects with a right click.

Figure 6-32. *Joining objects that belong together, before duplication, makes it much easier to position the copies.*

Because drum lugs are arranged in opposite pairs at the top and bottom of the drum, you can duplicate your joined lug object by choosing Object ➤ Duplicate on the lower toolbar (keyboard shortcut Shift+D), rotate the copied object, and move it into position next to the hoop at the other end of the drum. When that's done, you can join the upper and lower lugs to make a single object, duplicate this new object five times, and move the copies on the X and Y axes until they're evenly spaced around the outside of the drum shell object (see Figure 6-33). After rotating the copied lug and tension rod objects so that they face the drum shell object, you end up with a drum model with 12 lugs—6 holding down each hoop. All the lugs and tension rods should be identical, because they've been duplicated from the same original model.

Figure 6-33. *After duplication, join the opposite pair of lug and rod models into a single object so that they can be duplicated again.*

Your first drum model is complete, but it isn't much of a drum kit by itself. Use a lasso selection (hold down the Ctrl key, hold down the left mouse button, and drag around in a circle) to select the entire drum. Then, duplicate the drum so that you have two identical drums in your Blender workspace. To make a kick or bass drum, rotate the copy so that it sits on its shell, and scale it up a little. For reference, if your original drum model is a 16-inch diameter floor tom, the kick drum can be 20 inches in diameter for a jazz kit or 22 inches for a rock kit. If you aspire to play on a kit like the late John Bonham of Led Zeppelin, then you need a 24-inch bass drum. Snare drums tend to be 14 inches across the skin but relatively shallow, whereas the toms that sit on top of the kick drum may be 12, 13, or 14 inches in diameter but are deeper than the snare. Experiment with Blender's 3D Transform Manipulator and free scaling tools until the various drums look right (see Figure 6-34).

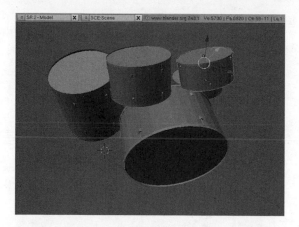

Figure 6-34. Duplicating, rotating, and scaling can make a five-piece drum kit in a fraction of the time it took to make the original drum model.

Real-life drums don't float in mid-air, so to increase realism you can model some legs for the drums to stand on. In the case of the original floor tom model, you can duplicate, scale up, and rotate a lug and tension rod joined object to look like one of three metal legs (see Figure 6-35).

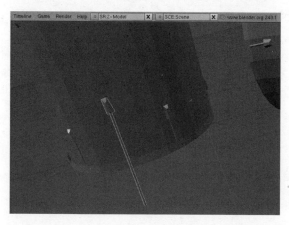

Figure 6-35. Duplicate legs for the floor tom from a lug and tension rod and then scale them up to the right size.

The two smaller toms need some hardware to support them, which in real life is usually attached to the top of the kick drum. One horizontal cylinder object to connect the toms, and a vertical cylinder to support the fitting, are a good start (see Figure 6-36). If you want to make this part of the model more realistic, you can make separate cylinder objects to support each tom.

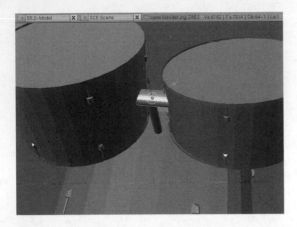

Figure 6-36. The small toms need a bracket to support them, which you can model using cylinder objects as a starting point.

You can quickly make a tripod stand for the snare drum from four cylinder meshes and a sphere object. Of course, you need to make only one of the cylinder objects from scratch, because when you have the right proportions and material, it's easily duplicated and rotated into position (see Figure 6-37).

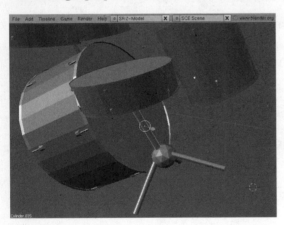

Figure 6-37. A snare stand modeled from four identical cylinders and a sphere mesh

Putting Text on the Model

Blender treats text much like any other shaped object. You can begin adding text to your model by selecting Add ➤ Text from the spacebar menu. The default word *Text* appears somewhere below the grid floor of the 3D scene (see Figure 6-38). To change this word into something more relevant, make sure it's selected, and then switch into Edit mode by pressing the Tab key. A gray cursor appears at the end of the word, which you can move with the Backspace key to delete the default letters. You can then type a new word the usual way, and switch back to Object mode to move, scale, or rotate it into the desired position.

Figure 6-38. Blender's text tool inserts the default word Text, *which you can change in Edit mode.*

In the lower part of the Blender interface is a panel labeled Font; but its drop-down menu isn't populated with names of the fonts installed on the system, on Ubuntu at least. Instead, you have to select a font file from the filesystem and click the Load button. There are also some text effects in this panel, including a button for putting text on a curve.

If you don't see the Font panel when a text object is selected, click the icon button in the lower Panels bar that looks like a small black square with four golden corner nodes (keyboard shortcut F9).

A text object can have a material attached to it, like any other object in Blender. With the text selected, go to the Link and Materials panel, click the New button, and create the material of your choice (see Figure 6-39).

Figure 6-39. When your text object is rotated into position, use the Link and Materials panel to color it.

Adding a Plane and a World

So far, your drum kit model is floating on an empty grid of nothingness. Any drummer will tell you that a piece of carpet underneath the kit helps prevent the kick drum from sliding around the stage while you hammer the foot pedal. For your purposes, a mesh underneath the model will also help create a sense of depth in the final image, adding to its realism. To create a virtual carpet in Blender's 3D scene, activate the spacebar menu, and select Add ➤ Mesh ➤ Plane. The default plane is rather small and doesn't have a material yet. Resize the plane and move it under the kit, and then add a material to it—just as you did before for the drum objects.

Figure 6-40. A plane underneath the model enhances the perspective and realism of the 3D scene.

Blender has a Worlds feature that enables you to create backgrounds quickly and easily. With the Shading icon button in the Panels bar selected (gray sphere, keyboard shortcut F5), on the far right of the second group of icon buttons is a very small blue and gray globe. Click this globe icon button, and a new Preview panel appears with a plain blue square. There are also World and Mist/Stars panels, among others (see Figure 6-41). In the Preview panel, a Blend button creates a gradient-filled background for your model; the Preview square updates as you click this button. In the Mist/Stars panel, clicking the Stars button creates an instant star field in Blender's world. Note that you can't see the currently set world in the main workspace while you're in Object or Edit mode, but it does affect the render preview.

Figure 6-41. Blender lets you rapidly create backgrounds via its World panel.

Using Lighting Effects

If the render preview shows your model to be a little on the dark side, look at the position of Blender's default lamp and camera. Is the lighting source putting the camera side of the model in shadow? Remember, the lamp can be selected and moved like any other object, with the 3D Transform Manipulator or free movement tool. As you move the lamp toward your model, notice how the effect of the lighting becomes brighter.

After you select a lamp, a Lamp panel appears in the lower part of the Blender interface. Next to it is another Preview window, with buttons including Lamp, Spot, and Sun. Needless to say, the Sun button makes for much brighter lighting than either Lamp or Spot. The Spot and Sun lights are directional, as their names suggest, so rotating the lighting object affects how much light falls on any part of the model (see Figure 6-42).

Figure 6-42. *The Spot light object is directional and can be rotated to focus its beam.*

In real life, more than one light source often affects an object, so Blender lets you have as many lamps as you require. On the spacebar menu, select Add ➤ Lamp, and position the new lamp in the 3D scene. Then, you can decide whether to make this lamp directional, how bright it should be, and the color of the light it emits, using the RGB sliders in the Lamp panel.

Final Render and Output

When your model is complete, choose Render ➤ Render Current Frame on Blender's top toolbar above the workspace (keyboard shortcut F12). You may need to adjust the camera object's position to get the framing you want.

To save the rendered image in a format that can be used by other graphics programs, click the far-right button in the first, main group on the left side of the Panels bar. This is the Scene button, which has an icon like a very small gray landscape, although this is hard to see (keyboard shortcut F10). The Format panel that appears includes a number of preset buttons for common video formats, including PAL, NTSC, and HD. For further use in a bitmap graphics program like the GIMP, choose the Full format button; unlike PAL or NTSC, it doesn't scale down the number of pixels in the output file.

Just to the left of these buttons is a drop-down menu for the output file format, which defaults to Targa. Several other obscure formats are listed here; if you don't have a preference, PNG format is a good choice for compatibility. On the top menu, select File ➤ Save Rendered Image (keyboard shortcut F3). A file-save dialog opens; the first field shows the directory path, and you type the file name in the field just below. Pressing Enter doesn't seem to be enough—click the Save PNG button (if that's the format you chose). Finally, check the rendered file in the GIMP or your photo manager of choice to be sure it's rendered correctly (see Figure 6-43).

Figure 6-43. The final render output to PNG, with HD pixel dimensions and aspect ratio. Note the star field background and the lighting effects in the foreground.

Further Reading

Many books about Blender are available, including introductory titles like *Blender for Dummies* by Jason van Gumster (Wiley, 2009, ISBN-10: 0470400188) and *The Essential Blender* by Roland Hess (No Starch Press, 2007, ISBN-10: 1593271662). More detailed coverage is available in specialist titles such as *Bounce, Tumble, and Splash! Simulating the Physical World with Blender 3D* by Tony Mullen (Sybex, 2008, ISBN-10: 0470192801) and *Foundation Blender Compositing* by Roger Wickes (Friends of Ed, 2009, ISBN-10: 1430219769).

Other Useful Programs

Although this chapter has been dedicated to Blender, you can check out other Free Software 3D tools, including the following:

- *K-3D* (GNU/Linux, Windows, Mac): A 3D modeling and animation package that features a procedural engine. `www.k-3d.org`.

- *Aqsis* (GNU/Linux, Windows, Mac): A 3D rendering system compatible with Pixar's RenderMan standard. `www.aqsis.org`.

- *Wings 3D* (GNU/Linux, Windows, Mac): A 3D modeler, rather than an animation package. www.wings3d.com.

- *YafaRay* (GNU/Linux, Windows, Mac): A raytracing rendering system that can be used with Blender. www.yafaray.org.

All of these packages are available in Ubuntu using the Add/Remove Programs application. YafaRay is a rewrite of an earlier program called YafRay, so you may find Ubuntu packages under the old name.

Using Lighting Effects

If the render preview shows your model to be a little on the dark side, look at the position of Blender's default lamp and camera. Is the lighting source putting the camera side of the model in shadow? Remember, the lamp can be selected and moved like any other object, with the 3D Transform Manipulator or free movement tool. As you move the lamp toward your model, notice how the effect of the lighting becomes brighter.

After you select a lamp, a Lamp panel appears in the lower part of the Blender interface. Next to it is another Preview window, with buttons including Lamp, Spot, and Sun. Needless to say, the Sun button makes for much brighter lighting than either Lamp or Spot. The Spot and Sun lights are directional, as their names suggest, so rotating the lighting object affects how much light falls on any part of the model (see Figure 6-42).

Figure 6-42. The Spot light object is directional and can be rotated to focus its beam.

In real life, more than one light source often affects an object, so Blender lets you have as many lamps as you require. On the spacebar menu, select Add ➤ Lamp, and position the new lamp in the 3D scene. Then, you can decide whether to make this lamp directional, how bright it should be, and the color of the light it emits, using the RGB sliders in the Lamp panel.

Final Render and Output

When your model is complete, choose Render ➤ Render Current Frame on Blender's top toolbar above the workspace (keyboard shortcut F12). You may need to adjust the camera object's position to get the framing you want.

To save the rendered image in a format that can be used by other graphics programs, click the far-right button in the first, main group on the left side of the Panels bar. This is the Scene button, which has an icon like a very small gray landscape, although this is hard to see (keyboard shortcut F10). The Format panel that appears includes a number of preset buttons for common video formats, including PAL, NTSC, and HD. For further use in a bitmap graphics program like the GIMP, choose the Full format button; unlike PAL or NTSC, it doesn't scale down the number of pixels in the output file.

Just to the left of these buttons is a drop-down menu for the output file format, which defaults to Targa. Several other obscure formats are listed here; if you don't have a preference, PNG format is a good choice for compatibility. On the top menu, select File ➤ Save Rendered Image (keyboard shortcut F3). A file-save dialog opens; the first field shows the directory path, and you type the file name in the field just below. Pressing Enter doesn't seem to be enough—click the Save PNG button (if that's the format you chose). Finally, check the rendered file in the GIMP or your photo manager of choice to be sure it's rendered correctly (see Figure 6-43).

- *Wings 3D* (GNU/Linux, Windows, Mac): A 3D modeler, rather than an animation package. www.wings3d.com.
- *YafaRay* (GNU/Linux, Windows, Mac): A raytracing rendering system that can be used with Blender. www.yafaray.org.

All of these packages are available in Ubuntu using the Add/Remove Programs application. YafaRay is a rewrite of an earlier program called YafRay, so you may find Ubuntu packages under the old name.

Figure 6-43. *The final render output to PNG, with HD pixel dimensions and aspect ratio. Note the star field background and the lighting effects in the foreground.*

Further Reading

Many books about Blender are available, including introductory titles like *Blender for Dummies* by Jason van Gumster (Wiley, 2009, ISBN-10: 0470400188) and *The Essential Blender* by Roland Hess (No Starch Press, 2007, ISBN-10: 1593271662). More detailed coverage is available in specialist titles such as *Bounce, Tumble, and Splash! Simulating the Physical World with Blender 3D* by Tony Mullen (Sybex, 2008, ISBN-10: 0470192801) and *Foundation Blender Compositing* by Roger Wickes (Friends of Ed, 2009, ISBN-10: 1430219769).

Other Useful Programs

Although this chapter has been dedicated to Blender, you can check out other Free Software 3D tools, including the following:

- *K-3D* (GNU/Linux, Windows, Mac): A 3D modeling and animation package that features a procedural engine. www.k-3d.org.
- *Aqsis* (GNU/Linux, Windows, Mac): A 3D rendering system compatible with Pixar's RenderMan standard. www.aqsis.org.

## CHAPTER 7

Publishing

The DTP Revolution

Although personal computers quickly replaced the humble typewriter, the art of typesetting and laying out high-quality printed documents took a little longer to go digital. True desktop publishing software is usually known by its acronym, DTP. This kind of program differs from word processors and home or small-office publishing packages in the precise level of control over the document that it enables. Designed for high-speed use by an experienced operator, a true DTP program doesn't try to suggest where a picture should be located on the page or correct your grammar. Its output format is designed for extremely accurate results when the document is transferred to the print shop.

Some proprietary DTP software was available in the 1980s, including Aldus PageMaker, but most printers were a technically conservative bunch of people. After all, the principles of moveable type printing had hardly changed in 500 years, since Gutenberg introduced this technology to Europe (see Figure 7-1). *Moveable type* means that each letter in a word or a line of text is an individual element, with a particular font style; letters can be rearranged quickly in any order for printing. Contrast the flexibility of this method to carved woodblock printing and the hand-inked parchments, produced slowly and carefully by monks and scholars, which the early printers were trying to emulate.

Figure 7-1. A German printing press from 1811, in the Deutsches Museum, Munich. Photo by Matthias Kabel, GNU FDL.

Right into the 1970s and 80s, some printers were still using typefaces cast from red-hot, liquid metal, just like Gutenberg (a goldsmith) had pioneered in Germany during the mid-fifteenth century. About 30 years ago, many printers switched to using electro-mechanical phototypesetting machines, but desktop computers were about to revolutionize the industry. Beginning in 1986, 5,000 print workers in London fought a bitter, year-long street battle with News International, publisher of *The Times* and other English newspapers, over its relocation to a brand new DTP-based printing plant at Wapping, east of the city center. The printers had been fired after refusing to move to the new facility, which was so controversial among members of their profession that it had been built in secret. Control was being taken away from the factory floor and put onto the computer user's desktop.

It wasn't until QuarkXpress 3 took hold in print shops during the early 1990s that the remaining traditional typesetters and layout artists were forced to retrain or lose their job to some teenager who knew how to work a Mac. QuarkXPress and PageMaker were also available for Windows, there was DTP software for home computers like the Amiga and Atari, and IBM had its own system based on the OS/2 platform; but Apple's integrated hardware and operating system became the de facto standard in professional publishing. The availability of Apple desktop laser printers played a part in that process, because they allowed sharp, accurate text proofs and final copy to be produced quickly and cheaply.

Digital preparation for mass-produced documents, sometimes called *prepress*, not only was much faster than the old typesetting and paste-up methods, but also enabled new designs and layouts that had been difficult to achieve before. However, much of the terminology and many concepts behind hot-metal printing were carried over into DTP software, which can make this kind of program hard to understand if you don't have a background in the industry.

Free Software Alternatives

Quark had a classic application software monopoly over the prepress industry throughout the 90s. Perhaps as a consequence, its flagship program was both very expensive and slow to add new features. Most print shops, in the United Kingdom at least, insisted on files being supplied in QuarkXPress native format. This situation prevailed until Adobe acquired PageMaker and launched its own implementation of the DTP concept, under the name InDesign 1.0, in 1999. As InDesign picked up users from QuarkXPress in the next decade, the proprietary monopoly became a proprietary duopoly, and most commercial design studios required prospective employees to have experience with one or both of these programs.

One factor that helped break the Quark monopoly was the rise in popularity of Adobe's Portable Document Format (PDF), which was initially proprietary but became an ISO open standard in 2008. PDF is suitable for prepress work because it preserves exact layouts and can have particular fonts embedded in it, ensuring reliable results. It meant that DTP users were no longer required to use a specific application to prepare their documents, because they could use the virtual printer in the Adobe Acrobat program to create PDF files.

Adobe decided to release the cut-down, reading-and-printing-only version of Acrobat as a free download, and pretty soon all print shops could handle PDFs. A bonus was that PDF files, being self-contained, could easily be sent over the Internet for proofreading or printing, whereas Quark projects usually comprised multiple DTP, image, and font files. Previously, a missing or corrupted font file could spell disaster for a Quark project on a tight deadline. Adobe Acrobat Reader, known later as Adobe Reader, also became a popular choice for bundling with PDF manuals and documentation, because it saved on printing and shipping costs.

In academic publishing, particularly of science and mathematics textbooks, a Free Software program called TeX (GNU/Linux, Windows, Mac) has been widely used for many years. Stanford University professor Donald Knuth created TeX in the 1970s after taking a dislike to the output of a phototypesetting machine, used for the second edition of the second volume in his epic book series *The*

Art of Computer Programming. Knuth preferred the accuracy and aesthetic qualities of the first edition, which had been typeset on a Monotype hot-metal machine, and went on to create a typesetting program that could emulate the traditional look. You can download versions of TeX via `www.tug.org/texlive/` or find packages included in most GNU/Linux distributions. However, TeX has a command-line interface and is therefore used in a completely different way from drag-and-drop programs like QuarkXPress and Adobe InDesign. The TeX command line is extremely precise and suits programmers very well; but designers and layout artists tend to think visually and so prefer to manipulate a document by eye.

In 2003, Franz Schmid, a software developer based in Germany, released the first version of a drag-and-drop Free Software DTP application called Scribus (GNU/Linux, Windows, Mac), with built-in support for creating PDF files. Versions of Scribus are also available for proprietary UNIX flavors and IBM's OS/2 operating system, making it a widely supported program. No doubt in part due to the high monetary cost of QuarkXPress and InDesign, which is a significant barrier to many prospective users of true DTP software, Scribus has attracted a considerable development and user community. In addition to relatively simple design projects, like posters and leaflets, a number of books, magazines, and newspapers have been produced with Scribus. The design agency Open Source Publishing, based in Belgium, used Scribus in its winning entry for the Plantin Moretus Award, given for the best-designed nonfiction book to come out of that country in 2009. All good GNU/Linux distributions should have a package of Scribus, and the latest version for the various platforms supported is available from the project home page at `www.scribus.net/`. In Ubuntu, you can install Scribus using the Add/Remove Programs application. You should also install the scribus-doc and scribus-template packages, which contain help files and sample layouts, respectively. These two extra packages aren't visible under Add/Remove Programs, but you can find them using the Quick search box in System ➤ Administration ➤ Synaptic Package Manager.

Working with Scribus

In Ubuntu, open Scribus from the Applications ➤ Graphics menu in GNOME. Some other GNU/Linux distributions place Scribus on the Office menu, although as you've read, a true DTP application is different from an office suite's word processor or wizard-led publishing tool. By default, Scribus opens with a New Document dialog window, with settings for a single page document and tabs for opening existing or recent documents (see Figure 7-2).

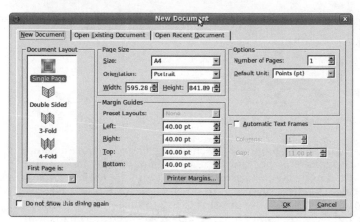

Figure 7-2. *Running Scribus for the first time opens the New Document dialog.*

Single-sided layout is fine for a poster; but for a book or newspaper, select Double Sided in the Document Layout pane at left. For leaflets, you may choose 3-Fold or 4-Fold. In the middle of the New Document dialog are settings for page size and orientation, and margin guides.

Notice that the Width and Height properties specified for the page look unusually large; this is because Scribus defaults to measuring in points. In common with other true DTP software, this is a hold-over from hot-metal printing, where typesetters were familiar with both fonts and little pieces of lead spacing made in point sizes. As you read in Chapter 4, computers have standardized the point as 1/72 of an inch. If you prefer to work in inches, centimeters, or millimeters, you can specify this in the Default Unit drop-down menu, in the Options area. You can also set the number of pages in your document, although it's fine to start with one—you can easily add more pages later.

Just below the Options section is an Automatic Text Frames check box. This is a very useful feature when you're running large amounts of text into the document—for example, from a book manuscript. You set the number of text columns and the gap between adjacent columns here. The margin guides around the edge of the page, which appear as light blue lines in the Scribus main window, are also set in this dialog. Unlike the margins in a word-processing application, these lines are only guides for the operator and don't constrain the placement of text. The only limitation is the minimum margin of the printer hardware.

Click OK to create a blank document, or click Cancel if you have the templates package installed and you'd prefer to start with one of its ready-made layouts. In the main Scribus window, choosing File ➤ New from Template offers several choices, from brochures to pizza menus (see Figure 7-3). If there isn't a suitable template available, you can create a template later from your own design, using File ➤ Save as Template.

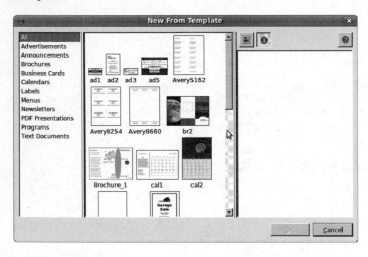

Figure 7-3. The optional templates package for Scribus offers a number of ready-made layouts.

After you've created a document, you can alter its properties by choosing File ➤ Document Setup. The resulting dialog contains many more options than the New Document dialog (see Figure 7-4). At left is a column of icons, with Document selected by default. This icon corresponds to the settings for layout, page size, and margins that you already saw. The check box and time-interval setting for the auto-save feature are useful if you're the kind of person who regrets not pressing Ctrl+S to save the document often enough. Scribus is a mature application, but like most computer programs it has been known to crash from time to time.

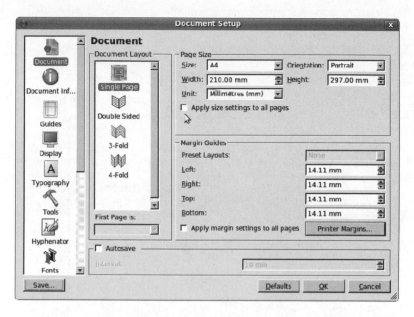

Figure 7-4. The Document Setup dialog in Scribus contains a great many options for your project.

The Concept of Frames

For the new Scribus user, the blank page that appears when you create a document from scratch may be confusing. It's not like a word processor, where you can click into the page area and start typing. All true DTP software is based on the concept of *frames*, much like the frames into which traditional typesetters placed their metal fonts, one character or line at a time. Without a frame on the page, there is nothing to hold the page contents in place. Frames can be made any size or shape, but they don't move or change unless you decide to make that happen. Typically, an individual frame can contain either text or an image but not both at once. Scribus also has a feature for creating tables with a fixed number of rows and columns. If there isn't enough room for the text inside a particular frame, the text flows into the next linked frame, providing one is available. Frames can be layered on top of each other—for example, to put a photo caption inside the area of the photo.

The main Scribus toolbar, at the top of the application window, has tool icons for inserting the three kinds of frames into the page as well as creating various shapes, polygons, and lines. The Insert menu shows the keyboard shortcuts for these functions. Press the T key on your keyboard, for instance, and the Scribus arrowhead tool changes to a small cross with a tiny text document at lower right. This is the cursor for inserting text boxes. Hold down the left mouse button and drag out the text box to the size you require. Only then can you click the toolbar icon for Edit Contents of Frame, which is a bold white letter A with an I-beam cursor on the right (keyboard shortcut E, for edit). As you press this key, the mouse pointer changes to an I-beam. Finally, you can type text into the frame. This may seem over-complicated; but as you learn more about Scribus, you may appreciate the level of control that the frame-based approach to layout offers.

By default, the text that you type into a text frame is small—too small for the headline on the poster you're going to make in this chapter, anyway. First, use the View menu on the main Scribus toolbar to zoom in a little. Choosing View ➤ Fit in Window shows the whole page vertically, whereas for detailed work you may prefer View ➤ 200%. There are also plus and minus magnifying-glass icons and a view-percentage scaling box in the lower-left corner of the main Scribus window (see Figure 7-5).

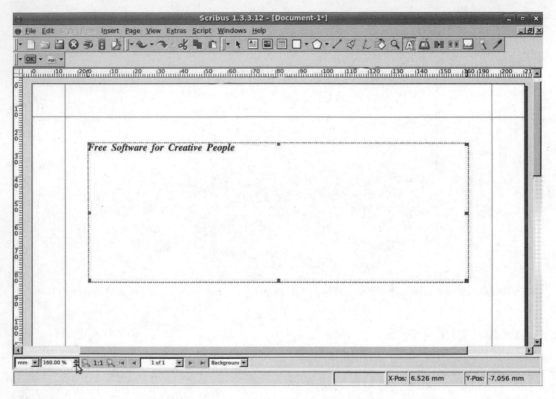

Figure 7-5. Zoom in to the page using the View menu, magnifying-glass icon, or percentage scaling box.

Working with Properties

All objects you add to the page, whether image frames, text frames, photos, graphics, text, or lines, are controlled from the Windows ➤ Properties dialog box (keyboard shortcut F2). With this dialog open and visible, click the frame you just created to select it, using the default arrowhead tool (keyboard shortcut C). The frame is highlighted in red with square handles on its corners and sides, and its details are displayed in the Properties dialog (see Figure 7-6). By default, your first frame is called Text1, but you can give it a more memorable name, to help you identify this particular frame later. You can adjust this frame's position, size, and rotation from the X, Y, Z tab of the Properties dialog, or use the red handles to drag and resize the frame with the arrowhead tool.

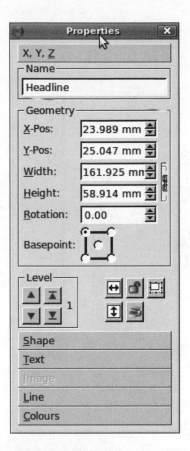

Figure 7-6. In Scribus, the Properties dialog controls all elements on the page. It includes six tabs—here, the Image tab is grayed out because a text frame is currently selected.

The Text Tab

Because the Properties dialog controls both the frame and its contents, you need to click the dialog's Text tab before you can manipulate the selected font's characteristics (see Figure 7-7). The X, Y, Z tab minimizes to make space for the Text tab when you do this. At the top of the Text tab is a drop-down menu for selecting the font family name, such as Norasi; another tab just beneath that lets you select variants of the font, such as BoldItalic or Oblique. Next are six scaling boxes, arranged in two columns of three. The upper-left box, for font size, is the one you're likely to use most often.

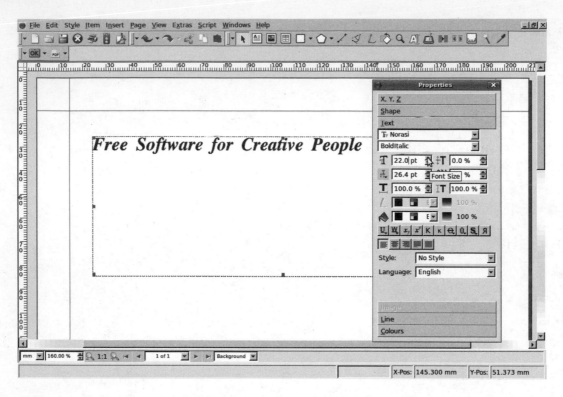

Figure 7-7. *The Text tab controls font family, variant, size, and other settings.*

Immediately beneath this box is the setting for line spacing, also known as *leading*, because hot-metal typographers used thin strips of lead to space lines of text further apart. Note that as the font size increases, the line spacing increases proportionally. Otherwise, the lines would get too close together as the font became larger and would eventually begin to overlap. In Scribus, the default setting makes line spacing 120% of the font size, which is reasonable for body text. You can adjust line spacing manually using the lower of these two boxes.

The box beneath these is for the scaling width of the font, which stretches and shrinks the characters rather than merely adjusting the spacing between them. That effect was nearly impossible to achieve with hot-metal type, because it would have meant recasting the entire font each time.

The first of the three scaling boxes on the right side of the Text tab is for baseline offset. If you imagine that a particular line of text is sitting on an invisible horizontal guide, this control sets how far above or below that guideline the font should be. Next down is the manual tracking box, which enables you to space out the font horizontally but without changing the proportions of individual characters. Again, this is a technique borrowed from hot-metal typesetting, where tiny slivers of lead were placed between letters. Last of the six boxes is the scaling height control; it's exactly the same as the scaling width box, except that it works in the vertical axis.

Below these six small boxes are two drop-down menus that control font color. The upper menu has a pencil icon and is for stroke color (for outlines, as you read about in Chapter 4) and also sets the color of drop-shadow effects. The lower menu has a paint bucket icon and controls the font's fill color. Scribus provides a palette of ready-made colors with names like BlanchedAlmond and BlueViolet—you take a closer look at colors later in this chapter. Both menus have a saturation control to the immediate right, which has a gradient icon. These percentage settings control how much ink should be put down on the digital paper. 100% means solid color; any less than that, and the effect of the color is lighter. Using the saturation controls enables you to make font effects less harsh, quickly and easily.

Text Effects

Immediately beneath the color controls on the Text tab is a row of small square effect buttons. Going from left to right, the first two buttons are for underlining text and underlining words only (see Figure 7-8). If you hold down the mouse button while clicking either of these two controls, a small dialog pops up that allows you to set options for the effect.

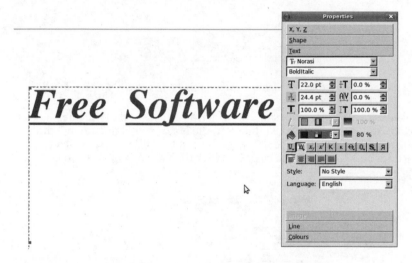

Figure 7-8. The Underline Words Only button leaves spaces in the underline below spaces in the text. The font fill color has been changed to 80% saturation black, which makes it dark gray.

Next are two buttons for subscript and superscript text, used when you're setting formulas such as $e=mc^2$. (The twentieth century might have ended very differently if Einstein's publisher had typeset $e=mc2$ instead, and no one had noticed at the proofreading stage.) Then come two buttons for all caps and small caps, respectively. These save you having to retype a section of text that is meant to be in capital letters—newspaper headlines, for instance. Small caps are uppercase letters, but only the first letter in each word is full size; the rest are scaled-down to lowercase size but retain the uppercase form (see Figure 7-9).

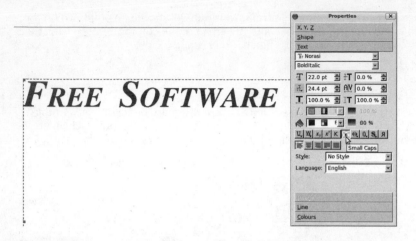

Figure 7-9. *The Small Caps effect scales down uppercase letters, except for the first letter in each word.*

After that is a button for strikeout text, which is the same as underlining except that the line passes through the center of the font's height. It seems a little redundant in the era of digital document editing, except to show on purpose where text has been removed. Next, is a button for outline text, which defaults to a subtle setting of 1% thickness. If the outline color is lighter than the fill color, it can be hard to see the effect (see Figure 7-10).

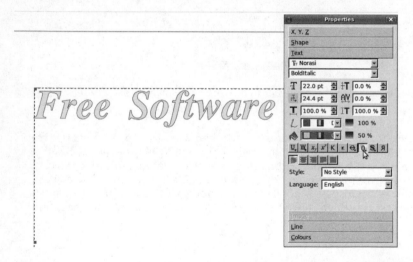

Figure 7-10. *You can adjust the thickness of outline effects by holding down the mouse button over the control. Here, the fill color has been lowered to 50% saturation so that the outline shows up better.*

Drop shadow, where the font is duplicated with a slight spacing to create a fake 3D effect, is commonly used for headings (see Figure 7-11). In the Text tab, you enable it using the second button from the right. You can adjust the strikeout, outline, and drop shadow effects by holding down the mouse button when you click the control button.

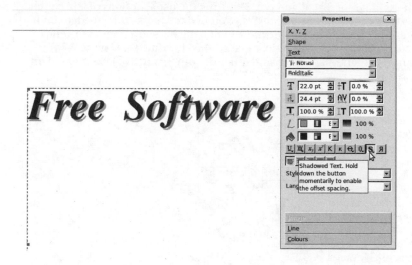

Figure 7-11. The Shadowed Text button creates a fake 3D effect by overlapping a copy of the letters.

Finally on this row is a button for flipping text to read from right to left, which is useful if you have to prepare a document in a language that reads that way, such as Arabic, Persian, or Hebrew (see Figure 7-12). Free Software is used all around the world, and so you find support in GNU/Linux packages for many human languages, including minority languages that aren't supported by proprietary software.

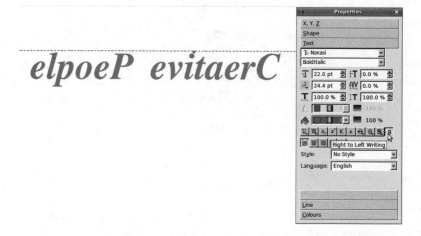

Figure 7-12. The final button in the row flips text to read from right to left. Note that the individual characters aren't reversed.

Text Alignment and Style

The next row of buttons on the Text tab is for text alignment, featuring the usual options of left, center, and right. There are also buttons for *justified* text, where text is stretched to create straight edges on both left and right margins (see Figure 7-13); and *forced justification*, which means short lines at the end of paragraphs are stretched right out, regardless of how widely spaced they become (see Figure 7-14). Justified text is usually found in newspapers, magazines, and other documents with a layout based on columns.

Figure 7-13. *Justified alignment is commonly used for text laid out in columns.*

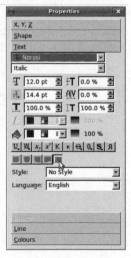

Figure 7-14. *Force-justified text can lead to over-wide spacing for short lines at the end of paragraphs.*

Scribus has sample text built-in, available in many languages, which you can use to test layouts. This dummy text is sometimes known as *lorem ipsum*, after a well-known passage written in Latin by the Roman philosopher Cicero. These particular words were once used in typeface catalogs as sample text and were later adopted by Aldus PageMaker. The function of this text is to show off a particular layout without the designer becoming distracted by the content of the text, because most people can't understand Latin these days. In Scribus, you can find the lorem ipsum by choosing Insert ➤ Sample Text on the toolbar at the top of the main window. The English sample text is by Bram Stoker, the author of *Dracula*; the source of this particular text is Project Gutenberg, an online library of public domain e-books.

Note Project Gutenberg is the oldest e-book library in the world, started by Michael Hart on July 4, 1971 at the University of Illinois. Its first text was the United States' Declaration of Independence, and the original mainframe computer that hosted the library was one of the first 15 computers on what would become the Internet. Find out more at www.gutenberg.org.

The frame containing the sample text has a small gray square with an X-shaped cross in the lower-right corner. This cross icon indicates that there is more text that isn't visible. Remember, a true DTP program doesn't attempt to shrink text to fit, generate additional pages, or move text frames without you telling it to do so; the layout is under full manual control. You read about text-frame linking later in this chapter.

Below the alignment buttons are drop-down menus for the current style sheet and hyphenation language. Using consistent paragraph styles helps a design look slick; the formatting for the body text should, ideally, be kept uniform throughout the document. Similarly, headlines, captions, and subheading styles look much better if they have a matching format. Rather than manually enter the specific font variant, size, and other settings for each line, it's a great time saver on a long document to define a particular style and then select it to set a paragraph or line in that style. Choosing Edit ➤ Paragraph Styles on the main Scribus toolbar opens a small dialog box that allows you to create and manage style sheets.

Click the New button to open a larger Edit Style dialog box. Here, you can define a style sheet according to a name you choose, font family and variant, sizes, colors, and effects like outline text. Most of the controls in this dialog are similar to the Text tab of the Properties dialog, except that there are additional settings for drop caps and tabulation. *Drop caps* are a feature of medieval manuscripts, carried over into traditional hot-metal printing, where the first letter of a paragraph is larger than all the other letters, covering two or more lines vertically. At the bottom of the Edit Style dialog is a preview window containing lorem ipsum text, so you can see what your new style looks like before you apply it (see Figure 7-15).

Figure 7-15. Good design requires consistent style. Here, a style sheet based on Bitstream Vera Sans Roman, 18 point size, center aligned, in blue, with drop caps has been defined.

After creating your style sheet, click OK to return to the small Edit Styles dialog (see Figure 7-16), and click the Save button. You can duplicate and edit a style sheet to make variations on your original choices without having to remember all the settings. This feature helps a great deal with maintaining consistency between style sheets.

Figure 7-16. The small Edit Styles dialog allows style sheets to be duplicated, edited, and deleted. A headline style has been created, based on the previously defined body text style.

Some headings with large font sizes may look better when the spacing between the letters (the *tracking*) is reduced. In the Edit Style dialog for your headline style sheet, you can reduce the percentage value in the Manual Tracking box, in the Distances section.

By clicking the Edit Contents of Frame button (the capital A and I-beam icon on the main Scribus toolbar), you can select inside a piece of text and manually alter the individual spacing in between two letters (the *kerning*) as well.

Importing Text and Images

Right-clicking inside a Scribus frame opens a context menu that gives you the option to paste or import a previously prepared text or image. The keyboard shortcut for right-click ➤ Get Text is Ctrl+D. It's possible to make alterations to the imported text using the Edit Contents of Frame button (keyboard shortcut E), but an alternative suits longer passages of text. The right-click ➤ Edit Text action brings up the Story Editor, which lets you manipulate text a little like a simple word processor (see Figure 7-17). The keyboard shortcut for opening the Story Editor is Ctrl+Y, which works as long as the relevant text frame is selected with the Select Item tool.

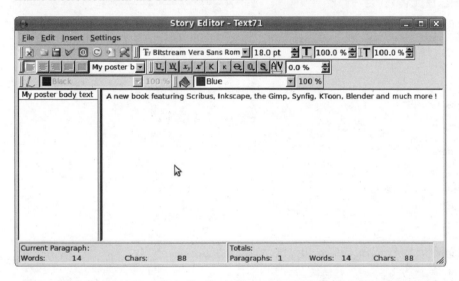

Figure 7-17. The Story Editor lets you modify text independently of the design.

True DTP programs aren't primarily designed for text editing within the main layout, because in a typical publishing workflow, the text has been finalized before it reaches the layout artist. However, the Story Editor lets you make last-minute changes independently of the layout design. This dialog includes a drop-down menu for setting the style of the current story, which applies automatically to the main document layout.

■ **Note** The Story Editor doesn't have an Undo feature, but if you make a mistake, you have the option to choose File ➤ Exit Without Updating Text Frame. This menu item has an icon button like a small red power switch in the upper toolbar of the Story Editor. The Edit Contents of Frame tool doesn't have an Undo function for text either, but if things go wrong you can delete and reimport your text.

After finalizing your text, click the small green check icon button in the upper toolbar to update the selected text frame in the layout and close the Story Editor (keyboard shortcut Ctrl+W); see Figure 7-18. To update a text frame without closing the Story Editor, use Ctrl+U instead.

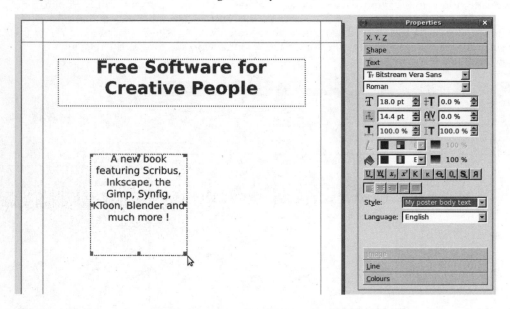

Figure 7-18. After you close the Story Editor, the active text frame is updated.

Importing pixmap image files is similar to importing text, except that empty image frames are shown with two diagonal lines running across them in an X. First, create an image frame in the document by choosing Insert ➤ Image Frame (keyboard shortcut I). The Scribus toolbar has an icon button for this function, which depicts a small square landscape picture; it's just to the right of the document icon button used for inserting text frames.

When your image frame has been dragged out to the correct size and is in position, it's time to locate the image file that you want to place in the document. Right-click ➤ Get Image has the same keyboard shortcut as Get Text, which is Ctrl+D. Supported pixmap formats in Scribus include JPEG, PNG, PSD, and TIF. The EPS and PDF vector formats can also be placed inside image frames (see Figure 7-19).

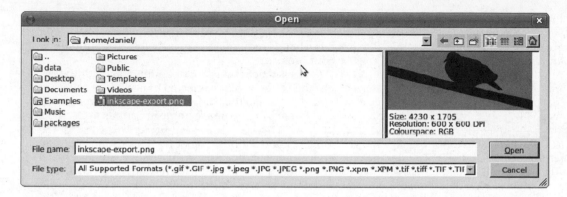

Figure 7-19. *Scribus image import supports most popular pixmap formats, plus EPS and PDF.*

When you click the Open button and the image fills the selected frame, you probably see that it doesn't fit all that well, particularly if it's a small frame containing a high-resolution image. In the Properties dialog, click the Image tab, and click the Scale to Frame Size radio button (see Figure 7-20). Make sure the Proportional box is checked, unless you want the image stretched to fit the frame in both dimensions. Alternatively, leave the Free Scaling radio button selected, and use the X-Scale or Y-Scale percentage control to set the image size your require. Hovering your mouse pointer over these controls and using the mouse scroll wheel is a convenient way to adjust the scale. A chain icon to the right of these two controls toggles proportional scaling on and off.

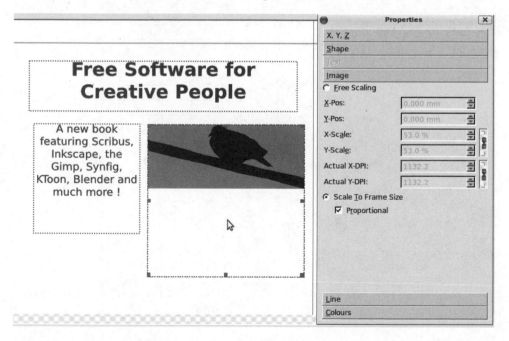

Figure 7-20. *The Image tab enables scaling by both frame size and numerical values.*

Just beneath these controls are settings labeled Actual X-DPI and Actual Y-DPI that you can use to set a specific image resolution in pixels per inch. Because these values update in real time as you adjust the size of the image in its frame, they also provide a handy reminder not to go below the minimum print resolution that you have set for the pixmaps in your project.

Another difference between image and text frames is that Scribus doesn't offer image-editing features internally. Right-click ➤ Edit Image opens the contents of the selected image frame using an external pixmap-editing program, which on Ubuntu defaults to the GIMP. After modifying and saving the image file, you may need to right-click ➤ Update Image on the image frame in Scribus to see the new version of the image in your layout.

You can choose Extras ➤ Manage Images from the main Scribus toolbar to check the current status of all the images included in your document. This feature is particularly useful should an image be missing from a long document, which you otherwise may not notice until it's too late. You can also choose Windows ➤ Outline from the main toolbar to quickly navigate through the pages of a document and find a particular image that you need to edit.

Scalable Vector Graphic (SVG) files, like those created by Inkscape, can be imported directly into Scribus without creating an image frame first. Choosing File ➤ Import ➤ Import SVG brings up a file-browser window in which you can select a suitable graphic. Click Open, and Scribus draws a dotted outline of your SVG to help you position it, with the upper-left corner attached to your mouse pointer. The outline of the SVG file moves with your mouse pointer until you click to release the image, which sets it at your chosen location in the document layout.

Placed SVG files behave like a text or image frame once imported. Because they're vector-based, they can be resized without any loss of quality (see Figure 7-21).

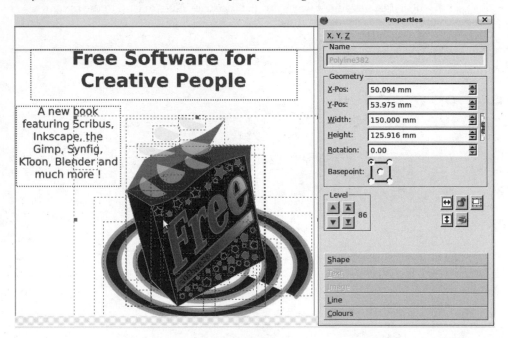

Figure 7-21. A placed SVG file can be scaled to any size in the Scribus document.

Frame Shapes and Colors

In the Properties dialog, in addition to from the X, Y, Z and Text tabs that you've already read about, the Shape tab controls frame shape, boundaries, and text flow. Frames don't have to be rectangular; there are a number of ready-made shapes to choose from, including circles, triangles, and arrowheads. To access the pop-up menu of shapes, click the button with the white square icon at upper right on the Shape tab (see Figure 7-22).

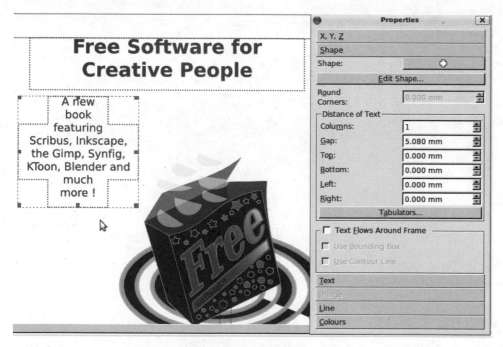

Figure 7-22. Scribus offers a number of ready-made frame shapes, including the cross shown here. Text flows inside the shape automatically.

If none of the preset shapes suits your needs, you can click the Edit Shape button on this tab to open the Nodes dialog (see Figure 7-23). This feature lets you edit the shape of a frame any way you choose and has path tools similar to those found in Inkscape.

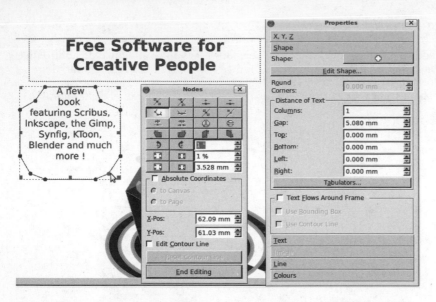

Figure 7-23. You can edit frames into any shape using the Nodes dialog.

Frames are transparent by default, so if you select a new frame and switch to the Colors tab of the Properties dialog, the fill color is set to None. You can choose a solid fill color for the selected frame or use the drop-down menu to set a gradient as the frame's background (see Figure 7-24). You can also set a stroke color for the frame, but you probably won't be able to see this outline accurately unless you uncheck View ➤ Show Frames on the main Scribus toolbar.

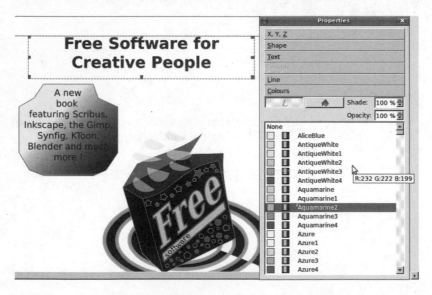

Figure 7-24. Use the Colors tab to give frames outlines or fills, including gradient fills.

Placing text on curves is also relatively straightforward. First, import or type the chosen text into a text frame, as usual. Next, click one of the line-drawing icon buttons on the main Scribus toolbar. You have a choice of three line tools: Insert Line (keyboard shortcut L), Insert Bezier Curve (shortcut B), or Insert Freehand Line (shortcut F). If you choose the Bezier curve tool, draw the shape you want by clicking and dragging the curves out and then clicking where you want the end point to be (see Figure 7-25). Next, right-click the mouse button to anchor the end point. Whichever tool you choose, select both the line and the text by holding down the Shift key and clicking each one. The final step is to choose Item ➤ Attach Text to Path on the main Scribus toolbar. You may need to adjust values in the Text tab of the Properties dialog to get the effect right. In Figure 7-26, the font size has been reduced to fit all of the text on to the Bezier curve, and the font color has been darkened in the Text tab.

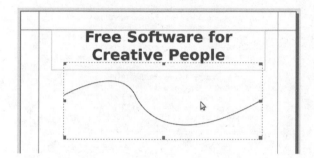

Figure 7-25. Attaching text to a line first requires that you use one of the three line-drawing tools.

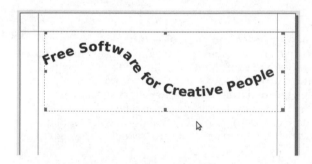

Figure 7-26. Then, select both the text and the line by Shift+clicking, and choose Attach Text to Path from the Item menu.

To separate an item of text so joined, choose Item ➤ Detach Text from Path. You can adjust the curve using the Edit Shape button in the Shape tab of the Properties dialog. When you're happy with the frame's position and properties, you can lock it to prevent accidental edits with right-click ➤ Is Locked (keyboard shortcut Ctrl+L). When you do, the red handles around the selected frame disappear.

Managing Fonts

Scribus has built-in features for managing fonts. Choosing File ➤ Preferences on the main toolbar and clicking the Fonts icon on the left menu brings up the global font Preferences dialog (see Figure 7-27).

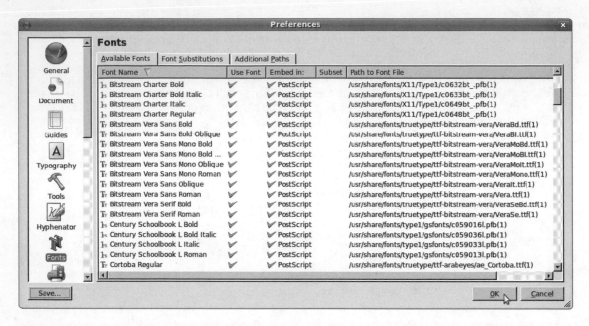

Figure 7-27. *The font Preferences dialog offers an overview of installed fonts and potential typeface troubles, such as missing fonts.*

Here you can check which fonts are available on your system, add font directory paths that aren't currently included, and make substitutions for fonts that are unavailable. Typically, missing fonts cause problems when a DTP document is moved from computer to computer, or a machine's disk is wiped and reinstalled. Suddenly, as you attempt to open the native DTP file, you realize that no one remembered to back up an obscure font that was downloaded from the Internet years ago.

Scribus, like all true DTP programs, is very fussy about fonts. It doesn't create fake italic or bold fonts if they don't exist in a given font family, like some other programs do by modifying the regular (also known as *Roman*) version. These automatically modified fonts can look OK on screen, but they have the potential to cause printing headaches later.

Spot and Process Colors

You can create and manage custom colors by choosing Edit ➤ Colors on the main Scribus menu bar, which brings up the Colors dialog (see Figure 7-28).

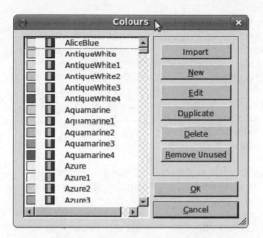

Figure 7-28. Scribus comes complete with predefined colors, using names of its own.

Note that most of the ready-made color names, like AliceBlue and Burlywood, have a small icon with red, green, and blue stripes. This denotes that these shades are defined as red, green, and blue (RGB) colors, which are useful for web design, video work, and PDFs destined to read on screen, but not so useful for matching colors on a printing press.

Because mixing ink to make a particular color is the opposite of mixing light on your computer screen, instead of RGB, color printing typically uses the direct opposite primary colors of cyan, magenta, and yellow (CMY); see Figure 7-29. In practice, it can be tricky to mix black accurately from these three primary ink colors, so most color printing is done with an additional key color of pure black ink. The letter K, for *key*, is added to the acronym CMY to make CMYK. Other color models used in commercial printing presses use six or more inks, plus varnishes and other translucent finishes; but CMYK is the most common model in the world of DTP.

Figure 7-29. Subtractive mixing of colors with cyan, magenta, and yellow light absorbers. Note the red, green and blue parts where the colored glass filters cross over. 3D image modeled in POV-Ray by Mirsad Todorovac, GNU FDL.

If you've ever opened a cereal box and wondered about the cryptic symbols printed on the inside flaps, they're alignment and color proofing marks from litho printing. The offset litho technique can print only one color at a time, using a metal plate that transfers the ink onto a roller; then, the roller puts the ink onto the paper. A full-color image therefore requires at least three different inks for the primary colors plus key ink, which means a minimum of four different plates and four runs through the press.

Registration marks, which are on every plate and look like cross hairs, help the printer make sure each subsequent color is printed exactly on top of the color before. If the paper in the litho machine or the printing plate is even slightly misaligned between runs, you see colored fringes around the edges of an image; you may have noticed this common error in a newspaper or a comic book, if you have a keen eye. *Cropping marks*, which show the print finisher where to line up the paper cutting machine, are often printed using the registration color.

Sometimes you can get away with black ink and one other color, which means the printing press runs only twice, making the litho job cheaper. For example, if you're printing stationery for a company that has only black text and a logo that is always the same shade of green, there's no need to use three different color plates as well as the black plate. These specific colors are known as *spot colors*, and they're usually specified by designers using the proprietary Pantone system of color swatch numbers. That swatch number translates into ratios of basic ink colors so that the printer can mix up a batch of ink for that one job.

Mixing inks for litho is a lot like what you do when you're painting a house—you take the paint company color chart to the hardware store, and they have a machine that adds precise amounts of pigment to a can of ordinary white paint. It saves the printer or hardware store from having to keep vast numbers of different spot colors ready mixed, which they may never need. Printers also use spot colors for inks that can't be mixed using CMYK ratios, such as metallic and fluorescent finishes.

Scribus doesn't support Pantone numbers by default, because their proprietary nature is difficult to reconcile with Free Software—not least because the owners of the Pantone system require license fees to be paid before you can reproduce or distribute their swatches. Instead, you can use the New button in the Colours dialog to open an Edit Colour dialog where you can specify a CMYK color by the percentages of the four inks (see Figure 7-30). To help you mix colors by eye, Scribus provides a hue, saturation, value (HSV) color map, similar to the GIMP's color picker. The drop-down menu at upper right lists the predefined swatch values you saw earlier.

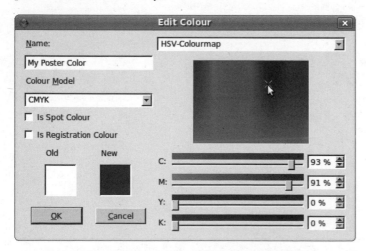

Figure 7-30. *Choose a color model, and then specify the percentages of each primary color plus black in the case of CMYK.*

Choose a memorable name for your new color; select the color model from CMYK, RGB, or the very limited web-safe RGB palette; and click the check box for spot color or registration color if appropriate. Then, click OK to close the Edit Color dialog. Back in the main Colors dialog, your new color is displayed; if it's a CMYK color, it has a different icon than the ready-made RGB colors (see Figure 7-31). Click OK again to close this dialog, and you can use your new custom color in the Edit ➤ Paragraph Styles dialog.

Figure 7-31. *After creating a new color and giving it a name, you're no longer limited to the ready-made swatches distributed with Scribus.*

Managing Document Layout

Much like images in the GIMP, Scribus documents can have layers, which you manage by choosing Windows ➤ Layers from the main menu bar (keyboard shortcut F6). These layers can be convenient for separating backgrounds and images from text and other content. You can toggle individual layers as visible, as ready for printing, or as locked against accidental edits by checking the boxes in the Layers dialog (see Figure 7-32).

Figure 7-32. *Using layers in Scribus helps to isolate different parts of a layout, which can be locked into position.*

Choosing Edit ➤ Master Pages from the main Scribus menu bar opens a small Edit Master Pages dialog with one page entry: Normal. This is the master page you've been working with so far, which sets the default state of each new page in the document. The content of your document disappears for a moment, because a master page is normally blank to start with. While you're in Edit Master Pages mode, you can set up guidelines by choosing Page ➤ Manage Guides from the main menu bar. It's also possible to set up the location of page numbers or add any text or image that you want to appear on every page in the document that is based on this master page.

Clicking the New button, which has an icon like a sheet of paper, creates a new master page with the name of your choice (see Figure 7-33). This dialog also includes icon buttons for duplicating master pages, importing them from another document, and deleting them. Double-click the current name of a master page to rename it—but note that you can't delete or rename the Normal master page. Clicking the X close button in the upper-right corner of the dialog saves the master pages and returns you to the document you were working on.

Figure 7-33. Use master pages to define custom layouts for different sections in your document.

The next time you choose Page ➤ Insert on the main Scribus menu bar, you're offered a choice of master pages to base the new page on, in a Master page drop-down menu (see Figure 7-34).

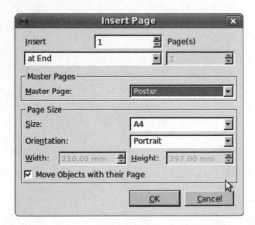

Figure 7-34. New inserted pages can be based on any previously defined master page.

Choosing Windows ➤ Arrange Pages brings up a dialog that lets you drag available master pages into gaps in the Document Pages pane (see Figure 7-35); you can structure the layout of the entire document that way. By clicking any of the page icons in the Document Pages pane, you can quickly skip to the corresponding page layout in the main Scribus window. You can also drag pages or master pages onto the trashcan icon in the Arrange Pages dialog to delete them, or switch the document layout from single-sided to double-sided, three-fold, or four-fold.

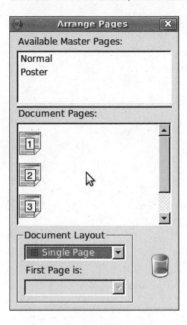

Figure 7-35. You can drag and drop master pages to create new pages in the Arrange Pages dialog.

Linking and Unlinking Frames

When you're working on long, continuous text, such as a book, it's unwise to break the imported text file into chunks the size of an individual frame. Small changes in formatting or minor edits to the text can result in the frame being redrawn on the page and words being lost. To link text frames, first create two or more frames; then, using the arrow Select Item cursor, click the first frame to select it. Click the Link Text Frames icon button on the main Scribus toolbar, which is represented by two sets of lines with a blue triangle between them (keyboard shortcut N). Then, click the frame you want the text to flow into next, and so on. Press the Esc key or click away from the text frames when you've finished linking to return to the Select Item tool.

Using the Link Text Frames feature can sometimes mean that certain words end up in the wrong frame. If you chose automatic text frames when you set up your document, you may see the same effect. A sentence that has lost a word from the end is known among DTP operators as a *widow*, whereas a single word that has lost its parent sentence is known as an *orphan*. To avoid widows and orphans, make sure each text frame is large enough for the text it's meant to contain. Then, click into the frame with the Edit cursor (the I-beam) at the end of the last paragraph intended for that frame, and choose Insert ➤ Spaces & Breaks ➤ Frame Break from the Scribus main menu (keyboard shortcut Ctrl+Enter). If you can't remember where you put the frame breaks, select View ➤ Show Control Characters. Frame breaks are shown as small arrows pointing downward to the right, in the same color as the font, and can be deleted like any other character. Because inserting a break is essentially a text edit, Scribus doesn't offer an undo for it, so you must rely on deleting the control character if you change your mind.

Choosing View ➤ Show Text Chain uses much larger black arrows to show the direction of text flow, which is useful for a complex document (see Figure 7-36). You can break text chains using the appropriate icon button on the main toolbar, which shows two sets of lines with two opposing red triangles (keyboard shortcut U, for *unlink*).

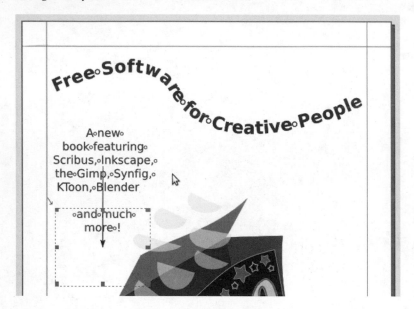

Figure 7-36. *Small arrows show frame breaks, and large black arrows show the direction of text-chain flow.*

Generating PDFs

In addition to the Scribus native, XML-based file format, which has the extension `.sla`, the program also supports export to pixmap formats including JPEG and PNG, as well as the vector formats SVG and EPS. You can find these options by choosing File ➤ Export from the Scribus main menu bar. You can also choose File ➤ Collect for Output to gather all the components used in your document into a single directory, including the native Scribus file and any fonts used, so you can send it to another Scribus user.

However, most DTP users want to produce PDF files, which are suitable for sending to any print shop without the risk of compatibility problems. Fortunately, Scribus is strongly orientated toward the creation of sophisticated PDF output, including interactive PDF forms with support for several PDF field types and JavaScript actions. Interactive PDFs aren't intended for prepress use. They have special features like hyperlinks, notes, bookmarks, and navigation features, similar to a web page. The Insert PDF Fields button on the Scribus toolbar has an icon of a gray button with the label OK. It enables you to draw a frame, into which you can set interactive controls by double-clicking to open the Field Properties dialog (see Figure 7-37).

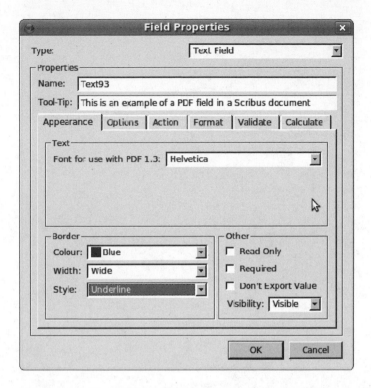

Figure 7-37. *The Field Properties dialog controls special features for interactive PDFs.*

Next to this is another button, which has a yellow icon like a well-known brand of self-adhesive square note paper, with the letters *PDF* on it. This button is for creating PDF annotations, links to other files, and web links.

When your document is complete, to create a PDF, click the Save as PDF icon on the Scribus toolbar, which has an icon like a white piece of paper with a red stylized letter *A* on it (the Adobe Acrobat logo). To the left of the PDF icon is a traffic light icon button for the Preflight Verifier feature that reports any problems found, such as overflowing text. When you try to save a document as a PDF, the Preflight Verifier runs automatically. You can click the problem items in the list to be taken to the relevant location in your document. Fix any errors reported, click the X button in the upper-right corner to close the Preflight Verifier dialog, and run Save as PDF again. If the verifier finds no errors, you go directly to the Save as PDF dialog.

Examine the options presented in the Save as PDF dialog. The defaults are perfectly sane and usable, although it's worth paying attention to a few of the options. First, look at the Compatibility drop-down menu, on the General tab, in the File Options pane. There is a choice of PDF specification version 1.3, 1.4, or 1.5. Older versions of the PDF format have the broadest compatibility, but newer versions support more features. If your system is set up for it, Scribus is also capable of producing the PDF/X-3 flavor, which is an ISO standard specifically intended for prepress work; it contains ICC color profiles, so your document should look the same wherever you get it printed (see Figure 7-38).

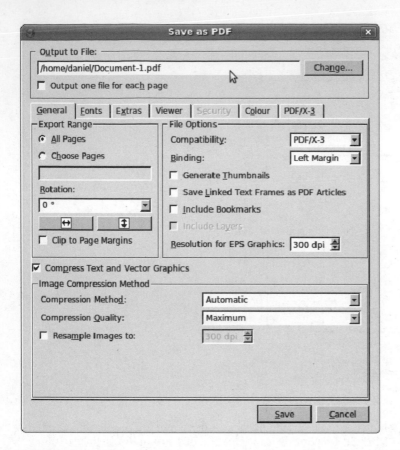

Figure 7-38. *Scribus specializes in producing PDF output to ISO standard, suitable for sending to any print shop on the planet.*

■ **Tip** If the PDF/X-3 tab is grayed out, cancel the Save as PDF dialog. You need to install the icc-profiles package in Synaptic, if you haven't done so already on this system. Then, restart Scribus, choose File ➤ Document Setup from the main Scribus menu bar, click the Color Management icon in the left column, and check the Activate Color Management box in the Color Management panel.

On the Fonts tab, choose to embed or outline all the fonts listed in the left column; otherwise, no one will ever get to see your wonderful homemade typefaces. Finally, in the Color tab, set Output Intended For to Screen/Web or Printer (for CMYK), as appropriate. There is also a setting for Grayscale, should your document lack color. If you've selected PDF/X-3 output, this field is locked to Printer and grayed out. If the Save button is grayed out too, note that the PDF/X-3 format requires that you complete the Info String field in the PDF/X-3 tab with the name of your document before attempting to save it.

When the export is complete, you should check your PDF for errors in Adobe Reader or another PDF viewer (see Figure 7-39).

Figure 7-39. The final poster, viewed in GNOME's PDF reader program, Evince.

Output and the Litho Process

When your document is free of errors and you've generated a final PDF file, you have a number of options for printing it. The method you choose depends chiefly on the quantity of copies required; but you should also consider the number of colors you need and the level of quality that is acceptable for your project. Here are three common options:

- *Inkjet printing*: Good for short print runs of up to 50 copies, but very costly for medium to long runs because the cartridges are expensive and usually contain tiny amounts of ink. Relatively slow, and the colors can be affected by moisture or sunlight—but you can do small-sized page printing at home. Special paper is required for best results, which costs extra. Commercial inkjet machines can print very large sheets of paper, such as banners, but printing these can be expensive.

- *Laser printing*: Ideal for medium-length print runs of 500 copies; cheaper per page than inkjet printing, but a color laser printer is more expensive to buy in the first place. A laser printer usually prints more pages per minute than an inkjet machine when printing across the whole page. The toner-heating process used by a laser printer doesn't soak cheap, thin paper with ink, and the colors are more durable.

- *Litho printing*: Expensive for short to medium runs due to setup costs, but much, much cheaper than either inkjet or laser for long runs of 1,000 copies or more. Excellent quality when done correctly. Looks good even on thinner paper. Coated paper, which features a surface impregnated with china clay (kaolinite), is a commonly specified option.

For short to medium print runs, it's cost-effective to use direct digital printing, with a home inkjet or small-office laser printer. If you're on a really low budget, you can prepare a master copy and duplicate it on a photocopier at your local copy shop. Using colored paper is a cheap way to make photocopies look more interesting—and you can sometimes find colored toner for mono, black-and-white copiers. If you don't have access to good printing equipment, online services will print short book runs for you using all-digital methods, including `www.lulu.com` for text books and `www.snapfish.com` for photographic books. Some local printers also offer digital print-on-demand services.

Like moveable type, lithographic printing, which uses metal plates and rollers to put the ink onto the paper, is hardly a new technique. The offset press has been around for a century, and the original idea of lithography is at least 200 years old; but litho still hasn't been fully replaced by digital printing. This is because for the time being, litho is cheaper than all-digital printing presses for large print runs. The difference is in the way the printing plates are prepared.

In the early days of computer prepress, layouts were printed on paper as camera-ready copy, which was photographed to make film images of each page for the plate-making machine. The camera side of the process had not changed from earlier prepress methods in which type was literally cut (with a scalpel) and pasted (with a glue brush). Later, DTP software was used to print to film instead of paper, using a machine called an *image setter*. Again, the text and pictures on the image-setter film were transferred photographically onto the litho plates. Now, many print shops have machines that can produce the litho plates directly from PDF files on a hard disk.

Further Reading

The official manual for the Scribus application is *Scribus: Open-Source Desktop Publishing* by Christoph Schäfer and Gregory Pittman (FLES Books, 2009, ISBN-10: 0956078001). There aren't many other books about Scribus, although the program has been featured in some magazine tutorials. Plenty of online documentation is available, including the official Scribus web site, its user-contributed wiki at `http://wiki.scribus.net`, and other web sites.

Other Useful Programs

Tools that complement Scribus for DTP work include the following:

- *LProf* (GNU/Linux, Windows, Mac): A Free Software color profiler that creates ICC-compliant profiles for devices such as cameras, scanners, and monitors. Having calibrated equipment helps match colors more accurately. Available from `http://sourceforge.net/projects/lprof`.

- *Pdftk* (GNU/Linux, Windows, Mac): A Java-based command-line tool for manipulating PDF files, including merging, splitting, and rotating. Free Software under the GNU GPL, available from `www.accesspdf.com/pdftk`.

- *PDFjam* (GNU/Linux, Mac): Another collection of command-line PDF utilities, this time based on TeX. Also Free Software; available from `http://go.warwick.ac.uk/pdfjam`.

LProf is available in Ubuntu using the Add/Remove Programs application. You can install pdftk and PDFjam by choosing System ➤ Administration ➤ Synaptic Package Manager.

CHAPTER 8

■ ■ ■

Making Music

The Beat Goes On

A DJ isn't a human jukebox—skill is required to play the right records in the right order and to be creative with the mix. Ask any DJ about the industry-standard tools of the trade, and they're still a pair of the Matsushita Electric Industrial Company's high-end hi-fi turntables from the early 70s, repurposed as club decks in the disco era and known as the Technics SL-1200s, or 1210s (see Figure 8-1).

Figure 8-1. The Technics SL-1200 Mk 2. Many DJs still prefer vinyl, but it can be hard to find new music in the format.

Vinyl offers hands-on control; and because the traditional setup is all-analogue, there are no latency problems or software glitches to contend with. The downside of vinyl is that a lot of new music isn't being released in the format; and unless you own your own cutting lathe, it isn't convenient or cost-effective to make one-off remixes on acetate, known as *dub plates*. Vinyl is easily damaged, having no error correction built in; even if well looked after, the soft plastic wears eventually under the pressure of a diamond stylus. To top all of that, unless you live in a large town or city, you probably don't have access to a decent record shop. The combined effect of supermarkets and online stores selling CDs and downloads have seen to that.

In the digital music era, there have been several attempts to snatch the SL-1200's crown, including DJ-orientated CD players and hybrid embedded systems that offer playback of material imported from CDs or flash memory cards. Windows-based DJ software has a more checkered reputation, partly because a general-purpose operating system isn't what you need for real-time responsiveness, and

211

partly because of all the headaches that come with depending on proprietary software. You don't want to be reaching fever pitch on a club stage when a message pops up inviting you to download an update to Windows Media Player, while mysterious disk thrashing begins in the background. And of course Digital Rights Management (DRM, also known as *copy protection*) is a complete nonstarter for DJs, who need to be able to do exactly what they want with the music they purchase, including remix and rerelease it.

A Question of Control

A further limitation of computer-based DJing is that laptops and PCs, having descended from the Victorian typewriter, don't have the same physical controls as a vinyl-based system. In addition to the hands-on aspect of the vinyl, there are mixer faders and knobs to take into consideration. One of the first attempts to solve this problem was start-up N2IT's Final Scratch, in which special vinyl with proprietary time-code on it was played into a USB device attached to a laptop. To the DJ, it was meant to feel exactly like playing records; but the audio came from files stored on the laptop's hard drive. Final Scratch was originally developed on the now long-dead BeOS platform, but by the time it was released under the Stanton brand name, the laptop was running a custom version of Debian GNU/Linux. Later, this software was ported to OS X and Windows XP, with mixed results. Despite legal battles over software patents, a number of me-too products appeared, each featuring incompatible vinyl time-code and hardware. The main drawback of this type of system is that if you don't already own a pair of turntables and a mixer, proprietary time-coded vinyl or special hardware aren't much use.

An alternative approach is to remove the need for traditional analogue equipment by providing a dedicated control surface: essentially, a dumb set of faders, knobs, and jog wheels (see Figure 8-2). This connects to the host computer via USB; and although it's not exactly the same experience as using vinyl, it does mean you have less equipment to carry around. These control surfaces are generally supported by one or more proprietary DJing applications for Windows or Apple platforms, often bundled with the hardware.

Figure 8-2. *Specialized DJ control surfaces like this Hercules RMX overcome some limitations of the PC interface.*

Before *beat matching* (perfect synchronization of two rhythms) became popular among DJs, a mixer usually had only one level control for each turntable, which could be a rotary knob or a vertical fader. It took a lot of practice to drop the level of one record while bringing up the other, maintaining the average volume so that there were no sudden quiet or loud passages. The introduction of the *crossfader*, usually operated horizontally, meant that the electronics could take care of the balancing act between turntable levels. As one recording fades out, the other fades in, with the main output level staying constant. Contemporary DJ mixers also feature controls for bass, midrange, and treble frequencies, with kill switches that cut these frequencies. There may be effects on board, such as a *flanger*, which changes the sound of the record. Both control surfaces and DJ software have to emulate these frequency and effects features to enable the transition from analogue to digital mixing.

Mixxxing It Up

In the Free Software arena, the *terminatorX* application (GNU/Linux, download from `www.terminatorx.org`) has offered entertainment by way of scratching and mixing for some time. Cross-platform upstart Mixxx (GNU/Linux, Windows, Mac) has the edge for the beat-matching style of mixing, where two recordings are synchronized together to create seamless fades or cuts. Mixxx has support for most popular time-coded vinyl formats and hardware control surfaces, offering a choice of interface, but you can also use it with QWERTY keyboard shortcuts on a standard PC or laptop. If you're running Ubuntu, you can download Mixxx using the Add/Remove Programs application; many other GNU/Linux distributions also have packages available. For Windows or Mac versions, visit the project homepage at `www.mixxx.org`—that's spelled with three *X*s.

If you've checked out Mixxx before but decided it wasn't ready to replace an analogue setup, it's well worth looking at the application again. A bunch of new features have been added recently, including native Free Lossless Audio Codec (FLAC) format support, which is useful if you care about sound quality. Some laptop-based DJs include in their mixes MP3 files they find on the Internet, and the degradation in quality is all too obvious when the computer is connected to a large sound system. If you're going to build up a substantial collection of music for digital DJing, it makes sense to start out with a lossless format like the Free Software FLAC standard, which doesn't throw away any of the audio data. FLAC files are typically much larger than MP3 files but remain significantly smaller than WAV files copied from audio CDs. If stereo WAV files use up roughly 10MB per minute, an MP3 made from that WAV may be only 1MB per minute, and a FLAC file converted from the WAV is half way between, at around 5MB per minute. This extra storage space required by FLAC isn't much of a problem now that even small, mobile computers have many gigabytes of disc or memory card space.

You can use any ordinary PC or laptop soundcard to DJ with Mixxx. However, for beat matching, most DJs rely on a stereo headphone cue output as well as the main stereo output. This separate headphone output helps the DJ make sure the two recordings are synchronized correctly before making the crossfade from one piece of music to the other. Unfortunately, most computers have only one independent audio output, which has two channels for stereo. The main exceptions among PCs are those machines designed for home cinema, which can have separate front and rear stereo output sockets, designed for connection to a 5.1 speaker system. You can often configure these audio cards to provide main output and cue outputs for DJing with Mixxx.

Some digital DJs invest in a specialized audio interface with at least four output channels, but these aren't strictly necessary to get started. A cheap trick is to use a pair of USB headphones for monitoring the music, because Mixxx is happy to use two different hardware devices for main and cue outputs. The kind of USB headphones sold for voice-over-IP (Internet telephony) and gaming use will do the job as long as they go loud enough, although specialized USB headphones for DJs are starting to become available. Without the extra volume, it may be difficult to hear the cue output in a noisy club environment; but of course, there are limits. You have to look after your hearing, because tinnitus or even permanent hearing loss will shorten your DJing career significantly.

Running Mixxx for the First Time

On Ubuntu, you can find Mixxx on the Applications ➤ Sound & Video menu, when installed. When you run it for the first time, Mixxx needs to know where on the local file system you keep your DJing music (see Figure 8-3). In the case of Ubuntu, a subdirectory called `Music` is in your home directory by default, although you need to put some `.flac` or `.wav` files in it.

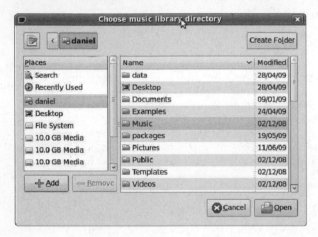

Figure 8-3. On the first start up, Mixxx invites you to indicate where you keep your DJing music files.

Mixxx also supports MP3 and the Free Software Ogg Vorbis format playback; but if the only copy of a particular song you have is in MP3 format, you may want to track down a higher-quality version for DJing, particularly if the bitrate of the file is 128kbps or less. Vorbis typically sounds better than MP3 at the same bitrate and very obviously better at low bitrates, but there is no compelling reason to choose Vorbis over FLAC for DJing purposes unless you're short on storage space. On the other hand, if you have a large collection of Vorbis files and no access to original `.wav` or `.flac` versions, you won't gain any quality by converting them to FLAC—because Vorbis, like MP3, is a lossy compression format.

If you don't have any good music on your computer, then see the links at the end of this chapter for tools you can use to convert audio CDs to files that Mixxx can use. Otherwise, look around the Internet for new music being made available for legal download, some of which is under Free Software or similar licenses, on sites such as `www.jamendo.com`, `www.magnatune.com`, and `www.newgrounds.com`.

When you specify a directory, the lower window of the Mixxx GUI, by default in Library view, fills with a list of sound files from that directory. If you want to locate audio files elsewhere on the filesystem, you can click the combo box just above the left side of this dialog, labeled Library by default, and select Browse. If your music library is large, use the Search box above the window to the right, which enables you to narrow the list of files to a particular artist or title keyword.

Troubleshooting Mixxx

The first time you run Mixxx, you may see an error message about the program not being able to open the default audio device on the system (see Figure 8-4).

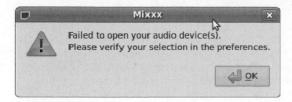

Figure 8-4. Mixxx tries to open the first sound card on the system by default, but this doesn't always work.

On Ubuntu GNU/Linux in particular, the PulseAudio sound server can prevent Mixxx from getting direct access to the soundcard. To correct this problem, go to Options ➤ Preferences on the main menu bar of Mixxx, and, in the Sound Hardware tab, set Audio Output Master to pulse. Click OK, and the warning dialog goes away. However, using PulseAudio this way does seem to add extra *latency*, or delay, to the sound output, so I recommend that you uninstall the pulseaudio package for best results with Mixxx. You can remove packages by choosing System ➤ Administration ➤ Synaptic Package Manager. Use the quick search box in Synaptic to locate the pulseaudio package, right-click it, and select Mark for Removal. Then, click the Apply button on the Synaptic main toolbar. You may need to reboot your computer after this step in order to get the audio system working correctly.

If you aren't running Ubuntu or PulseAudio, it may be that the first sound card in your system only supports 48000Hz sample rates. This is common with on-board sound chipsets and generic USB audio devices. By default, the output of Mixxx is set to 44100Hz, the sample rate of an audio CD, which is a sensible rate if your material is mostly copied from CDs. If your sound card refuses to open at the 44100Hz rate, you see the same error, but it's easily fixed. If the Preferences dialog box isn't open already, choose Options ➤ Preferences ➤ Sound Hardware, and set "Sample rate (Hz)" to 48000 (see Figure 8-5). Then, click OK to close the dialog.

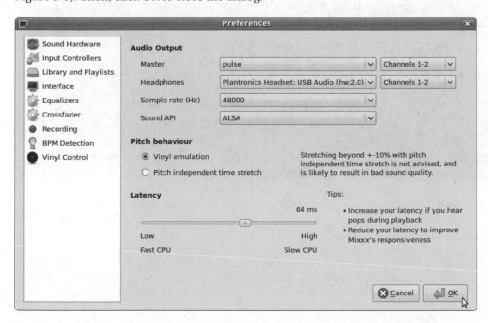

Figure 8-5. Correct setting of output sample rate avoids sound-card troubles.

In common with Blender, which you read about in Chapter 6, Mixxx uses OpenGL to draw its interface, specifically the waveforms of the audio files. If your PC's or laptop's video card isn't set up for the hardware-accelerated Direct Rendering Infrastructure (DRI), Mixxx warns you on startup that performance will suffer and that you should set Preferences ➤ Interface ➤ "Waveform display" to Simple. Although this setting improves performance on machines without decent OpenGL capabilities, it means losing the ability to check the alignment of your beats by eye. Unless you're already a skilled turntablist with a well-tuned ear, this feature is extremely useful (see Figure 8-6).

Figure 8-6. Mixxx's waveform display is so useful that accelerated video is well worth the upgrade.

I recommend leaving "Waveform display" set to Waveform, unless your machine is very old and slow. In that case, you may consider upgrading to a video card or integrated video motherboard with support for DRI. Hardware with this support in a Free Software driver is conveniently listed on the www.free3d.org website. I use Mixxx with a Matrox G550 card, toward the bottom of the performance table, which nevertheless offers crisp 2D output, is fanless, and has a mature Free Software driver with DRI support. You should be able to pick up a used model for a few dollars. If you need stronger 3D performance for use with Blender or other software, you're probably better off with an ATI Radeon or

NVIDIA card—but be careful about noisy, whining cooling fans, which can be a distraction in the creative studio.

On GNU/Linux, if you're running a compositing window manager such as Compiz, you may notice that Mixxx's waveform display appears to float on top of all other windows. This is because 3D desktops like Compiz are poorly integrated with OpenGL, at least in the package versions in current mainstream distros. The simplest workaround is to switch back to a 2D window manager, such as Metacity, when running Mixxx (see Figure 8-7).

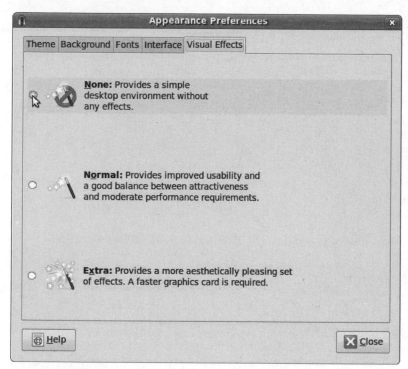

Figure 8-7. Disable Compiz if you see strange effects when running Mixxx on Ubuntu.

If you're running Mixxx in full-screen mode (Options ➤ Full Screen), you won't notice the window manager anyway. To fix this on Ubuntu, select System ➤ Preferences ➤ Appearance from the main GNOME toolbar, click the Visual Effects tab, and click the None radio button.

Back in Mixxx, choose Options ➤ Preferences ➤ Interface ➤ Skin to select a GUI that fits the display you're using. Figure 8-6 shows the default outlineSmall skin, which works on most sizes of screens. Other skins work more or less the same way, although the layout of the controls can be different.

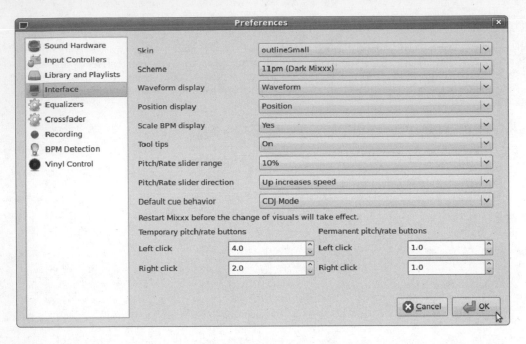

Figure 8-8. *In the Preferences window, select a skin that fits your display and suits your mixing style.*

Hit the Top, My Selector

Double-click any file in the Library view, and it loads automatically into the first available player—channel 1 is the left player, and channel 2 is on the right. Mixxx won't load a file into a channel where a track is already playing, which is a useful safety feature (for avoiding sudden, embarrassing silences on the dance floor). You can also load a track into a specific player by right-clicking it in the Library view. After a short delay while Mixxx analyzes the beginning of the file, calculating the beats-per-minute of the track, the audio's waveform is drawn in one of the player windows. Play this file by clicking the appropriate button on the interface or pressing the keyboard shortcut for start/stop (D for the channel 1 player, L for the channel 2 player).

The crossfader knob, just above the Library view, sits in the center—which isn't a good place to start, unless you already know exactly how you're going to mix the first two tracks. Drag it all the way to the left so that only the output from channel 1 is audible. Now, load up a second track in channel 2, and start it playing. If you have a four-channel or secondary audio device set up in Options ➤ Preferences ➤ Sound Hardware ➤ Headphones, press the headphone cue button; otherwise, you must rely on the waveform in the GUI or your memory of the track to know when to make the fade.

If one track is faster than the other, you can drag the Pitch fader on either player to attempt a match (see Figure 8-9). By default, this control is in vinyl-emulation mode, which means faster tempo equals a rise in musical pitch; but because this is a digital system, you can also use the CPU to stretch and shrink the timing of audio without changing its pitch. If you want to try this feature, enable it by choosing Options ➤ Preferences ➤ Sound Hardware ➤ "Pitch behavior." If you'd rather click than drag, there are buttons next to each pitch fader for precise adjustments, permanent or temporary.

Figure 8-9. Mixxx's pitch control can either emulate vinyl or time-stretch digitally.

The Sync button in this section of the GUI attempts automatic adjustment between channels, which works on the basis of the previously assessed tempo of each track. This beat-detection feature works pretty well for four-to-the-floor dance music like techno or house, less well for the complex rhythms found in drum and bass.

If beat detection fails and is displayed as 0.0, you have the option to enter the tempo of a track manually. To do this, right-click a file in the Library window, and select Properties to open the Track Editor dialog box. With the track in question playing, click the "Push to tap tempo" button in time with the song, which in dance music usually means in time with the kick drum. The better you are at console games like Guitar Hero, the closer the result will be to the actual tempo of the song.

Sometimes, beat detection doesn't work because the tempo is outside the range that Mixxx expects (by default, 70 to 140 beats per minute). To correct this for a fast song, use the Track Editor dialog to increase the maximum end of the BPM range, perhaps to 150 (see Figure 8-10). Then, click the Go button to begin detection. If the song has a slow introduction that unbalances the result, check the Analyze Entire Song box, and try again.

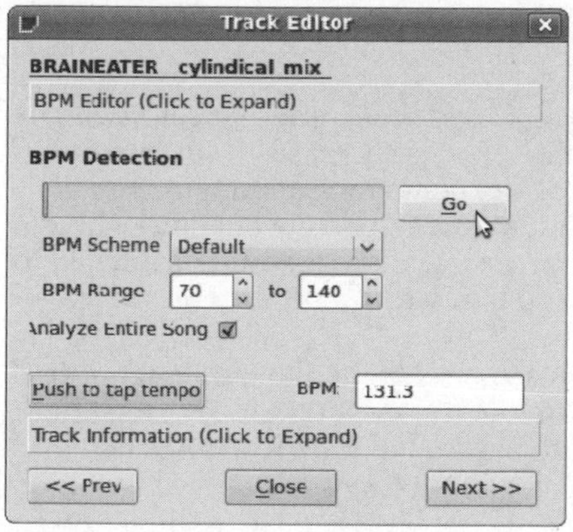

Figure 8-10. You can fix beat-detection problems manually in the Track Editor dialog.

Beat Matching

Of course, there's more to mixing than just having two songs playing at the same speed. To enable smooth crossfades, beats and bars have to be lined up in a musical way. Although that's largely a matter of the DJ's skill and judgment, Mixxx gives you full control over the position in the track of the two waveforms. Click anywhere in the waveform display, and drag the mouse—the farther you pull the mouse to the right, the faster Mixxx scrubs through the file. Move the mouse to the left, and the track slows to a stop and then plays backward at progressively greater speed.

Mixxx draws lines on the waveforms to indicate the positions of the beats, but unless you're mixing very similar tracks, these beat lines can be misleading. There's no substitute for using your ears, and that's where the fun begins. You can also play with the built-in equalizer (the knobs labeled High, Mid, and Low on each channel) and the flanger effect to make your mixes more creative (see Figure 8-11). When you've practiced a little and you're happy with the results, use Options ➤ Record Mix to prove your abilities to the nonbelievers.

Figure 8-11. *The EQ controls are useful for making house mixes more interesting.*

Making a Custom Skin

Perhaps you don't like the arrangement of the controls in Mixxx, you would prefer another color scheme, or you find that the skins supplied don't make the best use of your display size. Creating your own skin for Mixxx is straightforward, because each skin is made up of a directory containing a human-readable XML file and a set of graphics. Recompilation of the application isn't required to make or adjust a new skin. If you can put together a simple web page, then the syntax that Mixxx skins use won't be difficult to understand. On GNU/Linux, look in the **/usr/share/mixxx/skins/** directory to see the skin files supplied with the program.

It's a good idea to start with one of these existing skins and make a copy of the skin directory with a new name. You need to copy your new skin under the **/usr/share/mixxx/skins/** directory or the equivalent location on platforms other than GNU/Linux, so that Mixxx can find it. When you restart Mixxx, the new skin name is visible when you choose Options ➤ Preferences ➤ Interface.

In each skin's directory is a file called **skin.xml** and a background PNG file, as well as graphics for the various knobs and faders. Mixxx skins aren't currently dynamically resizable; but you can create a skin background that is exactly the width of your display, if you want to work in full-screen mode all the time. Even then, you must allow some space, about 25 pixels, for Mixxx's top menu bar.

The background PNG file provides all the static elements of the GUI, including borders between sections and the labels for controls. The x,y positions of the knobs and sliders, their tool tips, and the sizes of adjustable elements are specified in the `skin.xml` file like so:

```
<Tooltip>Playback rate factor</Tooltip>
<Channel>1</Channel>
<Pos>50,210</Pos>
<Size>47,16</Size>
```

Creating the skin background in the GIMP allows you to use the multilayered XCF file format; making small adjustments to static elements is much less tedious if you put each element on its own layer. You can then export the background to a flat, single-layered PNG file for use in your custom Mixxx skin (see Figure 8-12). Using a combination of screenshots of Mixxx and the GIMP's measurement tool helps you to get the dimensions right.

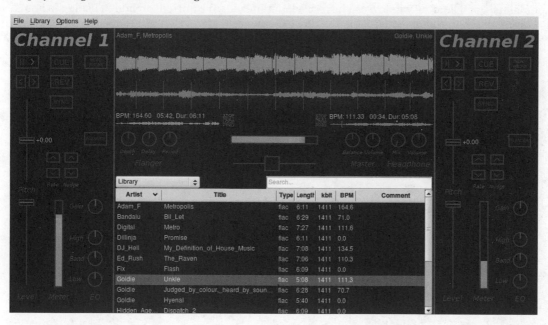

Figure 8-12. Wideboy, a custom Mixxx skin I adapted from outlineSmall for the Indamixx tablet computer. Note the unusual aspect ratio; the dimensions of the skin background are 1024 x 575 pixels.

Beats from Scratch

When you've had fun playing other people's music, you can move on to creating some of your own. For all kinds of dance music and any other kind that's meant to be mixed live by a DJ, a steady beat is essential; otherwise, beat matching is near impossible. Even for acoustic music, a computer can often be useful for creating drum tracks, because a programmed beat works like a metronome to keep the tempo steady. On top of that, a real drum kit takes up space and upsets the neighbors. If you're lucky enough to have access to a real drum kit, and your neighbors don't care, then you may find that learning drum-machine programming informs your own playing style. It used to be that a drum machine was a separate piece of hardware, but even an old PC is more than capable of emulating the very simple computers found in the classic beat boxes of the 1980s and 90s.

Several Free Software drum machines are available, but perhaps the most developed is Hydrogen (GNU/Linux, Windows, Mac). Although this is now a cross-platform application, it was originally developed for GNU/Linux, so that version is the most mature. Windows and Mac installers are available from www.hydrogen-music.org but are currently considered experimental. In Ubuntu, you can install Hydrogen using the Add/Remove Applications tool; packages are also available in many other GNU/Linux distros.

When you open Hydrogen from the Applications ➤ Sound & Video menu in Ubuntu, a welcome dialog box provides some details about the current version of the program. When you close the welcome dialog, Hydrogen fills most of the screen with its main window (see Figure 8-13). Inside this, three floating subwindows are visible: a song editor, a pattern editor, and a mixer. At the top of the main window is a conventional menu bar, and at the bottom are fixed panels for time, mode, tempo, and indicator lights. Each floating window can be resized, minimized, maximized, or hidden using the items on the View menu. This menu includes two floating windows that aren't shown by default—the drumkit manager and the instrument editor. You look at those later.

Figure 8-13. Hydrogen's interface includes up to five floating windows, plus several control panels in the lower bar.

The "Pattern editor" subwindow is a good place to start experimenting with Hydrogen. Unlike its chemical namesake, this drum machine won't literally explode and burn down your house, although it may burn up the dance floor. Down the left side of this subwindow is a list of the various components of the current drum kit, with an empty four-beat timeline in the main part of the window. If you click Snare Rock or Hand Clap in this window, you should hear the corresponding sound from your computer's speakers or headphones. If not, check the settings on the Audio System tab under File ➤ Preferences. Using the default of Auto for the "Audio driver" setting is recommended for now.

Each pattern represents a single bar of music, which could be the drum part for a verse, a chorus, or a fill. (A *drum fill* is the tricky bit that a drummer lays on top of the basic beat, often at the introduction to a song or to emphasize a change in pattern). Along the top of the pattern editor are various boxes that let you alter different parameters of the current pattern. The first box allows you to cycle through the pattern numbers used in the song editor; the pattern name in the second box changes accordingly. The Size box lets you choose the pattern length in eighth notes; the default setting of 8 gives you a conventional time signature of 4/4, used for almost all house and techno music and most rock songs. Setting it to 7 gives you a 7/8 bar, setting it to 10 creates a 5/4 bar, and setting it to 16 creates a double 4/4 bar pattern, effectively. The Resolution box affects the *quantization*—the number of playable beats in the bar expressed as note-length values. If you choose 16, this lets sixteenth notes be played. It's also possible to select triplet quantization, so 16T divides a 4-beat bar into 24. The late John Bonham was able to play triplets on a single bass drum, fact fans, but most drummers aren't that talented.

This time signature and quantization stuff will be familiar to anyone who has learned to read sheet music, but DJs, producers, and musicians who play by ear may be new to it. Nevertheless, it's important in the creation of more complex rhythms.

The last panel in the pattern editor is the Recording panel. There are two ways to record into Hydrogen: in real time or with the mouse. For real-time work you probably need all three buttons engaged—Hear New Notes, Record Keyboard/MIDI Events, and Quantize Keyboard/MIDI Events to Grid. If you don't have a MIDI piano keyboard or drum kit attached to your computer, you can use the keys of your QWERTY keyboard to trigger the notes. With the Record button enabled at least, click the Play/Pause button in the lower panel, to the right of the time clock (keyboard shortcut space bar). A black triangle cursor zips along the beat numbers at the top of the "Pattern editor" subwindow. Now, try pressing the Z, X, and C keys, and you hear sounds and see black diamonds representing the notes added to the pattern.

If you're entering notes using the mouse, then you don't need the Record button activated (see Figure 8-14). Click the horizontal line for each part of the drum kit—for example, Snare Rock—at the position on the grid of the beat number that you require. You can remove individual notes by clicking them. You can also use mouse editing to correct a pattern that has been triggered in real time without having to record the whole pattern again.

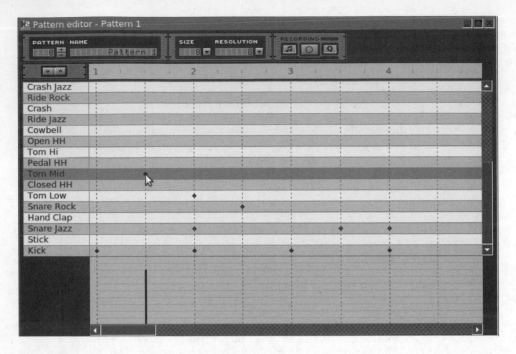

Figure 8-14. You can trigger the pattern editor using a MIDI instrument or a QWERTY keyboard in real time, or make adjustments with the mouse.

Laying Down the Groove

Start by laying down a basic beat: for example, eighth notes on Closed HH (hi-hat cymbal), Kick (bass drum) on beats 1 and 3, and Snare Jazz on 2 and halfway between 3 and 4. Next, adjust the tempo by mousing over the number in the BPM indicator on the lower panel and rolling the mouse wheel up or down. Hydrogen sets the song's beats per minute accordingly and displays that information in the BPM indicator. You can also alter the song's BPM manually using the small plus and minus buttons to the left of the indicator.

If you're working with another musician or instrument, you can adjust the pattern to fit their playing better. For instance, you can thin out the hi-hats to four in a bar, add a few grace notes and open hi-hats, or change the timing of one of the bass drum beats. Real drummers know that not all beats in a bar have the same weight, so edit the velocities displayed along the bottom of the "Pattern editor" subwindow by clicking and dragging the vertical lines (see Figure 8-15).

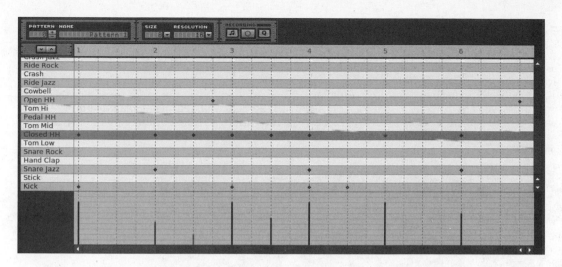

Figure 8-15. Adjust the vertical velocity lines for a more natural feel to your rhythm.

Right-clicking any of the instruments in the "Pattern editor" subwindow presents a pop-up menu of options to Mute, Solo, Clear, or Fill notes relative to the grid resolution set, or create pseudo-random velocities for that instrument. The Lock function sets the particular instrument sound belonging to the current drum kit on that pattern, which lets you mix and match sounds from different drum kits.

When you have a pattern you're happy with, save the song in Hydrogen's native `.h2song` file format by choosing File ➤ Save As from the main menu bar. Choose File ➤ Show Song Properties to fill in metadata for your new project (see Figure 8-16). This information means that if you share your Hydrogen files with your community, they can look up who made the beat and why.

Figure 8-16. The "Song properties" dialog enables you to save and share details about your beat.

Chaining the Song Together

So far, you have a good basic beat, but it will start to get repetitive after a while. The Song Editor subwindow lists the patterns in the left margin; the main area is a timeline matrix. This subwindow lets you arrange the patterns you've already created in sequence, making a more complex beat possible. By default, when you create a new song in Hydrogen, one little blue square in the grid represents one bar of Pattern 1 at the start of the song. If you click the square to the right of it, it turns blue, and another bar of that pattern is played after the first bar. When you've created another drum pattern for variety, named Pattern 2, you can activate squares in that row to make Hydrogen play that pattern wherever you like in the song (see Figure 8-17).

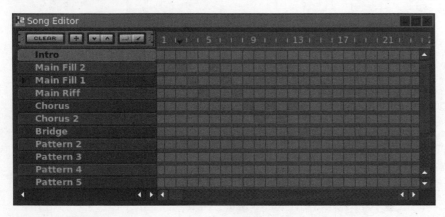

Figure 8-17. *The Song Editor allows numerous patterns to be chained together in any sequence.*

At the top of the left margin is a row of buttons that let you completely clear all patterns, a plus icon for creating new patterns, and up and down arrowheads for reordering the pattern list. Finally, a pair of buttons switch between Select mode (which enables selecting and then copying/pasting or moving the little blue squares) and the default Draw mode, in which you click the grid to add or delete squares. In Select mode, click a blue square until it turns orange (showing that it's selected), and then drag the mouse to move it. Alternatively, hold down the Ctrl key before selecting and dragging to copy and paste the original pattern square. If the cursor changes to a cross, which is triggered by moving the mouse as the button is held down, a selection rectangle is dragged out; you can then move or copy/paste multiple patterns simultaneously.

Right-clicking the pattern names in the left margin gives you the further choices of editing the pattern (in the pattern editor), copying or deleting the selected pattern, filling or clearing bars of the song sequence with that particular pattern, and editing the pattern's name via the Properties option. For instance, you can change Pattern 1 to Main Riff and then copy it to Main Fill 1 and Main Fill 2. Remember to select the pattern you want to edit with a click before continuing; otherwise, you can screw up the original.

To hear how all the patterns work together, you need to switch to Song mode, using the mode selector on the lower panel bar of the main Hydrogen window. By switching backward and forward, copying and altering sections, you can soon build up enough parts for a complete verse and chorus structure. Live musicians or singers also need an introduction bar to help them come in at the right time, just as a real drummer clicks their sticks four times before the song begins. To create an intro bar, copy a bridge pattern, rename it Intro, and edit it, removing everything but the final fill. Then, move the pattern sequence along by one bar to make room for the intro. By switching to Select mode, you can click and drag to select an area of patterns, and then click and drag them to the desired position.

Selecting the Right Sounds

If you're already bored with Hydrogen's default drum sounds, you'll be pleased to know that a number of extra ready-made drum kits are available. In Ubuntu, use Synaptic to install the hydrogen-drumkits package, and then restart Hydrogen. Select View ➤ "Show drumkit manager," and look at the alternative kits available on the Load tab (see Figure 8-18). Alternatively, visit the download page on the Hydrogen web site for links to individual kits, which you can install using the Import tab of the "Drumkit manager" subwindow.

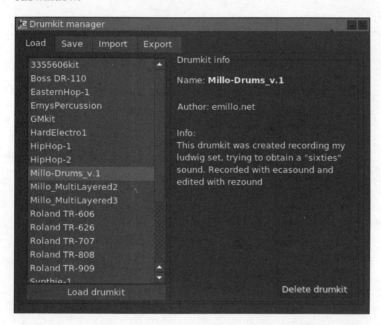

Figure 8-18. *Choose an alternative kit of drum sounds in Hydrogen's drumkit manager.*

By selecting a kit name and clicking the "Load drumkit" button, you can load the new kits while the song is playing, which enables you to easily preview the different sounds. The drum kits available for Hydrogen vary widely in sound, from samples of real acoustic kits to entirely synthesized bleeps and breaks, and can strongly affect the final feel of the track.

For more fine-grained control of the sounds, Hydrogen provides the facility to edit the individual components of the kit, via View ➤ "Show instrument editor." This small window displays detailed controls for the instrument that is currently selected in the pattern editor. Using this interface, you can create a custom drum kit with up to 32 samples and 16 velocity layers for each sample (see Figure 8-19). These layers are required for accurate simulation of an acoustic kit because real drums change sound depending on how hard you hit them. You can also adjust the envelope of the sound, or add filter and pitch effects for each instrument in the kit.

Figure 8-19. Hydrogen's instrument editor lets you tweak ready-made kits or create completely new, multilayered kits.

Next, you can add more effects to give the track some atmosphere. This type of effect is controlled via the Mixer subwindow. The main part of this window is laid out similarly to an analog sound mixer that you might find in a recording studio or live venue. Each component of the drum kit gets its own mixer strip, with controls to preview, mute, solo, and pan the sound; four rotary knobs to control effects (FX) level, and a vertical fader for the output level (see Figure 8-20).

Figure 8-20. Each instrument in the drum kit gets its own mixer strip.

Some interesting controls are in the mixer's right panel. Next to the Master Fader, which controls the overall output volume, are the Humanize functions, which you can use to add a touch of realism to Hydrogen's output (see Figure 8-21). These three knobs make it possible to adjust the influence of a random factor on the velocity and timing of each note played, and also to specify a *swing factor*—the amount of bounce applied to the rhythm. This can be essential for some jazz, reggae, and hip-hop feels. Careful use of these controls can really bring a drum track alive and make it sound almost organic.

Figure 8-21. *The Humanize controls allow for a more natural feel than the robotic beat that drum machines are typically known for.*

Below the Humanize knobs are two buttons: the top one toggles the peak level meters on and off, and the lower one opens the FX panel. Here you can have some fun with the four effects channels available to you. Click the Edit button for the first channel at the top, labeled "No plugin" by default. Doing so opens a plug-in properties window for that channel. Next, click the Select FX button, which brings up a further selection window with all the plug-ins installed on the system listed in the left-hand window. Hydrogen supports plug-ins in LADSPA format, which is the standard for audio effects on GNU/Linux. Ubuntu doesn't install any LADSPA plug-ins by default, but you can find hundreds by searching for *ladspa* in Synaptic Package Manager. If you install the swh-plugins, tap-plugins, and caps packages, that will get you off to a good start.

With the plug-ins installed, restart Hydrogen, and open the Select LADSPA FX window again. Plug-ins are listed by category, such as distortions, reverbs, and flangers (see Figure 8-22).

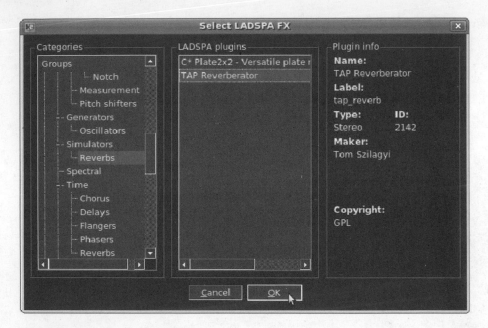

Figure 8-22. The Select LADSPA FX window lists effects plug-ins by category.

For instance, select TAP Reverberator, and click OK. The first of the four effects strips in the FX panel show that plug-in name.

Figure 8-23. The FX panel in the mixer shows selected effects plug-in names.

A small floating window with the controls for that individual effect plug-in also pops up (see Figure 8-24). If you're not familiar with the operation of recording studio effects boxes, then some of these controls may seem a little mysterious. By manipulating the faders, you can create a range of sounds from silence to ear-splitting noise; you're aiming for somewhere between these two extremes! Using this TAP Reverberator plug-in as an example, there is a control for *decay* in milliseconds, which is the amount of time it takes for the reverberation to fade away. This factor is related to the physical size of the room, building, or cavern for which the plug-in is trying to emulate the sound. There is also a control for the *wet level*, which means how much of the effect is applied to the original sound. Subtle effects often work better than obvious ones, so try dropping the wet level if the sound you're hearing is too harsh.

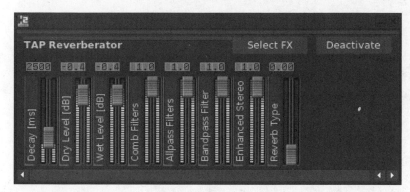

Figure 8-24. *Each effects plug-in has its own control window.*

The level of the effect applied to each specific instrument in the drum kit is controlled by the first of four knobs in that instrument's mixer strip. This is what is known as an *effects send control* on an analog mixer. You can turn up the reverb effect on the mixer strip of the snare and cymbals while leaving the bass drum *dry*, which means without the effect.

Exporting from Hydrogen

In order for this drum track to be used in other applications, you need to export it as a stereo audio file in .wav format. Hydrogen exports the file at whichever sample rate it's currently running at. Go to the Audio System tab of the File ➤ Preferences dialog if you want to change the sample rate setting. When all the details are set, choose File ➤ "Export song" to open a file browser dialog where you can give your project a name. Then, click the Export button, and wait for the progress bar to reach 100%. It's also possible to export the track as a MIDI file or hook up Hydrogen to an external MIDI source directly, so it can be run synchronously with other sequencers or multitrack recorders. The File ➤ Preferences dialog has tabs that enable you to control MIDI settings and Hydrogen's visual appearance.

If you've never used MIDI or don't know what it is, you need to read the next section. Synthesizer gurus and experienced digital music producers can skip ahead.

Sequencing with MIDI

In the early days of electronic music, there was no remote control or automation for synthesizers. You had to play all the notes on a keyboard in real time (see Figure 8-25), and the many and varied parameters of the instrument had to be set with knobs and patch cables before each session. Classical music notation, intended for a limited range of acoustic instruments, doesn't feature methods to represent these settings; even if you knew what the notes were meant to be, it was difficult to recall a particular synthesized sound without copious details being written down.

Figure 8-25. *A Minimoog synthesizer from the 1970s. Photo by Krash, public domain.*

As Moog early adopter Wendy Carlos discovered in the late 1960s, with the recording of *Switched-on Bach*, it was possible for a single musician to synthesize the sound of an orchestra. However, getting all the individual parts to synchronize on a tape recording was a serious technical challenge. It wasn't until the early 1980s that synthesizer manufacturers came up with a workable solution, in the form of the Musical Instrument Digital Interface protocol (MIDI). A testament to the power of open standards, MIDI was almost universally adopted in music hardware devices and remains a standard feature on electronic instruments today.

The original MIDI standard uses five-pin DIN sockets, which look uncannily like those found on cheap and nasty music-center stereos of the disco era (see Figure 8-26). However, no audio signal passes down the MIDI cable, digital or analog. Instead, a series of messages trigger particular notes at a given velocity, changes in instrument sound, and other parameters. The amount of data involved is therefore relatively small, compared to sampling the output of the synth in a `.wav` file.

Figure 8-26. *The obsolete five-pin DIN plug is still used for MIDI data. Photo by Boffy B, public domain.*

Programming a MIDI synthesizer and having it play back music on demand, without necessarily having to play a piano keyboard, became known as *sequencing*. Computers of the mid-1980s could be used to record, edit, and display MIDI data, even though multitrack audio recording on PCs was still a few years away. In particular, the Atari ST, with its built-in MIDI sockets, proved very popular with electronic artists and spawned whole new genres of music. Later in that decade, sampling sequencers like Akai's MPC range of embedded devices became essential tools for hip-hop and dance music producers. These limited data requirements mean that obsolete PCs and low-powered embedded systems are still good for fun with MIDI, when GNU/Linux and Free Software have been installed.

Conventionally, MIDI networks use a ring topology, so you can chain together multiple devices and trigger them all from the same sequencer. To avoid clashes between instruments, 16 MIDI channels are available; according to the General MIDI standard, drum instruments are usually triggered on channel 10. General MIDI dictates specific types of sounds for specific program-change messages, with a piano sound being the first of 128 instrument presets. It enables a MIDI file created on one machine to sound similar when played back on another; but unless you need this type of compatibility, it's not compulsory to use General MIDI presets.

MIDI on GNU/Linux

The Advanced Linux Sound Architecture (ALSA) sound-card drivers found in the Linux kernel have MIDI support and a built-in sequencer as standard. You can't use this sequencer to make music directly, but it's useful for connecting between hardware MIDI sockets, sequencer applications, and software instruments.

If you have the on-board type of soundcard, you may not have hardware MIDI sockets available. Connecting an external piano keyboard with five-pin MIDI sockets to a PC like this can be achieved with a small MIDI USB adaptor, which should work with ALSA as long as it's *class compliant*. (This means it meets the standard for these devices and doesn't need a special driver.) Some MIDI interfaces from M-Audio and Tascam aren't class compliant, although they can be supported with a firmware upload available from the web site `http://usb-midi-fw.sourceforge.net` and in several GNU/Linux distros. Other, newer MIDI instruments have USB sockets built in, removing the need for the DIN socket adaptor.

To list the MIDI output ports available on a GNU/Linux system, first open a terminal (on Ubuntu, choose Applications ➤ Accessories ➤ Terminal). Next, type in the following command:

```
$ aconnect -lo
```

The system responds:

```
client 14: Midi Through [type=kernel]
    0 Midi Through Port-0'
```

In a similar fashion, you can list input ports with

```
$ aconnect -li
```

to which the response may be

```
client 0: System [type=kernel]
    0 Timer
    1 Announce
        Connecting To: 15:0
```

```
client 14: Midi Through [type=kernel]
    0 Midi Through Port-0'
```

This example is from a typical desktop system with an on-board sound chipset, so only ALSA's MIDI through port is listed; there are no MIDI hardware ports with which to connect external devices. This need not prevent you from sequencing MIDI data and making music, because any PC made in the last decade or so has enough CPU power to use a virtual instrument. That means the synthesis is done in software, instead of having a MIDI-capable chip on the sound card or motherboard. Go back to the PCs of the mid-90s, like the original Pentiums, and you'd often find a Yamaha OPL3 chip inside—a crude synthesizer by today's standards, but a real MIDI instrument in its own right. Cost-cutting in PC manufacturing means that contemporary systems rely on the CPU instead, but due to increase in execution speed over the years this is no longer a big deal. A recent machine can run many concurrent virtual instruments without strain, as long as the code is written with efficiency in mind.

In the next section, you use the sequencer seq24 (GNU/Linux, Windows) to trigger AlsaModularSynth (GNU/Linux), also known by its initials as ams. This virtual instrument is a software emulation of the original Moog Modular synth of the 1960s and is a useful tool for learning about synthesis principles. It also makes great bass sounds; and, unlike the real thing, it doesn't go out of tune or weigh half a ton.

Getting Seq24 and AlsaModularSynth

The seq24 sequencer (download from www.filter24.org/seq24/) at first glance is easy to dismiss as a simple application (see Figure 8-27). It doesn't have the bells and whistles of contemporary proprietary sequencing applications, and it looks minimal compared to its Free Software counterparts. In this simplicity lies seq24's great strength—it does one job well, and perhaps because of that, it's stable and doesn't take long to learn. Former users of the Atari ST or Akai MPC should find the interface very familiar.

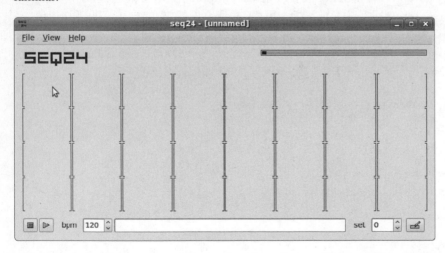

Figure 8-27. Seq24's opening window. Not much to see here, but don't be fooled by the simplicity.

■ **Note** If you're running Ubuntu, make sure you install seq24 version 0.9.0 or later. The seq24 package 0.8.7 in Ubuntu Jaunty is buggy and crashes as soon as you try to create a sequence. You can install version 0.9.0 on Jaunty using the package from Debian Sid (available via `http://packages.debian.org/sid/seq24`) and the Gdebi helper application. On Ubuntu Karmic or later, use the Add/Remove Applications tool to install seq24.

You should be able to find a ready-made package of seq24 for other GNU/Linux distros. If there's no menu entry for the application after you install it, you can start the sequencer from a terminal by typing `seq24` and pressing the Enter key. For the Windows version, it's probably best to download direct from the seq24 homepage; you also have to download a couple of Free Software library packages that seq24 needs to run.

AlsaModularSynth is available via the project's homepage—`http://alsamodular.sourceforge.net`— although you're likely to find a package available for your existing GNU/Linux distro. It's included in Ubuntu as well as in various multimedia package repositories, under the name ams. Note that the Ubuntu package of ams doesn't work unless the JACK (GNU/Linux, Mac) sound server is running, which is a reasonable default in an environment where multiple synthesizers are likely to be used (see Figure 8-28). Therefore, you should also install the jackd (server) and qjackctl (control panel) packages in the Add/Remove Applications tool before attempting to run AlsaModularSynth. After installation, you can find the qjackctl program in Ubuntu on the Applications ➤ Sound & Video menu, under the more user-friendly name of JACK Control.

Figure 8-28. The JACK sound server shares audio hardware between applications.

To get started with JACK, click the Setup button. Unless you already tweaked your system, uncheck the Realtime box, and check the Soft Mode box (see Figure 8-29).

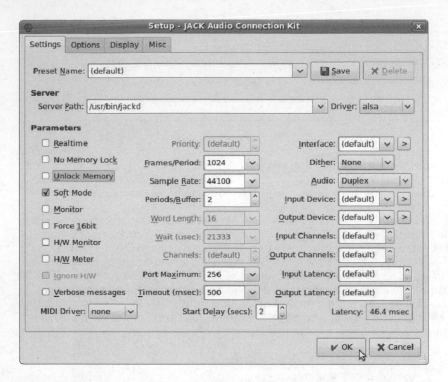

Figure 8-29. *Unless your system is already set up for it, disable the Realtime feature, and enable Soft Mode for now.*

On a stock Ubuntu Jaunty system, JACK won't start unless Realtime mode is switched off this way. Soft Mode disguises some of the limitations of running JACK on a standard Linux kernel. (You look at more advanced settings for JACK and the kernel in the next chapter.)

Click OK to close the Setup window, and click the Start button with the green triangle. This tells JACK to take control of your sound card and share it among all compatible audio applications, which are known as JACK *clients.* The JACK Control window displays the word *Started* in yellow at upper left in its black window. The current load on the system is also displayed as a percentage, alongside the JACK sample rate (see Figure 8-30).

Figure 8-30. *JACK Control displays the load on the system and the current sample rate.*

Running AlsaModularSynth

On startup, AlsaModularSynth offers a blank window by default. The Ubuntu version sometimes displays an error dialog with the text "Could not open file"—it's harmless, so click OK to close the dialog. To get some sound out of this synthesizer, you need to load a patch by choosing File ➤ Load Patch from the main menu. Synthesizer parameters are still called *patches*, even though the patching cables from the Moog days are now virtual—just a line drawn on the display. The ams package for your distro should provide plenty of demo patches, located in a directory such as `/usr/share/doc/ams/demos/` (see Figure 8-31).

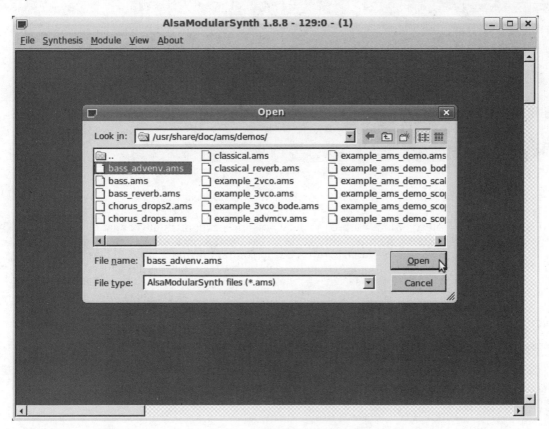

Figure 8-31. *You must load a patch file before AlsaModularSynth makes any sound.*

When the patch is loaded, you can see the modules of the synthesizer and how they're connected (see Figure 8-32). The last module is PCM Out, which is where the audio leaves the synthesizer and goes to the JACK sound server. You can rearrange the patch cables in any order you like to create different sounds, although if you're new to synthesis concepts, it's best to start from the demo patches provided.

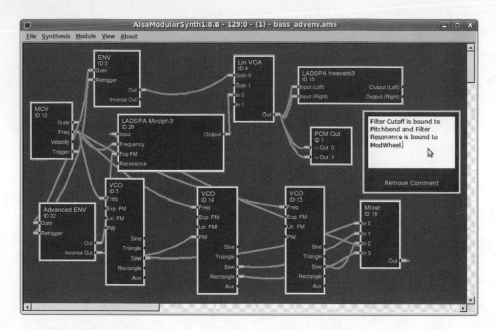

Figure 8-32. AlsaModularSynth with the demo bass_advenv patch loaded

You may need to connect the ams output to the JACK sound server manually, depending on how your GNU/Linux distro has this program set up. To do so, use the Connect button in JACK Control. When the Connections window opens, make sure you're looking at the Audio tab, and find the entry for ams on the left side, listed under Output Ports. On the right side, your sound card is labeled system, listed under Input Ports. Highlight both sets of ports by clicking them, and then click the Connect button in the lower-left corner of this window. A diagonal line indicates that the ports are connected, and the synthesizer can now send audio to the sound card (see Figure 8-33). You can manage all kinds of complex connection paths this way.

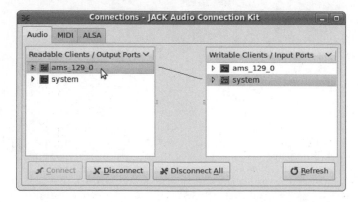

Figure 8-33. Use the Audio tab of the Connections window to hook up the output of music programs to the hardware.

You can also connect an external MIDI keyboard or virtual keyboard, such as Virtual Keyboard (GNU/Linux), to test that the synth is working. You can download the vkeybd package from www.alsa-project.org/~tiwai/alsa.html or install it in Ubuntu using the Add/Remove Applications tool. You can play either with the mouse cursor or with the QWERTY keys Z to M for the natural notes, and A to L for the sharps and flats. Notes are highlighted in blue when they're triggered (see Figure 8-34).

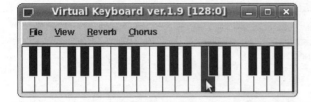

Figure 8-34. Virtual Keyboard is great for testing your MIDI setup if you don't have the hardware available.

Although you can manage these MIDI connections using aconnect on the command line, the ALSA sequencer tab of the JACK Control applet makes the task much more user friendly.

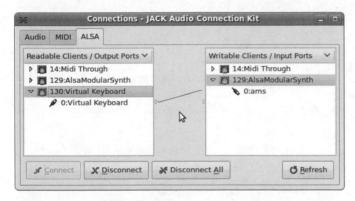

Figure 8-35. You can use the JACK Control applet to make a MIDI connection from Virtual Keyboard to AlsaModularSynth.

Between the Audio tab and the ALSA tab is another connection tab labeled MIDI, which is provided to manage routing under the new JACK MIDI standard. You don't need to use this tab for most MIDI applications on GNU/Linux yet, so its label is a little confusing.

Beginning the Sequence

Returning to seq24, you're now in a position to sequence your first loop. The application's main window is divided into an eight-by-four grid of brackets, each of which can contain an individual sequence. Right-click inside the upper-left bracket, and select New from the pop-up menu. A *piano-roll* window appears, so-called because it resembles the paper rolls fed into mechanical pianos. In this early form of automation, punched holes of various lengths represented the length and pitch of musical notes. Here, you can right-click the paper of the piano roll, and the mouse pointer changes into a pencil icon. Keeping the right button held down, you can click anywhere on the piano roll to place notes.

To edit a note, click to select it; it turns orange. Then, click and drag to move it on the piano roll, or press the Delete key to remove it. By default, these are sixteenth notes; but you can easily change this setting using the Note Length button in the second row of controls from the top of the window. The top row of controls allows you to set the time signature and the loop's length in bars—by default, it's 4/4 time and a one-bar loop, which can get a little repetitive (see Figure 8-36).

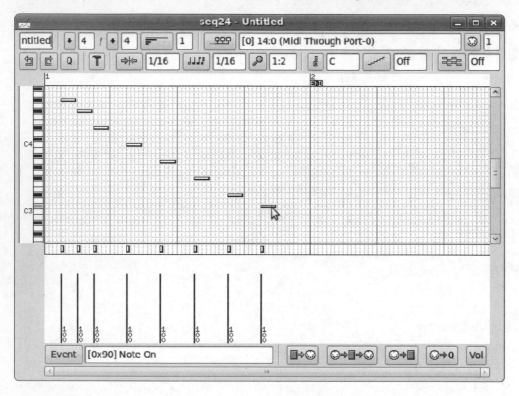

Figure 8-36. *A simple descending bassline one-bar loop, set up in seq24*

At the bottom of the window, vertical bars indicate the velocity value of the Note On message, equivalent to how hard the key on a MIDI piano is pressed. This is the same as the velocity control in Hydrogen, which you read about earlier in this chapter. By clicking and dragging, you can adjust these bars to vary the velocity of the note messages sent to the synthesizer. One difference between this velocity control and the equivalent in Hydrogen is that seq24 shows the numerical velocity value to the right of the vertical line (see Figure 8-37). 100 is the default velocity for each note, but the MIDI standard allows a maximum velocity of 127.

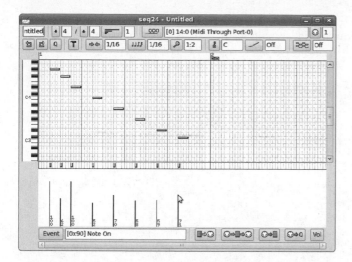

Figure 8-37. Note-on velocities are adjusted in the same way as in Hydrogen, but the velocity number is also shown.

In the upper-left corner, give the sequence a name that's more interesting than the default of Untitled. Then, in the upper-right corner, change the MIDI output device from (MIDI Through Port) to (ams) by clicking the Select Output Bus button, to the left of the output device label. The default setting of MIDI channel 1, in the box to the right, can be left alone for now. You next have to click the button in the lower-right corner with the green arrow pointing to a five-pin MIDI socket, for which the explanatory tooltip is "Sequence dumps data to MIDI bus." Otherwise, seq24 doesn't send any notes to AlsaModularSynth.

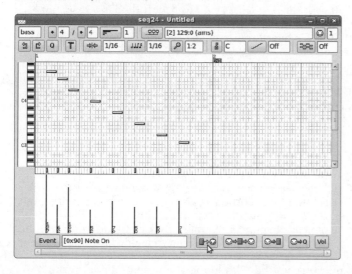

Figure 8-38. Name the loop, connect the MIDI output to the synth, and then make sure seq24 is in the right mode to send data.

Close or minimize this window, and click the green play button in the lower-left corner of the main seq24 window. A cursor line scrolls across your named loop in its bracket. If the loop has a white background and the synthesizer isn't being triggered, click it. It should then turn from white to black (see Figure 8-39); and if AlsaModularSynth is connected correctly, you start to hear your loop.

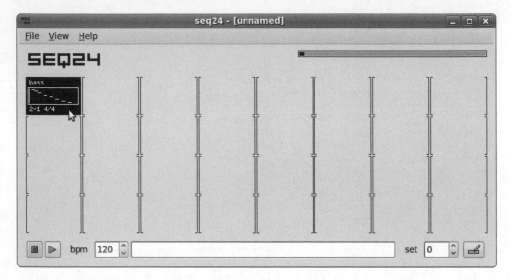

Figure 8-39. *The seq24 loop doesn't trigger the synthesizer until it's activated, when its background turns black.*

You can create as many loops as you want, pointing to different software or hardware synthesizers, and then turn individual sequences on and off with clicks. It works very well with a touchscreen, not unlike triggering loops on a hardware sequencer via its rubber pads. A low-budget alternative is to get the seq24 window in focus and then use QWERTY keyboard shortcuts to trigger the loops. The first row of loops is triggered by the number keys, starting with 1; the second row is triggered by the keys QWERTYUI; and so on.

You're not limited to the 32 loops in the brackets—in the middle of the main window, you can name any number of sets, numbered from 0 to 31. A loop that's playing in a particular set keeps playing when you switch to another set. Loops can be cut and pasted from one set to another with a right-click.

The Seq24 Song Editor

If clicking the loops to trigger them live doesn't appeal to you, you can also chain sequences together into a complete song. Click the stop button in the lower-left corner of the seq24 main window to halt playback, and then click the pencil button in the lower-right corner. The song editor appears, with any loops you've made listed at left. You can insert these loops into the song in the same way as for individual notes; by right-clicking to make the pencil icon appear, then left clicking in the window while keeping the right mouse button held down (see Figure 8-40). Click the green triangle Play button to hear your song played back.

Repeating the sequence isn't enabled until you click the "Play looped between L and R" button, which is to the right of the play button. By default, the song is set to repeat after four bars. You can set the start and end of the repeating section using left and right clicks, respectively, in the timeline above the individual loops.

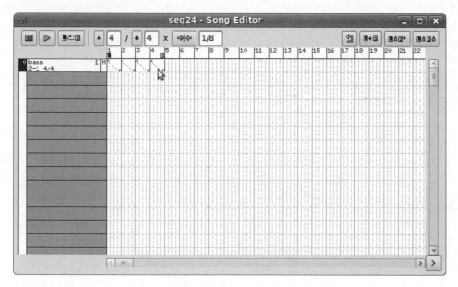

Figure 8-40. Seq24's song editor lets you construct complete compositions.

You can save your project as a standard MIDI file in binary format by choosing File ➤ Save As in the main window of the program. Seq24 doesn't object if you neglect to give the MIDI file a suffix, but by convention these files are usually given the **.mid** extension.

The Seq24 Configuration File

On startup, seq24 reads in preferences from the file ~/**.seq24rc** (a hidden file in your home directory). Close seq24 first, and you can then modify this human-readable file in a terminal with a text editor—for example, using the nano editor:

```
$ nano ~/.seq24rc
```

By default, seq24 manages MIDI connections itself, indicated in the following stanza of the **.seq24rc** file:

```
[manual-alsa-ports]
# set to 1 if you want seq24 to create its own alsa ports and
# not connect to other clients
0
```

This 0 in the last line is a user-friendly setting, because as you've seen, you can select the name of the output device or application from a drop-down list in the piano-roll window. Setting this value to 1 means the drop-down list instead lists 16 MIDI ports, which you can then connect to software instruments or hardware sockets using JACK Control.

Another option is to use JACK's transport features. This means several applications can have their start position and tempo synchronized. It's switched off by default, but you can enable seq24 as the transport master by setting the following 0 values to 1:

```
[jack-transport]

# jack_transport - Enable sync with JACK Transport.
0

# jack_master - Seq24 will attempt to serve as JACK Master.
0

# jack_master_cond -  Seq24 will fail to be master if there is already a master set.
0
```

Save the `.seq24rc` file (using Ctrl+O in nano), and restart seq24 to see this feature in action. In the central window of JACK Control, with the black background, look at the lower line, in green. When you click the play button in seq24, JACK Control says Rolling; the tempo of the transport is displayed, and a time clock counts up on the right (see Figure 8-41). Just beneath this are blue icon buttons for rewind, backward, play, pause, and forward. These are remote controls for JACK's transport, which you can use to manipulate seq24's song sequence as well as any other JACK transport-compatible applications that are running. Some other Free Software applications can output their audio to JACK but don't support the transport feature.

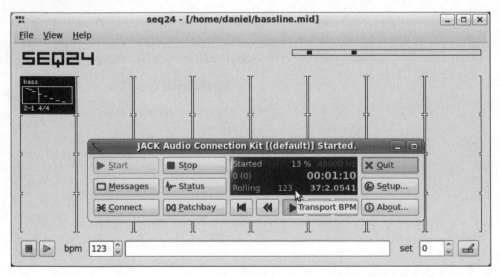

Figure 8-41. Seq24's play button gets JACK's transport moving. Notice that the tempo figure of 123 beats per minute is in sync.

Triggering Hydrogen Drums with Seq24

Because the Hydrogen drum machine accepts both MIDI input and JACK transport control, you have two options for synchronizing it with sequences created in seq24. You can either make a drum pattern in seq24 and trigger Hydrogen on MIDI channel 10 or create the pattern in Hydrogen's sequencer and use seq24's play button to get the transport rolling. Hydrogen accepts MIDI input on any channel, but you can get specific by choosing File ➤ Preferences ➤ MIDI System ➤ Channel. If you want to, you can use both methods at once to synchronize different drum patterns created in each application (see Figure 8-42).

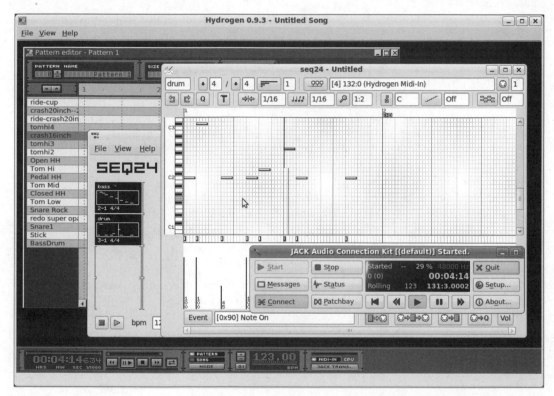

Figure 8-42. *Seq24 triggering AlsaModularSynth and Hydrogen at the same time*

Remember to deactivate the "Record keyboard/MIDI events" button in Hydrogen before you attempt this link-up; otherwise, Hydrogen's pattern editor fills with notes when you click the vertical note preview piano bar to the left of seq24's piano roll.

Further Reading

Not many books are available about making music with Free Software, but you can find quite a few tutorials online. Try the home pages of the applications mentioned in this chapter for specific information, and go to the `www.linuxaudio.org/resources` portal for links to more general help.

Other Useful Programs

There are many, many Free Software music-making applications. Here are some that follow directly from this chapter:

- *Sound Juicer* (GNU/Linux): A *ripper*, meaning a program that extracts music data from audio CDs and turns it into a format you can use with programs like Mixxx. It's straightforward and easy to use. Sound Juicer's home page is `www.burtonini.com/blog/computers/sound-juicer/`.

- *Grip* (GNU/Linux): Another CD ripper that can be used with Mixxx, available from `http://nostatic.org/grip` and in many GNU/Linux distros. Grip is more complicated than Sound Juicer, but it gives you greater control over the ripping process.

- *Jackbeat* (GNU/Linux, Mac): Another Free Software drum machine, available from the project homepage at `http://jackbeat.samalyse.org`. It's simpler in appearance than Hydrogen but has some interesting features.

- *Rosegarden* (GNU/Linux): A more complex MIDI sequencer than seq24, with audio recording and music notation features. Its home page is at `www.rosegardenmusic.com`.

- *Qtractor* (GNU/Linux): An alternative MIDI and audio sequencer, aimed more at dance music producers than notation-reading musicians. The Qtractor home page is at `http://qtractor.sourceforge.net`.

All of these programs are available in Ubuntu using the Add/Remove Programs application.

CHAPTER 9

■ ■ ■

Recording Audio

From Disc to Tape to Disk

Since Victorian inventors first recorded sound onto cylinders and discs, many competing technologies have been used to capture audio and play it back. Disc cutters and wire recorders gave way to magnetic tape as the primary medium after an American serviceman, Jack Mullin, "liberated" two Magnetophon recorders from a Nazi radio station in the final months of World War II. Returning to the USA, Mullin demonstrated the recorders to Bing Crosby in Hollywood. Crosby saw the potential for prerecording his own radio shows and invested in the Ampex company in order that the machines could be produced commercially (see Figure 9-1). (If you don't know who Bing Crosby was, ask your grandmother.) Analog recordings on tape dominated the music industry for decades, ranging in size from gigantic Studer two-inch tape machines down to miniature Nagra eighth-inch machines, used in any spy movie of the period.

Figure 9-1. An Ampex tape recorder from 1965, with its cover removed. Photo by Gregory Maxwell, GNU FDL.

In the 1980s and 90s, digital tape formats including DASH, DAT, and ADAT became popular, only to be replaced in turn by computer-based recorders that use hard disk, CD-R, or Flash memory card storage. A major advantage of computer recording is that the format is file-based, which means any part of the audio can be accessed at random, almost instantaneously. Contrast this to the linear, time-consuming process of having to spool through tape to find the part you want to change. This is why computer-based manipulation of audio and video is sometimes called *nonlinear editing*.

Recording direct to files on disk can make it faster to transfer material from machine to machine, too. Tapes need to be played back into the digital audio workstation (DAW) before editing, which can take up to an hour each time depending on the length of tape and the speed of the machine. The transfer time adds up if you've got a lot of audio to work on. However, for restoring or remixing older material that exists only on tape or vinyl, this is a valid approach. That's because digital audio editing on a computer offers great control without the generation loss of analog copies or the risks involved in slicing tape with razor blades.

The DAW part of the chain was desk-bound initially, because the hardware requirements for editing audio in real time were beyond the capabilities of the CPUs found in PCs and laptops. Specialized and proprietary digital signal processing (DSP) cards, each costing thousands of dollars, were required to do the job. As CPU capabilities improved about a decade ago, DAW software could be run on the host processor without needing the expensive DSP cards. It then became possible to run some DAW software on a laptop, away from the studio—recordings could be made and edited in the field.

The Input Side

One major drawback to this approach was that the audio hardware on PCs and laptops was universally poor and didn't begin to approach professional standards. As a workaround, recording engineers use external audio interfaces, typically connected by PCI cards or FireWire, to obtain acceptable input quality. Meanwhile, audio chipsets on PCs and laptops have begun to improve, partly driven by the home cinema market; it's not uncommon to find a digital audio output on an ordinary PC now.

The results you can achieve from digital, computer-based recording still depend greatly on the analog signal you put into the machine. When you record acoustic instruments and the human voice, a better-quality microphone and interface make an obvious difference. The cheap plastic microphones that are bundled with PCs and domestic hi-fi's aren't much good for audio recording projects, because they reproduce the audible frequency range unevenly and generate obvious noise in the signal.

For the last 50 years or so, professional recording studios have relied on a microphone design that hasn't changed much over time. Indeed, the original Neumann and Telefunken branded condenser microphones, devised in Berlin in the late 1940s and early 1950s, are highly sought after by contemporary studios. In more recent decades, millions of Neumann copies have been turned out by Russian and Chinese factories at a tiny fraction of the price of the originals (see Figure 9-2).

Figure 9-2. *The Oktava MK-319, a Russian condenser microphone based on the classic German designs of the 1940s and 1950s. Photo by Gregory Maxwell, GNU FDL.*

The typical large-diaphragm condenser microphone has a circular capsule about an inch across, suspended inside a wire basket to protect it from damage. The circuit inside the main body of the microphone is powered using voltage across the conductors of the microphone cable, instead of a separate power lead; this arrangement is known by audio engineers as *phantom power*. If you have a microphone that needs phantom power, which by convention is usually 48 volts, then you also need equipment that can provide that power in the cable. Not all equipment that has the standard three-pin XLR socket has phantom power, and some battery-powered condensers and vintage ribbon microphones can be damaged by the voltage, so this is something to watch out for. Dynamic microphones, which don't require phantom or battery power, are generally safe to be plugged into a powered socket—but if you aren't sure, check the manufacturer's documentation.

■ **Tip** Phantom-powered microphones shouldn't be plugged in or unplugged while the mixer or other equipment they're connected to is switched on. This can make a loud, nasty bang noise in your speakers or headphones, and probably isn't good for the microphone either. Instead, connect the microphone first, then power up the mixer or push the phantom power button, and finally, turn up the speaker or headphone level control. Preferably, do this half an hour before recording begins, so the microphone can warm up; this dries out any moisture that has collected in the condenser capsule. Moisture in a phantom-powered microphone can add random spikes of noise to your recording. This is why new microphones are often packaged with sachets of silica gel.

For recording one voice or instrument at a time, you can now buy a low-cost condenser microphone with a USB interface built in. Instead of the traditional analog interface with a three-pin XLR plug (see Figure 9-3), these newer microphones feature an analog-to-digital convertor chipset that is often USB class-compliant, advertised under the misleading slogan "works without a driver." In fact, these interfaces use a generic USB audio driver, which is provided on GNU/Linux systems by ALSA. The great thing about these USB condenser microphones is that they bypass the need for a separate hardware interface with XLR sockets, which is particularly advantageous in a laptop or mobile recording situation. They aren't so useful if you already have a collection of analog condenser microphones or need to use several of them at once. In that case, you need a separate audio interface and possibly an analog mixer with phantom power, too.

Figure 9-3. *Decent analog microphones standardized on the three-pin XLR connector, shown here in female and male variants, many years ago. Some newer microphones connect via USB instead. Photo by Michael Piotrowski, GNU FDL.*

However, to get started, any microphone that works enables you to begin learning the techniques of sound recording and editing. Particularly if you're using a condenser microphone, it's a good idea to buy or make a *pop filter* for recording speech or vocal tracks. This is a simple circular wire or plastic frame about five or six inches in diameter with a covering of mesh fabric, attached to the microphone stand. You can make a pretty good one out of a wire coat-hanger and a nylon stocking! The function of this device is to sit between the sensitive microphone capsule and the human mouth, in order to disperse excess energy from plosive sounds like the letter *P*. Otherwise, these sounds can sometimes be too loud on a recording, because of the rush of air hitting the microphone capsule.

Making a Podcast

The podcasting phenomenon means that more people than ever before have the ability to produce and distribute audio content worldwide. You don't need a broadcast license or to be affiliated with an established media outlet, and the equipment is very affordable and accessible.

The name *podcasting* is misleading, because an Apple iPod has never been required to make or listen to podcasts. This name caught on after web developers began to offer automated syndication of audio files over the Internet in the early 2000s. Audio files had been shared through simple web links for years before that, but podcasting used the power of the Web's emerging Really Simple Syndication (RSS) standard to alert subscribers to fresh content. RSS enabled podcast producers to build a regular audience quickly and at minimal cost, to the consternation of traditional broadcasters who had millions of dollars invested in infrastructure and government licenses.

One of the most popular tools for creating podcasts is Audacity (GNU/Linux, Windows, Mac), which is both an easy to use multitrack recorder and a fast editor (see Figure 9-4). Audacity is probably the most widely used of all Free Software multimedia applications, having enjoyed more than 60 million direct downloads from the `http://audacity.sourceforge.net` web site by mid 2009.

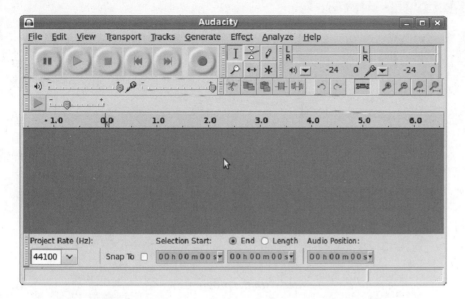

Figure 9-4. *Audacity is a popular Free Software audio editor, available for several platforms.*

The program is also distributed by microphone manufacturers with podcasting bundles, typically comprising a USB condenser microphone, headphones, and accessories. Audacity packages are included in most GNU/Linux distributions; and in Ubuntu you can install this program using the Add/Remove Programs application. The 1.3.x series of Audacity releases are officially beta versions, but they are very usable and contain so many new features that the stable 1.2.x series isn't worth installing unless you have a specific requirement for it.

After installation on Ubuntu, Audacity appears on the Applications ➤ Sound & Video menu. Running the program for the first time causes a dialog to pop up, which invites you to select the language you prefer for Audacity's user interface (see Figure 9-5).

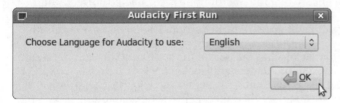

Figure 9-5. *Choose your preferred language from Audacity's drop-down menu.*

Next, a window displaying Audacity's built-in help tutorials appears. There is also a link to a PDF file of the full Audacity manual (see Figure 9-6).

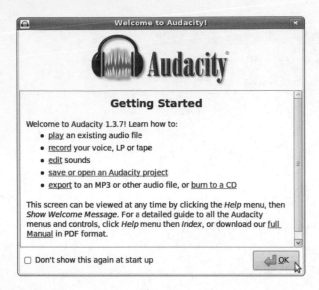

Figure 9-6. *Audacity has a number of tutorials integrated with the program.*

Close this help window by clicking the OK button, to view the main Audacity interface. You see the large, obvious buttons for pause, play, stop, rewind, fast-forward, and record, in the manner of a tape recorder. However, Audacity isn't a real-time editor, based on a tape machine analogy; instead, it uses a design in which edits and effects are applied as quickly as the computer can manage. Internally, large audio files are broken into blocks of approximately 1MB each, which means processing happens only on the relevant blocks of the file. This is the main reason Audacity can apply edits quickly to very large audio files, even on older, slower computers.

The First Recording

To begin making your podcast, you must first ensure that the microphone is connected correctly and that the sound level is about right. Too quiet, and noise will be apparent in the recording when the listener turns up their volume control. Too loud, and there will be distortion. Digital distortion sounds much worse than the same problem on an analog tape machine, where you can sometimes get away with running the meters hot. In this context, *hot* means into the part of the scale past the 0 on the sound-level meter—the place you're not supposed to go. Sound meters are labeled backward, so 0 is the maximum loudness and quieter sounds are expressed as numbers decreasing below 0. Therefore, on a sound meter, -3 is louder than -6. (You read more about audio metering in the next chapter.)

Plug in your microphone, and click Audacity's record button; the red recording meter at upper right in the Audacity window flickers toward the 0 mark on its right. As the timeline cursor begins to roll, a new audio track with a waveform is drawn in the middle of the interface. The blue waveform displayed by Audacity is really a graph of amplitude (or subjectively, loudness) against time of the digital audio data being captured.

If you're lucky, you'll get the input level about right the first time. More likely, you'll need to make some input level adjustments. When the recording is too quiet, the waveform drawn in the new track is shown as a series of small bumps near the blue horizontal center line (see Figure 9-7). You may recall from school lessons that sound in real life is a wave of pressure variations in air. The quieter the recorded sound is, the smaller the digital representation of that sound wave is drawn on the screen.

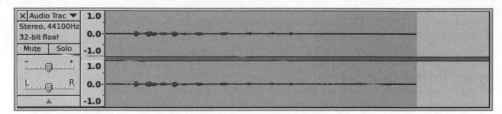

Figure 9-7. The first attempt at stereo recording results in a level that is too low.

Audacity records in stereo by default, even if the microphone is mono; so you see two waveforms, one above the other. Also by default, each time you click the record button, a new track begins at the current position on the timeline. If you want to append a recording onto the currently selected track, hold down the Shift key as you click the record button. The currently selected track has a darker gray panel and a bright yellow outline around its window.

Audacity has a built-in microphone level control located below the tape recorder controls, but you probably need to open the system's audio mixer applet and change some values there too. In Ubuntu, this applet has a loudspeaker icon next to the clock, in the upper-right corner of the GNOME desktop. Click the Recording tab, be sure the Capture and Microphone fader aren't muted, adjust the level of the fader, and try another recording (see Figure 9-8).

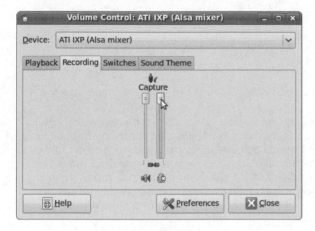

Figure 9-8. You probably need to adjust the system's input-level controls and capture switches.

With the sound mixer applet open, if there is no control for the microphone input, it's possible that the fader has been hidden by default. On Ubuntu, right-click the speaker icon, and select Open Volume Control. Then, click the Preferences button. In the small window that pops up, you can set which controls are visible in the main Volume Control window (see Figure 9-9).

Figure 9-9. *Hidden parts of Ubuntu's volume control can be made visible using the Preferences dialog.*

If your recording level is too high, Audacity's waveform display makes the problem obvious. The blue waveforms are *clipped* above the 0 level, which means data from the sound recording has been lost; audible distortion is the result. Instead of smooth, rounded peaks at different levels, the tops of the waveforms are flat and at the same level, like a garden hedge that's been cut with electric clippers (see Figure 9-10). Because clipping involves the loss of audio data, it's almost impossible to repair perfectly; that's why it's so important to get your input level right and avoid clipping in the initial recording. In a well-recorded track, none of the waveform peaks should reach the top of their respective window. You're aiming for a happy medium: not too quiet, not too loud, and certainly not clipped.

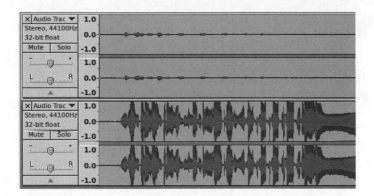

Figure 9-10. *Clipping, the loss of audio data, spells trouble. In this example, the upper track is too quiet, but the lower track is too loud and clipped.*

In the days of analog tape recorders, it was necessary to get the recording as loud as you dared, because the inherent noise of the system punished a sound engineer who allowed too much headroom between the peaks in amplitude and the maximum 0 level. With digital recording and a decent microphone, there is much less inherent noise, so you can afford to leave significantly more headroom. This extra headroom lets you capture a greater range of sounds without distortion, including sudden loud sounds that you hadn't allowed headroom for when setting the input level (see Figure 9-11).

To the left of each track window is a panel containing the track name, whether it's mono or stereo, and the sample rate in Hertz (Hz). There is also a label for the track's bit depth, which indicates the resolution at which Audacity processes the data. Normal audio CDs are made with 16-bit data, but now 24-bit recording and 32-bit processing are common in PC and laptop-based audio software. The more bits of data you have for each sample, the more subtle and natural the recorded track—just as when you're working with greater color depth in digital photography.

The panel includes Mute and Solo buttons, which are useful when you're working with multiple tracks. Below these buttons are horizontal level and stereo pan faders, which enable you to adjust the balance of different tracks in the overall mix. To rename a track, click the small black triangle on the right side of the top bar, and then select Name; a small dialog box pops up.

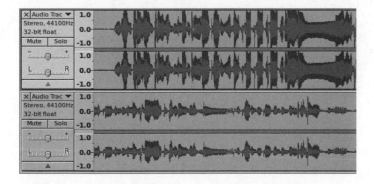

Figure 9-11. *Below the track that's too loud, and therefore clipped, another track has been recorded, where the level is just about right.*

Splitting, Cutting, and Pasting

It's very unlikely that your podcast will be recorded in one take without any mistakes or level problems. Fortunately, the ability to have fine control over edits is one of the strengths of computer-based recording. Audacity has six icon buttons on its main toolbar, to the right of the big record button, arranged in two rows of three. At upper left is the Selection tool, which has an I-beam icon and cursor. Immediately below this is a magnifying glass icon, which represents the Zoom tool. Pause the rolling timeline cursor at the appropriate point, and use the magnifying glass cursor to zoom into a part of the audio that you want to edit out.

Make sure the correct track is selected, if you have more than one, by clicking in the panel beneath the stereo pan control. Then, switch to the Selection tool, and click and drag horizontally to select part of the waveform in that track. The selected part of the waveform has a darker background than the rest of the track (see Figure 9-12).

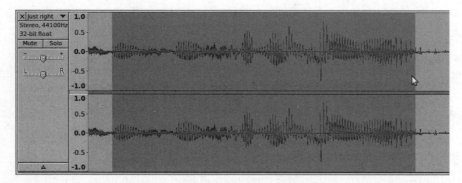

Figure 9-12. The background of the selected part of the waveform turns darker.

If you now click Audacity's play button, with the green triangle, you hear just the selection; if the Solo button isn't set for the selected track, you also hear any other tracks that aren't muted. On Audacity's Edit menu, a number of editing features are available for the selection, including Cut, Copy, Paste, and Delete.

However, because working with audio is slightly different from working with text or images, a couple of other editing features are very useful for fast and accurate work. Before you take any editing action, use the Edit ➤ Find Zero Crossings feature (keyboard shortcut Z) to make sure your selection begins and ends at points where the waveform crosses the blue center line. Otherwise, your spliced audio segments may be left with ugly joins, making an audible glitch where the two waveforms meet. Another useful feature is Edit ➤ Trim, which removes all of the audio in the track except the selection (see Figure 9-13).

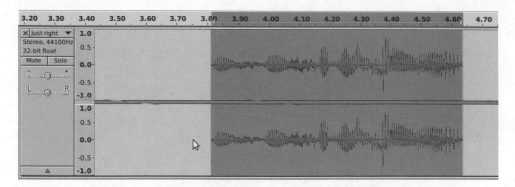

Figure 9-13. Audacity's Trim feature deletes the part of the audio outside the selection.

When you're editing a complex or lengthy recording, it makes sense to take advantage of Audacity's multitrack features to organize your project. It's a bit like using layers in the GIMP so that you can edit certain parts of the project, or apply effects to them, in isolation. The Edit ➤ Split Cut command cuts the current selection out of the timeline without moving other parts of the audio (see Figure 9-14). By choosing Tracks ➤ Add New ➤ Stereo Track and the Edit ➤ Paste command, you can arrange the audio clips that you cut anywhere on the timeline and manipulate them independently from the original recording.

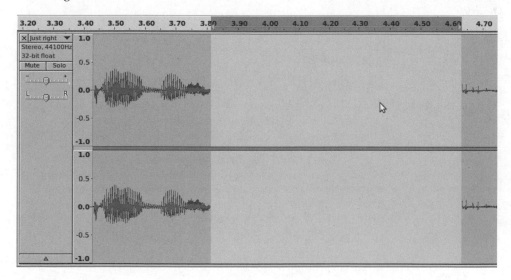

Figure 9-14. Use Split Cut to remove audio clips without joining the remaining material automatically.

Alternatively, choose Edit ➤ Split New to preserve the position of the selected clip on the timeline but place it on a new track of its own (see Figure 9-15).

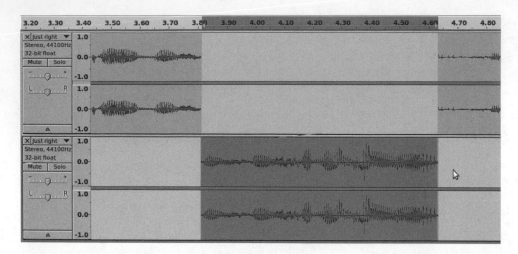

Figure 9-15. *Split New doesn't move the audio clip on the timeline—it only moves the clip to a new track.*

When an audio clip is on its own track, you can move it along the timeline using Audacity's Time Shift tool (see Figure 9-16), which has a small black double-headed horizontal icon in the toolbox, to the right of the big record button.

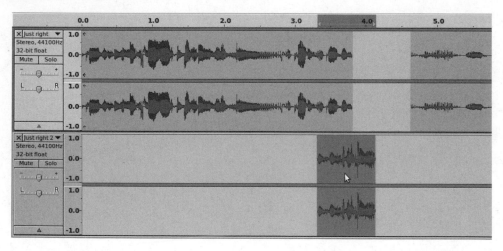

Figure 9-16. *The Time Shift tool enables you to position a clip anywhere on the timeline.*

You can add existing audio material to your project using the File ➤ Import Audio command, which opens a dialog box. Remember, though, if you're making a podcast for public distribution that includes other people's material, you need to have permission from the copyright holder or a copyright license for that material. Try searching on the Internet for *podsafe* music and other content that is explicitly allowed to be included in third-party podcasts.

Exporting the Podcast

When your podcast sounds good, or you want to safeguard it against accidental edits and computer crashes, save the project by choosing File ➤ Save Project, or File ➤ Save Project As with a new name. These commands save the project in Audacity's native format, in the directory of blockfiles that you read about earlier in this chapter. Although this native .aup format is good for preserving audio quality and is the best for making further edits in Audacity, it isn't understood by other audio programs. Because an Audacity project contains uncompressed audio data at up to 32-bit quality, it also tends to be relatively large in disk space terms, compared to a typical podcast.

Choose File ➤ Export to begin the process of saving the project in a format suitable for distribution on the Internet. This opens the Edit Metadata window, in which you can specify details such as your name and the name of the podcast or episode (see Figure 9-17). This metadata is displayed by compatible players when your podcast is being heard by the listener. The standard metadata tag names are set by Audacity and relate more closely to music than podcasts, but you can edit them in this dialog using the Add and Remove buttons. The Genre tag has a drop-down menu that includes a Speech category, but genre categories can also be edited. To alter the preset genres, use the Edit and Reset buttons at lower left in the Edit Metadata window.

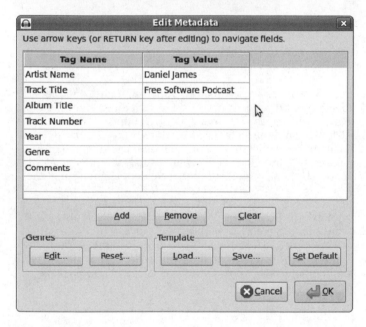

Figure 9-17. The first step in file export is to enter the metadata for your project.

Click OK, and a standard file-export dialog opens. Specify the filename of your exported audio project, and then choose a format from the drop-down menu at lower right.

Typically, podcasts are distributed in the widely supported MP3 format, although because the audio files are specified in the RSS feed, they can potentially be in any suitable format. Ogg Vorbis, the Free Software replacement for MP3, is a suitable format for podcasts because it features good compression and reasonable quality at low bit rates, which correspond directly to the amount of disk space used by the file and the time it takes to download it. Unfortunately, not all computers have an Ogg Vorbis player installed; but if you can download a podcast, it isn't a big deal to download a Vorbis-compatible player, too. Pretty much all Free Software media players support the Vorbis format out of the box.

If you decide to use MP3 format for backward-compatibility reasons, click the Options button in the Export File dialog to set the mode and quality of the MP3 file (see Figure 9-18). Variable mode adjusts the bit rate according to the specific material being encoded, which increases compression compared to Constant bit-rate mode. However, constant bit rate MP3s are the most compatible with older players. As when encoding most lossy formats, the Quality setting is a trade-off between bit rate and file size. MP3 bit rates below 128kbps aren't recommended for podcasts including music, because high-frequency reproduction suffers (as on AM radio). These low bit rates may be acceptable for speech-only material, however. Click OK to close the Specify MP3 Options dialog, and then click Save to begin the export.

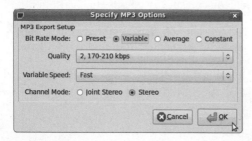

Figure 9-18. Set the mode and quality for your MP3 file export.

The problem with MP3 is that despite its popularity as a cross-platform open standard, encoders and decoders for the format remain encumbered by software patents. This makes it difficult for Free Software developers to distribute binary programs around the Internet with MP3 support built in; the validity of patents on software in general is disputed, and the legal position varies from country to country. Even Microsoft, having already paid off one patent claim, found itself on the wrong end of a very expensive patent lawsuit over MP3. So, making MP3s with Free Software usually requires that you download the encoder and decoder yourself, thereby bypassing the threat of a patent claim against the developers of the host program.

If Audacity can't find the LAME MP3 encoder (GNU/Linux, Windows, Mac) installed on your system, the program prompts you for the location of its library (see Figure 9-19). Helpfully, it also provides a Download button that is a link to the Audacity web site, with a list of places where you can download LAME for several different computer platforms. Ubuntu users can download the ready-made package libmp3lame0 from the multiverse repository, which you can find with a search in System ➤ Administration ➤ Synaptic Package Manager. In other GNU/Linux distros, the LAME library package may be named slightly differently.

Figure 9-19. If LAME isn't installed, Audacity tells you so.

After you install this package and restart Audacity, the MP3 export proceeds without the warning message about LAME's missing library. If you want to test your MP3 before distributing it around the Internet, which is a very good idea, you can do this in Ubuntu by double-clicking the file in the File Browser—for example, under Places ➤ Home Folder on the main GNOME menu. The Totem movie player opens. If the file won't play, it's probably because of a lack of MP3 decoder support; again, because this is a common problem with MP3, a workaround is built into Ubuntu. A dialog pops up, asking if you'd like to search the currently enabled software repositories for a suitable plug-in (see Figure 9-20).

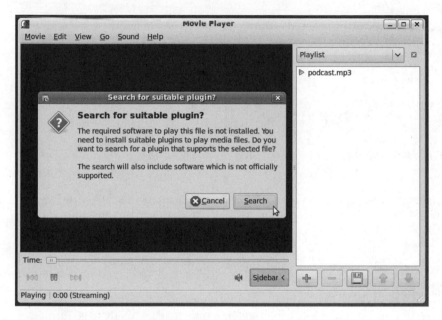

Figure 9-20. Ubuntu can automatically search for the correct plug-in needed by Totem.

■ **Note** A legal warning about software patents may pop up, asking you to confirm that software patents don't apply in your country, that you have a patent license, or that you're using the software for research only. Although the Ubuntu developers have their reasons for playing it safe, there have been no known cases of end users being sued for patent infringement after using an MP3 player with a Free Software decoder. Commercial use of MP3 is a different matter—if in doubt, consult a patent lawyer in your country.

If you click the Search button, the system should find at least one plug-in to enable MP3 playback in Totem (see Figure 9-21). Click the Install button to download the plug-in.

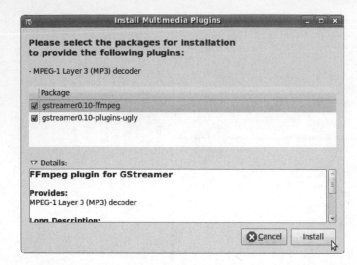

Figure 9-21. *The Install Multimedia Plugins dialog lists any plug-ins available that support the required format.*

Finally, after plug-in installation, Totem plays your MP3 format podcast for a final check before you upload it to your web server. By default, Totem displays colorful patterns in time with the audio; you can disable these visual effects by selecting Edit ➤ Preferences, clicking the Display tab, and deselecting the "Show visual effects when an audio file is played" check box.

Ardour: Rock Harder!

If you've made some audio recordings with Audacity on your PC or laptop and are ready to go further, or you're new to recording music with computers but are keen to find out what can be achieved, Ardour (GNU/Linux, Mac) is definitely worth checking out. Ardour's interface is densely packed with features and has been known to throw the newbie into a state of confusion, but time spent learning the program is well rewarded. Rather than being designed for simplicity and ease of use, like Audacity, Ardour is intended to provide professional users with the features and performance they need. In this respect, Ardour is similar to Blender—steep learning curve, but high-quality results.

The Ardour interface is meant to be familiar to users of proprietary recording studio software like Digidesign's Pro Tools or Steinberg's Nuendo. These systems carry over concepts from the mixers and multitrack tape machines used in recording studios before computers arrived. For example, Ardour features buttons for record arming, which you read about shortly. Effects are applied in real time, just as in an analog studio, which enables you to hear exactly what's going on as you adjust effect parameters; the reason for this becomes apparent in the next chapter. If you don't have studio experience, you have more to learn; but most of what you learn from using Ardour can be applied to other recording systems, too.

As Free Software, Ardour is accessible to a potentially far wider group of users, and not just because it's a gratis download from the http://ardour.org web site. Although a relatively expensive multichannel audio interface is recommended for serious use, Ardour has no special hardware requirements. It's very efficient and runs on pretty much any contemporary PC with an ordinary soundcard. A fast 7200rpm hard disk helps if you intend to record a lot of audio tracks, and newer processors are advantageous when it comes to adding CPU-intensive effects to those tracks, as you read later.

Most GNU/Linux distributions have Ardour binary packages available. You also need the JACK (GNU/Linux, Windows Mac) sound server installed to run Ardour (http://jackaudio.org). Unlike Audacity, Ardour relies on JACK for routing audio internally as well as to and from sound hardware and between other applications. As in the last chapter, the use of the qjackctl applet (JACK Control) is highly recommended. In Ubuntu, you can install the ardour, jackd, and qjackctl packages using the Synaptic Package Manager.

The Real-Time Linux Kernel

For the best results with Ardour, you need a real-time Linux kernel. It's possible for you to compile your own kernel with real-time patches if you know how, but it's a lot easier to use a ready-built multimedia kernel package for your GNU/Linux distribution of choice. These real-time kernels come as standard in multimedia distributions like 64 Studio (based on Ubuntu), JackLab (based on OpenSUSE), and Ubuntu Studio (based on... er... Ubuntu). To install a real-time kernel on Ubuntu Jaunty, open Synaptic and install the linux-rt package. Then, open a terminal and run the following commands, replacing the example of *daniel* with your own username:

```
sudo adduser daniel audio
sudo su -c 'echo @audio - memlock unlimited >> /etc/security/limits.conf'
sudo su -c 'echo @audio - rtprio 99 >> /etc/security/limits.conf'
sudo su -c 'echo @audio - nice -10 >> /etc/security/limits.conf'
```

The first of these four commands adds your username to the audio group on the system, and the second tells the system not to lock memory when members of the audio group run programs. The last two commands give members of the audio group the ability to run JACK with real-time priority.

Now, reboot to run the new kernel by selecting its entry in the GRUB boot manager. This kernel entry has a line ending in -rt, such as

```
Ubuntu 9.04, kernel 2.6.28-3-rt
```

■ **Note** If you ran JACK while reading the last chapter, without the real-time kernel, then after performing the steps just outlined, you can run the JACK Control applet, click the button to open the Setup window, check the Parameters box for Realtime, and uncheck the box for Soft Mode.

Configuring JACK

When the ardour, jackd, and qjackctl packages are installed, you need to tweak JACK for your particular system. Just as in the previous chapter, if you're using Ubuntu, it's highly recommended that you remove the pulseaudio package in Synaptic and reboot before running JACK. In theory, the PulseAudio system is compatible with JACK; but in practice, running both sound servers at the same time can lead to problems, including extraneous noise in recordings.

Close any programs that may be using the soundcard, and run the JACK Control applet from the Sound & Video menu. If you haven't run JACK before, click the Setup button on the right side of the JACK

Control applet, and look at the settings available (see Figure 9-22). If you already ran JACK while working your way through the last chapter, it's a good idea to take another, closer look at the options before running Ardour. For your purposes, the most important settings are as follows:

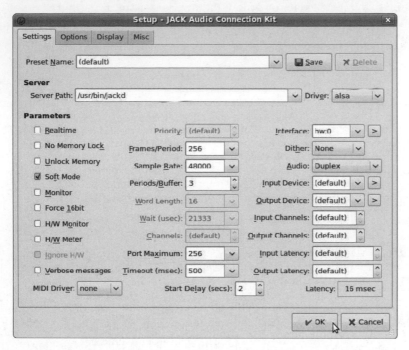

Figure 9-22. *These are good initial jackd settings for a modern PC with a standard (non-real-time) Linux kernel and a USB sound device.*

- *Parameters—Realtime:* This check box, on the left side of the Setup window, should be checked if you have a real-time kernel running and you've made the tweaks to the system's audio group suggested previously. It enables the jackd daemon to obtain real-time privileges, which is to say that audio becomes the machine's most important task. You can run jackd without these privileges, but audio streams may be interrupted, causing a buffer under-run (which jackd calls an *xrun*). These xruns are heard as glitches in the recording, which is something you want to avoid, of course.

- *Frames/Period:* This setting, in the middle column, determines the size of the buffer (and therefore the audible latency of the system). A big buffer is safer; but the bigger it gets, the worse latency will be. In an audio context, *latency* is the time that elapses between the moment when the computer does something and the moment you hear the associated sound. Musicians with well-trained ears can hear latencies of 10 milliseconds or less, which can upset their timing. On a modern machine with a real-time Linux kernel, 256 is a reasonable Frames/Period setting to start with. If you see xruns, set this to a higher number; if your PC is old and slow, you may need to go as high as 1024. Watch the figure in the Latency box (lower-right corner) change as you adjust the Frames/Period setting.

- *Sample Rate:* The higher the sample rate, the better quality your recording should be—at the expense of using up more disk space and requiring more data throughput. 44100Hz is the sample rate of a standard audio CD, but 48000Hz and 96000Hz are also popular recording rates. Many contemporary consumer sound chipsets can only do 48000Hz sampling and rely on software to convert material at other rates. If you start jackd at a different sample rate but get 48000Hz reported regardless, then you have one of these chipsets in your machine. It's no big deal, because 48000 is a reasonable sample rate setting, and you can downsample your recording to burn a CD later.

- *Periods/Buffer:* This should be set to 2 for most PCI sound cards. USB audio devices usually prefer a setting of 3. Experiment, and see which setting gives you the best results for your hardware. If you're having trouble with xruns at any Frames/Period setting, this is a good place to look.

- *Driver:* The Driver setting is near the upper-right corner of the Setup window. For PCI, on-board, and USB sound hardware, this should be set to alsa. For FireWire audio interfaces, which don't use ALSA drivers, you should select freebob. The FreeBoB driver project is working on a second-generation FireWire audio driver called FFADO, so if your distribution is very up to date, you may see ffado listed in place of freebob.

- *Interface:* This setting in the right column dictates which audio hardware jackd uses. The first soundcard in your system is called hw:0 by ALSA. Don't leave this set to default, because performance isn't as good, due to the use of ALSA's plug layer. You may have an onboard chipset, a multichannel PCI card, and a USB sound device such as hot-plug headphones, in which case you have a total of three ALSA devices. Sometimes the audio chipset on a software modem shows up here as well. Fortunately, you can click the arrowhead to the right side of the Interface box and select the correct hardware from a drop-down list by its real name—such as AMD8111, which is an on-board chipset.

- *Audio:* With this control, you can select Capture Only, Playback Only, or Duplex. The latter option means "play back and capture at the same time," which you need to have for *overdubs* (recording a second track in time with the first, by ear). Duplex mode requires more throughput, so you can switch to Capture Only or Playback Only mode if your system is struggling to keep up.

With all these settings tweaked, click OK, and you return to the main JACK Control window. Click the Start button at upper left in the GUI, and the display lights up with information about the JACK server. If it stays dark, then the jackd *daemon* (background process) has failed to start, in which case you should look at the Messages pop-up window for a diagnosis. In the event that this information doesn't help you find the problem, you can go back to the Setup window and select the "Verbose messages output" check box, which should provide additional clues.

The top line of output in the JACK Control display, in a yellow font, is most pertinent for now. The word *Started* indicates that jackd is running, and to the right of this you can see the letters *RT* if jackd is using real-time privileges. Going to the right again, you can see the DSP load figure as a percentage, which indicates how well jackd is coping. It's just over 1% in Figure 9-23 because not much audio processing is happening. If this figure approaches 100%, you're in trouble, because your system isn't capable of the task you're asking it to do. Because Ardour is efficient, you shouldn't see a high DSP load figure when making basic recordings unless your PC is antique.

Figure 9-23. The JACK Control window offers many useful statistics.

Finally, on the top row, you see the sample rate jackd is running at, in Hz. All JACK clients and interfaces should run at this rate, or you hear frequency shifts in the audio (like when you play a vinyl record at the wrong speed—if you're too young to know a 45rpm single from a 33rpm album, ask your dad). Fortunately, most JACK programs set their sample rate to whatever JACK requests. Some soundcards, like the M Audio Audiophile 24/96, allow you to lock the sample rate to a specific frequency, which can cause a mismatch with JACK. If you're having trouble of this nature, check the sample rate options in the control panel tool for your soundcard. In the case of the Audiophile 24/96, the GNU/Linux control panel is called envy24control and is available on Ubuntu by installing the alsa-tools-gui package in Synaptic.

Starting Ardour

Ardour doesn't open fully on launch from the Applications ➤ Sound & Video menu in Ubuntu, but instead presents a small Session Control window. You can't open Ardour without an associated project; a named session must be loaded, even if it doesn't contain any audio yet. So, at this stage, the window has two tabs: New Session and Open Session. Click the small triangle to the left of Advanced Options to look at the default settings. You want Create Master Bus checked, because you route all of Ardour's audio outputs through this. (A *bus*, sometimes spelt *buss*, is the part of an audio mixer that groups the signals from several other channels and sends them to a common destination.) The Master Bus is usually connected to the first two hardware outputs on the soundcard, in order to monitor the recording in stereo with loudspeakers or headphones. In some situations, you may activate the optional Monitor Bus for this task instead. For instance, you may want to monitor individual tracks without affecting the Master Bus output, which is a common requirement in a live music scenario where the Master Bus is connected to a public address (PA) system.

Automatically Connect to Physical Inputs is a good option, because it means the capture ports on your soundcard are connected to new tracks in Ardour without you having to remember to do it. The Automatically Connect Outputs to Master Bus option is also useful; otherwise, you don't hear anything by default. When you've set the advanced options to your liking, type a name for your session in the Name box, and click New (see Figure 9-24).

Figure 9-24. *Name the new Ardour session, and check the connection defaults.*

The main Ardour editor window now appears, with a gray box for the master bus displayed at left (see Figure 9-25). Click Help in the top menu bar; the only entry is About, which displays a box with the Ardour logo and the version number. Contrary to the implication that no help is available, a comprehensive manual is available on the Ardour web site, which is a good reference for details of advanced functions. Several Ardour tutorials are also available online.

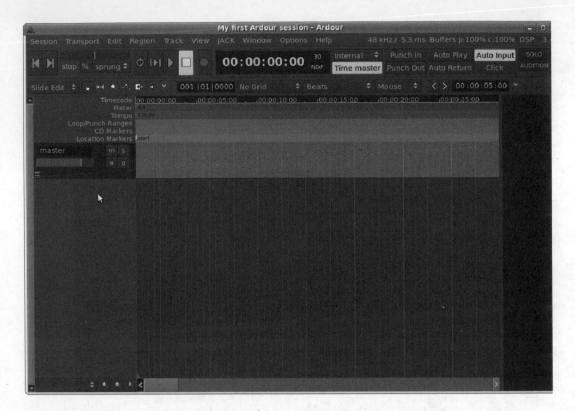

Figure 9-25. Ardour's main window, the editor. The master bus is visible, but there are no tracks yet.

On the Session menu, in the upper-left corner of the editor window, select Add Track/Bus. A small pop-up window appears—for your first recording, select 1 from the Add drop-down, and click the Tracks radio button. Under Channel Configuration, select Stereo and Normal (see Figure 9-26).

Figure 9-26. The "add track/bus" pop-up window lets you set up multitrack recordings.

Click the Add button, and a new Audio 1 box appears at left in the editor window. There's one of these boxes for each track or bus in the session, and each track has two rows of three buttons. (A bus has only four of the buttons.) At upper left of the six buttons on the track box is a button with a small red circle icon, which arms an individual track for recording. This feature allows you to re-record some tracks while preserving others. Click the red circle now: its surround changes to pink, to indicate that recording is active for this track.

You need to do one more thing before you can begin recording. Among the transport controls, below the top menu bar and to the left of Ardour's time clock, is another, larger, record arm button. This is the master recording control, and unless it's clicked, no recording takes place—regardless of the state of individual track record buttons. Click it now, and it flashes pink; this alert reminds you that you may record over irreplaceable audio material if you aren't careful (see Figure 9-27).

Figure 9-27. Recording is armed and dangerous.

Recording Drums

It's time to lay down a drum track. In a live band recording session, the first track laid down is usually the drums, so that all subsequent tracks can be recorded with the correct timing. (It also means the drummer can be sent to the pub early, and the rest of the band can discuss cheating the drummer out of his or her songwriting royalties.)

If you're lucky enough to have a real drum kit but are lacking in equipment on the computer side, you can get a pretty good recording with an ordinary sound card and a couple of mono microphones. Dangle one microphone directly above the kit, as high as practically possible, and place the other in front of the bass drum. For a stereo recording, use both microphones overhead: one each side of the kit, pointing slightly inward.

Although studio snobs insist that you need a bare minimum of eight microphones and a big mixing desk to record a drum kit, many great records were made using these simpler techniques. A definite advantage of the old-school methods is that you don't spend days remixing the drum sound; you just move your microphones around until the result sounds good, and then leave them there. Ron Parker, the first sound engineer to use Ardour in a commercial studio, has an answer prepared when clients ask him to make them sound like John Bonham, Led Zeppelin's late drummer. He says, "First you have to play like Bonham, then I'll take care of the rest." In other words, don't become fixated on your (lack of) equipment—concentrate on the performance. You can use a pair of bongos or even an old wooden box for percussion; it doesn't matter. Buddy Holly's drummer, Jerry Allison, didn't use a drum kit at all for the recording of the Crickets' hit single "Everyday"—he just slapped his hands on his knees.

With your percussion instrument set up and the microphones in place, select Window ➤ Show Mixer from Ardour's top menu bar. One vertical strip near the left side of the mixer window represents the track Audio 1, and a strip for the master bus appears at right (see Figure 9-28).

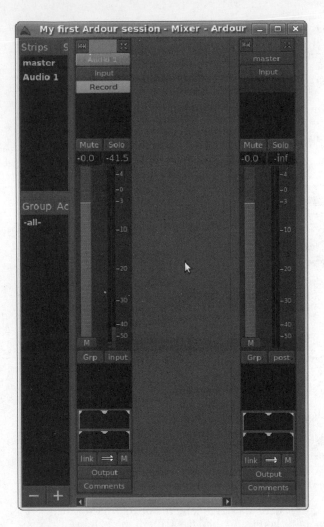

Figure 9-28. Ardour's mixer includes a strip for each track.

These separate Editor and Mixer windows are great if you have two displays; but even on a computer with a single display, it's convenient to put the Mixer window on a separate workspace from the Editor window. To do this in Ubuntu, right-click the brown title bar of the Mixer window, and select Move to Workspace Right. You can then switch between Editor and Mixer windows using the little workspace applet in the lower-right corner of the Ubuntu desktop, next to the trashcan icon.

On the mixer, near the top of the strip for Audio 1 is an Input button. Click this button, and select Edit from the pop-up menu. A new "Audio 1 input" window opens, and two boxes list which soundcard ports are connected to the inputs of this track. Because you asked Ardour to auto-connect physical ports in the New Session dialog, you normally see a port called system:capture_1 connected to *in 1* (Ardour's first input for the track, corresponding to the left stereo channel) and a port called system:capture_2 connected to *in 2* (for the right stereo channel); see Figure 9-29.

Figure 9-29. The mixer input editing window allows you to check JACK connections.

If all is well, click Close to return to the Mixer window. Because the record arm buttons are active, if you hit a drum, the Audio 1 meter moves (the blue-green vertical lines). If the meter goes into the red bar area, above 0 on the scale, you need to move the microphone further away from the drum kit. Dropping the recording level in Ardour's mixer, using the light grey fader control to the left of the meter, won't help if the microphone is distorting on the analog side of the system.

When you're happy with what the meters are telling you, return to Ardour's Editor window and click the Play button in the transport controls (it has a green triangle icon and is two places to the left of the master record arm control you clicked earlier). The red vertical cursor line in the Editor window begins rolling to the right. After a short delay, the recorded waveform appears in a horizontal region to the right of the track controls.

Your first track is laid down (see Figure 9-30)! Click the square stop button (between the play and record controls), and then select Session ➤ Save from the top menu bar.

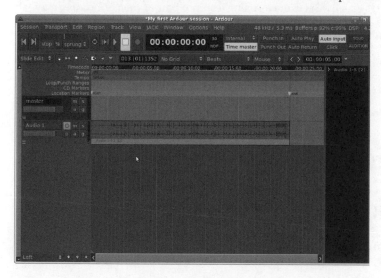

Figure 9-30. The recording has been made, and the waveform of the drum track is displayed in the Audio 1 strip.

Next, select the track by clicking the background of its panel, next to the six small buttons; it turns purple. Select Track ➤ Height ➤ Largest from Ardour's main menu bar, which enables you to see the peaks of the recorded waveform in more detail. This detail is a great help when you edit individual tracks. Alternatively, choose Track ➤ Height ➤ Fit Selected Tracks to stretch the height of the tracks to fill the available space in the display (keyboard shortcut F, for *fit*). This option is particularly useful if you're making a detailed inspection of a track or tracks on a large, high-resolution display (see Figure 9-31).

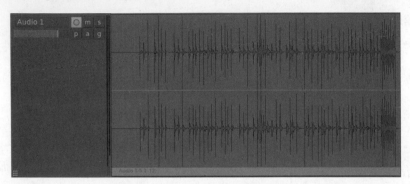

Figure 9-31. The Track Height control enables a closer look at the recorded waveform.

No Drums or Microphones?

If you don't have a drum kit, can't play one, or lack understanding neighbors, Free Software comes to your rescue again in the shape of Hydrogen. As you read in Chapter 8, this is a very flexible drum machine that can play samples of both acoustic and electronic kits. By default, Hydrogen auto-detects JACK on start-up, so recording from it is exactly the same as using a stereo pair of microphones on a real drum kit—except that the port names are different. When you click the Input button and select Edit in the Ardour mixer with Hydrogen running, an extra tab visible lets you select Hydrogen's left and right outputs. Click the "out_L" connection in the Hydrogen-1 tab, and it appears in the "in 1" box at left (the Ardour inputs side). Then, click the "out_R" connection so it appears in the "in 2" box (see Figure 9-32). You can then hide the track input box with the Close button. Try some of Hydrogen's demo patterns and sampled drum kits until you get ideas for your own patterns.

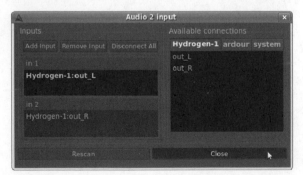

Figure 9-32. The Hydrogen drum machine is running and ready for recording in Ardour. Note the extra tab for Hydrogen-1 in the "Available connections" box.

To lock Hydrogen to Ardour's timeline, you can use the transport features in JACK. Just to the right of Ardour's clock is a small drop-down menu with the tooltip "Positional sync source," which defaults to Internal. Change this setting to JACK, rewind to the start of the Ardour session, and click the play button. You should now hear the current Hydrogen pattern playing back in sync with the Ardour session, if you have a pattern loaded.

Should you decide to dispense with the drums (real or machine programmed), Ardour has a handy click-track feature that can help you keep your timing. In the upper-right corner of the editor window is a group of six buttons, with the Click button at lower right. Activate this control, and the button turns light green to show that the click track has been enabled (see Figure 9-33). Press the rewind button (gray triangle and bar icon, furthest left on the transport controls), and then click the play button (gray triangle). You hear a 4/4 pattern of clicks (high, low, low, low), which sounds like a small child playing a xylophone.

Figure 9-33. The click track has been enabled, so the Click button lights up green.

By default, this click track plays at 120 beats per minute. To change this setting, look at the area above the individual track button boxes, on the left side of the editor window. Horizontal gray Meter and Tempo strips with small red markers next to them appear below the Timecode strip. Right-click the marker in the Tempo strip, and select Edit (see Figure 9-34). When you change the tempo setting and click Apply, more than the marker changes: the faint vertical lines in the editor window shuffle along to reflect the new setting, because the tempo markers don't just control the click track—they set timing for the entire session.

Figure 9-34. You can set any tempo you like, using the markers in the Tempo strip.

The same goes for the Meter setting; but for most contemporary music tracks, 4/4 time is fine. If you're using obscure time signatures, then you may be playing progressive jazz rock fusion—*beware.* There's no need to play at the same tempo or use the same meter throughout the session; right-click in the appropriate horizontal strip beneath the timeline at the point where you want to place another marker, and select New Tempo or New Meter (see Figure 9-35). Press the play button again, and listen for the change in the click track as the play cursor passes each marker.

Figure 9-35. You're not restricted to the same tempo or time signature for the entire session.

Of course, the click track isn't meant to be heard on the final recording. The usual practice is to play the click track in headphones, and Ardour provides a special JACK port for this task. If you have a multichannel audio interface, you can route this port to a separate output from the Master Bus, or even several different headphone outputs, one for each member of the band. Look at the Connections window in JACK Control to get an idea of the possibilities (see Figure 9-36). Should the drummer return from the pub, having lost his or her ability to keep time (which has been known to happen), then a click track can be particularly useful. It can also be a helpful learning aid if you're just starting to play the drums.

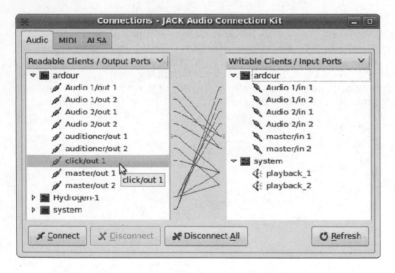

Figure 9-36. A separate JACK port for the click track can be routed to any output.

Hey Mr. Bassie

When you're happy with the drum recording, it's time to move on to the bass line. If you have an electric bass guitar but no amplifier, making the use of a microphone impractical, you can get a pretty good sound by plugging directly into a mixer with a 1/4" high-impedance socket (sometimes marked Hi-Z). Going direct from a bass guitar into a soundcard usually results in a thin sound, due to impedance mismatch, but there is a low-cost solution. A direct input (DI) box is a small, usually battery-operated, device that presents the correct, high-impedance input for a guitar pick-up, with a low-impedance output. You should be able to get the correct one in any decent music shop, if you explain that it's for connecting to a computer soundcard and needs a line level unbalanced output.

If you don't have a bass guitar, it's possible to record your bass line using a Free Software synthesizer. This doesn't mean you have to go electropop; Ray Manzarek of The Doors used an electric piano and an organ in place of a bass guitar. Ideally, you use a piano-style keyboard connected to the computer via MIDI to play or input the notes. If you're on a low budget, you can use a QWERTY keyboard to emulate a digital piano with vkeybd, as you read about in Chapter 8.

A good bass-line synth you can use to get started is AlsaModularSynth, also covered in the last chapter. You can program your bass line as a MIDI sequence, or play it live—Ardour doesn't care which. In favor of MIDI sequencing, using JACK's transport synchronization features means you can line up the bass and drum parts for multiple recording takes without the rest of the band getting bored.

Return to Ardour, and choose Session ➤ Add Track/Bus to add a new stereo track; it's called Audio 2 by default if you have a drum track laid down already. Click the track record arm button (the small red circle to the right of the track label), and its surround turns pink. You now need to connect AlsaModularSynth's outputs to the inputs of Ardour's Audio 2 track; otherwise, the bass line won't be recorded. You can make these connections either in Ardour's mixer window, using the Input button, or in the Connect window of JACK Control; the result is the same (see Figure 9-37). Note that in JACK Control, whenever you click a port on one side of the Connect window, the currently connected port on the opposite side changes to a blue font.

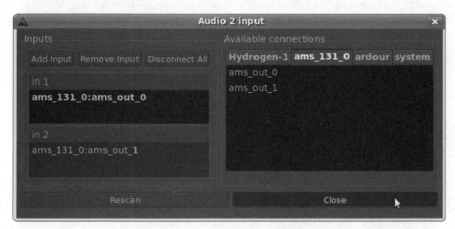

Figure 9-37. AlsaModularSynth is connected to the Audio 2 track in Ardour.

Switching back to AlsaModularSynth, with the vkeybd virtual MIDI keyboard connected and in window focus, you can play some notes on your QWERTY keyboard. On a U.K. keyboard, the bottom row from Z to ? represents the white piano keys (natural notes), and the row from A to L corresponds to the black keys (sharps and flats). You can also play directly on the screen with a mouse; but it's hard to play a bass line that way, unless you're going for a Stylophone sound. (Kids, look on Wikipedia under Dubreq Stylophone to find out what one of those is.)

A good AlsaModularSynth preset to start with is `bass_reverb.ams`; but of course it's a programmable synthesizer, so you can create any sound you want. To play low bass notes using the virtual keyboard, select View ➤ Key/Velocity, and drag the Key slider to around 24; otherwise, you're playing a couple of octaves above where you need to be.

In the Ardour editor window, use the transport buttons at upper left to rewind to the beginning of the session. Click the play button, and you hear the drum track as you play a bass line on the keyboard (as long as the virtual MIDI keyboard is in window focus). This can get complicated if you're using multiple workspaces in Ubuntu, so let the window manager help you out: right-click the brown title bar of the virtual piano window, and select Always on Visible Workspace. When you're ready to record your bass line, activate Ardour's master recording control in the transport buttons, rewind, and click play to set the transport rolling. As you play the notes, the waveform of the bass line recording is visible in the Audio 2 strip (see Figure 9-38).

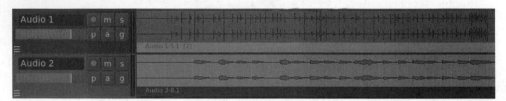

Figure 9-38. The drum and bass tracks are laid down on tracks 1 and 2.

If, after deactivating the master record control, rewinding, and playing back your first take, you aren't happy with the results, repeat the process. The new audio is recorded as a separate region, layered on top of the first. By default, the two takes aren't mixed together—you only hear the region on the top layer. Because layers are semitransparent, lower layers are visible underneath as grayed-out regions.

Guitars and Keyboards

Recording electric guitar is pretty much the same as recording electric bass, except that the straight DI method doesn't work as well. The clean tone you get from plugging an electric lead or rhythm guitar direct into a line input isn't very interesting compared to the sound you get using a good amplifier and speaker cabinet. This is because a guitar amplifier alters or distorts the tone of the analog signal that comes from the guitar pick-up considerably, as does the specially selected speaker cone in the cabinet. The reverberation of the room the amp and microphone are in can also color the recorded sound, particularly if the room is small with lots of reflective hard surfaces and the microphone is some distance from the amp. If you're amp-less, you can buy acoustic modeling hardware devices that are designed to emulate the amplifier, speaker, and microphone combination. There are Free Software applications that can do the same job, using the impulse response technique, including Guitarix (available from the `http://guitarix.sourceforge.net/` site). These programs also emulate traditional analog effects pedal hardware, which you can use to add distortion and reverberation to your guitar sound.

Creox (GNU/Linux) is a software guitar effects processor available as source from `http://zyzstar.kosoru.com/?creox`, with links to prebuilt packages for various distros (see Figure 9-39). Ubuntu users can find it using the Add/Remove Applications tool. There are other techniques for creating amp/speaker models and effects, but Creox is a good starting point because it sets up several of the commonly used effects pedal sounds for you. You can also use it to add extra crunch to your bass guitar or external keyboard sound, if the DI or amp sound you're getting is too clean for your tastes. Because it's a JACK application, you can use it to alter the sound of software instruments like AlsaModularSynth or drum machines like Hydrogen.

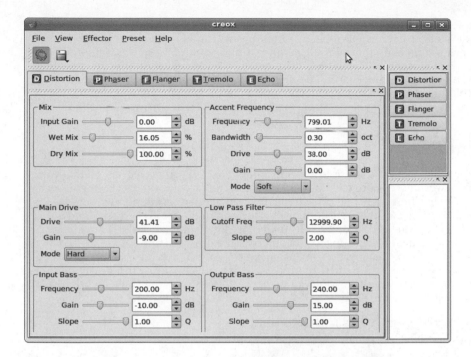

Figure 9-39. Creox is a collection of guitar effects pedals, re-created as a Free Software application.

Ardour lets you hear and see the effect of using Creox on a live audio input, when placed in the JACK signal chain before the track input. Figure 9-40 shows two takes: on the left, the Main Drive mode in Creox's Distortion tab has been set to Clean; on the right, the same control has been set to Hard, and there's an obvious difference in level. Note also that the hard distortion has caused clipping, which is shown in Ardour by red dots at the tips of the waveform. This clipping problem is something to watch out for with any effect that creates an increase in output level.

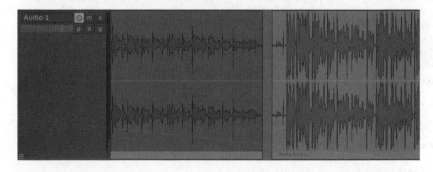

Figure 9-40. Creox distortion in two Main Drive modes, Clean and Hard. Clipping is apparent in Hard mode, on the right.

Laying down tracks from an external MIDI keyboard is much simpler than with electric stringed instruments, because most electronic keyboards have a line-out socket that is close enough in impedance and level to your soundcard that a simple adaptor cable should suffice. Even so, some keyboard players prefer to put a microphone in front of an amplifier and speaker cabinet for recording purposes. Some organs have an electromechanical Leslie speaker that features a rotating sound horn for the high frequencies, coloring the keyboard sound considerably. That's not an effect you want to lose by recording the organ directly.

Editing in Ardour

Now that you've laid down several tracks, it's time to begin editing. Even if you played so well that you didn't make any mistakes, when you record with microphones there are usually bits of extraneous noise that need to be cut out. The beginning and end of each region often need some attention to remove the sound of someone counting the beats, or a foot shuffling on the floor. There are also creative and aesthetic reasons for edits; they can help make the recording more interesting, or make room in the audible spectrum for individual instruments that would otherwise be drowned out.

You can divide single or multiple regions with the playhead cursor, which is the thin red vertical line that moves along the timeline. Below and to the right of the Ardour main clock is a drop-down menu with the tooltip "Edit point," which defaults to Mouse (see Figure 9-41). Switch this to Playhead, which is a much more precise mode.

Figure 9-41. Change the edit point from Mouse to Playhead to enable precise edits.

Click the small red downward-pointing triangle at the top of the playhead cursor to drag it to the edit position you want, if you can't wait for it to get there during playback. Alternatively, click the numbers in the horizontal timecode strip to make the cursor jump to that point. With the playhead cursor now in position, right-click in the region to be edited. Doing so opens a pop-up menu with the first submenu labelled with the name of the track and the selected region, separated by a hyphen—such as Audio 1-5.1. Navigate down this submenu with your mouse, and select Trim ➤ Start to Edit Point, or Split. Trim is used when you want to throw away the audio before or after the edit point, whereas Split leaves it in place. The great thing about playhead editing mode is that you can select multiple regions by Shift+clicking them and trim or split them at the exact same point on the timeline.

Ardour supports four main editing modes, each of which has its own small button under the transport control:

- *Select/Move Objects mode:* This mode treats each region of audio as a building block that can be dragged and dropped on to any track at any point on the timeline. It's good for making broad, general edits, or for more precise work when the recording is already divided up neatly into regions.

Another feature of Object mode is start- and end-point trimming. Often, all you want to do with a region is cut a little bit from either end on the timeline. When you mouse over the ends of the colored bar at the lower edge of a region, a small white double-headed horizontal arrow appears. Click and drag with this arrowhead tool to trim the start or end point of the region (see Figure 9-42). The timecode of the trim point is shown in a yellow font, to help you get it right. If you go too far, don't worry—Ardour is a nondestructive editor, so if you move the start or end point back later, the audio that was hidden by the trim is still there.

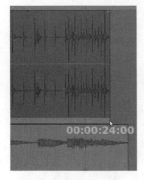

Figure 9-42. Use the mouse in Object mode to trim region start and end points.

- *Select/Move Ranges mode:* In this mode, audio is selected with the mouse and can be cut, copied, and pasted within regions (see Figure 9-43). It's useful when you have to make lots of small edits on individual tracks, and you can also use it to create multiple regions from a single one. Ardour uses the conventional shortcut keys of Ctrl+X for cut, Ctrl+C for copy, and Ctrl+V for paste. Note that by default, pastes occur at the current edit point on the timeline.

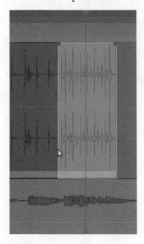

Figure 9-43. Range editing mode lets you cut, copy, and paste within regions.

- *Draw Gain Automation mode:* Sometimes, instead of an absolute cut, you want the region in question to change level dynamically. Gain Automation mode allows you to draw points (shown as small red squares) on the waveform with mouse clicks, which correspond to relative boosts and cuts in level on playback (see Figure 9-44). Points above the green center line are level boosts, and points below the line are level cuts. The size of the boost or cut in level is indicated as a number of decibels (dB) in a bold yellow font, with a cut shown as a negative number. You look at the decibel scale in Chapter 10.

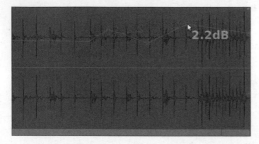

Figure 9-44. *Draw points for automated playback in Gain Automation mode.*

This automation drawing tool controls the gain of both channels of a stereo track with the same points. The graph line you draw isn't directly related to the waveform shown underneath, but instead uses the full height of the stereo track to represent the range from a 6dB boost at the top to a cut of around -120dB (or - infinity for total silence) at the bottom.

- *Stretch/Shrink Regions mode:* In certain kinds of music, particularly electronic dance music, you need to make an audio sample fit a programmed drum beat, aligning it with the bar and beat lines dictated by Ardour's Meter and Tempo settings. Time *stretching* or *shrinking* lets you manipulate the length of a sample without changing its pitch. This is a computationally complex technique to get right, especially when the audio source material is *polyphonic* ("with many voices"). When you use Ardour's Stretch/Shrink Regions mode, a number of alternative detection categories are provided on a drop-down menu, such as "Balanced multitimbral mixture" (see Figure 9-45). You probably need to experiment to find the method that works best for the material you're stretching or shrinking.

Figure 9-45. *Ardour's Stretch/Shrink Regions mode offers a range of alternative methods.*

After you save your recording session by choosing Session ➤ Save (keyboard shortcut Ctrl+S), try each of these editing tools on the regions in your recording. You can always use the Ctrl+Z keyboard shortcut to undo, or choose Edit ➤ Undo from the main menu bar.

Exporting the Session

The multitrack approach to recording and editing is very flexible, but a native Ardour session isn't in a format most people can listen to. You need to export the session so that the results can be played back on a normal hi-fi, portable, or media player. CD audio, from which most lossy Internet formats are encoded, is 2-channel, 16-bit, with a sample rate of 44100Hz. So far, you've only been working with a stereo master bus, and therefore two export channels are no problem. Ardour and JACK use 32-bit audio by default internally, for quality reasons, so that has to be reduced to 16-bit depth on export. As you read earlier in this chapter, many soundcards only work at 48000Hz, meaning the sample rate of your session may have to be reduced too. Fortunately, Ardour provides a dialog box that covers all of these parameters and more.

When you're ready to export the session, the Session ➤ Export menu presents three options. The first, "Export session to audiofile," is simple enough—the entire session from the small green start to end markers in the horizontal Location Markers strip is exported. The second, "Export selection to audiofile," affects only that part of the session selected with the mouse in Range edit mode. This is useful if you have a long session, such as a live concert, and you only want to export one song from the concert.

The final option is "Export range markers to audiofile." To specify a range for export, first click and drag over it with the Select/Move Ranges tool. Right-click inside this range, and select Add Range Markers from the pop-up menu that appears. These range start and end points are visible as small green draggable triangles in the horizontal Range Markers strip, which is hidden by default. You can make this strip visible by right-clicking in the blank gray area to the left of the strips and selecting the Ranges item so that it's checked (see Figure 9-46). The advantage of range markers is that you can name them and save them with the session, unlike selections, which are transient.

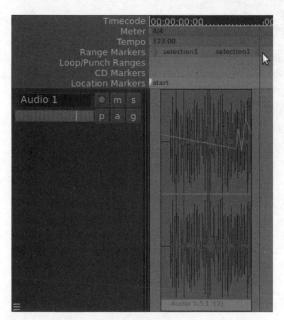

Figure 9-46. *You can use range markers to set and save the precise length of the export.*

The Export dialog begins with the name of the file to be exported, which by default is created in the **export** subdirectory of the session directory. This has the benefit that you're less likely to lose the exported file or get it mixed up with another project, but it does increase the size of the session directory. This may be a consideration when you're copying a session onto media like a DVD-R or USB memory stick.

You can now select the appropriate options for your target media. Under Channels and File Type, stereo and WAV, respectively, are the correct options for CD production (see Figure 9-47). Set Sample Format to "16 bit." When you're exporting to a 16-bit file, it's a good idea to choose one of the dither types provided, because *truncating* (simply throwing away) the extra bits in the exported file loses the benefit of processing at a higher bit rate. It's arguable which form of dither is the best, but you have a choice of Rectangular, Shaped Noise, or Triangular.

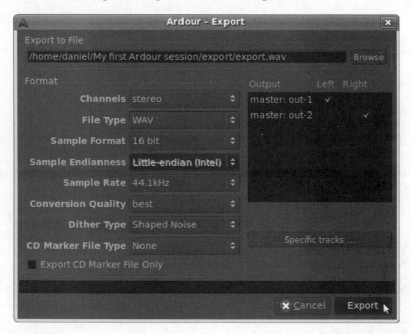

Figure 9-47. *The Export dialog allows you to specify which channels go where, as well as the format of the exported file.*

At right in the Export dialog, a black box lets you specify which channels in the master bus are to be exported to which channels of the export file. It's very important to look at this, because by default none of the boxes are checked, and so exports are silent. Normally, for a stereo project exported directly to a WAV file, you check one box so that the first channel on the master bus goes to the left channel in the export and the second channel on the master bus goes to the right channel. For a more complex setup, you can click the "Specific tracks" button and export only some of the tracks in the session. For example, you can export everything but the vocal tracks, which creates an instant instrumental dub version without requiring any changes to the session.

Finally, click the Export button, and the gray progress bar at the bottom of the dialog box zips across. If you have Ardour's Editor window in the background, you also see the Play cursor move through the session. You now have a WAV file that you can burn to CD.

After your first export completes, a dialog box pops up, asking you to consider making a one-time financial donation to the Ardour project or to become a regular subscriber (see Figure 9-48). This is optional and doesn't affect the operation of the program. If you do decide to donate and click the appropriate option, a web browser opens at the donation page of the http://ardour.org web site. It's an innovative way to approach the funding of a major Free Software project.

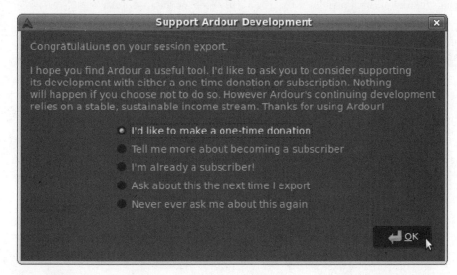

Figure 9-48. Ardour's first export triggers a dialog box asking for an optional financial donation.

In the next chapter, you look at ways of making your Ardour project sound even better and how to use the graphics skills you've acquired in earlier chapters to make your CD look good too.

Further Reading

Not many books are available about recording audio with Free Software, except the forthcoming book on Audacity by Carla Schroder (No Starch Press). However, a great many books are available on the recording studio generally. A good all-round introduction is *Practical Recording Techniques* by Bruce and Jenny Bartlett (Focal Press, 2005, ISBN-13: 978-0240811444).

Other Useful Programs

All of the following software is available in Ubuntu using the Add/Remove Programs application:

- *Audio Tag Tool* (GNU/Linux): An editor for the metadata in MP3 and Ogg Vorbis files, enabling you to add or correct tags in your podcast and music releases. It can be used to edit tags one by one, or to tag and rename hundreds of files at once. http://pwp.netcabo.pt/paol/tagtool/.

- *ZynAddSubFX* (GNU/Linux, Windows, Mac): A software synthesizer with many advanced features, some excellent preset sounds, and support for JACK. Windows and Mac versions are at `http://zynaddsubfx.sourceforge.net`.

- *Mx44* (GNU/Linux): Another software synth with JACK support, only with a more radical interface featuring a 4x4 oscillator matrix. `http://web.comhem.se/luna/`.

- *Aeolus* (GNU/Linux): A realistic church organ emulator synth, with support for JACK and multiple manuals (keyboards). `www.kokkinizita.net/linuxaudio/aeolus/`.

■ ■ ■

## CHAPTER 10

Mixing and Mastering

Optimizing Your Sound

In Chapter 9, you looked at recording your first Ardour session, with drum, bass, synthesizer, and guitar tracks exported to a stereo WAV file. If you burned your exported file to an audio CD and tried it on your stereo, then unless you're a naturally talented sound engineer, you probably found that it sounded quiet and, in subjective terms, lacked clarity and punch. This is most likely because you're comparing it to the commercial releases you're used to hearing on the radio, on TV, or on the Internet, which have gone through a lot of sonic mangling to make them sound that way. Since the 1950s, popular music producers have used ever-greater amounts of analog (and now digital) processing to make their recordings stand out from the rest.

Broadly speaking, there are two parts to this process. *Mixing* means making the different tracks in a session fit together sonically and musically. *Mastering* comes later and is all about making the various mixes sound as good as they possibly can when assembled into the final project. If you look on the back of a CD or at the inlay notes, you often see different people and different studios credited for the mixing and mastering, because each craft is a specialism of its own. With Free Software, you have the tools to tackle both tasks. As in all creative endeavors, close study of the efforts of others and a great deal of practice are required for best results.

Whether mixing or mastering, good audio engineers depend first and foremost on their ears to make the right judgments. However, you can use certain features of the software to help you when you're learning and as a reference check later on. In particular, to measure how the sonic enhancement involved in mixing and mastering is achieved, you need to read up on audio metering. If you're already familiar with the decibel scale as applied to digital audio, you can skip the next section.

Digital Audio and the Full Scale

A *decibel* (dB) is one tenth of a *Bel*, but hardly anyone uses the Bel for anything. In contrast, the Bel's smaller brother is used for a many different measurements in science and engineering. To quote a number of decibels without any context is meaningless, because a decibel reading is based on a comparison with a known reference level that differs according to that context. Even in the specific field of acoustics and human hearing, there are a variety of uses for the decibel. If someone says their guitar amplifier was measured at 110 decibels, making it about as loud as an aircraft's jet engine sounds when you're standing beside a runway, they're talking about *sound pressure level*. The reference level for decibels of sound pressure is the threshold of human hearing—the quietest sound the average person is supposed to be able to hear. This reference level is abbreviated 0dBSPL, which stands for *zero deciBels of Sound Pressure Level*.

Digital audio metering has a completely different use for the decibel. The Pulse Code Modulation (PCM) system used by audio CDs and computer soundcards is based on sampled, numerical values for the amplitude of a waveform at different points in time. Sampling amplitude values many thousands of times per second allows that waveform to be approximated and reconstructed inside a computer. (As you read in Chapter 9, 44100Hz and 48000Hz are commonly used sample rates in digital audio).

A standardized PCM system must have a fixed number that represents the maximum sample value allowed, or the full scale. Because the actual sample values are long binary numbers and not very user-friendly for making comparisons, the decibel is used to describe how close a particular sample is to the full scale value. The maximum possible level of digital audio equipment is therefore referred to as *zero deciBels from Full Scale*, or 0dBFS. This dBFS value isn't related to sound pressure level (dBSPL) until the digital audio is converted to analog waveforms, amplified, and sent to loudspeakers or headphones. Amplitude levels below the maximum level of 0dBFS are expressed as negative numbers, which you can see displayed on the Ardour meter strips in the mixer in Figure 10-1.

Figure 10-1. Ardour's mixer scale is calibrated from +4dBFS all the way down to -50dBFS.

In theory, any signal that exceeds 0dBFS, going into the red on the Ardour meter, should introduce *clipping*—the nasty-sounding digital distortion you read about in the last chapter. When the top of the waveform is clipped off, it turns a sine wave into a kind of square wave shape, changing the sound (see Figure 10-2). This isn't the same as the analog distortion you get from a guitar amp or tape machine being overdriven, which some people describe subjectively as *warm*; digital distortion is tiring on the ear. So, you want to avoid it if at all possible.

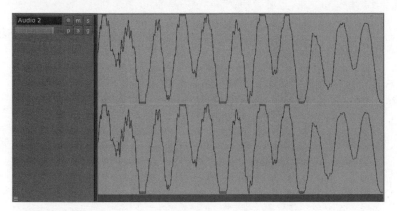

Figure 10-2. A clipped waveform shown close up in Ardour. The peak areas where sample information has been lost are shown in red.

Ardour and JACK can forgive overs that take place during the mixing process as long as they aren't too extreme; but you have to take care of these before you finalize a CD or produce a FLAC or Ogg Vorbis file for your web site. This is because the export process and the playback equipment aren't accommodating when it comes to clipping. The meter on the Ardour mixer's master bus strip is the one to watch for overall output level, and like the other meters, it shows the highest peak level reached during the session as a numerical value. This is useful in case you miss a transient over, too short in duration to hear at first. These transient overs are often caused by drum tracks and percussive sounds generally (see Figure 10-3). If the clipping is in the source material, rather than the result of excessive level boosts at the mixing stage, then the material should be rerecorded if at all possible.

Figure 10-3. *Transient overs. Although the flickering vertical meter bars currently read around minus 9dBFS, the positive number at the top of the master bus meter indicates there has previously been a peak of +4.7dBFS. The two small red bars at the +4dBFS line tell you the most recent peak level.*

As you read in Chapter 9, it was once the fashion to run the recording meters *hot*, which means to go as close to the maximum level as possible for each track. This was due to the inherent background noise of analog tape formats, which meant that quiet recordings had more hiss when they were amplified. You may recall similar advice if you were in the habit of making cassette compilations back in the 1980s—to keep the recording level meters *in the red*. (Yes, I know some of you weren't even born in the 80s. It really wasn't as cool a decade as they claim on VH1.)

With digital audio recordings, there is usually no need to run hot. The background noise level— sometimes referred to as the *noise floor*—is very low in any half-decent audio interface designed for a PC or laptop. This means you can record and mix each track without the meters glowing red all the time and leave raising the average level to the mastering stage, which you look at later in this chapter. Perceived loudness is a subjective measure that depends on several factors, but the Ardour meters give you a good general idea of what's going on in the session, level-wise.

The best way to record and mix is to leave yourself some headroom between the waveform peaks and the 0dBFS point on the meter, because after you've manipulated the track with fades and effects, it may come back louder. Remember, though, that you can't improve the *signal-to-noise ratio* by boosting level in the mix, because you boost the noise on the track at the same time. Aim for a track that is recorded loud enough to mask background and equipment noise but with at least a few decibels of headroom at the top of the meter during the mixing stage.

Finding the Balance

Start JACK, and open the Ardour session you created while reading Chapter 9; or, record a new session. Click the transport rewind button, click the play button, and then switch to the mixer view by choosing Window ➤ Show Mixer. You see the meters flickering, with two blue-green colored vertical bars: one each for left and right channel output. The meter is in Post mode by default, which shows the post-fader playback level after any adjustment made in the mixer strip. You can switch modes between Pre-fader, Post-fader, and Input monitor level using the small grey button directly below the meter. If you click the record arm button on any particular track, the meter switches into Input mode automatically.

As the level increases toward 0dBFS, the meter bar color changes to pale green and then to red if there is an over. If this happens, the peak level box above the meter strip changes to a white number on a red background, to alert you that you have a potential clipping problem. Click this peak level box to reset it to the current peak value.

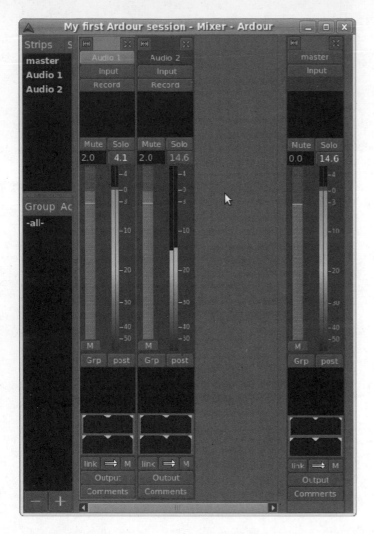

Figure 10-4. You're running way too hot here—a session mixed like this will sound pretty rough on CD.

You can use Ardour's mixer with a digital mixing desk or a dedicated control surface; but if you're just starting out, adjusting track levels with your mouse works fine. If you click the light grey bar to the left of each pair of meter bars and hold down the button, you can move the gain fader up and down with mouse movements. (*Gain* means a change in output level; a cut in level can be described as *negative gain.*)

By default, each fader begins at 0 decibels, which means that neither boost nor cut is being applied to the track. The reference level for this decibel measurement is the track level before gain is applied, as shown on the prefader meter. You can see the number in the box at the top of the fader change as you move your mouse up and down. A single click brings the fader up or down in small increments, depending on whether you click above or below the thin white 0dB line. The decibel scale is logarithmic, which means each 3dB boost makes the level twice as loud as it was before. Each 3dB cut makes the sound only half as loud.

Balancing levels in the mix isn't just about making sure there are no overs. You must also make subjective and aesthetic decisions. For instance, in some gentler styles of music, the drums are meant to sound like they're off in the distance, which corresponds to a lower level in the mix. In other genres, they're right up front, which means loud. The only way you can get this right is to practice, trying out your mixes on different playback systems until they sound good to you. Friends and family will also volunteer their advice, which will probably be negative at first: "The guitar is too loud," "I can't hear the singing," and so on.

The Pan Control

Most live instruments and vocals are recorded with mono microphones, and yet the output format is usually stereo. Although it's possible to produce a retro all-mono record, like Seasick Steve's 2006 album *Dog House Music*, since the mid 1960s most recordings have featured a fake stereo sound field created by panning individual tracks. Ardour's panning control is located toward the bottom of the mixer strip and features a thin green line that you can click and drag to either side of the stereo field. You can also click the small triangles at the top of each panning control to select hard-left, center, or hard-right panning automatically. For stereo tracks, there are two controls, with channel 1 (left channel, by default) at the top. You can pan the left channel to the hard right, and vice versa, if that takes your fancy (see Figure 10-5).

Figure 10-5. *Stereo track on the left, featuring two-channel panning. Mono track on the right, panned to center.*

There are some conventions for panning in popular music recording, which approximate to vocals in the center and guitars and bass panned slightly to left and right. This supposedly represents the positions in which musicians would stand on a stage. Live drum recordings are usually panned to the rough positions of the microphones on the kit. It's not like you'll be taken away by the mixing police for breaking these rules, so experiment if you want to. Some early stereo recordings put the band entirely in one speaker and the singer entirely in the other, which allowed the listener to use the balance control on their hi-fi to create their own mix. (A balance control is often confused with a pan control, but it's not the same. The balance knob controls the level of each channel, not which tracks are sent to each channel.) Watch out for using too much panning—this can leave a hole in the middle of the stereo image if you're not careful.

Mixer Automation

Balancing the tracks in a mix works best when it's done dynamically—making the lead guitar louder during a solo is a classic example. You can also use fades creatively to remove instruments from different parts of the session timeline without time-consuming edits. So far, you've been controlling faders and pans manually. In the analog days, this was the only way to mix, and sound engineers had to adjust controls in real time while the mix was being *dubbed* (copied) to a second tape machine. Hand-written notes were kept for the benefit of engineers who might have to remix the material later, but these were easily lost. Because you're using a computer, you can have the software record your mix decisions and play them back later; this is known as *mixer automation*. Ardour saves mixer automation data in the session directory, so you should be able to recall exact mix parameters many years later, even when the original rationale for the mix has long been forgotten.

You control Ardour's gain fader automation using the small gray button directly beneath the fader. By default, it has the letter *M* for Manual as a label. Click this button, and you see the other options: Play, Write, and Touch. The functions of Write and Play modes are obvious—you set Write mode when you want to record moves on an individual fader, and you set Play mode to recall them. Try it now; as the red playhead cursor in the Ardour editor moves to the point on the time line where you wrote a fade, in Play mode the fader moves in a ghostly fashion. You can't make manual adjustments to a fader when it's in Play mode.

Touch mode lies somewhere between Write and Play modes, in that existing automated fades are played back, but if you touch the fader, new automation data is recorded. Touch mode is handy if you're happy with most of the fades you've written to the automation file, but you need to make some adjustments here and there.

Pan automation works exactly the same way as gain fader automation and is controlled independently by its own Play/Write/Touch button. This small button is on the right side of the mixer strip, just below the pan controls.

Compression, Limiting, and Equalization

Now you've got the tracks in balance, with fades up and down in all the right places, it's time to address three common mix problems:

- Some of the tracks are at an inconsistent level, and it would take forever to sort out with gain fader automation. (This is often the case with vocal tracks, particularly when the singer doesn't have much studio experience.)

- Transient bursts of sound push the meters into the red, even though the rest of the track is quiet.

- Many of the instruments have a muddy, booming sound, and it's hard to hear them individually.

Sound engineers like to attack these problems using the triple whammy of compression, limiting, and equalization. These are traditional techniques used since the early days of rock 'n roll, when the aim was to make recordings sound more exciting when played on a jukebox. Fortunately for you, these methods translate well into the digital domain, and Free Software plug-ins for Ardour cover all these effects and many more. LADSPA has been the audio plug-in standard on GNU/Linux for several years, and the API of its successor, LV2 (LADSPA version two), is starting to gain acceptance. For the time being, you're likely to find that the original LADSPA versions of the plug-ins are packaged for your

GNU/Linux distro of choice. The following examples use the swh-plugins package (available from `www.plugin.org.uk`). Ubuntu users can install swh-plugins using the Synaptic Package Manager.

Compression is the tool used to solve the problem of inconsistent level. Every time the signal passes a predetermined threshold, the compressor plug-in applies a preset gain reduction on the part of the audio above the threshold. The effect is to make the loudest parts a little quieter, while the quiet parts are left alone. This creates more headroom, which is why a compressor often includes a boost control—raising level after the compression stage, for gain with reduced risk of clipping, but at the cost of an increased noise floor.

In Ardour's mixer, right-click in the black box above the Mute and Solo buttons for the track you wish to compress. This is the prefader plug-ins box; there's a corresponding post-fader plug-ins box further down. Select New Plugin from the pop-up menu, and then select Plugin Manager from the sub menu. A LADSPA plug-in selection dialog opens, if your plug-ins are correctly installed (see Figure 10-6). (You can use the same right-click menu to delete a plug-in when you no longer need it.) Plug-ins are listed alphabetically by default—you may find it helpful to click the Category button, which resorts the plug-ins by their function. Under the Compressors category is SC4, which is a stereo in, stereo out plug-in. An alternative SC4 Mono compressor is available for tracks with a single channel. Select SC4 or SC4 Mono, click the Add button, and then click the Insert Plugins button to close the dialog box.

Figure 10-6. Ardour's Plugin Manager dialog, featuring a broad range of LADSPA effects. A bug in Ubuntu means that each plug-in is listed twice in this screenshot.

The name of the plug-in you selected, SC4, appears in the prefader plug-ins box of the mixer strip. If a plug-in's name is in brackets, the plug-in is bypassed in the mixer's signal chain until you choose to activate it. Double-click SC4 to bring up the plug-in's dialog, and click the Bypass button—this plug-in's name is shown in brackets in the mixer strip. Click the Bypass button again, and the brackets disappear—the plug-in is ready for use. The name of the plug-in author is displayed proudly in the brown top bar of the plug-in's dialog—just as there is a community of Free Software application developers, there is a community of Free Software audio plug-in creators.

Next, start session playback with the play button in Ardour's transport controls; the Amplitude meter in the SC4 dialog shows some activity. The Gain Reduction meter probably isn't doing anything yet, because the default settings don't do any compression. You may need to bring the threshold level down to about -20dB or lower; and if the track is mostly transient sounds, you probably need to reduce the attack time to 10 milliseconds or so. The Attack control determines how long the compressor waits before applying the effect; if attack is set too long, the plug-in will miss transients, such as snare or bass drum hits. Finally, set the compression ratio to around 4.0. The "Gain reduction" meter starts to move (see Figure 10-7).

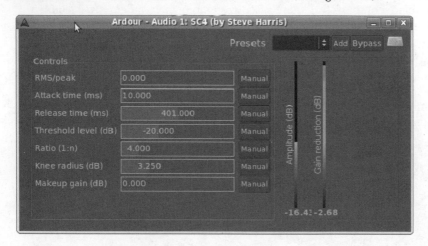

Figure 10-7. Some typical settings for the SC4 compressor. The "Gain reduction" meter shows a -2.68dB cut on the Audio 1 track, but this value varies continuously according to the input amplitude.

If only a few loud transients are reducing headroom across the track, as in the second typical problem, then a limiter may be the best solution. The swh-plug-ins package includes a plug-in called Hard Limiter, which, as the name suggests, produces a harsh clipped sound if overused (see Figure 10-8). However, with more subtle settings, you can use it to catch the occasional transient without audible side effects. Increasing the "Residue level" control softens the effect by mixing in some of the untreated signal, but allowing too much of this residue into the track's output works to negate the limiting.

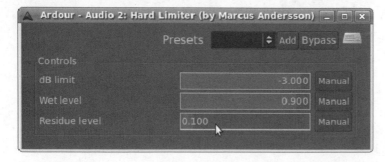

Figure 10-8. You can use the Hard Limiter plug-in to prevent transients from causing overs.

To fix the third problem, muddy and indistinct tracks, you can use a frequency equalizer, such as the LADSPA plug-in Multiband EQ (see Figure 10-9). This equalizer plug-in is a little like the graphic equalizer on some hi-fis, which is designed to compensate for acoustic deficiencies in the listening room. Alternatively, a parametric EQ plug-in allows you to specify any problematic frequency you choose and apply boost or cut as required. The bandwidth control on a parametric EQ lets you set a wide or narrow boost or cut across the frequency range, as desired. Knowing the exact frequencies to boost or cut is part of the mixer's art; but generally speaking, you're looking to avoid large overlaps in frequency bands between different tracks—and cuts usually work better than boosts.

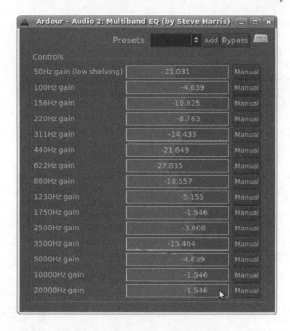

Figure 10-9. This multiband EQ with a low shelf enables you to shape the frequency curve of your track.

Mastering Principles

You've learned how to use Ardour to mix, using plug-ins and automation to make your session sound clearer, more exciting, and punchy. Now it's time to look at mastering and final export, which involve yet more processing of the digital audio. Back in the vinyl days, there was a maximum loudness a recording could reach before the stylus jumped off the record; and so a mastering engineer was employed to supervise the production of the master discs used in the vinyl-stamping machine. As CDs became the norm, mastering engineers found ways to make the average sound level higher. They figured out how to do this without breaching 0dBFS, the new maximum level imposed by digital audio systems; as you read earlier, exceeding this limit produces clipping, a distortion that is unpleasant and fatiguing to the human ear.

Although the peak level of an audio CD can't go any higher than 0dBFS, the average level has crept up steadily over the last 25 years. This is generally assumed to be for commercial reasons, because in a direct comparison, the average human prefers a louder track to a quieter one. There's been a kind of arms race to make the loudest, brightest recordings possible; and when records are played on the radio, even more processing is applied at the broadcast end of the chain. Flip between a pop radio station and a classical station on FM, and you hear a massive difference in average level. This is because of what is known as *dynamic range*. The classical recording has a high dynamic range, which means it has some very quiet bits—like a vocal solo—and some extremely loud bits, when all the instruments in an orchestra are going at full blast. By contrast, most contemporary music records are made to be loud all the time, which means their dynamic range is relatively small. Instead of quiet, loud, quiet, it's loud, really loud, extremely loud, using every trick in the digital audio book.

There's a growing consensus (among people who care) that some of these techniques are being over-applied in the pursuit of subjective loudness, which equates to a high average level. You can examine the waveforms of commercially mastered CDs by ripping (converting) them to WAV format and opening them in Ardour using Session ➤ Import. If there's no headroom between any of the peaks and 0dBFS, and a dense lump of data appears in the middle of the waveform, the CD has probably been hard-limited at the mastering stage. This is the crudest way to raise average level—just slice off all the peaks, and boost what's left. It's not all that different from clipping done on purpose. You can say goodbye to musical subtlety and hello to a headache in about five minutes.

In the extreme and rather ridiculous juxtaposition that follows, you look at Peter Lawson's recording of Erik Satie's "Three Gymnopédies" for EMI (CD-CFP 4329). This was recorded on analog tape at the Wigmore Hall in London during 1979 and remastered for CD at the famous Abbey Road studios in 1989. Then, you examine Snoop Dogg's track "Doggfather," from the 1996 album *Tha Doggfather*, on Death Row/Interscope (IND-90038), right beneath it.

First, you can see in Figure 10-10 that the Satie recording has a great deal of headroom. It may be one of the quietest recordings ever released commercially on CD. The neophyte may ask, "Why didn't the engineer at Abbey Road run this track through a normalizer plug-in to boost the level?" The reason is that professional mastering engineers don't rely on a plug-in to calculate and apply the maximum possible gain to each track. They listen to the material first and then adjust track levels by ear until all the tracks play well together. The engineer in this case may have decided that "Three Gymnopédies," being a very softly played solo piano piece, deserved to be quiet. Louder tracks come later on the CD, and making the opening track quiet preserves the natural dynamic range of the instrument. No law says that dynamics processing must be applied at all. But stick this CD on the average car stereo in rush-hour traffic, and many people will wonder if the speakers are broken.

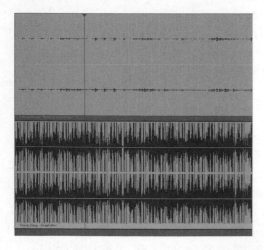

Figure 10-10. Two very different styles of mastering. "Three Gymnopédies" is at the top, and "Doggfather" is on the track below.

In contrast, not only does the Snoop Dogg recording peak at 0dBFS on every kick-drum hit and hand clap, but the average level is many, many times higher than the Satie recording. True, you can hear the song clearly, even when the volume control on your amplifier is turned down low; but the hand claps sound very harsh, and any dynamics present in the studio mix have been squashed flat. What you're aiming for is a happy medium between these two extremes, with enough processing to enable your mix to be heard, but without damaging the qualities that you were able to hear for yourself during the recording.

Of course, some records deserve to be played loud. But by over-using limiting techniques, the mastering engineer makes that decision for you. Excessive processing during the CD mastering stage may be one reason why many critical listeners still prefer the 'warm' and 'natural' sound of vinyl, even though the vinyl mastering process can produce artifacts of its own. Consider that a complex musical waveform is the product of many superimposed sound waves of various shapes and frequencies. It usually ends up looking something like a sine wave, but with lots of smaller ripples in it. Using hard limiting, all the musical information over 0dBFS is lost, and only a flat-topped waveform remains. It's a bit like having the complete works of Shakespeare, except with every fourth word replaced by *blah*:

Shall I compare blah to a summer's blah?
Thou art more blah and more temperate:
Blah winds do shake blah darling buds of Blah,
And summer's lease blah all too short blah date

You'd get pretty sick of hearing the word *blah* by the end of a three-hour play. Your ear feels the same way about square waves.

Hope You Like JAMin Too

The core tools of the digital audio mastering engineer aren't all that different from those used in the mix—compression, limiting, and equalization again. The main difference is that mastering plug-ins are generally less invasive, because they're not meant to have an obvious effect. You're only supposed to notice the increase in average level and how much better the mix translates to different playback systems, not any change in tonal color or increase in distortion. It's possible to master a session using Ardour's LADSPA plug-in support, but the Ardour mixer isn't geared to the task. Instead, you can use JAMin (GNU/Linux), the name of which stands for the JACK Audio Mastering Interface. JAMin is available from http://jamin.sourceforge.net or in most good GNU/Linux distributions. Ubuntu users can install the jamin package with the Add/Remove Applications tool. Because it's a stand-alone program, you can use JAMin with any JACK application, not just Ardour.

JAMin provides a custom interface for a collection of the most frequently required stereo mastering plug-ins and provides global preset save and recall facilities for them. It includes a 1023 band equalizer with parametric controls and a neat hand-drawn frequency curve feature. There's also a more traditional 30-band equalizer with faders and a built-in spectrum analyzer. Next in the signal chain is a three-band mastering compressor, which means you can adjust bass, middle, and treble frequency bands independently. On the output stage, a look-ahead brick-wall limiter catches any transient peaks that exceed 0dBFS. The look-ahead feature means the effect of limiting isn't as harsh and obvious as a simple hard limiter that square-waves every peak.

You must have JACK running before you attempt to start JAMin, or it won't work. Next, open your previous Ardour session. You need to use JAMin's bypass button to make subjective comparisons between processed and unprocessed sound, which means JAMin has to sit in the signal chain between Ardour's master bus outputs and your soundcard's playback ports (see Figure 10-11).

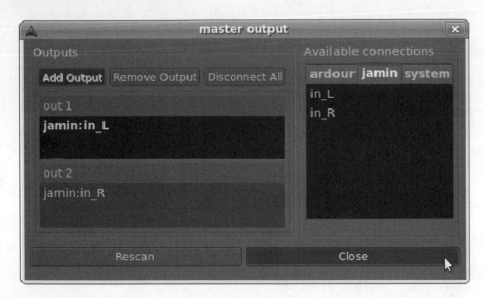

Figure 10-11. JAMin connected between Ardour's master bus outputs and the first two ports of the internal soundcard

Because JAMin connects to your soundcard by default on startup, the easiest way to accomplish this is to use Ardour's mixer to disconnect the master bus outputs from the soundcard and then connect them to JAMin's inputs. You can use JAMin to manage JACK connections by using JAMin's own Ports menu, but make sure you disconnect any previous direct connection from Ardour's master outputs to your soundcard first.

Don't be too alarmed if the DSP load figure reported by JACK shoots up. JAMin is CPU hungry—it has to be, to perform complex audio processing tasks in real time. Just like Ardour, JAMin works best on a system with a real-time kernel, but you shouldn't need one just to check out how the program works.

Back in Ardour, to the right of the clock on the top bar is a small drop-down menu that says Internal by default; switch this to Jack. (You may recall setting this menu option when working with Hydrogen in the last chapter.) You can now remote-control Ardour's transport using the play, rewind, and pause buttons at upper left in the JAMin window. You can also press the space bar on your keyboard to toggle play or pause, just as in Ardour. This saves a lot of clicking back and forth between windows during the mastering process.

Now you're ready to begin mastering. First, click the left-pointing arrow in the JAMin transport controls to rewind to the beginning of your Ardour session. Then, click the triangle play button, and the JAMin clock to the immediate right starts counting upward. To the right again, the transport indicator says Rolling. If all is well, the green input and output meters at the extreme left and right of the JAMin window, respectively, flicker, and you hear your Ardour session playing back through your soundcard (see Figure 10-12).

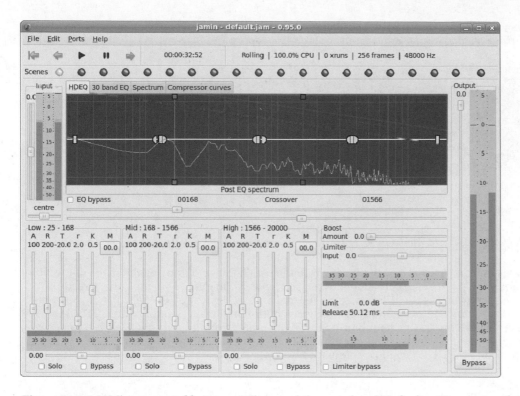

Figure 10-12. JAMin connected between Ardour and the soundcard. Default settings mean that not much processing is apparent yet.

The Equalizer

The first thing to check is the input level meter, at left in the JAMin interface. If the thin blue horizontal lines, which represent peak level, are well below 0dBFS on the scale, you've got headroom for a level increase. If you increase input level too far and have to drop it down using the fader to the left of the meter, right-click anywhere on the meter scale to reset the blue peak lines.

Next, check out the dancing pale green line in the main hand-drawn equalizer (HDEQ) window in the center of the JAMin interface. This dancing line represents the frequency curve of your session at that moment. (There's also a bar graph analyzer on the Spectrum tab, if you need it.) If there are any extreme peaks, you can use the HDEQ to make cuts by drawing them on the waveform and get back some headroom. But before you go to town with the HDEQ's pencil tool, bear in mind that bass frequencies usually have a lot more energy than treble frequencies; it's normal to see a downward slope toward the right of the HDEQ window.

As you move the pencil cursor over the waveform, the line of characters immediately below the window reports the audio frequency at the point you're hovering over, from 25Hz (low bass) on the far left to 20000Hz (high treble) on the far right. Like digital audio sample rate, audio frequency (musical pitch) is measured in Hertz (cycles per second), but these are two very different measurements. 25Hz to 20000Hz approximates to the range of audio frequencies that a good pair of loudspeakers can reproduce (their *frequency response*). The pencil tool also reports the EQ adjustment if you click at that point, as well as the current reading from the spectrum analyzer (see Figure 10-13).

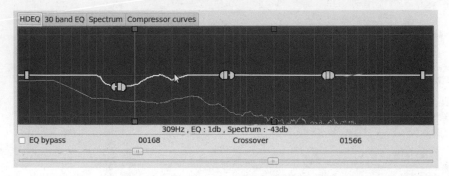

Figure 10-13. *JAMin's hand-drawn equalizer feature is unique to this Free Software mastering tool.*

Try making some boosts and cuts by clicking with the pencil tool and drawing the shape of the white EQ line you require. Click again to complete the line, and have JAMin join it with the curve already on the screen. If you screw up, right-click with the pencil tool to reset the white EQ line to flat. If you're not sure if you're making any improvement, click the Bypass button in the lower-right corner of the JAMin window to neutralize all processing temporarily. And if you prefer a traditional equalizer, you can click the 30 band EQ tab to see the more usual representation of the same settings. Any changes you make on this tab are applied to the HDEQ window automatically.

Heavy Dub Pressure

Look at the three-band stereo compressor, which sits beneath the HDEQ window. The single-letter labels on the vertical faders aren't all that obvious, but they stand for *Attack, Release, Threshold, ratio* (note the small *r*), *Knee*, and *Makeup gain*. Beneath each panel of the compressor is a right-pointing green meter that shows the input level in the relevant frequency band—Low, Mid, and High (see Figure 10-14). Immediately below this is a left-pointing meter that shows the gain reduction applied by the compressor. It has a yellow bar by default, but I personally use the Colors drop-down menu under Edit ➤ Preferences to change the Meter Warning color to orange, because it shows up better.

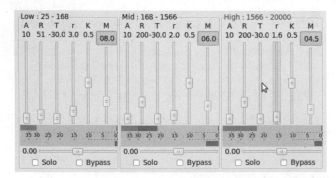

Figure 10-14. *JAMin's compressor is divided into three bands: Low, Mid, and High.*

Select the Solo check box beneath the compressor for the Low band. You hear just the bass frequencies of your session. Because of the relatively high energy of the bass frequencies, it's down here that compression can help the most. Lower the Threshold fader until the compression meter starts to work. If you've got a kick drum in the mix, you probably also need to reduce the Attack fader to a setting of around 50 milliseconds or less. Click the Auto button at the top of the Makeup gain fader, and you should hear an obvious increase of level in the low frequency band. Now, uncheck the Solo box, and repeat the process for the other two bands. Keep using the Bypass button to make sure you're making an improvement to the overall sound. You can click the "Compressor curves" tab above the main JAMin window to see a plot of input level against output level, which changes in real time as you make adjustments to the faders (see Figure 10-15). These graphs are especially useful to demonstrate what the Knee control does—try it and see.

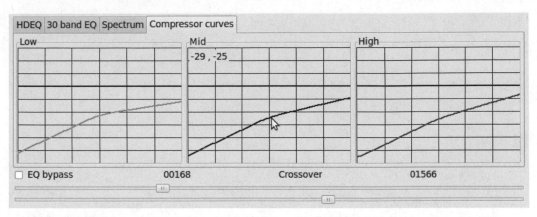

Figure 10-15. The "Compressor curves" window shows graphs for each of the three bands.

Reaching the Limit

Just above the Limiter, which is at lower right in the JAMin interface, is a Boost control. You can use it for a quick and dirty increase in output level, but do so with caution—unless you're deliberately aiming for a distorted effect. The Boost control is meant to simulate a mildly overdriven valve amplifier for a warm sound, but you have to judge for yourself whether an effect of this nature is useful to you, or if it should have been added back at the mixing stage.

Next is the look-ahead limiter. The default settings of Input 0.0 and Limit 0.0dB should probably be left alone for now. Certainly you can increase the input setting and get an instant increase in subjective loudness; but if your session is well mixed already, you'll be heading for Square Wave City. You may need to reduce the limiter Release control to less than the default 50 milliseconds if its effect is too obvious, but that's probably a sign that you're using the limiter too often. If you're curious to see the difference that the limiter makes, check the "Limiter bypass" box at the bottom and watch the output meter at right go into the red on transient peaks (see Figure 10-16). You can also use the limiter bypass control to hear how much distortion the limiter adds when you over-do the Boost and Input level settings.

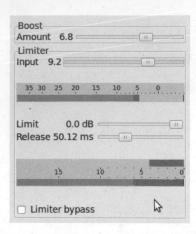

Figure 10-16. *How much is too much? This much. Note that the limiter is working hard, as shown by the upper orange bar.*

Making a Scene

With so many settings available to tweak, it's a relief that JAMin supports plug-in automation through its scene function. Look at the row of colored lights along the top of the JAMin interface; the first one on the left should be yellow and the rest should be red, for now. Right-click the yellow one, and choose Set from the pop-up menu—the light turns green. You can use the Name option to give it the same name as your session or part of your session—for example, Verse, Chorus, or Solo. If you mouse over a scene light that has been named, the name is displayed in a tooltip. Now, make some adjustments to JAMin's controls, and right-click to set the second colored light. You now have two green lights, with the active setting in a brighter shade of green.

This is the very cool part; if you click any green light, not only are the saved settings loaded, but the faders slowly morph and crossfade from one setting to the other. So, you can save and recall mastering settings several times within a single session, and JAMin handles the transition between scenes with ultra-smoothness. When you're happy with all your scene settings, choose File ➤ Save As to save the presets to the `.jamin` directory under your `/home` directory.

You're now ready to export the mastered version of your Ardour session to a WAV file for CD burning, or for encoding to FLAC or Ogg Vorbis formats. This process is exactly the same as exporting the Ardour session as you did before, except that you don't want to export Ardour's master bus—that would give you the unmastered version. Instead, choose Session ➤ Add Track/Bus in Ardour, create one new stereo bus, and change its name from Bus 1 to something like 'jamin return'. Make sure the output of this new bus isn't connected to Ardour's master bus before you perform the next step, or you'll get gigantic feedback in your loudspeakers or headphones. The easiest way to do this is to click the Output button at the bottom of the mixer strip for the new bus and select Disconnect from the pop-up menu.

Now, use the Input button in Ardour's mixer strip for this bus to select JAMin's left output as the first input and JAMin's right output as the second (see Figure 10-17).

Figure 10-17. JAMin's output ports show up in Ardour's "Available connections" window.

You should see the meter on the mixer strip for the jamin return bus move up and down. If JAMin is set up correctly, this new bus shows an average level that's similar to or higher than Ardour's master bus, but with no overs (see Figure 10-18).

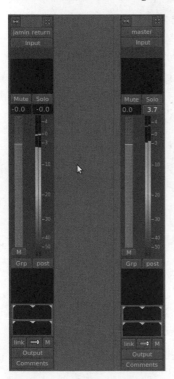

Figure 10-18. The jamin return bus in the Ardour mixer. The level coming back from JAMin has a peak level of exactly 0.0dBFS—but there's still more than 3dB of headroom at this point. The master bus is showing overs, peaking at 3.7dBFS, but JAMin has taken care of these.

Now, all you need to do is open Ardour's Session ➤ Export dialog, uncheck the master bus outputs, click the "Specific tracks" button, and check the boxes for the jamin return bus first and second outputs to go to the left and right channels, respectively, in the WAV file (see Figure 10-19). Because you need to reduce bit depth from JACK's internal 32-bit format to the 16-bit format required for an audio CD, it's advisable to enable the Dither option. *Dither* means adding a little random noise to the signal to smooth the effect of throwing away all those bits of digital audio information; it sounds crazy, but it works. Shaped-noise dither is supposed by some people to be the best option—try all three types, and see if you can tell the difference.

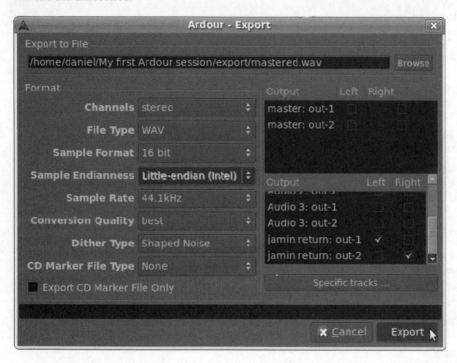

Figure 10-19. Make sure you check the correct output boxes when exporting from the jamin return bus.

Testing Your Results

The only sure way to know that you're on the right path with mastering is to test, test, and test again. You should use a variety of playback systems for the task, depending on the kind of listeners you're aiming your music at. Kitchen CD players, car stereos, portables with earbud headphones, and club sound systems are all very different in terms of frequency response across the audible spectrum. It's great if you're a professional mastering engineer and you can afford to invest in full-range reference speakers, like the Bowers & Wilkins 800D at around $23,000 a pair. But if most of your listeners have nasty plastic PC speakers like the models shown in Figure 10-20, available for under $20 in a chain store, then you've got to test your masters on them at least once.

Figure 10-20. *The PC Line PCL-201S—six watts of raw power for the price of a pizza!*

Audio CD Production

CD and DVD writers have been fitted to mass-market PCs for years, and the technology is now so ubiquitous that blank media is sold in supermarkets along with other everyday consumables like toothpaste and breakfast cereal. As a Free Software distributor, as well as a sound engineer and aspiring record producer, I'm probably one of the only customers of my local bulk blank media store who isn't actively involved in copyright infringement. It's no wonder that the established suppliers in the ready-made culture market are engaged in a collective panic over their future.

Nevertheless, the CD writer has brought the means of production into the hands of the individual, whether you want to make a disc of your own music, a 'mixtape' of a live DJ set, or a compilation of existing recordings. Subjective comparisons of digital audio with the 'warmth' of vinyl miss the point, as far as home production is concerned. It was never this straightforward or affordable to make your own releases back in the DIY days of punk rock and 7" singles.

With the advent of Blu-Ray, the price of a bare DVD writer for fitting to a PC has fallen below $40, and these cheap generic drives can easily burn a full-length audio CD in a few minutes. In cities like Los Angeles, it's common to be approached on the street by a young man holding a fistful of home-produced hip-hop CDs for sale, in a sort of twenty-first century take on busking. The URL of his MySpace page is invariably written on the CD-R with a marker pen.

The CD Still Rules

It's almost too easy to throw together a CD, scribble a name on the disc, and stuff it into a paper case, but Free Software and GNU/Linux distributions offer a range of tools that can help you create a more polished article. The artwork techniques described in this chapter are equally applicable to data or movie discs, but you can use the audio CD as a starting point.

The original Red Book specification for audio CDs was released jointly by Sony and Philips in 1980, describing a two-channel (usually stereo) format with 16 bits of signed PCM data. The Red Book specifies that recordings can be no longer than 74 minutes. The unlikely CD sample rate of 44100 cycles per second (Hertz) was derived from the frame rate of analog video tape. VCRs were used for digital audio master recordings in those days, before purpose-built DASH and DAT machines were invented.

In 1988, the Orange Book offered a new specification for recordable CDs, with a format close enough to Red Book that most standard audio CD players could play correctly formatted CD-Rs. In contrast with movie DVDs, a conventional audio CD has no filesystem and therefore no directory structure. Instead, a subcode is multiplexed with the audio; these are the PQ codes, containing basic metadata about the start position of individual tracks, publishing information, and so on. In 1996, the CD-Text extension to the Red Book standard was released, allowing more complex metadata, including artist and track names, to be embedded in the subcode. However, not all audio CD players support CD-Text, and not all burners have support for CD-Text in their firmware.

More recently, higher quality digital formats including SACD and DVD-Audio have flopped in the marketplace, a casualty of the rush to portability (the iPod and its clones) and downloaded lossy-compressed music at less than CD quality (MP3 and the AAC format found on iTunes). This has left the venerable Red Book format toward the high-quality end of the fidelity spectrum, as far as music distribution is concerned, despite the fact that recording studio technology now employs much higher sample and bit rates. Free Software offers a solution: the 24-bit version of the FLAC format, which has begun to be adopted by *audiophiles* (people who care about sound quality in music recording). The aforementioned Bowers & Wilkins company, maker of some of the finest loudspeakers available, has settled on 24-bit FLAC as the distribution format for its Society of Sound record label, fronted by musician and studio owner Peter Gabriel (see `www.bowers-wilkins.com` for details).

In the meantime, audio CDs remain a convenient way to distribute music on a widely understood and supported medium, especially when face to face with the intended listener. Because of the age of the Red Book format and its therefore relatively limited technical requirements, even PCs generally considered redundant are easily able to handle the amount of data involved in CD production, when your GNU/Linux distro of choice has been installed.

Burn, Baby, Burn

Many Free Software disc-authoring tools are available, both command-line and graphical, and practically all of them can make valid audio CD-Rs. Most of these tools, like their proprietary equivalents, treat the audio tracks as if they were generic files, listing them in a window with track-length information. In contrast, GNOME CD Master (GNU/Linux) draws the audio data as a waveform, which, as you read earlier, is a digital representation of the real-life audio wave. This feature allows you to see at once if the audio data is too loud or too quiet, or inconsistent in level between tracks. Superficially, GNOME CD Master resembles an audio editor such as Audacity, but in fact there are only limited cut and paste features available. Instead, the program is designed to let you append or insert audio from `.wav` files into a sequence of data that is then burned to disc. GNOME CD Master is available for download from `http://cdrdao.sourceforge.net/gcdmaster/` or ready-packaged in many GNU/Linux distributions. Ubuntu users can download it using the Add/Remove Applications tool, which adds an entry for the program to the Sound & Video menu.

The gcdmaster program is a front-end for cdrdao, the command-line tool for disc-at-once recording. Recording CDs this way, instead of track by track, gives you fine control over the gaps between tracks—or, alternatively, enables you to have track markers without any gaps. This feature is useful for dividing up a long recording without splitting it into individual files first. If you have to change track positions, it's a lot quicker to do it with markers than to go back to the source material and chop up .wav files again. The program also has some support for parallel burning to multiple drives, which could be very useful if you're thinking of going into mass production.

PERMISSION ERRORS ON UBUNTU

Some versions of Ubuntu, including Jaunty, have a bug that delays the start-up of GNOME CD Master by ten or more seconds. If you run gcdmaster in a terminal, you may see a message like this, over and over again:

```
Error trying to open /dev/sg0 exclusively (Permission denied)... retrying in 1 second.
```

On some computers, this bug prevents CDs from being written with this program, because GNOME CD Master runs but can't scan the burner hardware. If this is the case on your computer, you can use a different CD-burning program such as Brasero (GNU/Linux), which is installed on Ubuntu by default.

To get started with GNOME CD Master, gather together the .wav files containing the audio data you wish to put on the CD. These should be prepared as 44100 Hz, 16-bit files, to match the audio CD standard. You should also consider applying dither, if you're reducing bit depth in the conversion process. If you're using Audacity to export your audio material, the File ➤ Export menu item defaults to .wav at CD sample rate and bit depth as long as Project Rate (Hz) is set to 44100 in the lower-left corner of the Audacity window. The dither options are located under the Quality tab of the Edit ➤ Preferences dialog in Audacity. When you're exporting .wav files from Ardour, the sample rate, bit depth, and dither options are in the Export dialog, as you read a few pages ago.

Running gcdmaster from the command line or a menu item, the first thing you see is a small GUI inviting you to begin a new project. You're interested in the Audio button; it's subtitled "Create an audio CD from wav files" (see Figure 10-21).

Figure 10-21. Gnome CD Master has a simple start-up dialog.

Click this button to open a blank window titled `unnamed-0.toc`. This window title refers to GNOME CD Master's native project format, a text file listing the positions of the files relative to the start of the CD and where the track markers are (see Figure 10-22). The `toc` part of the filename stands for *table of contents*. It's a good idea to save your project at this stage with a more meaningful name; you must give it a `.toc` extension, because GNOME CD Master doesn't append the suffix automatically. File ➤ Save As does the trick. Then, select Edit ➤ Append Track. A file-selection dialog opens in which you can click on a suitably formatted `.wav` file. Next, click the Add button in the lower-right corner. The dialog doesn't close automatically, which lets you go on selecting files and clicking Add until your sequence of `.wav` files is complete. Then, click the Close button.

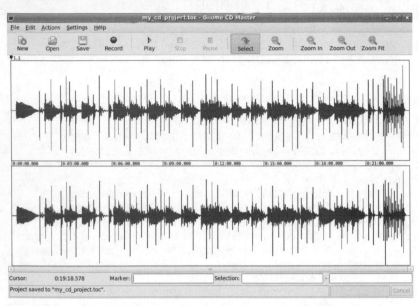

Figure 10-22. Add tracks one at a time, until your CD project is complete.

Returning to the main window of GNOME CD Master, you may have to resize or maximize the window before you can see the buttons to the right of the toolbar. The Zoom button allows you to inspect a selection of the waveform up close, perhaps to examine a section that is distorted. The Select tool enables cut and paste operations, which are found on the Edit menu. However, there is no Undo option, so edit carefully or prepare to restart the process of importing and appending `.wav` files.

When you're happy with the sequence of tracks, you can click the Play button to hear the entire CD via the default sound hardware on your system. Using the Select tool in combination with the Play button means you don't have to listen to the whole project from the start, just the part you're most interested in.

If you want to add a new track marker, click the waveform, and the cursor draws a red vertical line at that point. Then, choose Edit ➤ Add Track Mark, and the new mark appears (see Figure 10-23).

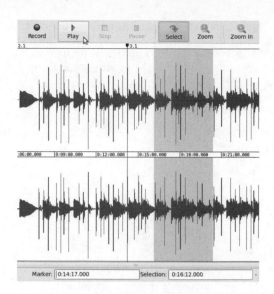

Figure 10-23. Gnome CD Master enables both visual and auditory inspection of the proposed CD data.

If you have a burner that supports the format, you can use the CD-Text–related options at the top of the Edit menu to input metadata (see Figure 10-24). Note that if you want to use the Track Info option, you need to click the track marker immediately above the waveform to select it; the marker is highlighted with a red background. You can also choose Edit ➤ Remove Track Mark when a particular track marker is selected.

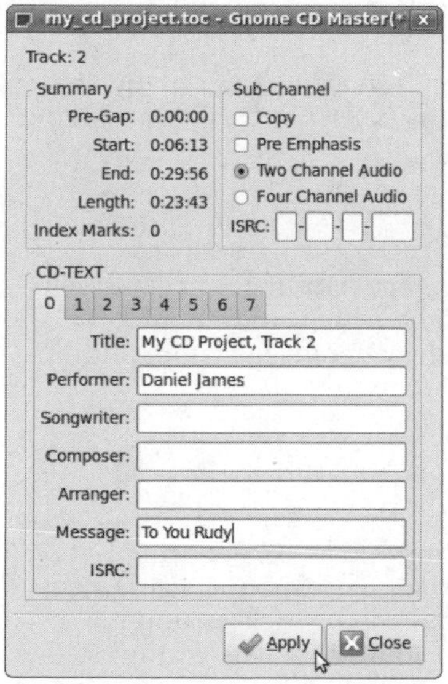

Figure 10-24. CD-Text lets you include metadata, but not all burners support the feature.

Click the Save button again to update the .toc file, and then click Record. A burning dialog opens, listing the available recorder devices and their status. By default, the Simulate option is selected, which is a hangover from the days when optical drives suffered from buffer under-runs and blank media was relatively expensive. In a well-configured GNU/Linux system, you should be able to go straight to Burn without problems, but try the Simulate option if you wish.

Figure 10-25. *You have the opportunity to simulate the burning process if you don't want to risk making coasters.*

After burning has completed, a dialog prompts you to eject the disc. Because your .toc file has been saved, you can return another day to burn the same sequence again using the Open button on the initial GNOME CD Master dialog, instead of starting from scratch each time. That is, as long as you don't move the .wav files. If you do, the program doesn't know where to find them. Because the .toc files made by GNOME CD Master don't use full system paths, it makes sense to store the .toc file and the .wav files in the same directory.

GNOME CD Master has a detailed manual page that explains all the advanced features of the program, in case you want to dig deeper. To read it, open a terminal on any GNU/Linux system with the program installed, and type

```
man gcdmaster
```

Then, press the Enter key. Doing so opens the manual page directly in the terminal; you can scroll through it using the up and down arrow keys on your keyboard. All old-school Free Software programs on GNU/Linux are packaged with this type of text documentation, for quick reference to command-line options. Just type man followed by a space and the name of the program binary.

Making It Pretty

Many self-produced CDs have a rough-and-ready look, but with a little care and an ink-jet printer, their appearance can be improved a great deal. First, there's the question of what to do with the disc surface. Sticky labels can be fed on a sheet into most kinds of printer, although they can be tricky to apply smoothly. Blank discs with printable surfaces are readily available, but of course you need hardware that explicitly supports printing directly on to CDs. My own experience is that printable-surface CD-Rs are slightly less reliable when it comes to audio CD player compatibility, but perhaps I've just been unlucky.

Either way, you need to prepare your artwork and find a driver that supports printing on to circular media. The good news is that the Free Software Gutenprint drivers offer support in GNU/Linux for direct CD printing on Epson ink-jets that have the feature. This includes print-size settings for both standard 5-inch (120mm) CDs and 3-inch (80mm) mini CDs (the latter size was once used for CD singles). Driver support on other printers with CD trays may be incomplete, so it's recommended that you check the OpenPrinting database at `www.openprinting.org` for details of your specific model.

Many GNU/Linux distributions include Gutenprint drivers by default. On Ubuntu, you can find these drivers in the cups-driver-gutenprint package, which is installed using the Synaptic Package Manager. You may also wish to install the gimp-gutenprint package; it's a plug-in that adds a new print dialog to the GIMP, with finer control over printing options.

Even with driver support, ink-jet printing onto CD surfaces can be a little hit and miss. I'm currently using an Epson Stylus Photo R200, which was the lowest-cost decent-quality model with CD printing features I could find (see Figure 10-26). The model is now discontinued, having been replaced by the Epson Artisan 50, which retails for around $100. The print quality of the R200 with Gutenprint is generally very good, although the CD feeding tray can be difficult to get working. The trick is to leave the cover of the printer open and check that the leading edge of the CD tray is engaging with the motorized rollers that drag it under the print head. If not, a slight shove gets it moving in the right direction.

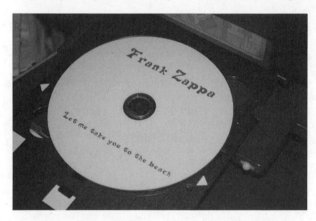

Figure 10-26. Epson's ink-jet printers can print on the CD surface, if you're prepared to coax them a little.

An application used for preparing artwork for CDs should support vector file formats and have PostScript output, because you want your fonts to be crisp and clear. Inkscape and Scribus are good choices, with Scribus being particularly useful if you need to generate PDF output for someone else to print. You can use the GIMP if you prefer, as long as you make sure your bitmap output has high resolution; but the following example uses Inkscape. Refer to Chapter 4 if you've skipped ahead and don't have Inkscape installed and running.

By default, Inkscape opens with a blank A4 canvas, but you need to set up the size that's required for your CD. Choose File ➤ Document Properties, and set the default units to millimeters. This setting is a lot more useful for a CD than points, the traditional typographer's unit of measurement. Then, in the "Custom size" box, change the Height and Width values to 120mm, or 80mm for a mini CD.

Figure 10-27. Set the Inkscape document size to ensure correct alignment in the printer.

Close the Document Properties box, and you see a square canvas. I find it useful to draw circles representing the outside and inside of the printable area of the disc, as a guide. This is easy to do with the Circle, Ellipse, and Arc tool on the toolbar at left (the pink circle). Hold down the Ctrl key while dragging to get a regular circle. The exact size of the printable area around the CD hub depends on your particular brand of blank media and your Gutenprint settings, but Figure 10-28 allows a generous diameter of 40mm. Before printing, you can right-click these guide objects, select Object Properties, and check the Hide box, so they don't show up on the printed disc. You can also drag vertical and horizontal guides from the rulers to give you an idea where the center of the CD hub is.

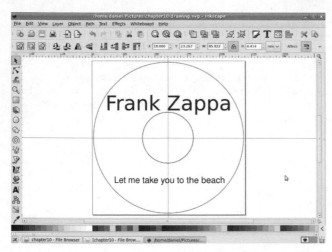

Figure 10-28. Guidelines and circles help you center the CD design.

Using the Text tool from the toolbar, labeled with an *A*, is straightforward, although the default font isn't very interesting. To fix this, open the Text and Font dialog from the top menu bar, labeled with a *T*. In this dialog, select a font family and style; you probably need to increase the font size for a title. The font in your artwork isn't updated until you click the Apply button. This example uses a font called Delta Hey Max Nine Regular by Ray Larabie, in 56 point and 30 point sizes (see Figure 10-29). You can find Larabie's TrueType fonts packaged for most GNU/Linux distros, or you can download them directly from `www.larabiefonts.com`. In Ubuntu, you can install the ttf-larabie-straight, ttf-larabie-uncommon, and ttf-larabie-deco packages using Synaptic.

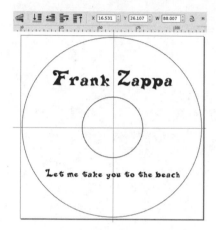

Figure 10-29. Ray Larabie's freaky font makes the CD look more interesting.

To color your fonts, use the Fill and Stroke dialog, which you open via the paintbrush icon on the top menu bar. *Fill* refers to the body color of the font, and *stroke* is the outline color; by default, there's no stroke on the font, but try different stroke paints and styles to see if you like the effect (see Figure 10-30).

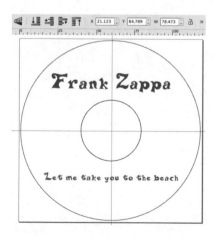

Figure 10-30. Adding a touch of color makes the font stand out even more.

When you're ready to print, check the printer control panel of your GNU/Linux distro to fine-tune your Gutenprint settings. Scribus allows you to do this from within the application, using the Options button in the Print dialog; but Inkscape appears to rely on the system's print dialog. When you run Inkscape on Ubuntu, on the Page Setup tab of the print dialog, you need to change "Paper source" to Print to CD so the printer knows which tray to feed (see Figure 10-31). On the Advanced tab, you can specify the CD hub size and fine adjustment values (see Figure 10-32). Make sure Backend is set to Vector, not Bitmap, on the Rendering tab. Then, click the Print button, and the job is sent to the printer.

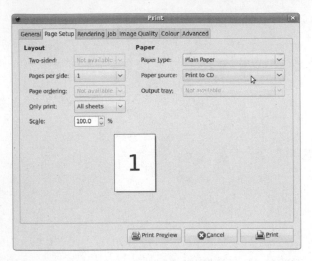

Figure 10-31. Check your print settings to make sure you're sending the artwork to the correct tray.

Figure 10-32. Careful review of advanced settings makes sure you don't waste ink and blank discs.

Printing packaging for your CD is much the same as printing on the disc, except that you have a lot more flexibility. It's simple enough to design inserts for standard jewel cases in Inkscape, although having a rotary paper trimmer available makes cutting the insert a lot more accurate than cutting by hand. The dimensions of the inserts should be available from your CD case supplier; if not, careful measurement and a little trial and error produces the figures that you need. But no law says a CD has to be in a plastic case—you can wrap it up like a parcel or get creative with origami if you want to.

Ardour Integration

If you're preparing your audio material in Ardour, integration with Gnome CD Master is pretty seamless (see Figure 10-33). In your Ardour project, use the CD Markers strip to show the beginning and end of tracks, or check the CD box in the Locations window to turn ranges into CD tracks. When it comes to exporting your session, set CD Marker File Type to TOC, and a .toc file is saved alongside your exported .wav file. You can open this .toc file in Gnome CD Master, just as if you'd created it manually in the program.

Figure 10-33. *Ardour and Gnome CD Master work very well together, thanks to Ardour's TOC export feature.*

Other Useful Programs

Neither of the following programs is available in Ubuntu yet, but you can download them as source code from the www.kokkinizita.net/linuxaudio/ web site along with a variety of other tools suitable for use in mixing and mastering:

- *Jconv* (GNU/Linux): A convolution engine for JACK. Reverberation is sampled from real spaces, such as cathedrals, using the impulse response technique. This naturalistic reverb can then be applied to a digital mix using convolution.

- *Jkmeter* (GNU/Linux): An audio mastering meter, based on the K-System designed by Bob Katz. This system allows masters to be compared against a reference for subjective loudness, providing a guard against excessive compression and limiting.

Further Reading

Mixing is a subjective art form, and listening to experienced mix engineers talk about their work can help you learn a lot. The techniques are basically the same for traditional analog or computer-based recording, and lots of relevant advice is available in print. *Mixing Audio—Concepts, Practices and Tools* by Roey Izhaki (Focal Press, 2008, ISBN-13: 9780240520681) is supported by a web site at `www.mixingaudio.com` that offers a sample chapter. The monthly magazine *Sound on Sound*, to which I am an occasional contributor, is an excellent resource for mixing and recording tips. Its web site at `www.soundonsound.com` features many archived tutorials and interviews with mix and recording engineers from the last 15 years.

If you're curious to know more about digital audio mastering, the definitive book on the subject is *Mastering Audio: The Art and the Science*, by Bob Katz (Focal Press, 2002, ISBN-13: 9780240808376). The only omission in the first edition was that Katz didn't mention JAMin, GNU/Linux, or Free Software, leaving the impression that the reader required a lot of expensive, specialized equipment to practice and improve their mastering skills. To be fair to Katz, JAMin was pretty new when the book first came out.

CHAPTER 11

■ ■ ■

Video Editing

With video-sharing web sites like YouTube and its clones firmly embedded in the mainstream consciousness, and the Firefox browser now having built-in support for the Free Software Ogg Theora video format, it's arguable that the Internet has outgrown its text-only origins. Whatever you think of the late Marshall McLuhan's theories on print versus TV, making videos and sharing them is just plain fun.

Unfortunately, out-of-the-box support for editing and publishing video shorts on the GNU/Linux platform has lagged behind the proprietary competition. It's not just that writing a nonlinear video editor is hard; after all, the Free Software development community has tackled other ambitious projects. It's more likely that the effect of software patent claims on video *codecs* (compression and decompression methods) is to blame. This issue has prevented many GNU/Linux distributions from shipping video-editing applications, damaging integration and restricting the user base to the seriously interested. Despite this situation, in addition to the tools covered in this chapter, several Free Software video-editing projects are under way. Some of the graphical applications aren't fully stable yet, and a couple of them are barely functional. However, with care and patience, it's possible to edit and complete video projects using only Free Software tools. Many of the popular video-based web sites use Free Software command-line video tools behind the scenes.

To complicate matters, two video files that appear to be in the same format can vary in playability on any specific computer. This is because a video file with an extension like .mpg (for MPEG), .ogv (for Ogg video), or .avi (for … er … AVI) can be used to contain any two codecs. There's one codec for the video data and another for the audio, which are chosen by the person who authored the project from a long list of the codecs currently available. Therefore, it's important to know which specific codecs you and your audience have installed, to guarantee a smooth playback experience.

Converting Video with Avidemux

Avidemux (GNU/Linux, Windows, Mac) is a Free Software video-editing application designed for simple cutting, filtering, and encoding tasks. Its strength lies in its support for a wide variety of video file formats, including AVI, the MPEG-2 files found on DVDs, and the newer MPEG-4 standard. Avidemux also handles a number of popular video and audio codecs out of the box. This makes the program an excellent conversion tool, either working alone or alongside other video-editing applications. You can download it via the project home page at www.avidemux.org in versions for all supported platforms. Ubuntu users can install the program with the Synaptic package manager from the multiverse repository.

Sometimes you have a complete video project that happens to be in the wrong format. This section's example uses a video that's already been shot, and converts it to a format suitable for YouTube or another video-sharing web site.

■ **Note** As you read a couple of chapters ago about making podcasts, it's important to check copyright details before you upload any media to the Internet. Most video-sharing web sites, including YouTube, ask you to swear that you have copyright for the material you're uploading, which is their way of passing the buck. It means that if the lawyers come knocking at YouTube's door, they can redirect those lawyers to visit you instead.

On Ubuntu, after you install Avidemux, you can find the program on the Sound & Video menu. Running it for the first time reveals a window with drop-down menus for codecs and format on the left side and a timeline and transport controls at the bottom. The codec drop-down menus for Video and Audio default to Copy, which means Avidemux preserves the codecs of the original video material (see Figure 11-1). In theory, this should keep the quality of the final video as high as possible, because *transcoding* (converting from one compressed format to another) can often result in artifacts, with the effects of compression all too obvious on-screen.

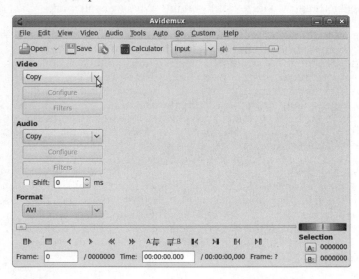

***Figure 11-1.** Avidemux is a popular Free Software video conversion tool. The simple interface hides a very useful and versatile program.*

Beneath these codec menus is the drop-down menu for Format, which defaults to AVI. The AVI format came originally from Microsoft Windows; like MP3, it's a legacy format that remains in use because of its wide support on viewers' PCs. However, third-party changes to the AVI standard, intended to add modern features, have been known to break its backward compatibility—so it's not quite a universal format.

Click the Open button in the upper-left corner of the Avidemux interface, select the video material you wish to convert from the file dialog that pops up, and then click Open. In addition to the video input formats that Avidemux supports, the program can also import numbered sequences of still BMP, JPEG, or PNG pixmap files. This is a very useful feature if you've been creating animated sequences as a series of still images in another program, such as KToon (see Figure 11-2). It's also useful for importing title frames previously created in Inkscape or the GIMP.

Figure 11-2. *It's the stick man from Chapter 5! Avidemux can assemble a series of still frames into a video file, as long as they're sequentially numbered.*

Creating the video output file is as simple as selecting appropriate choices from the drop-down menus at left in the Avidemux interface and clicking the Save button at left on the upper toolbar. An Encoding window pops up, offering statistics and a progress bar (see Figure 11-3). Video encoding is very CPU intensive, so this process may take a long time if you have a lot of frames to encode or your computer is an older model.

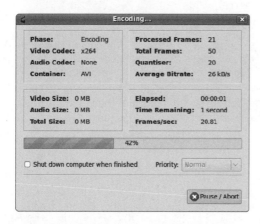

Figure 11-3. *The progress bar indicates how long you have to wait for your video to be encoded. If it's a long video and your computer is slow, it may be time to order a pizza. This simple example has only 50 frames of animation, which are being encoded at around 20 frames per second.*

Importing from DVD

As you read in Chapter 10, a movie DVD is different from an audio CD in that it contains a filesystem, like any other data disc. For video-conversion purposes, you usually only need the VOB file from the DVD, which contains the video and audio data. If you put a DVD in your computer and examine it in the system's file manager, you see that it contains a directory called `VIDEO_TS`, which in turn contains the VOB files. For example, `VTS_01_1.VOB` may be the first title and chapter on the DVD. It's easy to tell which files on the disc contain the video data: they're much, much larger than the IFO and BUP files, which contain metadata. There is probably also a directory called `AUDIO_TS`, but it doesn't contain the video soundtrack. This directory is included in the DVD specification to support the DVD-Audio standard for hi-fi media distribution—which, as you read in Chapter 10, flopped in the marketplace and is heading for obscurity.

■ **Note** Commercially released DVDs feature video and audio data mangled with the Content Scramble System (CSS). Copying the raw video file from a CSS-encoded DVD results in an unwatchable picture. This problem doesn't usually affect material for which you hold the copyright, because homemade DVDs aren't typically made with CSS encoding.

As you open the VOB file in Avidemux, the program asks if you wish to index the MPEG file (see Figure 11-4). This is essential for editing purposes, so there's not much point clicking No.

Figure 11-4. MPEG data imported from DVD VOB files must be indexed before it can be edited in Avidemux.

The indexing process takes a couple of minutes, again depending on the length of the video file and the speed of your computer (see Figure 11-4). It shouldn't take as long as encoding the output file will later.

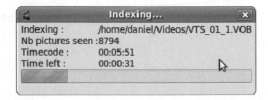

Figure 11-5. The MPEG indexing process takes a short while to complete.

When the video from the DVD is visible in the main window of Avidemux, click the Play/Pause button in the lower-left corner of the interface (a gray rectangle and gray triangle next to each other) to review your material. If you don't hear the soundtrack from the DVD, check the setting under the Audio tab of the Edit ➤ Preferences dialog (see Figure 11-6). On a GNU/Linux system, if the "ALSA device" field is set to "dmix", which is a software option not set up on all systems, this may be the cause of the silence. Change this setting to "default" (don't type the quotes) and click OK, and the audio should work. If you have multiple audio devices and you want to specify a particular one—for example, a pair of USB headphones—you can set the ALSA device name here. This is hw:0 for the first hardware audio interface in the system or hw:1 for the second. Typically on GNU/Linux, the on-board sound chip is hw:0 because it's loaded before any USB audio devices.

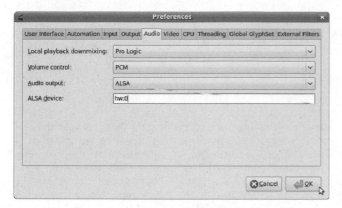

Figure 11-6. You can fix silent audio by setting the correct hardware device in the Avidemux preferences.

Format and Codec Choice

It's important to note that although you can choose any combination of file format, video codec, and audio codec, not all combinations are compatible with the majority of playback systems. Free Software video players like MPlayer (GNU/Linux, Windows, Mac; `www.mplayerhq.hu`) and VLC (GNU/Linux, Windows, Mac; `www.videolan.org`) can handle pretty much any format and codec combination you can throw at them; but proprietary video applications like Windows Media Player are much less versatile, restricted as they are by vested interests in the Internet formats war. It's a good idea to research not only the formats and codecs that your viewers can use, but also the combination in which to use them. (On Ubuntu GNU/Linux, you can install MPlayer and VLC using the Synaptic package manager.)

Video web sites like YouTube specify which formats and codecs are preferred for uploads in their user documentation. At the time of writing, the specification for uploads in the YouTube Handbook (available at `www.youtube.com/t/yt_handbook_produce`) is as follows:

- *Video format:* H.264, MPEG-2, or MPEG-4 preferred
- *Aspect ratio:* Native aspect ratio without letterboxing (examples: 4:3, 16:9)
- *Resolution:* 640×360 (16:9) or 480×360 (4:3) recommended
- *Audio format:* MP3 or AAC preferred
- *Frames per second:* 30
- *Maximum length:* 10 minutes (I recommend 2–3 minutes)
- Maximum file size: 1GB

H.264 is a currently fashionable codec for Internet video; it's provided in Avidemux by the Free Software implementation x264 (see www.videolan.org/developers/x264.html). The x264 encoder is used by the Google Video web site, among others. Video files encoded in H.264 are usually packed into the MPEG-4 container format rather than the older MPEG-2 format found on DVDs.

AAC is a lossy audio codec used by Apple for the iTunes Music Store, and in theory it's meant to sound better than MP3 at the same bitrate. However, there is little or no evidence that AAC files encoded with the Free Software FAAC encoder (GNU/Linux, Windows, Mac) sound any better than MP3 files created with the LAME encoder. Refer back to Chapter 9 for details on how to install LAME. If you want to give FAAC a try, you can download source code via the project's web site at www.audiocoding.com/faac.html or the binary package faac for Ubuntu via the Synaptic package manager.

As mentioned in Chapter 5, frame rates typically vary from 24 per second for film, to 25 per second for PAL format video, to just under 30 for NTSC format video. Although frame rates of 50 to 300 per second are under consideration for future high-definition TV standards, 25 to 30 frames per second are more than adequate for Internet video.

Cropping and Resizing

After your video material is loaded into Avidemux and is playing back correctly, and you can hear the sound, you can use the editing features in the program before you perform the output encoding. Often, if you're preparing video for the Internet, you have to reduce the resolution, change the aspect ratio, or cut it in length. Skipping this step may mean your video is edited or resized automatically by the video server, which can lead to unacceptable results. Suppose you have some digital camcorder footage shot with each frame 600 pixels wide and 480 pixels high. The screenshots in the following example are from a camcorder video shot underwater, courtesy of the www.xlighter.org web site (see Figure 11-7). They show the shipwreck of X127, a Royal Navy lighter sunk in 1942 at a harbor on the island of Malta, in the Mediterranean Sea.

Figure 11-7. Camcorder footage can be cropped, resized, and edited before encoding.

The camcorder footage has been burned to DVD, which has 720 pixels wide by 576 pixels high native resolution, without being resized. This has left a black border around the moving part of the video, although the pixels are in almost the same condition as when the video was in the camera.

Just as when you resize still images, adding extra pixels can't improve the quality of the original. If you aren't sure which resolution and codecs you're working with, choose File ➤ Properties to open a dialog that provides details about the source material (see Figure 11-8).

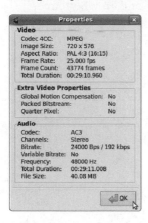

Figure 11-8. The Properties dialog provides details about the resolution and codecs of the source video.

You could leave the black border and resize the entire 720×576 pixel frame to the size required by the video web site. Unfortunately, doing so leaves the moving part of the picture quite small; it's much better in this situation to crop before resizing. To do so in Avidemux, select Video ➤ Filters from the main menu bar to open the Video Filter Manager window (see Figure 11-9). The first filter on the default Transform tab is Crop.

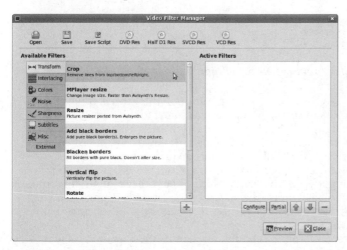

Figure 11-9. The Video Filter Manager offers a good selection of options for modifying the appearance of your project.

Double-click the Crop filter, and a Crop Settings window appears. Just below the preview of your video is a timeline slider control. You may need to drag this a little with your mouse to find the frames that need cropping if your video starts with a fade from black. Although it's possible to calculate how many pixels need to be cropped and enter the numbers in the four boxes under the timeline slider, Avidemux has a couple of features that make this task unnecessary. First, the crop has a bright green preview color, which means you can adjust the crop by eye (see Figure 11-10). To do so, click the small up and down arrowheads next to the values for Crop Left, Crop Right, Crop Top, and Crop Bottom.

Figure 11-10. Avidemux allows you to adjust crops by eye, using a bright green preview color.

Second, when you crop black bars, you can click the Auto Crop button in the Crop Settings dialog and adjust the result a pixel either way, if necessary, using the arrowheads next to the displayed crop values. If you make a mistake and want to start again, click the Clear button; otherwise, click Apply to make the crop, and click OK to close the dialog. The Video Filter Manager dialog lists your crop in its Active Filters window, at right. A short description of the filter's effect is displayed under the filter's name. You can click the Preview button in this dialog to check the result of the filters before going further. You can also click the Save button at upper left to preserve your filter choices for another time. Then, click Close to return to the main Avidemux window. The effects of the crop filter aren't shown in the main window, which may come as a surprise. Instead, any active filters are applied when you perform the export later.

Resizing is performed much the same as cropping, except that Avidemux offers a choice of two filters: standard resize and MPlayer resize, which is said to be faster. Using the MPlayer resize filter requires you to set the aspect ratio for both the source and destination files (see Figure 11-11). Then, you can use the resize slider control to set a scaling factor—for example, 80%. As you move the slider, compare the pixel numbers displayed in the Width and Height controls to the video web site's specification. If the Width is correct but the height is wrong, or vice versa, you need to go back to the Crop stage and decide whether to lose a few pixels from the top, bottom, or sides of the frame. Alternatively, you can leave in some black bars either side of the frame to preserve all of the original image. Just as when you're resizing still images, it's important to get the aspect ratio correct; people, in particular, will look strange otherwise.

Figure 11-11. Adjust the output frame pixel dimensions with the MPlayer resize filter. If you can't get the correct numbers, you may need to go back to the cropping stage.

Returning to the Video Filter Manager dialog, you can preview the results of each filter independently. Filters are applied in sequence from the top to the bottom of the list; in this case, cropping is first and then resizing. You can adjust the sequence of filters using the small arrow icon buttons beneath the Active Filters window (see Figure 11-12).

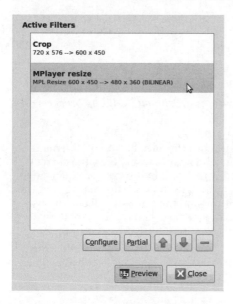

Figure 11-12. Check the filters that have been set up, and preview each one if required.

Cutting to Fit

You may have half an hour of video footage from the camcorder, but you probably need to make an editorial decision and select the most interesting three minutes or so for the exported Internet video. Avidemux has a simple editing feature, based on selection points, that can help you accomplish this easily; either by cutting out selected parts that you don't want or by exporting an individual selection that you do want.

In the lower-right corner of the Avidemux interface, under the label Selection, are the letters A and B with numbers next to them. These are the video frame numbers that correspond to selection points A and B. You set the points with the Selection start button (which has an A icon button) and Selection end button (with a B icon button) in the transport controls, at lower left in the main window. You may find it helpful to use the jog wheel, which is a gray control with a small red vertical line in the middle of it, just above the Selection A and B numbers. You can use the jog wheel to skip backward and forward through the video material and find your perfect start and edit points for the shortened video. When you're working with compressed video on the input side, it's best to cut at a *key frame* for the start point; otherwise, the first few frames of your edited video may be missing data. (Compressed video uses key frames that contain all the data and in-between frames where data is thrown away, as a means of reducing file size.)

When you know the start point of your edit, drag the timeline slider to that point, use the double-headed arrow icons in the transport to find the nearest key frame, and click the Selection start button. Then, drag the slider to the end point, and click the Selection end button. A small square bracket appears on the timeline at each position, and the Selection numbers at lower right display the corresponding video frame numbers (see Figure 11-13). The Time box below the transport controls gives you an idea of how long your edit is in minutes and seconds, which is more user-friendly than the frame count.

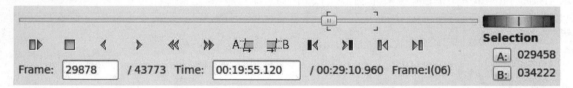

Figure 11-13. The selection points set with the A and B transport buttons are shown as square brackets on the timeline.

Exporting a selection is the same as exporting the entire movie; click the Save button on the main tool bar, beneath the main menu bar. A file export dialog opens, in which you must specify the correct file extension for your output video file (this isn't done automatically for you). In the case of H.264 video inside an MPEG-4 container, the standard filename suffix is .mp4, although Apple's iTunes store uses the nonstandard .m4v extension for the same thing. Click the Save button, and the Encoding dialog opens, showing the statistics from the x264 conversion (see Figure 11-14). If you have a lot of video material to encode, and you're leaving the PC or laptop on overnight, you can select the "Shut down computer when finished" check box. This handy feature enables you to go out for pizza instead of ordering another delivery!

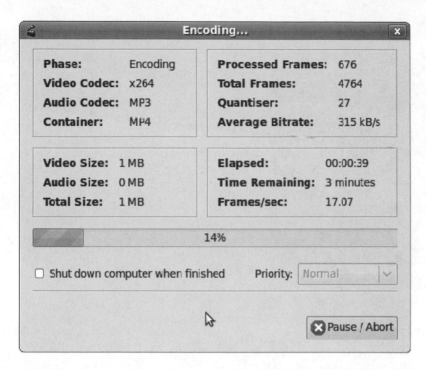

Figure 11-14. *Encoding a video with x264 can take some time, particularly if your computer is slow. Here, my laptop is managing 17 frames per second.*

When the encoding is complete, a small dialog box pops up to let you know. It's important to test the playback of your video before you upload it to the Internet: if you find mistakes after uploading, the web forms that web sites like YouTube use become tedious as you fill them in repeatedly. The GNOME interface for MPlayer (Ubuntu package gnome-mplayer) has the menu option View ➤ Details, revealing the format and codecs of the clip you're reviewing (see Figure 11-15).

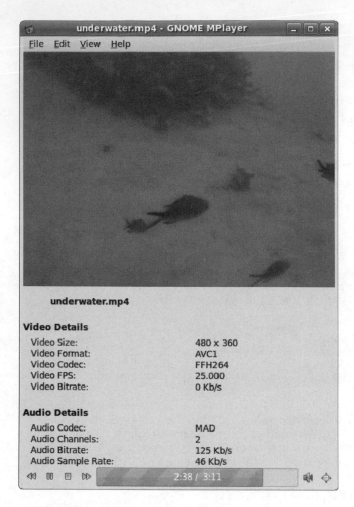

Figure 11-15. *Check your edited video in a program like GNOME MPlayer before uploading it to the Internet, so you don't waste time later. In this example, the statistic for Video Bitrate is clearly wrong, as is the Audio Sample Rate, but the rest of the details are useful. AVC1 is another name for the MPEG-4 Part 10 or H.264 video format. The codec labeled MAD here relates to the libmad decoding library for MP3.*

Getting Video from a Camera Tape

So far, you've looked at importing video as a file. The process of importing video from a camera with a hard disk and a USB socket, or a model that records onto memory cards, is similar to importing from DVD. However, many digital video cameras don't use file-based storage. The *Digital Video (DV)* standard has been around since the mid 1990s and is a linear format, not a random-access format like video files on a hard disk. DV cameras use a variety of tape cassette sizes, most often in the MiniDV version on affordable equipment. A few Sony camcorders use a similar format called Digital8, but the cassette size is larger than MiniDV. Some broadcast camera equipment uses other variants of DV called DVCAM (Sony) or DVCPRO (Panasonic); those cassettes are larger still.

Because DV is a linear format, tapes must be played back into the computer, or *captured*, before editing can begin. Almost all MiniDV camcorders (or their docking stations) have an IEEE 1394 socket to enable direct digital transfers of video material from the tape. If you have an older, analog camcorder that uses Video8, Hi8, or VHS tapes, you can usually capture video using a video output socket on the camera, an appropriate cable, and a specialized PCI card fitted to your computer. If you're running GNU/Linux, you should check driver support on the `www.linuxtv.org` site before purchasing an analog capture card, because many models are only supported under Windows. The driver problem may affect users of Apple's OS X or Windows 7 too. Because analog video capture is considered old-fashioned now, some PCI cards work only under obsolete versions of Windows, such as Windows XP.

Not all video-editing programs have features for getting video from a camcorder tape onto your computer. For that task, you can use Kino (GNU/Linux; `www.kinodv.org`). This deceptively simple DV capture and editing tool for IEEE 1394 hardware works well, as long as the camera you're using is supported (see Figure 11-16).

Figure 11-16. Kino is a useful tool for capturing video from DV cameras.

In my case, I use Kino with a Sony DCR-HC22E camcorder—a basic model that uses MiniDV tapes and has an IEEE 1394 socket (which Sony calls iLINK) on its docking station. I personally think Apple's name for IEEE 1394, FireWire, is catchier, even though the cable shouldn't actually catch fire in normal use. (If it does, you may want to have a word with your landlord about electrical safety regulations.)

Kino is available ready-packaged for most GNU/Linux distros, but it's worth checking on the Kino web site if your distro of choice ships the latest version of the application. Ubuntu users can easily install Kino using the Add/Remove Applications tool, which places the program on the Sound & Video menu. Before you run Kino for the first time, connect the camera or docking station to the GNU/Linux machine with a FireWire cable, and switch the camera on. If you don't have FireWire ports on your motherboard, then a PCI card for IEEE 1394 is a low-cost upgrade. Older laptops can be FireWire enabled with a PCMCIA card, but not all recent laptops have a PCMCIA socket. Again, checking driver support in GNU/Linux for any new piece of hardware is a good idea, particularly if it's an obscure device.

After Kino starts, click the Capture tab at right in the GUI. If a tape with a recording on it is loaded in the camera, you should see some video in Kino's main window. Kino has transport remote controls that allow you to rewind, fast forward, and otherwise manipulate the camcorder tape, so you shouldn't need to touch the camera during the capture process.

Before you click the Capture button below the main viewing window, choose Edit ➤ Preferences and click the Capture tab. Specify the file type you require; in this case, click the Raw DV radio button (see Figure 11-17). The DV AVI Type 2 option is said to provide better compatibility with Windows video-editing applications.

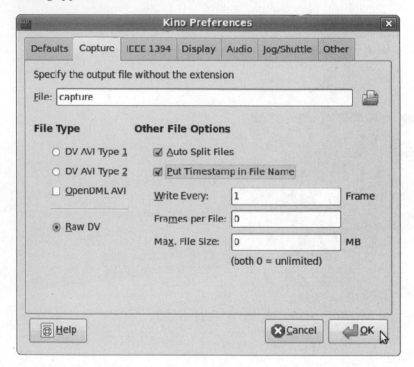

Figure 11-17. *Set Kino's preferences before you attempt your first video capture.*

It's a good idea to check the Auto Split Files box, which gives you a separate DV file for each continuous shot on the camcorder (not the same thing as a separate file for each still frame). In a drag-and-drop environment, it's much easier to make editing decisions about individual shots than about long, unbroken files. Personally, I also set the Put Timestamp in File Name option, because it makes it much more practical to manage a large number of individual files. If the clock is set correctly on your camcorder, each DV filename is then tagged with the date and time of the original shot.

If you click the Capture button and all goes well, the directory specified in the Capture tab of Kino's preferences dialog begins filling with DV files. Note that the process happens in real time, so a standard 60-minute MiniDV tape takes an hour to capture. You need around 13GB of hard disk space for each 60 minutes of DV captured.

It's well worth checking out Kino's editing, effects, and export features, because it may have all you need to prepare a simple YouTube-style video. A comprehensive user manual is available at www.kinodv.org/docbook/.

Command-Line DV Capture

If you don't need Kino's features, and you just want to get the video off the camera with as little fuss as possible, you can use the dvgrab (GNU/Linux) utility on the command line. The dvgrab source code is available via the Kino web site; like its sister project, there should be a binary package available for your GNU/Linux distro. Ubuntu users can install dvgrab using the Synaptic package manager. The dvgrab package has a man page (type man dvgrab into a terminal after installation) that details all of the program's parameters. For instance, you can use dvgrab with the following options:

```
dvgrab --autosplit --format dv2 --size 0 --opendml my_videofile-
```

The last part of the command, my_videofile-, is the prefix given to each sequentially numbered DV file captured from the camera tape.

Open Movie Editor

Open Movie Editor (GNU/Linux; www.openmovieeditor.org) features a drag-and-drop, timeline-based interface that will be familiar to users of other video-editing applications. It also has support for the JACK sound server and, crucially, JACK's transport control. This means that when you use Open Movie Editor, you can synchronize sound from other JACK transport-aware apps, like Ardour, without having to render the audio or video first; this is potentially a killer feature for soundtrack production. On the downside, Open Movie Editor can be laborious to install from source code, is sometimes quirky, and currently offers a limited range of rendering presets. At least, because it's a nonlinear editor, one that records edit decisions rather than mangle the input files, there's little chance of damaging your original video material when it does crash. Usually, you can restart Open Movie Editor and be right back at the point before the crashing bug was triggered. I hope the application gets the attention it deserves and the lone developer, Richard Spindler, gets the community help he needs to make Open Movie Editor stable and practical for everyday use.

You spend the rest of this chapter looking at the application, so you can find out what working with bleeding-edge Free Software is like. Ubuntu users can install Open Movie Editor using the Add/Remove Applications tool. Optionally, you can also install the Frei0r video effect plug-ins (GNU/Linux, Windows, Mac; www.piksel.org/frei0r), which are supported by Open Movie Editor and several other Free Software video applications. (That's a zero after the letter *i*, by the way, not an *O*—knowing this should help you find information about Frei0r on search engines.) In Ubuntu, you can install the frei0r-plugins and frei0r-plugins-doc packages using Synaptic.

Before running Open Movie Editor for the first time, you need to make sure you have the JACK sound server installed and working. Fortunately, the jackd daemon and its qjackctl applet (often labeled Jack Control) are available ready-packaged for most GNU/Linux distros and should be installed by default on any multimedia-specific distro. If you've skipped ahead in this book and haven't run JACK yet, refer back to Chapters 9 and 10 for JACK installation and configuration tips.

48000Hz is the most likely audio sample rate for a video project, so set JACK to run at that rate unless you know otherwise. If you have JACK installed but it isn't running when you start Open Movie Editor, the application starts JACK by itself. In this case, you can still open JACK Control after the fact to check on settings and connections.

Making the Interface Fit

When you start Open Movie Editor for the first time, it creates a directory called `Video Projects` in your personal home directory (`/home/daniel/` in my case). This new directory is where the program's native project files (but not necessarily imported video data) are stored.

The first thing to do in the running program is to resize the interface to fit your screen, because you need every available pixel of space to make the most of the editing features. Maximize the Open Movie Editor window, or choose View ➤ Fullscreen (keyboard shortcut F11); see Figure 11-18.

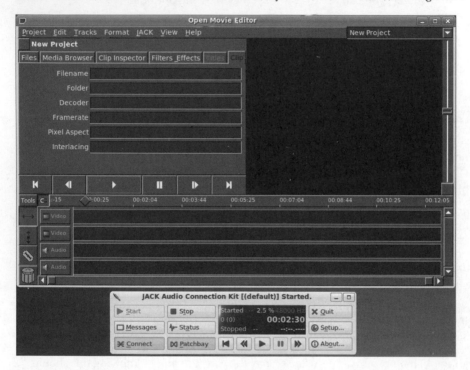

Figure 11-18. Start JACK, and then run Open Movie Editor and resize its interface so that you can see all the tabs on the left side of the main window.

Near the upper-left corner of the interface is a series of tabs labeled Files, Media Browser, Clip Inspector, Filters & Effects, Titles, and Clip. You probably can't see all of these unless you resize the box they're in by dragging its right edge further to the right.

To the right of these tabs is the resizable video preview window, which is black until you have video playing. The aspect ratio setting on the Format menu, which determines the output video file's proportions, defaults to 4:3. Before widescreen TVs and monitors, that was the aspect ratio that most camcorder footage was designed for; but now a 16:9 ratio is common. 2.35:1 ratio is even more "widescreen" than 16:9 and was used for epic movies in the late 1950s and the 1960s. Around 1970, the standard for this ratio was adjusted to 2.39:1, although some people round this figure up to 2.40:1 and others still call it 2.35:1 for old-times' sake. For a cinematic look with black borders at the top and bottom of the picture, you can apply a 16:9 or 2.35:1 mask to 4:3 footage, using the options in the lower part of the Format menu.

Having dragged the lower edge of the viewing window to make it your preferred size, you then have the option to make the video and audio tracks larger in height. Doing so makes the video thumbnails (the first frame of each clip) and the audio waveforms easier to see. If you later add more than the default two video and two audio tracks, you can scroll the edit window vertically, using the slider at right. To increase the height of a track, click the button to its left labeled Video or Audio, and select 2x or 4x from the pop-up menu. This menu also has options to remove or rename a track, or move it up or down in the track order.

Adding Opening Titles

All good movies start with the title and credits for the major protagonists. (The people who did the catering have to wait until the very end of the movie before they get to see their names, in a very small font, up on the screen.) Choose Project ➤ Save As or Project ➤ New Project, and give your video a name. Unusually, with Open Movie Editor, you don't need to remember to save the project as you go along, because all edit decisions are written to the project file.

Next, click the Filters & Effects tab, and click and drag the Titles icon at the top of the effects list onto a video track. The titles item that appears on the timeline defaults to a very small thumbnail, which is hard to select. Resize the Video track with the title to 4x height, and then use Open Movie Editor's zoom handle, on the gray slider beneath the Audio tracks, to take a closer look (see Figure 11-19).

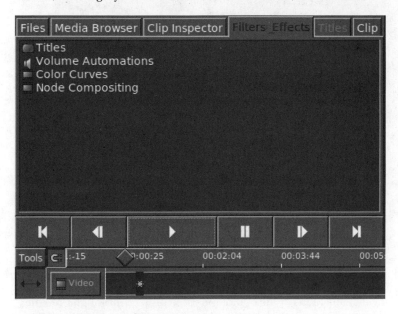

Figure 11-19. You drag titles onto a video track from the Filters & Effects tab. They appear as a small thumbnail on the relevant track.

You can click and drag the squares at either end of the handle to zoom in or out. Dragging the main central part of the handle lets you adjust the point on the timeline that's being viewed. The shorter you make the slider, the more zoomed in you are.

Now, click the titles thumbnail to select it; it becomes outlined in red. Only then does the Titles tab start to work (see Figure 11-20). By default, the title says "A movie by," but you can click in the large blue text box on the Titles tab to replace this with any text you wish. You can also set the title font, size, color, and position in this tab. Title frames in Open Movie Editor have a transparent background, so it's a good idea to put titles on the first video track and your camcorder material on the second or subsequent tracks. That way, your title frames are shown as a transparent overlay on top of the video material; video tracks in Open Movie Editor are a little like layers in the GIMP, with the first track as the top layer.

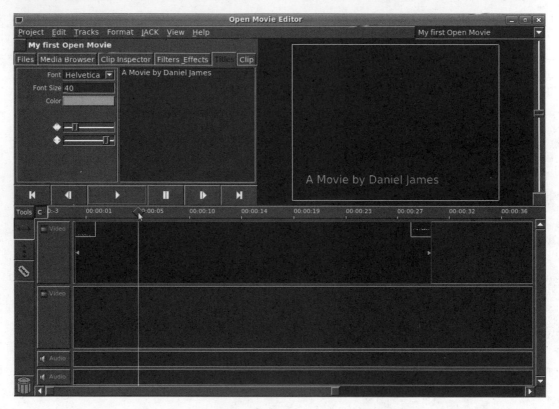

Figure 11-20. Select a title thumbnail, and then use the Titles tab to edit the title's text and its properties.

For sections on the timeline where there is no video, Open Movie Editor exports black frames. So, if you want titles against a plain black background, position the title thumbnail before the video material on the timeline. The same goes for movie-style credits at the end of the video project, although the Titles tab doesn't support scrolling credits. This type of animated sequence can be prepared in another program like KToon or Synfig, exported to a series of still PNG frames, and converted to a video file with Avidemux.

If you've dragged multiple title sections onto the video tracks, for basic title animation, you have to select the active section with the mouse before you can edit it. Like video and audio clips, titles can be clicked and dragged anywhere on the timeline or switched from track to track.

You can adjust the position of a title or clip on the timeline using the default Positioning tool, located to the left side of the video tracks, which has a double-headed horizontal arrow icon. To trim the start and end points of a particular title or clip, mouse over the left or right sides of the item; a handle icon appears, which you can click and drag.

Alternatively, you can create PNG title frames in the Gimp or from SVG files using Inkscape's Export Bitmap feature, and drag them from the Media Browser tab onto a video track (see Figure 11-21). Using transparent PNGs lets the video show through from the track beneath. You can also use this technique to create color overlays with logos, like those used on TV news channels like CNN for station identification. Other TV stations, including the BBC's digital channels, favor a less intrusive, near-transparent logo in the corner of the screen, to remind the viewer where the video material was originally created.

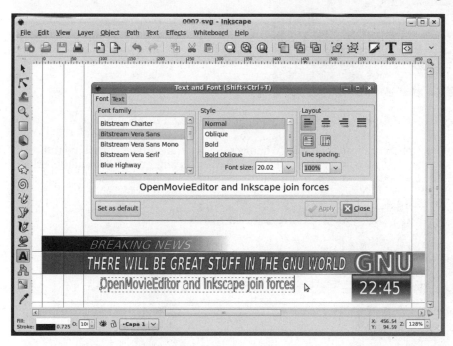

Figure 11-21. You can create titles and color overlays as SVG files in Inkscape and then export them to transparent PNG pixmaps for use in Open Movie Editor.

Static overlay files created in another application are much less flexible for quick editing than Open Movie Editor's built-in title tool, although they offer more creative possibilities. Some example SVG titles for use in Inkscape are offered at www.openmovieeditor.org/titles.html, if you need inspiration.

Working with Video Clips

It's time to start bringing in some video. Click the Media Browser tab, and then use the small white triangle icon button to navigate to the directory that contains your video files (see Figure 11-22). These may be DV files that you captured from a camcorder tape or AVI files exported by another program. Again, just as with the titles, click, drag, and drop the file onto an available video track. Note that any audio embedded in the video file is represented as a small green waveform underneath spaced image thumbnails of the video.

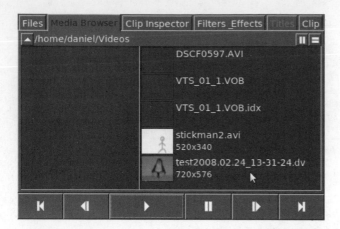

Figure 11-22. Select video material for dragging and dropping from the Media Browser tab.

The title-adjustment features come into their own, when you realize that you've placed the title right over the movie star's face. That's easily fixed by adjusting the vertical alignment slider in the Titles tab, which is the lower of the two sliders found beneath the font settings (see Figure 11-23).

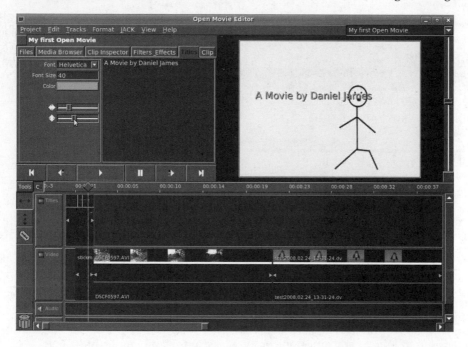

Figure 11-23. You can adjust title positions to fit the video material by using the horizontal and vertical sliders.

Continue adding video files until the shots of your movie are roughly in the correct order. Then, trim the start and end points of each shot by clicking and dragging the edge handles, to remove boring or irrelevant frames. By default, adjacent video clips snap together to ensure that there are no blank frames between them. You can switch off this snapping behavior using the small horseshoe magnet icon to the immediate left of the timeline indicator strip (see Figure 11-24).

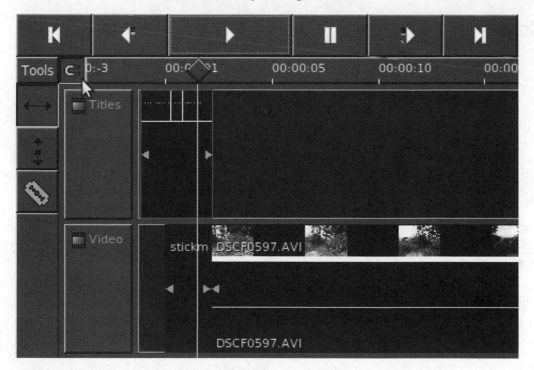

Figure 11-24. *Video clips snap together when the magnet icon is active.*

If you want crossfades between shots, drag one clip over another, and a blue and red area indicates the length of the crossfade (see Figure 11-25). To slice a shot into two parts, click the razor-blade tool to the left of the video tracks, and then click at the point where you want the cut made. To get rid of any unwanted material, drag it to the trashcan icon, also at the left side of the Open Movie Editor interface.

Figure 11-25. *To crossfade two video clips, overlap them.*

You may find that the default size of a video clip on your screen makes precise editing difficult; that problem is easily solved with the zoom handle beneath the timeline. In addition to clicking the timeline scale (in *hours:minutes:seconds* format) to jump to a particular point, you can click and drag the diamond-shaped icon on top of the vertical timeline indicator to scrub through your movie, frame by frame.

If you installed the Frei0r plug-ins and want to add a video effect, click the Filters & Effects tab and drag and drop the effect icon on top of the video clip you're interested in (see Figure 11-26). To remove an effect, select the Clip Inspector tab, click the clip in the timeline, click the effect listed in the tab's window, and then click the Remove Effect button. There's also an Edit Effect button in this tab for adjusting effect parameters. Alternatively, you can drag a fresh copy of the original material from the Media Browser onto another place in the video track, without the effect being applied.

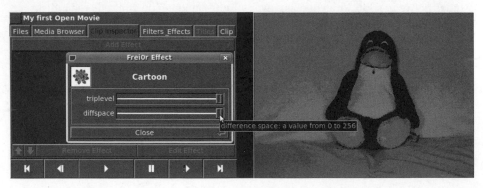

Figure 11-26. *Effects, like this cartoon-style plug-in, are dragged and dropped onto video clips.*

Importing Audio

No movie would be complete without a soundtrack. If you don't have suitable audio material of your own, lots of music tracks are available on the Internet under Creative Commons and other Free Software–inspired licenses. These licenses explicitly allow you to include the music in your project, although the exact terms vary, and commercial use of the music is sometimes prohibited. A few online music stores that offer music under Creative Commons licenses, including Jamendo (`http://pro.jamendo.com`) and Magnatune (`www.magnatune.com/info/licensing`) also license music for use in commercial video projects.

Dragging an audio clip from the Media Browser onto an audio track works exactly the same as with video or titles. If you want to mute the audio from the camcorder, such as unwanted dialogue or background noise, right-click that particular video clip, and select Mute Original Sound from the pop-up menu.

A common requirement is that a soundtrack drops in level while dialogue is heard. Open Movie Editor provides a volume-automation feature for this task (see Figure 11-27). It works in a similar way to the level-automation tool in Ardour's editor window. First, drag a Volume Automations icon from the Filters & Effects tab onto the audio clip in question. A red line appears at the top of the waveform, with a small red square at each end. You can then use the Automations tool, to the left of the video tracks (with the vertical, double-headed arrow icon) to place red automation markers on the waveform. A marker at the top of the waveform means audio is played back at full volume at that point on the timeline, whereas lower markers indicate a drop in level. You can also use this feature to create fade-ins and fade-outs on audio tracks.

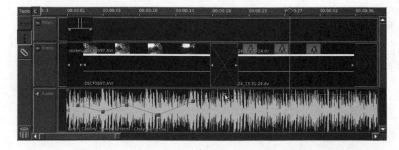

Figure 11-27. Open Movie Editor's audio volume automation works in a similar way to the Ardour editor's level automation.

Exporting the Finished Movie

Exporting the project to a playback file isn't difficult; choose Project ➤ Render to open the Export dialog. The difficulty comes in knowing which format to choose: a bewildering variety of codecs and containers are available, and there is only one preset, for PAL DV in a QuickTime container.

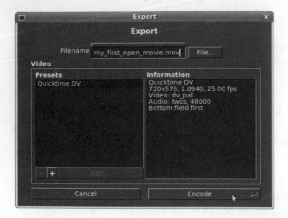

Figure 11-28. The Export dialog box offers only one codec and container preset.

The main emphasis in this program is on exporting projects to Apple's QuickTime format. Conversion tools like Transcode (`www.transcoding.org`) and ffmpeg2theora (`http://v2v.cc/~j/ffmpeg2theora/`) can put Open Movie Editor's output into pretty much any format you require, albeit with some loss of quality, as noted earlier. I personally use the QuickTime DV preset for rendering Open Movie Editor projects, a format that can be viewed directly in MPlayer. QuickTime format has the `.mov` file extension and is related to MPEG-4, without being identical.

To try rendering with different container formats and codecs, click the plus (+) icon button at lower left in the Export dialog. Doing so opens the Custom Video Format window, which enables you to name and save presets for format and codec combinations of your choice (see Figure 11-29). This is where things start to get complicated: the exact codecs available depend on the version of FFmpeg (www.ffmpeg.org) installed. As when you're using Avidemux, it's possible to create a custom format this way that no player software will ever support, so it's important to test the output video file on a variety of players. This is especially critical if you've never tried a particular video format before.

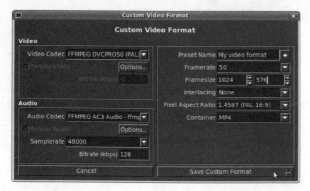

Figure 11-29. You can specify new presets in the Custom Video Format window.

The rendering process takes at least as long as your movie lasts and possibly longer, depending on the speed of your CPU. You have time to throw some popcorn in the microwave before settling down to view your cinematic masterpiece.

Compiling Open Movie Editor from Source

Most GNU/Linux distros don't have an up-to-date package of Open Movie Editor. Because the program is still under heavy development, it's worth getting the latest version if you intend to use the program regularly. This usually involves compiling the application from source code, which may be daunting if you've never tried it before. However, it's a step-by-step process, and when it goes wrong, the computer tells you why—even if the message is a little cryptic to the uninitiated. A search engine can usually provide a clue to get you on your way if you type in the exact error message, because it's very likely that you're not the first person to run into it. Mostly, compilation problems are caused by not having all the right packages (or up-to-date versions of those packages) in place.

To set up your system for building applications from source, you need a metapackage like Ubuntu's build-essential, which you can install with Synaptic. This metapackage contains links to other packages that go well together, to save you having to download them individually or missing one by mistake. It pulls down the GNU Project's compiler gcc, the g++ package, and the standard C++ development libraries. You also need doxygen installed, but you probably don't need to build that from source either. In a terminal, the commands

```
sudo apt-get install build-essential
sudo apt-get build-dep openmovieeditor
```

get you most of the packages you need. The `apt-get install` part is the command-line equivalent of clicking a new package in Synaptic, and the `apt-get build-dep` command means "get me the package dependencies I need to build the following program from source code." The `sudo` prefix gives you administrator rights so your user account is allowed to install packages. On a well-configured system, the sudo program prompts you for your login password, to make sure it's really you.

For a bleeding-edge application like Open Movie Editor, you also need to compile fresh versions of at least some of the libraries the program relies on. In other cases, you may wish to enable features in a library that your distro of choice has skipped. For instance, you probably want to compile your own version of FFmpeg, because many distros ship feature-limited versions of this package (software patents again). For most of the libraries, follow the standard routine of downloading the source tarball, unzipping it, opening a terminal, and changing to the directory where the tarball was unpacked. Then, you can compile the library or application with the following commands:

```
./configure
make
sudo make install
```

It helps if you build the packages in the correct order, because of their interrelated dependencies. At least the `./configure` step warns you if any libraries or development packages are missing. If you decide to compile FFmpeg yourself, the Open Movie Editor documentation recommends that you use these configure options:

```
./configure --enable-gpl --enable-shared
```

Other tips for building required libraries are provided in the README file in the Open Movie Editor source package and in the web site documentation. Building LAME (`http://lame.sourceforge.net`) is straightforward because it doesn't have many dependencies. That can't be said of libquicktime (`http://libquicktime.sourceforge.net`), which has quite a few.

When you build libquicktime from source, the Open Movie Editor documentation suggests using the `configure` option:

```
./configure --enable-gpl
```

If appropriate versions are available in your GNU/Linux distro of choice, you may be able to use ready-made packages of some of the libraries. When compiling from source code on Ubuntu, you need the -dev (development version) of the library package, not just the library itself. For example, the libfltk1.1-dev library package is required to build Open Movie Editor's graphical interface. Installing the libfltk1.1 package by itself isn't sufficient. If you install libfltk1.1-dev, the system installs libfltk1.1 automatically.

The swscale library is part of FFmpeg and may need to be built from source; but if you're happy to use your distro's packages of FFmpeg, then you can build Open Movie Editor without swscale support. The configure script complains about libswscale being missing, but the application still compiles. If you already have gavl and the other libraries required for building Open Movie Editor, then compilation of the Frei0r plug-ins should be straightforward.

If you attempt to run the freshly compiled `openmovieeditor` binary on your computer for the first time, and the program complains about not being able to find a couple of shared libraries, this is easily fixed. Having been compiled from source on the same machine, libraries are often installed into `/usr/local/lib` by default, rather than the `/usr/lib` directory where binary packages typically install their libraries. A couple of symbolic links can solve the problem. For example, in a terminal, you can enter commands something like these:

```
sudo ln -s /usr/local/lib/libgavl.so.0.0.0 /usr/lib/libgavl.so.0
sudo ln -s /usr/local/lib/libquicktime.so.0.0.0 /usr/lib/libquicktime.so.0
```

These commands place a link in the `/usr/lib/` directory to the actual library in `/usr/local/lib/`, so the program can find it. After you take this step, Open Movie Editor should spring into life.

Further Reading

Not many books have been written on video editing specifically with Free Software, although just as for audio, many general books are available. For detailed information about the main programs covered in this chapter, it's best to refer to the Avidemux documentation at `www.avidemux.org/admWiki` and the Open Movie Editor manual at `www.openmovieeditor.org/documentation.html`.

Other Useful Programs

Because most Free Software video-editing programs are still under heavy development, it's well worth checking out alternative projects that may suit your needs, including these:

- *Kdenlive* (GNU/Linux, Mac): A nonlinear video editor, similar in ambition to Open Movie Editor. You can download it from `www.kdenlive.org` or install it in Ubuntu using the Add/Remove Programs tool.

- *LiVES* (GNU/Linux, Mac): A little different from most video editors, in that it can also be used by video jockeys (VJs). You can download it from `http://lives.sourceforge.net`. LiVES isn't currently available in Ubuntu, although packages for Ubuntu are available on third-party sites.

CHAPTER 12

■ ■ ■

Web Content

This final chapter brings together all the skills you've acquired so far to put your creative projects on the Internet. Although you've read about creating physical media—printing, and burning CDs, for instance—most of the skills involved can be applied directly to creating web content. Indeed, some Internet media is intended to be printed out or burned to disc by the recipient; only the means and location of production have changed.

Distribution and Competition

It's no exaggeration to say that the Internet has offered more people the chance to distribute their creative work to the general public than ever before. Mostly, this phenomenon is due to the lower costs of digital rather than physical distribution. Another important reason follows from these lower, or even near-zero, costs. If there is little financial risk in offering a creative work for distribution, then it becomes possible for organizations to distribute many more individual projects than before. A direct financial return from any particular project becomes less important, as long as the hosting or enabling organization benefits overall. Arguably, the quality barrier is lowered in the process, although personally speaking, I don't accept this reasoning; plenty of lame books, records, and movies were made before the Internet was available to the public. I know—I bought some of them!

However, marketing or promoting that creative work still takes time, effort, and money. Perhaps it takes more work than ever, now that such a huge quantity and diverse range of published material is available. Taking the example of music, several web sites now offer large catalogs of music by independent artists, of which very few will ever gain a significant audience. This is because the web site operator barely has the resources to listen to all the new material uploaded, let alone actively promote it. In the long tail of the listener numbers graph, there are undoubtedly many fine artists who deserve wider attention but won't get it. These web sites usually rely on random visitors searching the huge catalog to find the worthwhile material and then promoting it to their friends. That model might have worked in the early days of web multimedia, due to the novelty of the format; but what happens when the ratio of creative musicians to interested listeners reaches 1:1? What if the number of would-be uploaders eventually outstrips the number of active downloaders on a particular site?

This is what I call the *MySpace effect*—everyone can put their own music on the Internet, but no one is listening. In case you think this is criticism from the sidelines, cynicism, or nostalgia for the pre-Internet days when making your own record actually meant something, I've been there—I have music on MySpace and other web sites. (If you're curious, drop by `www.myspace.com/ddjomp` to hear an album project on which I played bass guitar. It was recorded with Ardour and mastered with Jamin, all on GNU/Linux.)

Web sites like CD Baby (`www.cdbaby.com`) and Zimbalam (`www.zimbalam.co.uk`) charge a setup fee to distribute music. Sites like these offer to take a small cut of sales in return for distributing music to well-known online retailers, including iTunes, often on a non-exclusive contract. But if the distributor's cut is small and the deal is non-exclusive, it could be argued that the distributor has little incentive to invest in or promote any particular CD over another, particularly when the artist is unknown to the music-buying public. Consider these figures taken from CD Baby's web site in the summer of 2009:

- 278,510 albums available for sale on CD Baby

- 5,339,025 CDs sold online to customers

- $107,769,092 paid directly to the artists

The numbers look impressive, don't they? That's more than $100 million earned by independent artists from one web site. But let's take a closer look. From these figures, I calculate that the average album project on CD Baby sells 19 copies—and that average includes recordings by famous or established artists. (Typically, these are early indie recordings, or albums made after the artist left their record label for whatever reason.) Also, I reason that the $107,769,092 figure includes income from download sales. Otherwise, it would imply that each CD sale earns more than $20 for the artist, but the typical retail price of an album on CD Baby is $12. Including this extra income from downloads, it works out that each indie album project earns an average gross of $387 for the artists involved, before production costs and other expenses. It's not much, considering the work involved, and I guess that's why there are more solo artists than big bands around these days.

For physical CD sales, the web site takes a $4 cut, and the artist is responsible for manufacturing the CD, printing the artwork, and shipping it to CD Baby's warehouse in Oregon. That means the typical $12 album on CD, selling 19 copies, earns around $100 for its creators—if they aren't paying themselves for the work required to create the CD, that is. By the way, the $35 that CD Baby charges to listen to your album has to be subtracted from the average $100 earned. (My own band's CD is on CD Baby and has earned precisely zero to date, so I'm $35 out of pocket on the deal.)

What I offer from this analysis is that if you put your own creative projects on the Internet, don't be surprised or disappointed if the only people who notice are your family and friends. Certainly, don't bank on recouping your investment in recording equipment from online CD sales. If you want to be a rock star or famous artist, putting the material online isn't enough by itself. To stand out from the crowd, you need good-quality content on an attractive, well-designed web site that is regularly updated. Then, you have to figure out how your audience will find your web site, and implement that strategy. Whether you like it or not, you're effectively in competition with other creative people for a limited number of interested ears and eyes. It's up to each artist to promote their own work or accept a very modest response—regardless of the quality of the project. Although I've used music as an example, the same principle applies to self-published printed books, e-books, photographs, illustration, animation, video, or any other kind of digital artwork.

Free Content

If you conclude that you don't wish to promote or sell your work on a commercial basis, you can consider making it available under a Free Software-inspired content license in order to reach a wider audience. Licenses that actively encourage content sharing may mean that your work is republished on other web sites, if other people appreciate it enough. The Creative Commons project (`http://creativecommons.org`) offers the best known Free Content licenses, but there are plenty of others, including the GNU Free Documentation License used for several of the photos in this book.

Bear in mind that if you release your work under a Free Content license on the Internet, it's possible someone else may take that work, remix or reshape it, and make a huge hit out of it. This depends on the specific terms of the Free Content license you choose, because some licenses prohibit derivative versions. You may not get paid, although I suspect this derivative work would do your career no harm. On the other hand, you may object on artistic grounds that the integrity of your original work has suffered in the adaptation. Significantly, you can't stuff the genie back in the bottle and use copyright to prevent other people from using, adapting, and enjoying the original work according to the terms of the Free Content license. It's vital to get the agreement of everyone involved in your project (anyone who could reasonably claim copyright in it) to release the work under a Free Content license before you do so, to avoid potential legal trouble later.

Web 2.0 and Platform Choice

Having decided whether your project is commercial, noncommercial, "all rights reserved," or Free Content, you need to select a technical means of distribution. GNU/Linux and Free Software are the de facto standard in web hosting, but building and maintaining a static web site made of manually generated HTML pages can be a chore. This is particularly the case when the web site contains a large number of pages, images, or other files. Supposedly, programs like Adobe Dreamweaver, which provide some automation in web page production, make the process easier, but they're mostly used to generate static pages. The same goes for Adobe's Flash format, which is interactive only in the limited sense that users can click page elements and make things appear to happen. Flash animations are self-contained bundles of vector and application files that can't usually be directly manipulated or altered by the web site visitor.

Since about 2004, Internet pundits have used the term *Web 2.0* to describe user-driven sites that host social networking communities, including sites for music and video creators. MySpace and YouTube are examples of Web 2.0—these are sites that couldn't have been built using static HTML pages or Flash animation alone. Instead, web content is held in a database, and the pages seen by the visitor are generated on the fly by the server. The database is the feature that allows a social-networking site to display the day's most popular content, without anyone having to rebuild the home page manually. Many, if not most, Web 2.0 sites are based on Free Software, whether it's the Apache web server, the MySQL database, the PHP scripting language, or a content management system (CMS) written in PHP, such as Drupal.

Setting up your own Web 2.0 site is no doubt more complicated than using one of the many social-networking or content-sharing sites on offer. On the plus side, you're in control of your own web site, unrestricted by policies on the length, size, or type of material you can upload. (Some Internet hosting companies, which supply server hardware for rent, have user agreements that do restrict the material you can upload. And of course, certain types of video and photographic content are illegal in just about every country around the world.)

However, there's a more important reason to run your own show. Let's return to the importance of marketing and promotion for a minute. If you have your own web site, then as long as you pay the modest annual fee to renew the domain name—around $35 per year or less—you get to use the domain name for the foreseeable future. When you promote a MySpace URL for your band, such as www.myspace.com/ddjomp or similar, you send people to a web site that includes a lot of advertising for other bands, mobile phones, and TV shows on the parent company's Fox network. (It's a particular irony that MySpace, the host of so much independent music, has been owned by one of the world's largest media corporations since 2005.) Not to mention the hundreds of young, single people in your area who want to show you close-up photos of their body piercing experiments. It's likely that the web site visitor will become distracted and click one of these other enticements before taking the time to fully appreciate your work. Having got someone's attention to the point that they want to check out your web site, it's a shame to waste the opportunity.

Of course, you can create your own web site and then use pages on various social-networking sites to lead visitors back to it. The main drawback to this approach is that updating multiple sites can take up more of your time, unless you use automated syndication (like the RSS feeds that you read about in Chapter 9).

Installing the Apache Web Server

On GNU/Linux systems, no hard line exists between desktop and server machines. You can install server packages on your regular PC without having to change the operating system. A dedicated server machine runs only those packages required for the task, which greatly simplifies security and administration. However, by using localhost, the system's network address for itself, you can run both a server and a desktop with a web browser on the same machine. This approach is valid for experimentation or testing a site before it's copied to the production server. If you have a broadband Internet connection, you can usually serve a limited amount of material from your desktop PC or laptop without running into trouble. Your Internet Service Provider (ISP) may have set monthly limits on the amount of data that you can serve from a domestic Internet connection without a financial penalty; if in doubt, check the figures first.

Most web sites sit on dedicated servers in ISP data centers because they benefit from better bandwidth connections to the Internet than are typically available at home. Also, you don't have to leave your home PC switched on 24 hours a day, 7 days a week because web site visitors can arrive at any time. A good server installation benefits from multiple Internet connections, back-up power supplies, and a skilled network or system administrator on site. All these things help keep web sites going around the clock, when a simpler domestic setup could go down.

To get started, you need to install Apache (GNU/Linux, Windows, Mac), the most popular web server software on the Internet. The easiest way to do this on Ubuntu is to install the apache2 metapackage, using System ➤ Administration ➤ Synaptic Package Manager (see Figure 12-1).

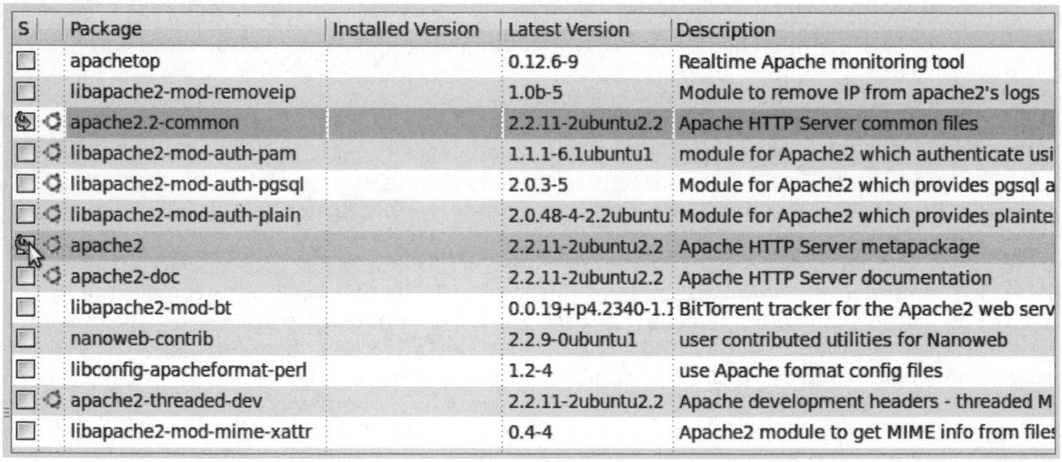

S	Package	Installed Version	Latest Version	Description
☐	apachetop		0.12.6-9	Realtime Apache monitoring tool
☐	libapache2-mod-removeip		1.0b-5	Module to remove IP from apache2's logs
☑	apache2.2-common		2.2.11-2ubuntu2.2	Apache HTTP Server common files
☐	libapache2-mod-auth-pam		1.1.1-6.1ubuntu1	module for Apache2 which authenticate usi
☐	libapache2-mod-auth-pgsql		2.0.3-5	Module for Apache2 which provides pgsql a
☐	libapache2-mod-auth-plain		2.0.48-4-2.2ubuntu	Module for Apache2 which provides plainte
☑	apache2		2.2.11-2ubuntu2.2	Apache HTTP Server metapackage
☐	apache2-doc		2.2.11-2ubuntu2.2	Apache HTTP Server documentation
☐	libapache2-mod-bt		0.0.19+p4.2340-1.1	BitTorrent tracker for the Apache2 web serv
☐	nanoweb-contrib		2.2.9-0ubuntu1	user contributed utilities for Nanoweb
☐	libconfig-apacheformat-perl		1.2-4	use Apache format config files
☐	apache2-threaded-dev		2.2.11-2ubuntu2.2	Apache development headers - threaded M
☐	libapache2-mod-mime-xattr		0.4-4	Apache2 module to get MIME info from files

Figure 12-1. Install Apache 2 using its metapackage, for instant gratification.

This installs all the basic packages that the second major release of the Apache web server requires, without your having to specify them individually. Other GNU/Linux distributions have Apache packages available, and Windows and Mac users can download the software from `http://httpd.apache.org`.

Now, open a web browser (which on Ubuntu is Mozilla Firefox by default), type the URL `http://localhost/` into the location bar, and press the Enter key on your keyboard. If Apache has been installed correctly, a simple but encouraging web page is served by your PC or laptop (see Figure 12-2). If you know the IP address of your machine on the local network, which is 10.0.1.91 in my case, you can type this into the location bar instead of `localhost`.

Figure 12-2. Apache confirms that it has been installed correctly with this very simple page.

This Apache test page can't be accessed by anyone else yet, unless your broadband router or other Internet connection is configured to allow incoming traffic on port 80, the traditional port for serving web pages. To enable public access to your computer, and all that implies, check the documentation that came with your router to see if it allows port forwarding.

Open a terminal (in Ubuntu, choose Applications ➤ Accessories ➤ Terminal), and change to the directory where web pages are kept by default. On Ubuntu, this is the `/var/www` directory:

```
cd /var/www
```

Then, issue a "list directory contents" command, which is `ls` on GNU/Linux. You should find the `index.html` file that you just saw the result of in the web browser. Using the `-l` switch at the end of the list command reveals more details about the `index.html` file (see Figure 12-3).

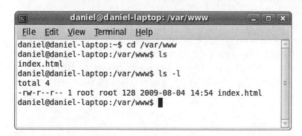

Figure 12-3. The `ls -l` command tells you more about the file.

In addition to the date the file was created or modified, this command informs you that the `index.html` file belongs to the user root and the group root. This *root* is the traditional name for the administrator account on a GNU/Linux system. Ubuntu doesn't have a root user account that you can log in to, but you can assume administrative powers using the sudo command instead, as you saw in earlier chapters. You need these powers to edit the index.html file that belongs to root because it's not one of your personal files, which are normally in your /home directory.

To perform the edit, you can use a command-line editing program called GNU nano (GNU/Linux, Windows, Mac). The nano program should be installed by default on any GNU/Linux or Apple OS X system. Windows users can download it from http://nano-editor.org. It may seem a little old-school, but nano is an awesome program to have in your toolkit when you're working directly on a remote server on the other side of the Internet, which may have no desktop. In the terminal, type the following:

```
sudo nano index.html
```

The sudo prefix elevates the command to administrator status. Otherwise, nano can read the file for you but not write out any edits you make. Ubuntu prompts you for your login password, to make sure you're not a random person who happens to be passing the keyboard, ready to abuse those root powers. Then, the nano editor starts up inside the terminal, showing you the HTML source code of the file specified (see Figure 12-4).

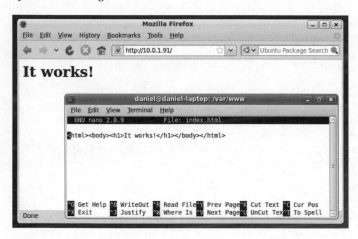

Figure 12-4. *GNU nano is a very useful command-line text editor for administering web servers.*

To make edits in nano, use the cursor keys to move around the text file, change the part you want, and then press Ctrl+O followed by the Enter key to write out a new copy of the file (save it to disk). (Most commands in nano are accomplished with Ctrl+key combinations, which are listed at the lower edge of the terminal window.) If you want to prove that the web server is running, edit the index.html file, write it out, and click the refresh button on your web browser (see Figure 12-5). Use Ctrl+X to close nano when you're done.

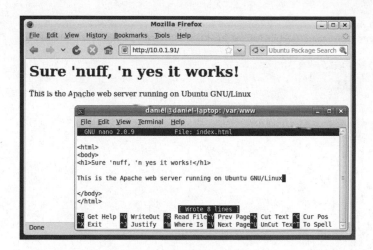

Figure 12-5. Editing Apache's default web page shows that the web server is really running.

If you've done any manual web-page editing, the HTML syntax of the file should be familiar—all page text is enclosed in tags made from angled brackets, with a corresponding closing tag. For example, text enclosed by the tags <h1> to </h1> represents a large headline font.

Installing the MySQL Database Management System

As you read a few pages ago, Web 2.0 sites are database driven, so you need to install a suitable database management system. Fortunately, you don't need to be an experienced database administrator to set up a contemporary web site, because any popular web content management system (CMS) offers step-by-step instructions for this task. Some CMS packages, including Drupal, create the database structure and initial data for you automatically during their installation.

First, you have to install the database management software. The MySQL (GNU/Linux, Windows, Mac) package is a popular choice. (Despite the similarity in name, MySQL has nothing specifically to do with MySpace, although the database server is used on a lot of well-known web sites.) Ubuntu users can install the mysql-server metapackage in Synaptic. Like Apache, MySQL is a standard package available for most, if not all, GNU/Linux distributions. Windows and Mac users can download MySQL Community Server from http://dev.mysql.com.

The installation of the MySQL server on Ubuntu is a little different from typical desktop packages, because the system asks you to set a database administrator password. This is for security reasons, because you don't want publicly accessible MySQL servers running all over the Internet with the same default password. Confusingly, the MySQL administrator account is called root, even though this is a completely different account from the system root user.

Choose a good, long password that includes letters and numbers. If you include uppercase letters, punctuation marks, and other keyboard symbols in your passwords, they should be harder to break by brute computational force. However, the number-one way that passwords get broken may not be evil super-villains with super-computers. That way is, in all probability, writing the password on a Post-It note and sticking it to your computer screen! Write down your MySQL root password if you must, but keep it hidden or locked away. Synaptic asks you to type the password a second time, to make sure it's typed as intended. The characters in the password are shown on the screen as a series of black dots, as shown in Figure 12-6, in case an evil super-villain, or co-worker, is looking over your shoulder.

Figure 12-6. Choose a good, strong password for the MySQL root user.

Installing the PHP Scripting Language

HTML is a markup language, derived from typesetting principles, and therefore it doesn't offer features that enable interactive elements on web pages. To achieve these interactive elements, web developers use a *scripting language*, which is a programming language that doesn't need to be compiled before it's run. Many Free Software scripting languages are available, but one in particular has been widely adopted in Web 2.0 sites: PHP (GNU/Linux, Windows, Mac). Ubuntu users should install the php5-mysql package in Synaptic, which also downloads the php5-common and libapache2-mod-php5 packages as dependencies. (Don't worry if Synaptic suggests removing the apache2-mpm-worker package and installing the apache2-mpm-prefork package instead; this is fine for your purposes.) You need all three of these PHP packages to run your CMS and connect it via PHP to the MySQL database and the Apache web server. Other GNU/Linux distributions have similar packages. Windows and Mac users can download PHP from `www.php.net`.

Installing the Drupal Content Management System

Ubuntu has a handy metapackage called drupal6 that conveniently downloads all the packages required to run this CMS. However, I believe it's still a good idea to run through the previous steps of installing and testing Apache, configuring a root password for MySQL, and installing PHP before you attempt to install Drupal. Otherwise, it's easy to skip through these vital steps without being able to remember them later.

Other GNU/Linux distributions are likely to have Drupal packages; but for those that don't, and for Windows or the Mac, you can also install Drupal manually on a web server. To do this, download the *tarball* (compressed archive) from `www.drupal.org`, unpack the tarball in the directory of your web server where the HTML files go, and follow the instructions in the supplied text file.

On Ubuntu, Synaptic asks if you wish to configure the database for Drupal automatically. Unless you know otherwise, leave the check box selected, and click the Forward button (see Figure 12-7).

Synaptic presents a graphical front end to debconf, the system that Ubuntu uses to manage package configuration. Like the `.deb` suffix on the end of Ubuntu package file names, debconf is named after the Debian GNU/Linux distribution on which Ubuntu is based.

Figure 12-7. *Let debconf run the database configuration tool for Drupal automatically, unless you know that you shouldn't.*

Next, the installer asks which database management system you intend to use with Drupal. Again, accept the default of mysql unless you have a better idea (see Figure 12-8).

Figure 12-8. *Debconf defaults to MySQL for database type when installing Drupal, which is a likely choice.*

After that, the installer needs to know the database administrator password you set when you installed MySQL (see Figure 12-9).

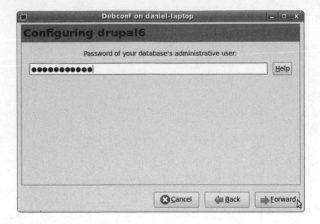

Figure 12-9. Enter the MySQL root password. Now, where did I put that Post-It note?

The installer also needs to know which password you want Drupal to use when it connects to the database. This should be different from the MySQL root administrator password, for security reasons. If you like, you can leave this field blank, and the installer generates a random password for you. Random passwords are likely to be more secure than those you make up yourself, although they can be harder to remember.

After the Drupal installation completes and you close Synaptic's pop-up window, you need to restart Apache so it can read in the new configuration for Drupal. On Ubuntu, you can do this by opening a terminal, and typing

```
sudo /etc/init.d/apache2 restart
```

This means to run the script that controls Apache (`/etc/init.d/apache2`) to make the server restart, and to do it with system administrator powers (`sudo`). You need to enter your password to use `sudo` again. Don't worry if Apache complains about not being able to reliably determine the server's domain name (see Figure 12-10); this is because the PC or laptop is set up for a local network rather than the open Internet. It won't stop you from experimenting with Drupal on this machine.

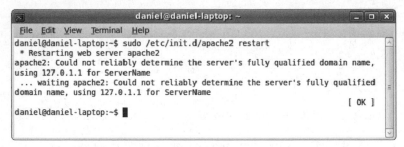

Figure 12-10. Restart Apache on the command line so settings for Drupal are loaded.

Configuring Drupal

The remainder of the Drupal configuration can be carried out using the web browser on your system. If you're installing on a remote web server, replace `localhost` in the following example URLs with the server's domain name (for instance, `www.freesoftwarecreative.com`) or IP address (such as `62.75.222.127`).

First, point your browser at the `http://localhost/drupal6/install.php` page (see Figure 12-11).

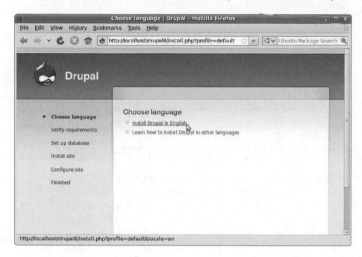

Figure 12-11. *Most Drupal settings are configured after installation, through the browser.*

Note that this page has the `.php` extension, not the `.html` extension you see on a static web site. It's very important that you type the entire URL, including the `install.php` part; otherwise, you may see a page of error messages instead of the Drupal installation page.

By default, Drupal is installed with the administration pages in English, but you can click a link to information about how to change this setting. Of course, just because Drupal's administration pages are in English doesn't mean all the content posted to the site has to be in the same language. However, adding multilingual support to Drupal helps non-English-speaking users of your site when they register or post content (if you decide to let them do that).

If you're using the Ubuntu installer, the package requirements are in place and the database is already set up, so Drupal skips the next two steps and jumps straight to the Configure Site page. On this page, the first field is for your new Drupal site's name, which you should choose carefully, because it appears on most pages of the site. The default of the server name, `localhost` in this case, won't do.

Below this is the field for the site's official e-mail address. On a production web server, which is permanently connected to the Internet and has a mail server running, this feature enables Drupal to send e-mail to new users when they register for membership on your site (if you decide to allow third-party registrations). This From address should normally be within the same domain as the web site, so that anti-spam programs don't get confused about which server the mail is coming from. In this example, I've used the address `robot@freesoftwarecreative.com` so people realize the e-mail isn't from a human being (see Figure 12-12).

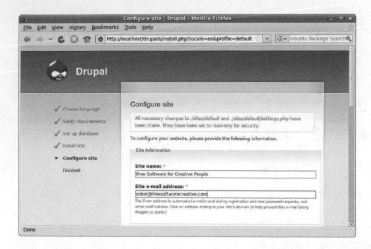

Figure 12-12. Set the name of your web site and the From address for automated system e-mails.

If you don't have a mail server on your test machine, put your own e-mail address in this box for now. Drupal won't be able to send out e-mails, but that need not prevent you from trying the software. If you're using Ubuntu and you've installed the drupal6 metapackage, the exim4 mail server packages will have been installed automatically. For the purposes of testing Drupal, you don't need to configure the Exim mail server, which is just as well. Exim is a powerful program, but tuning it can get complicated. An alternative mail server that is easier to configure and that works perfectly well with Drupal is Postfix (GNU/Linux, Mac; `www.postfix.org`). Ubuntu users can find a package called postfix in Synaptic. Installing this package removes the exim4 packages, because it doesn't make sense to run two mail servers on the same machine.

Scroll down the "Configure site" page to the next section, headed "Administrator account." Enter the username you'd like, your own e-mail address, and a good strong password (see Figure 12-13). It's not a wise idea to reuse a password from the same or another system for this. Enter the password a second time to confirm your typing. Then, click the Save and Continue button at the bottom of the page.

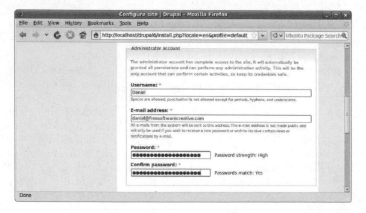

Figure 12-13. Enter a name, an e-mail address, and a password for the system administrator (that's you).

If you run into a "Fatal error: Allowed memory size exhausted" message in the web browser when configuring Drupal, this is because PHP's default settings on Ubuntu only allow a script to use a maximum of 16MB memory, and Drupal can easily exceed that limit. To fix this problem, open a terminal, and change to the directory where the PHP configuration for Apache is stored:

```
cd /etc/php5/apache2
```

Then, edit the PHP configuration file, php.ini:

```
sudo nano php.ini
```

Use the Ctrl+W search feature in nano to find the text *memory_limit*, because php.ini is a long file. Change the default value of memory_limit = 16M to memory_limit = 32M (see Figure 12-14), and then write out the file with Ctrl+O.

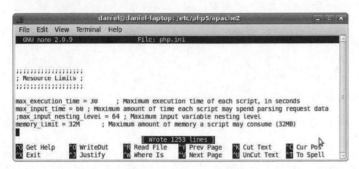

Figure 12-14. Memory limit problems during Drupal installation can be fixed with a simple tweak to the PHP configuration.

Refresh the Drupal install page, and the error message should go away. In its place is a message that Drupal is already installed (see Figure 12-15).

Figure 12-15. After fixing the PHP memory limit, Drupal confirms that everything is OK.

Navigate to `http://localhost/drupal6/`, or click the link that says "View your existing site." This takes you to the home page of your freshly installed CMS (see Figure 12-16). Of course, there is no content yet, and the graphical theme is a plain, default one, but the features you need to administer and start building the web site are all in place.

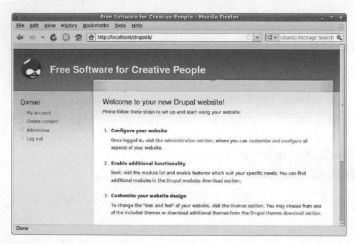

Figure 12-16. *The home page of your new Drupal site has little content and a plain blue theme, but you'll fix that later.*

Your administrator account should be already logged in, with your username shown at left on the web page. Below this are four key links: "My account," where personal settings are edited; "Create content," which is the route to uploading text, pictures, and video; "Administer", where you manage site content and users; and "Log out," which prevents others from tampering with your web site if you're using a shared computer.

Security Updates

First, click the Administer link. If there are any problems with your Drupal installation, the software warns you on this page. In Figure 12-17, Drupal says to check the "Status report" page for a problem report. It also warns that a security update is available for Drupal. It's important to take notice of these warnings; having a web site that only partially works is bad enough, but security holes can allow your web server to be taken over by spammers, phishers, scammers, and other criminally inclined low-lifes.

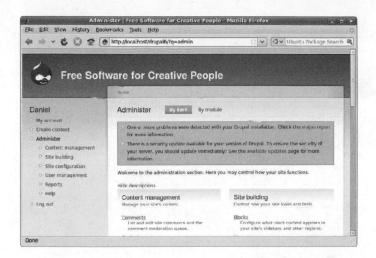

Figure 12-17. *There's a problem with the Drupal installation, which should be addressed before you go any further.*

The "Status report" page indicates that Drupal is running fine but that the version of the software has been superseded by one or more security updates (see Figure 12-18). Because fixing security holes is a high priority for the Drupal team, several updates may be made between the release of the Ubuntu or other GNU/Linux distro package and the time you install it. It's a good idea to check with the Drupal home page to be sure you have the latest version when installing from a distro package.

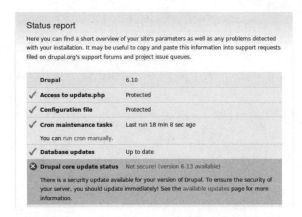

Figure 12-18. *Here's the problem: the Drupal version is out of date. At least one security update is available.*

The "Status report" page has a link to the "Available updates" page, which shows the currently installed version of Drupal and has links to download subsequent available versions (see Figure 12-19). These links aren't to Ubuntu `.deb` packages, but to the plain tarballs provided directly by the Drupal project, which require manual installation.

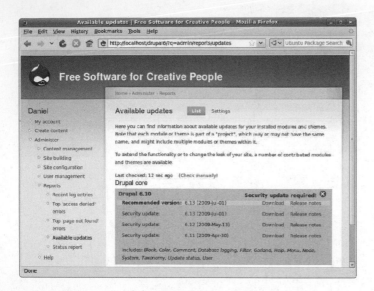

Figure 12-19. Drupal not only knows when it's out of date, but also can tell you the latest update versions available.

Click the Download link for the latest version shown. The browser usually asks what to do with the file. In Firefox, click the OK button to save the tarball file to your PC or laptop (see Figure 12-20). Ubuntu systems save the tarball to the desktop directory by default.

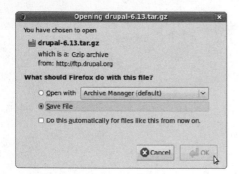

Figure 12-20. Save the tarball from the Drupal web site to your local machine.

Navigate to the "Site maintenance" page, which on a local Ubuntu installation is at `http://localhost/drupal6/?q=admin/settings/site-maintenance`. You can find a link to the "Site maintenance" page under the "Site configuration" menu on Drupal's left navigation menu. On this page, you can click a radio button to set "Site status" to Off-line (see Figure 12-21). For a production site, this step ensures that visitors don't click things during the upgrade and mess up settings. Then, click the "Save configuration" button. Don't log out of your Drupal session, and keep the browser window open— you'll need it shortly.

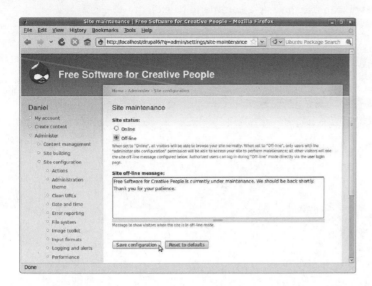

Figure 12-21. Take your new site offline before performing the security upgrade.

Next, you have to unpack the update tarball in Drupal's installation directory. For a production site on a real web server, you would back up the database and files first, as outlined in the file UPGRADE.txt included in the Drupal tarball. To back up the MySQL database, open a terminal and type

```
mysqldump -u root -p --all-databases > mydatabases.sql
```

This command means the user root (the database administrator, not the system root user), using the password (the -p switch) would like to dump all databases to a file called mydatabases.sql in the current directory. For a freshly opened terminal on Ubuntu, this is your home directory. If you still have a terminal open from earlier changes to the PHP configuration, you need to change back to your home directory first. You can accomplish this using the cd command and the shortcut of a tilde character ~, like so:

```
cd ~
```

The mysqldump program prompts you for the database administrator password and, if you supply the correct one, writes out the mydatabases.sql file. You can use this .sql file to restore your databases to the MySQL server later, should something go wrong and you make a mess of them.

Now, you can use the terminal to back up the current Drupal installation files. You need to use sudo for this task because you're working in a part of the filesystem outside your home directory. The location of the Drupal directory can differ, but the Ubuntu package puts it under the /usr/share/ directory and automatically configures Apache to find it there. You can use the cp command for this backup, which means "make a copy." The -r switch added to cp means "copy recursively"; in other words, go through the directories beneath this one, and copy everything—which is what you want:

```
sudo cp -r /usr/share/drupal6/ /usr/share/drupal6-backup/
```

To confirm that the backup worked, you can use the `ls -l` command (see Figure 12-22):

```
ls -l /usr/share/drupal6*
```

The asterisk (*) is a wildcard; it means the `ls` command should list everything that begins with the text *drupal6*.

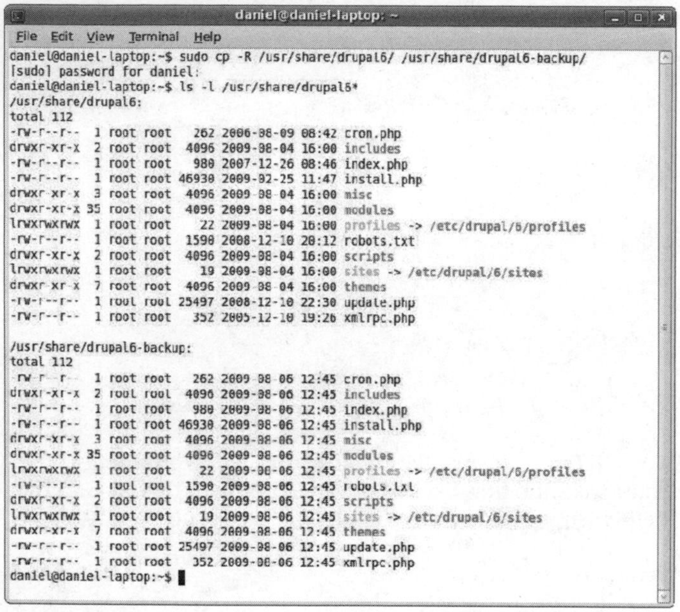

Figure 12-22. Double-check that the backup was copied correctly with the ls -l command. The directories should be identical, apart from the date and time stamps.

Remove Drupal's original installation directory with the `rm` command:

```
sudo rm -r /usr/share/drupal6/
```

Now, change to the directory where the new Drupal tarball was downloaded, which in my case is the Desktop directory underneath the `/home/daniel` directory:

```
cd /home/daniel/Desktop
```

Move the tarball to the directory where it will be unpacked, using the `mv` command. You will be using a version later than 6.13, but the rest of the command is the same for an installation under the `/usr/share` directory:

```
sudo mv drupal-6.13.tar.gz /usr/share/
```

Change to this installation directory:

```
cd /usr/share/
```

and unpack the new tarball in its place, using **sudo** and the **tar** command:

```
sudo tar -xvzf drupal-6.13.tar.gz
```

The **-xvzf** switches on the **tar** command mean "extract verbosely (with details) the **zip** file." (The **tar** command has many such options, which you can check out by typing **man tar** in any terminal.) Because you use the verbose switch, the **tar** command lists all the files it has extracted. These are placed in a directory with Drupal's full release number, such as **drupal-6.13**, but your Apache setup requires them to be in a directory called **drupal6**. No problem; you can copy the directory to the original name and keep the tarball version that you just unpacked as an additional backup of that release:

```
sudo cp -r drupal-6.13 drupal6
```

To check that you've done it right, issue another **ls** command to see what's in the Drupal directories you created:

```
ls drupal*
```

The results should include the **drupal6** directory from the Ubuntu package that you backed up, the tarball you downloaded, the directory unpacked from the tarball, and the copy you just made of that directory (see Figure 12-23).

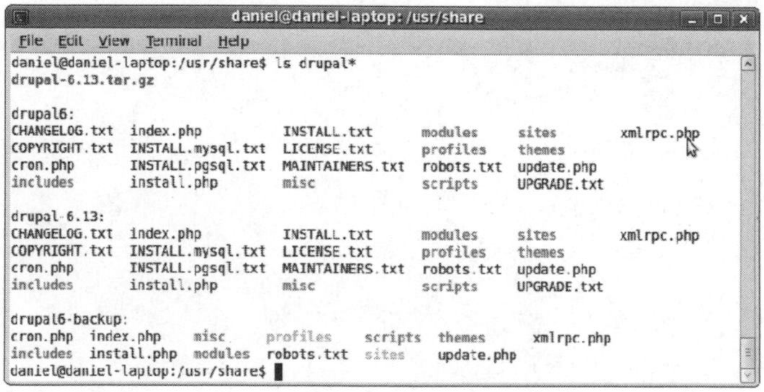

Figure 12-23. Look at the directories you've copied. Note that the Drupal tarball contains more files than the Ubuntu package.

Because the Ubuntu package puts Drupal configuration files in a different directory than the standard tarball, you need to take three additional steps when switching from one to the other. Otherwise, the site administration details, the database setup from your initial installation, and the files directory won't be preserved:

```
sudo cp /etc/drupal/6/sites/default/settings.php /usr/share/drupal6/sites/default/
sudo cp -p /etc/drupal/6/sites/default/dbconfig.php /usr/share/drupal6/sites/default/
sudo cp -rp /etc/drupal/6/sites/default/files/ /usr/share/drupal6/sites/default/
```

The **-p** flag used with the **cp** command preserves the user and group ownership details of the files and directory copied. This is necessary because these files need to belong to the **www-data** group of which the Apache web server is a member. That way, Apache can read the files, but your web site visitors can't by default. That's important, because the **dbconfig.php** file includes your Drupal database password, and the **files** directory can include media that you wish to remain private.

If you chose an automatic password during Drupal package installation, you can look at the contents of the file using **sudo** and the **less** command, and make a note of the password. This comes in useful later, if you move your Drupal site to another server. The **less** program is a simple file viewer, rather than an editor like **nano**. Because you don't need to edit the **dbconfig.php** file, **less** is what you should use. It prevents you from making edits to a critical file with an accidental slip of the keyboard. You can use the **less** command like this:

```
sudo less /usr/share/drupal6/sites/default/dbconfig.php
```

With that job done, it's time to go back to your web browser and access the **update.php** page: for example, **http://localhost/drupal6/update.php** in the case of a local installation on Ubuntu. This Drupal page reminds you to back up your database and any customized files, and put the site into maintenance mode (see Figure 12-24). Then, click the Continue button.

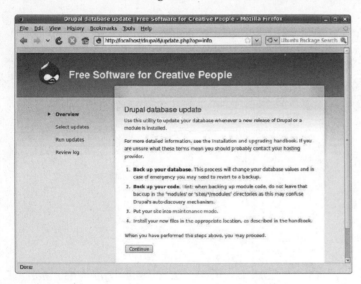

Figure 12-24. *There's one last reminder to back up and set the site to maintenance mode before the upgrade.*

Drupal asks you to select the update that you require in the next step, but if you're upgrading from a recent version, this is detected automatically (see Figure 12-25). Click the Update button.

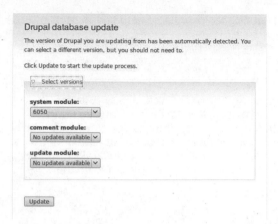

Figure 12-25. *The database update page allows you to select alternative versions, if available. Unless you know otherwise, go with the defaults.*

If all is well, a column of green check marks appears at left, and a message says that you can proceed to the main home page or administration pages (see Figure 12-26).

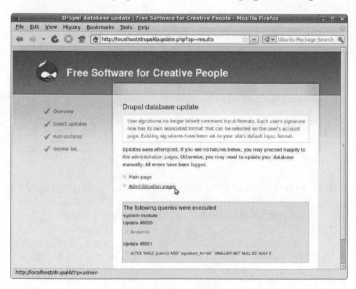

Figure 12-26. *The database update has completed successfully. Any error messages are logged, and you can view them by following the link.*

If you return to the status report page, for example at `http://localhost/drupal6/?q=admin/reports/status`, you see that the Drupal version has changed to the release number of the security update to which you just upgraded. You can now go back to the `http://localhost/drupal6/?q=admin/settings/site-maintenance` page, set "Site status" to Online, and click the "Save configuration" button. The security upgrade has been completed, and you're back in business.

Creating Initial Site Content

So far, your web site doesn't have much to say. The front page still shows a "Welcome to your new Drupal web site!" message, which is only intended to be seen by you, the site owner. You can remedy that by using the "Create content" link on the left navigation bar. The default installation provides links for two kinds of text content: Page and Story (see Figure 12-27). The Page content type is similar to the pages on a static web site, whereas the Story type is much more Web 2.0, with automatic links from the home page and the ability for site visitors to leave comments (if you want to allow them to do that).

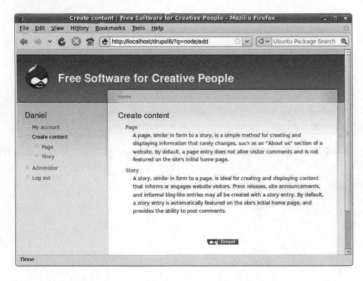

Figure 12-27. Drupal offers two kinds of text content by default.

If you follow the link to create a story, you see a simple web form with fields for the Title and Body of the story (see Figure 12-28). There are also expandable links for "Menu settings," "Input format," "Revision information," "Comment settings," "Authoring information," and "Publishing options." The Menu link allows you to set a title for an automatically created link to this story in the navigation bar, which saves a lot of time over creating and maintaining links manually. Comments are set to Read/Write by default, which means any user whom you allow can add comments to this particular story. The "Read only" option is useful when you decide that a particular discussion is no longer topical, and the Disabled option can be used if you don't want comments posted at all on this story.

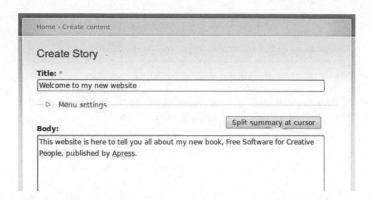

Figure 12-28. *Enter a title and body for your first text content, and then check out the various options that Drupal offers from the expanding links.*

Down in the "Publishing options" section, a check box indicates that this story will be promoted to the home page of the web site, until you decide otherwise. For an important story, you may wish to set the "Sticky at top of lists" option.

Click the Preview button if you aren't sure how your new story will look to the public; otherwise, click Save to publish the story (see Figure 12-29). You can revise it as many times as you want by clicking the Edit button—it isn't set in stone. This first piece of content is called `node/1` by Drupal, with a corresponding URL. If you decided to create an automatic menu link, it appears in the upper-right corner of the web page by default.

Figure 12-29. *The first story node on the new web site. Note the link "About this site" in the upper-right corner, which has been created automatically.*

Enabling Drupal Modules

Text pages and stories are all very well, but you want to create a multimedia web site with social-networking features. To do this, you need to enable some extra modules for Drupal. Click the Administer link at left on the page, and, on the page of links that appears, find the "Site building" section. Under this heading is a link to the Modules page; click it, and you see a list of "Core - optional" modules with check boxes, including Blog, Book, Contact, Forum, Poll, Search, and Upload (see Figure 12-30). To enable one of these modules, check the corresponding box and click the "Save configuration" button at the foot of the page.

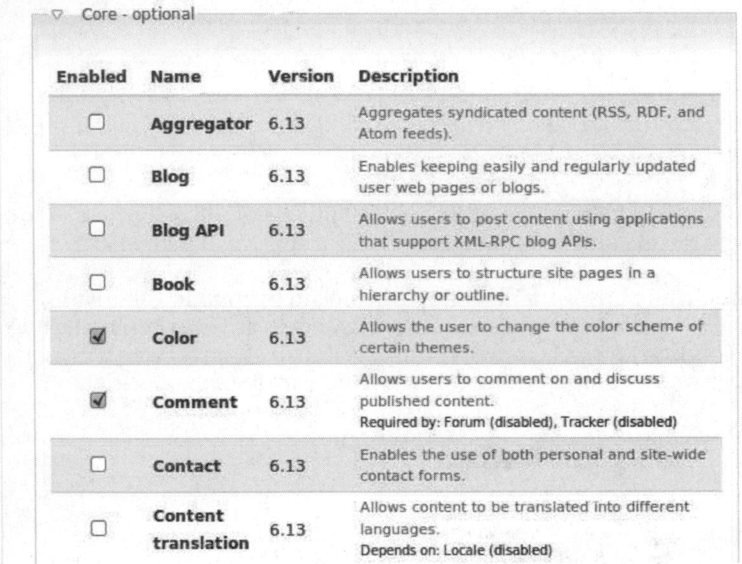

Enabled	Name	Version	Description
☐	**Aggregator**	6.13	Aggregates syndicated content (RSS, RDF, and Atom feeds).
☐	**Blog**	6.13	Enables keeping easily and regularly updated user web pages or blogs.
☐	**Blog API**	6.13	Allows users to post content using applications that support XML-RPC blog APIs.
☐	**Book**	6.13	Allows users to structure site pages in a hierarchy or outline.
☑	Color	6.13	Allows the user to change the color scheme of certain themes.
☑	**Comment**	6.13	Allows users to comment on and discuss published content. Required by: Forum (disabled), Tracker (disabled)
☐	**Contact**	6.13	Enables the use of both personal and site-wide contact forms.
☐	**Content translation**	6.13	Allows content to be translated into different languages. Depends on: Locale (disabled)

Figure 12-30. The Drupal tarball includes a number of optional modules you can use to add features to your site.

The optional modules that are bundled with the standard Drupal tarball don't include modules for handling image files, video, or audio specifically, although the Upload module allows site visitors to attach any one of these files to a page, story, blog entry, or forum post that they create.

To install one of the third-party modules available for Drupal, follow the link to contributed modules from the Modules page of your site, which points to `http://drupal.org/projects/modules`. (I usually open this page in a new tab in Firefox, side by side with the web site I'm working on.) The search feature on the Drupal site should find one or more modules that do what you need. There are many of these contributed modules available, and some work more smoothly than others. Module versions that are still under development may be tagged with a `-dev`, `-alpha`, or `-beta` suffix. For a production site, it's a good idea to go with the recommended release version of the module, even if that's a little older.

It's also important to make sure you're installing a compatible module, for Drupal 6 in this case. Plenty of people are still using the earlier Drupal 5 CMS, so modules are available for that version too. Some modules are being ported to the forthcoming Drupal 7 system, but that's strictly bleeding edge for now. The Drupal web site's Modules page has a handy "Filter by compatibility" link at right.

Contributed modules are supplied as tarballs, which must be unpacked in the correct directory on the server. In the following example you install the Image module. It's tagged as an alpha version in Figure 12-31, but it works well enough. First, download the tarball by clicking the relevant link on the Modules page of the Drupal web site.

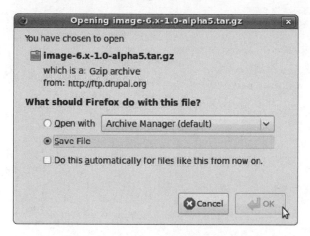

Figure 12-31. A wide variety of third-party contributed modules are available for Drupal, covering nearly all the features required for a typical Web 2.0 site.

Then, create the directory for contributed modules, which belongs under the **sites/all/** directory of your Drupal installation, using the `mkdir` command:

```
sudo mkdir /usr/share/drupal6/sites/all/modules
```

Change to the directory containing the module tarball—for example, the **Desktop** directory—and then move the tarball to the new directory you just created:

```
cd Desktop
sudo mv image-6.x-1.0-alpha5.tar.gz /usr/share/drupal6/sites/all/modules/
```

Now, change to the new contributed modules directory, and unpack the tarball:

```
cd /usr/share/drupal6/sites/all/modules/
sudo tar -xvzf image-6.x-1.0-alpha5.tar.gz
```

(The exact filename of the tarball will no doubt be different.) Return to the Modules administration page of your Drupal site, and refresh it in your browser. At the end of the page is a new section showing your freshly installed module, together with any dependent submodules the tarball contained (see Figure 12-32). New modules are switched off by default; check the boxes under the Enabled column for the modules you require, and then click the "Save configuration" button.

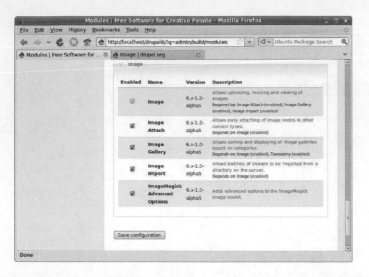

Figure 12-32. Don't forget to enable your new module after installation, or you won't see it working.

Finally, visit the Administer by Module page to set specific options for your newly installed module. On a local Ubuntu installation, this page is at `http://localhost/drupal6/?q=admin/by-module`. Scroll down until you find the section for Image. There are also sections for configuring the submodules, such as Image Gallery. For the parent module, Image, there are three links: "Configure permissions," "Images", and "Get Help"—the latter is a link to the locally installed Drupal documentation, within the web site. The Permissions page is very important, because here you set whom you allow to do what with your web site (see Figure 12-33).

Permission	anonymous user	authenticated user
image module		
create images	☐	☐
edit images	☐	☐
edit own images	☐	☐
view original images	☐	☐
image_gallery module		
administer images	☐	☐
image_import module		
import images	☐	☐

Figure 12-33. Think carefully about permissions for any newly installed modules before allowing just anyone to use them.

By default, Drupal site visitors fall into two categories: *anonymous*, which includes any random person browsing the site, and *authenticated*, who are the people you allow to register. You probably don't want anonymous users to be able to create image nodes (picture pages), for instance. If you want a private site and don't want strangers registering for accounts, you can specify this on the "User settings" page, for example on an Ubuntu machine: `http://localhost/drupal6/?q=admin/user/settings`.

By visiting the Images page, you can set the name of the directory where uploaded pictures are stored (the default is `images`), the maximum file size you allow site visitors to upload, and the pixel dimensions for full-size images and thumbnails (see Figure 12-34).

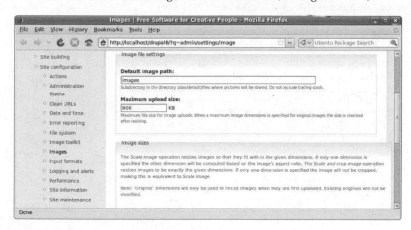

Figure 12-34. Set the default image path and maximum upload size allowed on the Images page.

Selecting a Drupal Theme

It would be dull if every Drupal site looked exactly the same. Fortunately, this CMS is fully themeable, allowing you to change the appearance of the site with a couple of mouse clicks. Under the Administer link at left, select "Site building" and then "Themes". This page initially displays the bundled themes, which are named Bluemarine, Chameleon, Garland, Marvin, Minnelli, and Pushbutton (see Figure 12-35). Click the Enabled check box or the Default radio button to try them. The changed theme takes effect immediately if you select it as the default. If you enable other themes, they're available to you and other registered users as a personal configuration option, which can be set by using the My Account link in the left-side navigation menu.

Figure 12-35. The Drupal tarball contains six different themes for you to try. The default is Garland.

If you don't like any of the supplied themes, plenty more contributed themes are available via the Drupal web site at http://drupal.org/project/themes and on many designer's web sites. These themes are supplied as tarballs, and the installation process is similar to installing a contributed module. For example, to enable the A3 Atlantis theme on an Ubuntu installation of Drupal, issue commands similar to the following in a terminal:

```
sudo mkdir /usr/share/drupal6/sites/all/themes
cd /home/daniel/Desktop
sudo mv a3_atlantis-6.x-1.2.tar.gz /usr/share/drupal6/sites/all/themes/
cd /usr/share/drupal6/sites/all/themes
sudo tar -xvzf  a3_atlantis-6.x-1.2.tar.gz
```

Refresh the theme administration page on your Drupal site, and the theme you just installed is available for activation (see Figure 12-36).

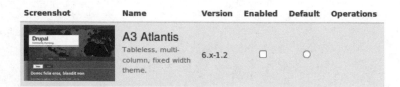

Figure 12-36. The contributed theme has been copied to and unpacked in the correct directory, and it's ready for use.

Check the box for the new theme, click the Default radio button, and refresh the page. You now see your web site in a whole new light (see Figure 12-37).

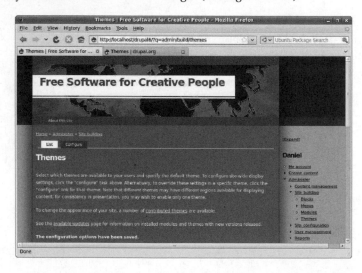

Figure 12-37. The look of your Drupal web site is transformed with a simple change to a contributed theme.

With a little HTML and Cascading Style Sheets (CSS) knowledge, it's possible to create your own Drupal theme. Rather than start from scratch, it's much easier to find a theme that you like most parts of and adapt it for your own web site. Because most Drupal themes are released under Free Software licenses, like Drupal itself, this adaptation is legitimate and even encouraged. It's good courtesy to give credit or a link from your web site to the creator of the original theme, though.

To get started with theme development, change to the `themes` directory, and copy the directory containing the Free Software theme you want to start from under a new name. For example, for a fictitious theme called 'cooltheme':

```
cd /usr/share/drupal6/sites/all/themes
sudo cp -r cooltheme mynewtheme
```

Then you'll need to change to the new theme directory, and modify the name of the copied theme's information file (which has the `.info` suffix) to show its new name:

```
cd mynewtheme
sudo mv cooltheme.info mynewtheme.info
```

Here, the `mv` command is used to rename the file, which, as far as the computer is concerned, is the same thing as moving it. Next, edit the metadata about the theme in the `.info` file:

```
sudo nano mynewtheme.info
```

Change at least the value of the `name` = line in this file, and write it out with `nano` using Ctrl+O. Refresh the Drupal theme administration page, and My New Theme should now show up in the theme list for you to select (see Figure 12-38). You can tweak the files of this new theme as much as you like, without affecting the original theme it was copied from.

Figure 12-38. After copying a Free Software theme you like and updating the `.info` file, you can begin to create a new custom theme.

Streaming Audio

Serving audio and video files as individual downloads from Drupal is one thing, but what about live streams? Some streams are of media as it happens, like a traditional radio or TV station with human presenters and DJs. Due to cost-cutting and consolidation in the media business, many radio stations and smaller TV stations are now partly or completely automated, streaming media files from a prearranged playlist on a hard disk. Either way, Free Software includes everything you need to stream audio and video via networks, with a variety of front ends available to do the encoding. At the end of this chapter, you read about setting up an Internet radio station; but you have to tackle some legal complexities first.

Show Me the Money

Independent music radio on the Internet isn't what it might have been, due to crippling royalty demands from SoundExchange in the USA and similar organizations in other territories. These royalty-collection societies require payment before you can stream just about any music released on a commercial CD to the general public—whether you make any money from streaming or not. It's not so much the percentage of revenue demanded, but the fact that you must usually pay an annual minimum fee, that hurts small stations disproportionately.

For example, in the UK, the MCPS-PRS Limited Online Exploitation License covers noncommercial music streaming by groups and individuals, as long as their gross revenue is less than £6,250 per year. The cost is on a sliding scale, up to £536 plus 15% tax per year for delivering up to 225,000 individual streams or serving 12,500 files; after that, you have to apply for a full MCPS-PRS Online Music License. That doesn't sound too bad at first, but 12,500 files per year works out to fewer than two downloads per hour for an around-the-clock web site. You also have to provide full statistical details to the MCPS-PRS Alliance of all music streamed or downloaded from your site. Even if your radio station is mostly speech, many limitations appear in the small print of these music licenses. For instance, you can't use music for promotional purposes, and you can't stream an entire opera without negotiating separate licenses. Weirdly, you aren't allowed to play a piece of music in a 'derogatory context' to the writer or performers; no drummer jokes allowed, then.

However, the biggest pitfall is that these MCPS-PRS licenses only cover listeners in the UK. If your Internet station picked up a significant number of listeners in other countries, you would have to pay for similar music licenses in those countries as well. It's no wonder that many not-for-profit radio stations have disappeared from the virtual airwaves over the last few years—not having a license could leave the operator liable to legal action. If you want to go down the paid-license route, and you can afford it, check out the www.prsformusic.com web site for UK license details (see Figure 12-39). In the USA, the www.soundexchange.com web site currently quotes a $500 minimum annual fee for noncommercial webcasters, plus a usage fee above a certain number of listener hours, for the right to stream music from its member record labels.

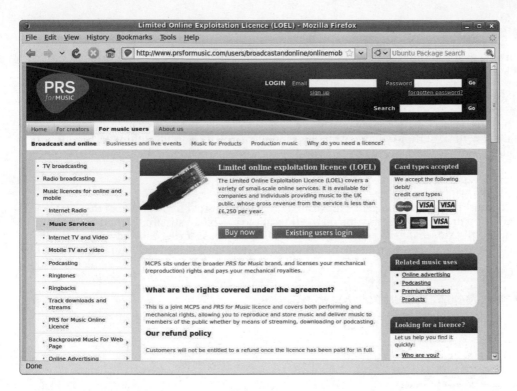

Figure 12-39. *The MCPS-PRS Alliance will gladly sell you a license for the right to stream commercially released music on the Internet, under certain conditions, to listeners in the UK only. But if you're not a member, streaming your own content is free.*

Free Content streaming offers the chance that DIY Internet radio could rise again. Because royalty collection societies like MCPS-PRS and SoundExchange can only represent the interests of their own members, it follows that if you aren't a member, you can stream your own self-produced content without paying for their license. If you state somewhere on your web site that the stream is of your own copyrighted material and is made available to the public under a specific Free Content or other license, then no one should misunderstand your intentions. You may be able to persuade other people to allow you to stream their content, too, as long as they don't have a conflicting legal obligation, such as having previously joined one of the many royalty-collection societies around the world. You can ask for permission to stream when web site visitors upload their own music files to you via a HTML form, much as the likes of MySpace do. Or you can collect files licensed under an appropriate Creative Commons or other Free Content license.

Explicit permission to stream on your server is always the ideal, so think about your own terms and conditions before you accept files from third parties for streaming. How, for example, do you know if someone uploads a file to your online radio station that unknown to you is ripped from a commercially released CD? That's the kind of thing that can get you in trouble with the licensing authorities and copyright holders.

373

Setting Up Icecast

Before you can stream any audio, you need a suitable server running. Apache can serve up static audio files as downloads on demand, but Icecast (GNU/Linux, Windows, Mac) is the most popular Free Software server for streaming Ogg Vorbis and MP3 audio in real time. Icecast also has support for video streaming in the Ogg Theora format. It's available for download from `www.icecast.org` as source code or Windows binary, but it's also available via Synaptic on Ubuntu. Make sure you install the icecast2 package, not the older icecast-server package, which can only stream audio in MP3 format.

After installation, the first thing you need to do is modify the Icecast configuration file, because its default passwords aren't secure. Open a terminal, and use `nano` with `sudo` to tweak the settings:

```
sudo nano /etc/icecast2/icecast.xml
```

For now, the most important changes to make are in the `<authentication>` section of this XML configuration file. You don't want just anyone on the Internet to be able to stream their audio content from your Icecast server. So, change the `<source-password>`, `<relay-password>`, and `<admin-password>` values to something a little more secure than the default of `hackme` for all three (see Figure 12-40).

Figure 12-40. The Icecast package is distributed with default passwordsand not very good ones either.

If you have a hostname set up for your server, put it in the `<hostname>` section of the configuration file. If not, the default of `localhost` is fine. You can connect to the web interface of an Icecast server from a remote machine using just the IP address and the port number if you wish, separated by a colon; the default Icecast port is 8000.

Save the file by pressing Ctrl+O and Enter in `nano`, and then press Ctrl+X to close the editor. Next, you need to start Icecast; but because of the weak passwords in the default configuration file, Ubuntu prevents the streaming server from starting automatically. You can fix this with `nano`:

```
sudo nano /etc/default/icecast2
```

Change `ENABLE=false` in this file to:

```
ENABLE=true
```

Then, save the file by pressing Ctrl+O and Enter, and quit nano with Ctrl+X. You're now in a position to run the Icecast initialization script:

```
sudo /etc/init.d/icecast2 start
```

To check that Icecast is running, you can use the administration pages of its web interface. Switch back to your web browser, and type in the URL `http://localhost:8000` into its location bar. In the Icecast web page that appears, click the Administration link in the top navigation bar. You're prompted for your username, which is *admin*, and the administrator password you just set. You now see a web page in the directory /admin (see Figure 12-41). Among the statistics on display, the line `server_start` shows the date and time at which Icecast began running. This page also shows the total number of `listener_connections`, which is a useful statistic if your stream becomes popular.

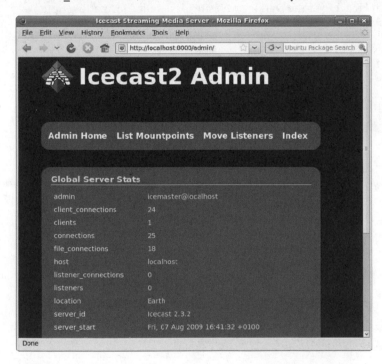

Figure 12-41. *Check the Icecast server status in your web browser.*

The Streaming Client

When the Icecast server is running, the next step is to select a streaming client. This is the application that assembles a playlist of files into the order you desire or, alternatively, forwards a live audio stream to the server. In a large-scale setup, it's most common to have the Icecast server sitting in an ISP's data center and the client machine in the radio studio. This is because Icecast is a unicast server, so the bandwidth required for streaming increases in proportion to the number of listeners. But for the purposes of this chapter, it's practical to have the streaming client and the Icecast server running on the same machine. The only limitation is that if the machine is on the slow side CPU-wise, audio frames may be skipped during the encoding of live audio, which sounds nasty when you're listening to the stream.

Various command-line and graphical streaming clients are available for Icecast, depending on the format of the stream and whether it's live or based on prerecorded files. A good, straightforward command-line client for live streaming is DarkIce (GNU/Linux, Mac), which you can download from http://code.google.com/p/darkice/. Ubuntu users can install the darkice package via Synaptic.

DarkIce supports JACK and so is very useful as a bridge between the JACK server and the Icecast server. Ideally, you should have JACK running first before you use DarkIce. (If you're not sure how to set up JACK, refer back to Chapters 9 and 10.) The inherent latency of audio streaming across the Internet means that having a small JACK buffer isn't as important as when you're recording multitrack audio, for instance.

To use DarkIce, you must create a configuration file for it at the location /etc/darkice.cfg by default. See the manual page at man darkice.cfg or the DarkIce web site for detailed formatting options. Just to get started, enter the command

```
sudo nano /etc/darkice.cfg
```

and then enter options like those shown in Figure 12-42.

Figure 12-42. DarkIce needs a configuration file to be created before it will run.

In the [general] section of the configuration file, duration=0 means "keep streaming until DarkIce is shut down," which is a suitable option for a permanent installation (you might find it used in a radio station). The streaming buffer is set to 5 seconds.

Further down in the [input] section, the program is configured to connect via jack, with the client name darkice. The sample rate setting for DarkIce must match the JACK sample rate, which is 48000Hz in this case. In the [icecast2-0] section, in addition to the server name and port and the stream format, mode, and quality, you have to set the *mount point* (the specific filename listeners connect to) and the source password you set in the Icecast configuration file. Of course, you shouldn't use *hackme* as the source password; it's only in the figure to remind you never to do the same.

CHAPTER 12 ■ WEB CONTENT

With the **/etc/darkice.cfg** file completed with suitable options and saved, you can run the following command in a terminal:

```
darkice
```

Check your JACK connections in the JACK Control applet; the darkice client should be visible (see Figure 12-43). You can now connect the soundcard capture inputs or any JACK-compatible audio program to DarkIce. That program can be Mixxx for a live DJ set, a simple media player with a prepared list of files, or even a full Ardour session.

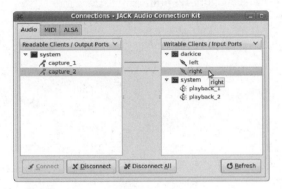

Figure 12-43. *Check that DarkIce is working in the Connections tab of JACK Control.*

Then, point your browser to the URL of the Icecast web interface, and you should now see the mount point from DarkIce listed on the home page. Visitors to this server can click the M3U (playlist format) link to open the stream in their media player of choice (see Figure 12-44).

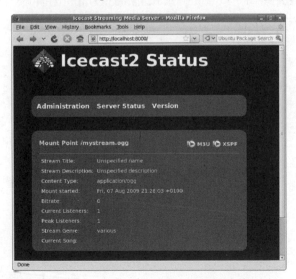

Figure 12-44. *Icecast lists all active mount points on the status page of its web interface.*

If you like, you can use the `darkice.cfg` file to specify stream metadata, which is displayed in the Icecast status page and in compatible clients. For example, suppose you add the following metadata to the end of the [`icecast2-0`] section:

```
name=My Stream
description=A test stream from my laptop
genre=Rock 'n roll!
```

When you restart DarkIce, re-create the audio connections in the JACK Control applet and look again at Icecast's web interface, the metadata should appear (see Figure 12-45).

Figure 12-45. Icecast shows the metadata for the audio stream, including title, description, and genre.

By using JACK, the studio can monitor exactly what the listeners hear, even when only one physical sound card is available. All you need is a JACK-compatible media player that can play Icecast streams, such as Aqualung (GNU/Linux; `http://aqualung.factorial.hu`). Aqualung is available in Ubuntu using the Add/Remove Applications tool. To get Aqualung to play your stream, right-click the M3U link in the Icecast web interface, and save it to disk. Then, in Aqualung, right-click the blank playlist window, choose "Load playlist," and open the saved `.m3u` file (see Figure 12-46).

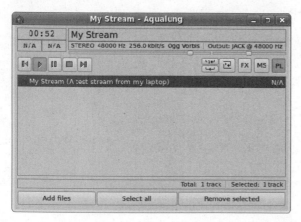

Figure 12-46. As Aqualung connects to the Icecast stream, you're on the air!

Launching Your Station

Now that you've tested Icecast and found that it runs smoothly, you can adjust the look of the web interface before you announce your streaming station to the public. First, stop Icecast with

```
sudo /etc/init.d/icecast2 stop
```

In the directory `/etc/icecast2/web/` are several XSLT and other files that are used to generate the Icecast web interface; anyone familiar with HTML can modify these pages, which are well commented. You do have to be careful with syntax, because something as simple as a missing bracket can cause the web interface to break down. For example, you can change this page:

```
sudo nano /etc/icecast2/web/status.xsl
```

Modifying the `status.xsl` page is a good place to start because it's the default page that site visitors see when they browse port 8000. The most obvious change to make in the XSLT pages is the content of the `<title>` and `<h2>` tags, to announce the name of your station. You can also modify the `style.css` file in this directory to change color and layout options.

Then, start Icecast again:

```
sudo /etc/init.d/icecast2 start
```

The new look should now be visible, as shown in Figure 12-47.

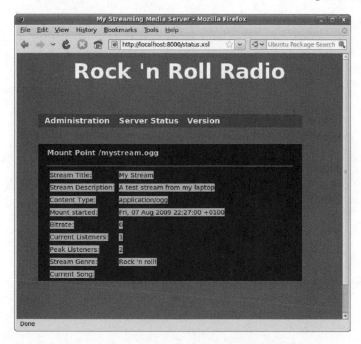

Figure 12-47. The Icecast status page, customized with a few simple tweaks to XSLT and CSS files.

When you're happy with the way the web interface looks and the sound quality you're streaming, you can uncomment the `<directory>` section in the `/etc/icecast2/icecast.xml` file to have your new station automatically listed on the `Xiph.org` web site, which should help you pick up a few listeners. You can also put a link to the Icecast status page at port 8000 on your Drupal home page, to help integrate the two sites.

Further Reading

Drupal comes with built-in help and also has comprehensive documentation on the project's own web site. If you want to go further, look at *Pro Drupal Development* by John K. VanDyk (Apress, 2007, ISBN-13: 9781590597552).

Other Useful Programs

Internet DJ Console (GNU/Linux) is an Icecast client that can handle both live and prerecorded material. It contains many other features useful to radio-style broadcasting, such as jingle buttons, microphone compression, and even VoIP integration so that you can host your own phone-in show. In Ubuntu, you can install the idjc, flac, and vorbis-tools packages via Synaptic. Other GNU/Linux users can download source code from the Internet DJ Console web site at `www.onlymeok.nildram.co.uk` if a binary package isn't available in your distro of choice.

PART 3

Appendixes

APPENDIX A

■ ■ ■

GNU/Linux Commands

Here is a quick reference guide to many of the most frequently used command-line programs on a GNU/Linux system. Although it's possible to rely on purely graphical Free Software applications, knowledge of the command line can often save time or get you out of trouble—particularly when you're working on a remote system such as an Apache, Drupal, or Icecast server located at your ISP.

This appendix was adapted from the Linux QuickRef Guide (© 2000-2003 David D. Scribner, download from `www.nichedevelopment.com`) and is made available under the GNU Free Documentation License (see Appendix 2).

■ **Note** All of the commands in this appendix should be issued on one line of the terminal without pressing the Enter key until you reach the end of the command. (Some of the longer commands are shown as wrapped over the line end for reasons of space.) On Ubuntu GNU/Linux, because there is no root user, many administrative commands must be prefixed with `sudo`. This rule doesn't apply when you're working on your own files, located in your personal `/home` directory.

Mounting Filesystems

`mount -t iso9660 /dev/cdrom /mnt/cdrom`	Mount a CD-ROM (iso9660 filesystem) at `/mnt/cdrom`.
`mount -t vfat /dev/hda1 /mnt/win`	Mount a VFAT (Windows) hard drive partition hda1 at `/mnt/win`.
`mount -t smbfs //system/share/ /mnt/samba`	Mount an SMB (Windows network) share located at `//system/share` at `/mnt/samba`.
`mount -t iso9660 -o loop image.iso /mnt/iso`	Mount an ISO image as a filesystem at `/mnt/iso` using the loopback device.
`umount /mnt/cdrom`	Unmount the CD-ROM.

Finding Files and Text within Files

find / -name *filename*	Starting at the / directory, find the file *filename*.
find / -name "**string*"*	Starting at the / directory, find the file containing the word *string*.
find / -perm +4000 -user root -print	Find existing files on the system that have their SUID root permissions set.
find / -perm +2000 -group \<group\> -print	Find existing files on the system that have their SGID permissions set.
find / -nouser -print	Find existing files on the system that don't belong to any user listed in /etc/passwd.
info	Lists the commands and utilities installed with brief descriptions of what they're used for.
locate *filename*	Locate a file *filename* using the updatedb database (see next).
updatedb	Create or update the database used by the locate command.
apropos *subject*	List man pages for *subject*, searching the whatis database for strings.
whatis	Search the whatis database for complete words.
which *filename*	Show the subdirectory containing the executable file *filename*.
grep -r *textstring* /dir	Starting with the directory */dir*, recursively find and list all files containing the string *textstring*.

Move, Copy, Delete, and View Files

mv *filename* /home/*dirname*	Move the file *filename* to the directory /home/*dirname*.
cp *filename* /home/*dirname*	Copy the file *filename* to the directory /home/*dirname*.
rm *name*	Remove the file or directory *name*.
rm -rf *dir*	Remove the entire directory *dir*, forcing the removal of included files and subdirectories recursively as well.
ls -l	List files in the current directory in long format.

`ls -F`	List files in the current directory, and indicate the file types.
`ls -aCl`	List all files in the current directory in long format, and display in columns.
`cat` *filename*	Display the file *filename*.
`more` *filename*	Display the file *filename* one page at a time. Advance pages by pressing the space bar.
`less` *filename*	Display the file *filename* one page at a time. Advance pages by pressing the space bar, or go back up with the *b* key.
`zless` *filename*	Same as above, but used with files compressed with gzip.
`head` *filename*	Display the first 10 lines of the file *filename*.
`head -25` *filename*	Display the first 25 lines of the file *filename*.
`tail` *filename*	Display the last 10 lines of the file *filename*.
`tail -25` *filename*	Display the last 25 lines of the file *filename*.

Metacharacters

`*`	Multiple-character wildcard
`?`	Single-character wildcard

File Permissions

When you use the command `ls -l`, a list of file names is displayed. The first column in this list details the file type, and the other columns show the permissions applied to the file. If a permission is denied for a set, User (the owner), Group, or Others, it's represented by a hyphen.

```
         User           Group          Others
d      r   w   x      r   w   x      r   w   x
```

385

File type labels

d=directory

-=file

l=link

b/c=block/char device

Permission labels

r=read

w=write

x=execute

Each type of permission is given a numerical value.

```
Read = 4
Write = 2
Execute = 1
```

These values can be added together to create a permission code. You can alter permissions on a specific file using the chmod command and the appropriate code for each set. For example, the command

```
chmod 764 filename
```

makes the file *filename* r-w-x for the user, r-w for the group, and r for any others.

chmod Modes

chmod 600	Apply read and write permissions for User only.
chmod 700	Apply read, write, and execute permissions for User only.
chmod 755	Apply full permission for User and read and execute for Group and Others.
chmod 711	Apply full permission for User and execute for Group and Others.
chmod 444	Apply read permissions only for everybody.
chmod +x *filename*	Make the file *filename* executable for everybody.
chmod go-w *filename*	Revoke write permissions for Group and Others on the file *filename*.
chmod ug=r *filename*	Set the permissions to readable only for User and Group on the file *filename*.
chmod a=r,u+w *filename*	Set the permissions to readable only for everybody, and add writeable for User on the file *filename*.

Symbolic Links

`ln -l` *linkname*	Display the link-path for a link.
`find . -type l -exec ls -l {} \;`	Find all symbolic links, and show what they point to.

User Administration

`useradd` *username*	Create a new user account named *username*.
`passwd` *username*	Assign a password to *username*.
`sudo` *command*	Run *command* with root powers. Requires the user's password.
`su` *username*	Switch user to *username*. Requires the other user's password.
`exit`	Exit, log off, or log out of account.

Printing

`/etc/init.d/cupsys start`	Start the print daemon.
`/etc/init.d/cupsys stop`	Stop the print daemon.
`/etc/init.d/cupsys status`	Display the status of the print daemon.
`lpq`	Query and display jobs in the print queue.
`lpq -a`	As above for all printers controlled by the **cupsys** daemon.
`lpr`	Print a file.
`lprm`	Remove jobs from print queue.
`lpc`	Start the printer control tool.

man Pages

`man -k word`	Display man pages containing *word*.
`man subject	col -b	lpr`	Print the man page *subject* as plain text.
`man -t subject	col -b	lpr`	Print the man page *subject* as Postscript.

Each man page is organized into sections:

`Name`	The name of the command and a brief description
`Synopsis`	How to use the command and command-line options
`Description`	An explanation of the program and its options
`Files`	A list of files used by the command and their location
`See Also`	A list of related man pages
`Bugs`	Known problems
`Author`	The program's main author and other contributors

Shutdown and Reboot

`shutdown -h now`	Shut down the system now, and halt (no reboot).
`shutdown -r now`	Shut down the system now, and reboot.
`shutdown -r +5`	Shut down the system in 5 minutes, and reboot.
`halt`	Stop all processes, and shut down.
`reboot`	Stop all processes, and reboot.

Installing Software

`./configure ; make ; make install`	Execute the scripts preparing the source files for compiling and installation on the system.
`apt-get update`	Update the package list.
`apt-get upgrade`	Upgrade installed packages.
`apt-get install name`	Install the package *name* (also resolve any dependencies).
`apt-get remove name`	Remove the package *name* (also remove any unneeded dependencies).
`dpkg -i pkg.deb`	Install the package *pkg.deb*.
`dpkg -r pkg.deb`	Remove the package *pkg.deb*.
`dpkg -iGRE temp`	Install all packages in the directory *temp* (including subdirectories) that are newer than the installed versions or not already installed.

Linux Kernel Modules (Drivers)

`insmod modulename`	Insert a module *modulename* into the running kernel.
`lsmod`	List the modules currently used by the kernel.
`rmmod modulename`	Remove a module from the running kernel (use `lsmod` to determine the *modulename*).
`depmod`	Create a dependency file for kernel modules (`modules.dep`).
`modprobe modulename`	Load *modulename* and any dependencies based on the `modules.dep` file created by `depmod`.

System Services

`/etc/init.d/<daemon> stop -or- start -or- restart`	Stop, start, or restart the individual service *<daemon>*.

Debian/Ubuntu Runlevels

0	Halt
1	Single-user mode
2	Multiuser mode (default)
3	Same as 2
4	Same as 2
5	Same as 2
6	Reboot

Networking

`ifconfig -a`	List IP address for all devices on the system.
`ifconfig eth0 192.168.1.12 broadcast 192.168.1.255 netmask 255.255.255.0`	Assign the IP address 192.168.1.12 to the first Ethernet device (`eth0`) using a standard Class C broadcast and netmask.
`route add -net default gw 192.168.1.100 netmask 0.0.0.0 metric 1`	Add a route for a default gateway located at 192.168.1.100 for the system.
`dhclient eth0`	Tell the interface `eth0` to grab an IP address from any DHCP server available on the local network.
`iwconfig wlan0 essid any`	Set up a Wi-Fi connection for the device `wlan0` (exact device names vary with driver) with any available access point.

Archiving

`tar -xvf archive.tar`	Decompress the files archived in the tarred file *archive*`.tar`, listing the contents to the console or terminal.
`tar -xzvf archive.tar.gz`	Decompress the files archived in the gzip compressed and tarred file *archive*`.tar.gz`.

`tar -xjvf` *`archive`*`.tar.bz2`	Decompress the files archived in the bzip2 compressed and tarred file *`archive`*`.tar.bz2`.
`tar -tvf` *`archive`*`.tar`	Display a list of the contents in the file *`archive`*`.tar`.
`tar -cvf` *`filename`*	Create a tar file, *`filename`*`.tar`, from the file *`filename`*.
`tar -czvf` *`filename`*	Create a gzip compressed tar file, *`filename`*`.tar.gz`, from the file *`filename`*.
`tar -cjvf` *`filename`*	Create a bzip2 compressed tar file, *`filename`*`.tar.bz2`, from the file *`filename`*.

Bash Shell (Terminal)

`history`	Search through the history file.
`history 20`	List the last 20 commands entered.
`history | grep` *`variable`*	Pipe the output of `history` though the `grep` command, searching for *`variable`*.
`!!`	Execute the last command entered in the history file.
`!#`	Execute the command numbered *#* in the history file.
`!`*`string`*	Execute the command with the most recent matching string *`string`*.
`env`	Run a program in a modified environment.
`printenv`	Display the environment variables in use.

X Windows

Alt+Esc	Cycle through active windows.
Alt+Tab	Display a list of active windows, and cycle through them.
Ctrl+Alt+F*n*	Switch to virtual console *n*, where *n* is a number from 1 to 6.
Ctrl+Alt+F7	Return to the current X session.
Ctrl+Alt+BkSpace	Kill the X-server.

391

Tips and Tricks

`df -h`	Display the disk filesystems mounted, including space used and available, in human-readable form.
`/sbin/e2fsck hda5`	Execute the filesystem check utility on the hard drive partition `hda5` (`umount hda5` first).
`dd if=/dev/hda of=/dev/hdb`	Create a data dump of one hard drive onto another (ghosting).
`cat /var/log/messages | less`	Display the system log, with paging.
`cat /var/log/dmesg | less`	Display the boot messages log with paging; useful for troubleshooting.
`dmesg | less`	Same as above.
`ps -u username`	List the current running processes for the user *username*.
`ps -e`	List all current running processes for all users and daemons.
`kill 1234`	Kill (stop) a process with job ID *1234*.
`kill -9 1234`	Same as above, but the kill may not be blocked.
`ulimit -c`	Display the current limit on core file size.
`ulimit -c 1000`	Set the allowable size limit on core files to 512KB (1000×512-byte blocks).
`uname -a`	Display system info (OS, host name, kernel version, date, time, time zone, year, processor type and label).
Alt+F*n*	When in a text console, switch to virtual console *n*, where *n* is a number from 1 to 7 (the default maximum).
Alt+right arrow	Switch to the next highest virtual console.
Alt+left arrow	Switch to the next lowest virtual console.
`reset`	Reset your terminal console if a binary file was displayed.
`split -b 1420K bigfile`	Split *bigfile* into smaller 1420KB files *xaa, xab, xac,* and so on that fit on a floppy disk. Adjust the `1420K` value to `500M` or `1G` for larger media, such as USB memory sticks.
`cat xaa xab xac > bigfile`	Reassemble *bigfile* from smaller files created with `split`.

APPENDIX B

■ ■ ■

GNU Free Documentation License

This Free Content license is used by several of the photos in this book as well as the text of Appendix 1.

GNU Free Documentation License

Version 1.3, 3 November 2008
Copyright © 2000, 2001, 2002, 2007, 2008 Free Software Foundation, Inc. http://fsf.org/

Everyone is permitted to copy and distribute verbatim copies of this license document, but changing it is not allowed.

0. PREAMBLE

The purpose of this License is to make a manual, textbook, or other functional and useful document "free" in the sense of freedom: to assure everyone the effective freedom to copy and redistribute it, with or without modifying it, either commercially or noncommercially. Secondarily, this License preserves for the author and publisher a way to get credit for their work, while not being considered responsible for modifications made by others.

This License is a kind of "copyleft", which means that derivative works of the document must themselves be free in the same sense. It complements the GNU General Public License, which is a copyleft license designed for free software.

We have designed this License in order to use it for manuals for free software, because free software needs free documentation: a free program should come with manuals providing the same freedoms that the software does. But this License is not limited to software manuals; it can be used for any textual work, regardless of subject matter or whether it is published as a printed book. We recommend this License principally for works whose purpose is instruction or reference.

1. APPLICABILITY AND DEFINITIONS

This License applies to any manual or other work, in any medium, that contains a notice placed by the copyright holder saying it can be distributed under the terms of this License. Such a notice grants a world-wide, royalty-free license, unlimited in duration, to use that work under the conditions stated herein. The "Document", below, refers to any such manual or work. Any member of the public is a licensee, and is addressed as "you". You accept the license if you copy, modify or distribute the work in a way requiring permission under copyright law.

A "Modified Version" of the Document means any work containing the Document or a portion of it, either copied verbatim, or with modifications and/or translated into another language.

A "Secondary Section" is a named appendix or a front-matter section of the Document that deals exclusively with the relationship of the publishers or authors of the Document to the Document's overall subject (or to related matters) and contains nothing that could fall directly within that overall subject. (Thus, if the Document is in part a textbook of mathematics, a Secondary Section may not explain any mathematics.) The relationship could be a matter of historical connection with the subject or with related matters, or of legal, commercial, philosophical, ethical or political position regarding them.

The "Invariant Sections" are certain Secondary Sections whose titles are designated, as being those of Invariant Sections, in the notice that says that the Document is released under this License. If a section does not fit the above definition of Secondary then it is not allowed to be designated as Invariant. The Document may contain zero Invariant Sections. If the Document does not identify any Invariant Sections then there are none.

The "Cover Texts" are certain short passages of text that are listed, as Front-Cover Texts or Back-Cover Texts, in the notice that says that the Document is released under this License. A Front-Cover Text may be at most 5 words, and a Back-Cover Text may be at most 25 words.

A "Transparent" copy of the Document means a machine-readable copy, represented in a format whose specification is available to the general public, that is suitable for revising the document straightforwardly with generic text editors or (for images composed of pixels) generic paint programs or (for drawings) some widely available drawing editor, and that is suitable for input to text formatters or for automatic translation to a variety of formats suitable for input to text formatters. A copy made in an otherwise Transparent file format whose markup, or absence of markup, has been arranged to thwart or discourage subsequent modification by readers is not Transparent. An image format is not Transparent if used for any substantial amount of text. A copy that is not "Transparent" is called "Opaque".

Examples of suitable formats for Transparent copies include plain ASCII without markup, Texinfo input format, LaTeX input format, SGML or XML using a publicly available DTD, and standard-conforming simple HTML, PostScript or PDF designed for human modification. Examples of transparent image formats include PNG, XCF and JPG. Opaque formats include proprietary formats that can be read and edited only by proprietary word processors, SGML or XML for which the DTD and/or processing tools are not generally available, and the machine-generated HTML, PostScript or PDF produced by some word processors for output purposes only.

The "Title Page" means, for a printed book, the title page itself, plus such following pages as are needed to hold, legibly, the material this License requires to appear in the title page. For works in formats which do not have any title page as such, "Title Page" means the text near the most prominent appearance of the work's title, preceding the beginning of the body of the text.

The "publisher" means any person or entity that distributes copies of the Document to the public.

A section "Entitled XYZ" means a named subunit of the Document whose title either is precisely XYZ or contains XYZ in parentheses following text that translates XYZ in another language. (Here XYZ stands for a specific section name mentioned below, such as "Acknowledgements", "Dedications", "Endorsements", or "History".) To "Preserve the Title" of such a section when you modify the Document means that it remains a section "Entitled XYZ" according to this definition.

The Document may include Warranty Disclaimers next to the notice which states that this License applies to the Document. These Warranty Disclaimers are considered to be included by reference in this License, but only as regards disclaiming warranties: any other implication that these Warranty Disclaimers may have is void and has no effect on the meaning of this License.

2. VERBATIM COPYING

You may copy and distribute the Document in any medium, either commercially or noncommercially, provided that this License, the copyright notices, and the license notice saying this License applies to the Document are reproduced in all copies, and that you add no other conditions whatsoever to those of this License. You may not use technical measures to obstruct or control the reading or further copying of the copies you make or distribute. However, you may accept compensation in exchange for copies. If you distribute a large enough number of copies you must also follow the conditions in section 3.

You may also lend copies, under the same conditions stated above, and you may publicly display copies.

3. COPYING IN QUANTITY

If you publish printed copies (or copies in media that commonly have printed covers) of the Document, numbering more than 100, and the Document's license notice requires Cover Texts, you must enclose the copies in covers that carry, clearly and legibly, all these Cover Texts: Front-Cover Texts on the front cover, and Back-Cover Texts on the back cover. Both covers must also clearly and legibly identify you as the publisher of these copies. The front cover must present the full title with all words of the title equally prominent and visible. You may add other material on the covers in addition. Copying with changes limited to the covers, as long as they preserve the title of the Document and satisfy these conditions, can be treated as verbatim copying in other respects.

If the required texts for either cover are too voluminous to fit legibly, you should put the first ones listed (as many as fit reasonably) on the actual cover, and continue the rest onto adjacent pages.

If you publish or distribute Opaque copies of the Document numbering more than 100, you must either include a machine-readable Transparent copy along with each Opaque copy, or state in or with each Opaque copy a computer-network location from which the general network-using public has access to download using public-standard network protocols a complete Transparent copy of the Document, free of added material. If you use the latter option, you must take reasonably prudent steps, when you begin distribution of Opaque copies in quantity, to ensure that this Transparent copy will remain thus accessible at the stated location until at least one year after the last time you distribute an Opaque copy (directly or through your agents or retailers) of that edition to the public.

It is requested, but not required, that you contact the authors of the Document well before redistributing any large number of copies, to give them a chance to provide you with an updated version of the Document.

4. MODIFICATIONS

You may copy and distribute a Modified Version of the Document under the conditions of sections 2 and 3 above, provided that you release the Modified Version under precisely this License, with the Modified Version filling the role of the Document, thus licensing distribution and modification of the Modified Version to whoever possesses a copy of it. In addition, you must do these things in the Modified Version:

- A. Use in the Title Page (and on the covers, if any) a title distinct from that of the Document, and from those of previous versions (which should, if there were any, be listed in the History section of the Document). You may use the same title as a previous version if the original publisher of that version gives permission.

- B. List on the Title Page, as authors, one or more persons or entities responsible for authorship of the modifications in the Modified Version, together with at least five of the principal authors of the Document (all of its principal authors, if it has fewer than five), unless they release you from this requirement.

- C. State on the Title page the name of the publisher of the Modified Version, as the publisher.

- D. Preserve all the copyright notices of the Document.

- E. Add an appropriate copyright notice for your modifications adjacent to the other copyright notices.

- F. Include, immediately after the copyright notices, a license notice giving the public permission to use the Modified Version under the terms of this License, in the form shown in the Addendum below.

- G. Preserve in that license notice the full lists of Invariant Sections and required Cover Texts given in the Document's license notice.

- H. Include an unaltered copy of this License.

- I. Preserve the section Entitled "History", Preserve its Title, and add to it an item stating at least the title, year, new authors, and publisher of the Modified Version as given on the Title Page. If there is no section Entitled "History" in the Document, create one stating the title, year, authors, and publisher of the Document as given on its Title Page, then add an item describing the Modified Version as stated in the previous sentence.

- J. Preserve the network location, if any, given in the Document for public access to a Transparent copy of the Document, and likewise the network locations given in the Document for previous versions it was based on. These may be placed in the "History" section. You may omit a network location for a work that was published at least four years before the Document itself, or if the original publisher of the version it refers to gives permission.

- K. For any section Entitled "Acknowledgements" or "Dedications", Preserve the Title of the section, and preserve in the section all the substance and tone of each of the contributor acknowledgements and/or dedications given therein.

- L. Preserve all the Invariant Sections of the Document, unaltered in their text and in their titles. Section numbers or the equivalent are not considered part of the section titles.

- M. Delete any section Entitled "Endorsements". Such a section may not be included in the Modified Version.

- N. Do not retitle any existing section to be Entitled "Endorsements" or to conflict in title with any Invariant Section.

- O. Preserve any Warranty Disclaimers.

If the Modified Version includes new front-matter sections or appendices that qualify as Secondary Sections and contain no material copied from the Document, you may at your option designate some or all of these sections as invariant. To do this, add their titles to the list of Invariant Sections in the Modified Version's license notice. These titles must be distinct from any other section titles.

You may add a section Entitled "Endorsements", provided it contains nothing but endorsements of your Modified Version by various parties—for example, statements of peer review or that the text has been approved by an organization as the authoritative definition of a standard.

You may add a passage of up to five words as a Front-Cover Text, and a passage of up to 25 words as a Back-Cover Text, to the end of the list of Cover Texts in the Modified Version. Only one passage of Front-Cover Text and one of Back-Cover Text may be added by (or through arrangements made by) any one entity. If the Document already includes a cover text for the same cover, previously added by you or by arrangement made by the same entity you are acting on behalf of, you may not add another; but you may replace the old one, on explicit permission from the previous publisher that added the old one.

The author(s) and publisher(s) of the Document do not by this License give permission to use their names for publicity for or to assert or imply endorsement of any Modified Version.

5. COMBINING DOCUMENTS

You may combine the Document with other documents released under this License, under the terms defined in section 4 above for modified versions, provided that you include in the combination all of the Invariant Sections of all of the original documents, unmodified, and list them all as Invariant Sections of your combined work in its license notice, and that you preserve all their Warranty Disclaimers.

The combined work need only contain one copy of this License, and multiple identical Invariant Sections may be replaced with a single copy. If there are multiple Invariant Sections with the same name but different contents, make the title of each such section unique by adding at the end of it, in parentheses, the name of the original author or publisher of that section if known, or else a unique number. Make the same adjustment to the section titles in the list of Invariant Sections in the license notice of the combined work.

In the combination, you must combine any sections Entitled "History" in the various original documents, forming one section Entitled "History"; likewise combine any sections Entitled "Acknowledgements", and any sections Entitled "Dedications". You must delete all sections Entitled "Endorsements".

6. COLLECTIONS OF DOCUMENTS

You may make a collection consisting of the Document and other documents released under this License, and replace the individual copies of this License in the various documents with a single copy that is included in the collection, provided that you follow the rules of this License for verbatim copying of each of the documents in all other respects.

You may extract a single document from such a collection, and distribute it individually under this License, provided you insert a copy of this License into the extracted document, and follow this License in all other respects regarding verbatim copying of that document.

7. AGGREGATION WITH INDEPENDENT WORKS

A compilation of the Document or its derivatives with other separate and independent documents or works, in or on a volume of a storage or distribution medium, is called an "aggregate" if the copyright resulting from the compilation is not used to limit the legal rights of the compilation's users beyond what the individual works permit. When the Document is included in an aggregate, this License does not apply to the other works in the aggregate which are not themselves derivative works of the Document.

If the Cover Text requirement of section 3 is applicable to these copies of the Document, then if the Document is less than one half of the entire aggregate, the Document's Cover Texts may be placed on covers that bracket the Document within the aggregate, or the electronic equivalent of covers if the Document is in electronic form. Otherwise they must appear on printed covers that bracket the whole aggregate.

8. TRANSLATION

Translation is considered a kind of modification, so you may distribute translations of the Document under the terms of section 4. Replacing Invariant Sections with translations requires special permission from their copyright holders, but you may include translations of some or all Invariant Sections in addition to the original versions of these Invariant Sections. You may include a translation of this License, and all the license notices in the Document, and any Warranty Disclaimers, provided that you also include the original English version of this License and the original versions of those notices and disclaimers. In case of a disagreement between the translation and the original version of this License or a notice or disclaimer, the original version will prevail.

If a section in the Document is Entitled "Acknowledgements", "Dedications", or "History", the requirement (section 4) to Preserve its Title (section 1) will typically require changing the actual title.

9. TERMINATION

You may not copy, modify, sublicense, or distribute the Document except as expressly provided under this License. Any attempt otherwise to copy, modify, sublicense, or distribute it is void, and will automatically terminate your rights under this License.

However, if you cease all violation of this License, then your license from a particular copyright holder is reinstated (a) provisionally, unless and until the copyright holder explicitly and finally terminates your license, and (b) permanently, if the copyright holder fails to notify you of the violation by some reasonable means prior to 60 days after the cessation.

Moreover, your license from a particular copyright holder is reinstated permanently if the copyright holder notifies you of the violation by some reasonable means, this is the first time you have received notice of violation of this License (for any work) from that copyright holder, and you cure the violation prior to 30 days after your receipt of the notice.

Termination of your rights under this section does not terminate the licenses of parties who have received copies or rights from you under this License. If your rights have been terminated and not permanently reinstated, receipt of a copy of some or all of the same material does not give you any rights to use it.

10. FUTURE REVISIONS OF THIS LICENSE

The Free Software Foundation may publish new, revised versions of the GNU Free Documentation License from time to time. Such new versions will be similar in spirit to the present version, but may differ in detail to address new problems or concerns. See http://www.gnu.org/copyleft/.

Each version of the License is given a distinguishing version number. If the Document specifies that a particular numbered version of this License "or any later version" applies to it, you have the option of following the terms and conditions either of that specified version or of any later version that has been published (not as a draft) by the Free Software Foundation. If the Document does not specify a version number of this License, you may choose any version ever published (not as a draft) by the Free Software Foundation. If the Document specifies that a proxy can decide which future versions of this License can be used, that proxy's public statement of acceptance of a version permanently authorizes you to choose that version for the Document.

11. RELICENSING

"Massive Multiauthor Collaboration Site" (or "MMC Site") means any World Wide Web server that publishes copyrightable works and also provides prominent facilities for anybody to edit those works. A public wiki that anybody can edit is an example of such a server. A "Massive Multiauthor Collaboration" (or "MMC") contained in the site means any set of copyrightable works thus published on the MMC site.

"CC-BY-SA" means the Creative Commons Attribution-Share Alike 3.0 license published by Creative Commons Corporation, a not-for-profit corporation with a principal place of business in San Francisco, California, as well as future copyleft versions of that license published by that same organization.

"Incorporate" means to publish or republish a Document, in whole or in part, as part of another Document.

An MMC is "eligible for relicensing" if it is licensed under this License, and if all works that were first published under this License somewhere other than this MMC, and subsequently incorporated in whole or in part into the MMC, (1) had no cover texts or invariant sections, and (2) were thus incorporated prior to November 1, 2008.

The operator of an MMC Site may republish an MMC contained in the site under CC-BY-SA on the same site at any time before August 1, 2009, provided the MMC is eligible for relicensing.

ADDENDUM: How to use this License for your documents

To use this License in a document you have written, include a copy of the License in the document and put the following copyright and license notices just after the title page:

> Copyright (C) YEAR YOUR NAME.
>
> Permission is granted to copy, distribute and/or modify this document
>
> under the terms of the GNU Free Documentation License, Version 1.3
>
> or any later version published by the Free Software Foundation;
>
> with no Invariant Sections, no Front-Cover Texts, and no Back-Cover Texts.
>
> A copy of the license is included in the section entitled "GNU
>
> Free Documentation License".

If you have Invariant Sections, Front-Cover Texts and Back-Cover Texts, replace the "with … Texts." line with this:

> with the Invariant Sections being LIST THEIR TITLES, with the
>
> Front-Cover Texts being LIST, and with the Back-Cover Texts being LIST.

If you have Invariant Sections without Cover Texts, or some other combination of the three, merge those two alternatives to suit the situation.

If your document contains nontrivial examples of program code, we recommend releasing these examples in parallel under your choice of free software license, such as the GNU General Public License, to permit their use in free software.

Index

■H

You Need the Companion eBook